Consolation
of Philosophy

BOETHIUS

Consolation of Philosophy

Translated, with
Introduction and Notes, by
Joel C. Relihan

Hackett Publishing Company, Inc.
Indianapolis/Cambridge

For further information, please address:
  Hackett Publishing Company, Inc.
  P.O. Box 44937
  Indianapolis, IN 46244–0937

  www.hackettpublishing.com

Cover and interior design by Abigail Coyle
Cover art courtesy of www.corbisimages.com.

Library of Congress Cataloging-in-Publication Data
Boethius, d. 524.
    [De consolatione philosophiae. English]
    Consolation of philosophy / Boethius ; translated, with introduction
and notes, by Joel C. Relihan.
    p.   cm.
    Includes bibliographical references (p.).
    ISBN 0-87220-584-3 (cloth)—ISBN 0-87220-583-5 (paper)
        1. Philosophy and religion. 2. Happiness. I. Relihan, Joel C.
II. Title
  B659.C5 E52   2000
  100—dc21   2001026401

ISBN-13: 978-0-87220-583-3 (pbk.)
ISBN-13: 978-0-87220-584-0 (cloth)

To Elise
again and always

PREFACE

As I prepared to send this manuscript to the press I was struck by the realization that I was at the age at which Boethius may be supposed to have been executed. My first temptation was to say that I had spent more of my life in contemplation of his *Consolation of Philosophy* than he ever did, two decades that have seen a dissertation and two literary studies as well as the painstaking work that has resulted in this, what I hope will be seen as, not only a new translation, but a new sort of translation, of *Consolation*. But the truth rapidly displaced this boast: Boethius did spend more time on *Consolation* than I have. I do not mean that he composed it over twenty years; rather, it had become clear to me that this book encapsulates and consummates a lifetime of work, embracing in subtle and remarkable ways both the volumes of translations and commentaries that he had been able to commit to paper and all of those projects for which he would never be given the opportunity or the time. I do not refer just to the well-known hopeful statement of the young Boethius that he intended to translate and comment on all of the works of Plato and Aristotle and demonstrate their harmony and consistency. Rather, the spirit of St. Augustine, whose *Confessions* presides over many aspects of this work (the general structural principle of dialogue as self-examination, for example, and the anguished doubts about the nature of rational inquiry at V.3 and V.m.3), directed Boethius to compose as his last work what may in many ways be seen as a parallel to Augustine's *Retractions*. Augustine was once able to contemplate all the works that he had written and comment on their strengths and weaknesses; Boethius, I would argue, does the same here in these *retractions*, meaning not "withdrawals" but "going over one more time."

It is an unfortunate and incurious simplification that sees *Consolation* as merely inspirational; it is also confessional, and the prisoner's struggle to locate himself within the world of time, Book V's capstone to Philosophy's presentations, is no mere step in an impersonal argument. Frank Kermode, toward the end of *The Sense of an Ending*, quotes Philip Larkin:

> Truly, though our element is time,
> We are not suited to the long perspectives
> Open at each instant of our lives.
> They link us to our losses . . . .

Kermode comments: "Merely to give order to these perspectives is to provide consolation. . . ."[1] Boethius the author belongs to two worlds, perhaps to a number of pairs of worlds, all of which find their place in *Consolation*: active and theoretical, Aristotelian and Platonic, temporal and eternal, Christian and pagan. His life's work was dedicated to one particular world, to Aristotle and commentary on Aristotle, to toil on the lower slopes of Parnassus: In the world of Neo-Platonism, Aristotle was, after all, only considered an adjunct to the study of Plato and the higher studies of the metaphysical architecture of the universe and the myth of the soul's return to its source. Might not Boethius, like any author, pause to regret the limitations of his past choices, to try to create something newer and bigger, and to hope for a chance to write again? Surely, *Consolation of Philosophy* is like nothing else that the author had written before, or that any philosopher had written before. How and why such an eccentric work came to be written is worthy of all our attention.

In what follows, I try to make clear, if nothing else, at least how complex and many-layered a work Boethius' *Consolation of Philosophy* is; I hope also to provide the means to make this complexity comprehensible. I have a number of people to thank who have helped me in this enterprise: Deborah Wilkes of Hackett Publishing Company, who encouraged me to undertake this translation; Wheaton College, which, for the sabbatical in which the first draft was done, gave me a lovely office in the library through whose windows the ivy grew; my colleague Jonathan Brumberg-Kraus, who in a lapidary phrase suggested to me that Philosophy may be what Boethius speaks *through*, but religion is what he talks *about*; Joseph Pucci of Brown University, "the present truth of Providence," who gave every word of this translation meticulous scrutiny; my family, a source of inspiration greater than Philosophy. I did not, of course, take all the advice that I was given; for the errors and infelicities that remain because of my injudicious refusals, I take lonely responsibility.

J. C. R.
Wheaton College
Norton, Massachusetts

---

[1] Frank Kermode, *The Sense of an Ending: Studies in the Theory of Fiction* (New York: Oxford University Press, 1967), 179.

INTRODUCTION

The philosophers of the sixth century neither sought nor prized original-ity. Their labors took the form of commentary (or, in the case of the Latin Boethius, translation and commentary) on the established corpus of Platonic and Aristotelian works. A new idea may occasionally find expression in a commentary, decently obscured by the verbiage around it; but the philosophical system most characteristic of this period, which we call Neo-Platonism, did not present itself as, or even imagine itself as, anything other than the literal meaning of a systematized Plato. Philoso-phers were the guardians of inherited truth; their views were conserva-tive; their contributions lay in the ever-more-elaborate presentation of the harmonies of the philosophical thoughts that came before them. It is now possible to read portions of Boethius' own Aristotelian commentar-ies in English translation, and this is in fact a highly desirable exercise, to appreciate the vast gulf in style, structure, tone, and intellectual goal that separates his commentaries from this, his final work.[1] If *Consolation of Philosophy* were in any way a typical product of this era, it would today be scarcely read or remembered.

The reader must not be misled by the fame of the book into thinking that it is in any way ordinary. The philosophical views expressed within it may be quaint by modern standards, but *Consolation* is in fact a work of surprising originality.[2] This originality is communicated more by the

---

[1] Most important are the translations from Boethius' *First and Second Com-mentaries on Aristotle's On Interpretation* in Blank and Kretzmann 1998, 129–86. Boethius' analysis of Chapter 9 of *On Interpretation*, in which Aristotle intro-duces his famous example of tomorrow's sea battle in a discussion of future con-tingents, makes a number of important appearances in Book V of *Consolation*. See also Spade 1994, 20–25, for a translation of Boethius' discussion of the three questions about universals that Porphyry refuses to discuss in his *Isagoge* (*Intro-duction to the Categories of Aristotle*) from his *Second Commentary on the Isagoge*.

[2] Curley 1986, 211–12, begins with a brief discussion of the gulf that sepa-rates modern Western philosophy from Boethius, and of the modern inability to respond literarily to a philosophical work.

structures into which it fits its arguments than by the arguments themselves. Not only is it not a commentary; it chooses in preference to align
itself with a number of other literary forms that would seem to have little
to do with systematic philosophy. The first is announced in the title,
which is not merely a poetic fancy but a generic labeling: *Consolation*
lays claim to the genre of consolation, a moral exhortation, an address to
one who is bereaved, an argument that death is not to be feared.[3] But
here too is a surprise for any reader whose sole exposure to ancient consolatory literature is Boethius. The title is a paradox at best; Philosophy's
consolation is not a consolation according to the practices of the genre.
It avoids what is the most characteristic function of the genre: to explain
why death is not to be feared.[4] If anything, *Consolation* is about the consolation that death itself provides (Philosophy encourages the prisoner
to embrace it; cf. I.3.6, 9; II.7.21–23, IV.6.42).[5] An ancient reader who
expected a consolation would have been frustrated in that expectation;
the modern reader must be encouraged to wonder about the author's
provocative title.

There is another false promise associated with this one: All consolations conclude with some sort of explanation of the rewards of the
blessed or the punishments of sinners, some view of the life after death
and the abode of the good. Philosophy in fact frequently offers to take
the prisoner to his fatherland, from where he can look down on the
world below (cf. IV.1.8–9, IV.m.1, V.1.4; so also the conclusion of
III.m.12); one may see the rewards of virtuous philosophers and the
punishments of wicked tyrants *in this world*. In this regard, *Consolation*
could be called *Apocalypse Denied*; for some reason, the beatific vision is
never achieved. Death hangs over this *Consolation*, but something other
than the fact that our soon-to-be-executed author chooses not to make
himself die in this work of fiction is responsible for this deferral. It is
another frustration for the reader: Why does *Consolation* so often evoke
the expectation of such a vision and then refuse to satisfy it?

But there is a genre whose rules and conventions Boethius the
author does follow in writing this strange *Consolation*: This is the comic
genre of Menippean satire, which delights in multiple points of view,
the presence of many genres of literature within a single work, and the

---

[3] An excellent presentation of the conventions of consolatory literature in
antiquity and late antiquity may be found in the introduction to Scourfield 1993.

[4] Despite its vast medieval authority, Boethius' *Consolation* had no influence
on medieval consolatory literature for this simple reason.

[5] Cf. Shanzer 1984, 362–66.

frustration of expectations. Named after the Cynic philosopher and author of the third century B.C.E., the genre is best known for its mixture of prose and verse; but as I have argued, the function of such a mixture is to make the resulting work unclassifiable by ancient literary standards, which strictly separate prose and verse genres.[6] By mixing prose and verse organically together, not merely quoting poetry but incorporating it; by having speakers within a dialogue speak in verse; by having a narrator who will at times communicate in verse as well as in prose; by making a problem out of the very fact of the composition of the text[7]—by all of these means the genre creates unreliable narrators, authors of questionable authority, and texts with ever-shifting points of view. It undermines the consistency that a reader expects of a work, and makes the interpretation of the work problematic. It may seem surprising that *Consolation* with all its sincerities belongs to such a genre; but it is in fact an ideal genre for describing two worlds, and for suggesting that such worlds do not easily coalesce into one. Prose and verse within *Consolation* have long been thought of as representative of two different avenues to the truth, logical and emotional, discursive and affective. But I would argue that *Consolation* is in fact trying to enclose all of human experience within it; and true to its Menippean origins, it expresses the difficulty inherent in trying to reduce such human experience to theory and rule.

Consolation may not seem to have much in common with the *Satyricon* of Petronius, the best-known Menippean satire, though it is worth noticing that Death is a powerful presence in both of them; more important is what happens to the genre in late antiquity, and particularly in two works (of the early and late fifth century, respectively) close to Boethius' own time that clearly have left their stamp on it. These are both encyclopedias of sorts, each an attempt to encapsulate human wisdom, each depicting the embarrassment of a theorist who thought that the world could be so easily categorized and understood. The first is the allegorical extravaganza of Martianus Capella, *The Marriage of Philology and*

---

[6] Relihan 1993, 12–48: "A Definition of Ancient Menippean Satire."

[7] Nowhere in *Consolation* does Philosophy tell the prisoner to write; he is first seen taking dictation from his Muses, and then setting his pen down. At II.7.20, Philosophy tells a story of a false philosopher, who would have proved himself a true philosopher had he kept quiet; the fact that the philosopher Boethius has written *Consolation* down, evidently after the fact of his conversation with Philosophy, may be seen as a sort of rejection of Philosophy's expectations for what constitutes a true philosopher. Only one who did not escape with Philosophy to his true fatherland could have done so.

Mercury.[8] In it, Philology is chosen to be Mercury's bride; she prepares herself for her wedding; she ascends to Olympus, catching briefly a view of the abode of the Unknown Father that lies beyond, offers a prayer to the Father, and arrives on Olympus where the Seven Liberal Arts are presented to her as wedding gifts, explaining to her in encyclopedic fashion their knowledge.[9] The prayer to the Unknown Father, in epic hexameters (2.185–93), is the model for the hexameter central poem of *Consolation* (III.m.9), also an address to the Creator. Also of interest is that the work is presented in the form of a debate between the author and Satire, the Muse of the work; they struggle with questions of propriety, and at the end the Muse abandons the work in disgust as unworthy of her lofty goals; the narrator has had too much influence in it.

Still closer to Boethius' own time is the *Mythologies* of Fulgentius, three books of simple-minded allegorical interpretations of Classical myths accommodated to Christian thought. The appearance of Calliope, the Muse of the work, to the sleeping and incompetent narrator in the introduction is one of a number of epiphanies that work their influence in the opening prose section of *Consolation*. Here, too, in Fulgentius, is a debate between the author of the work and his Muse; Calliope finds him boldly proclaiming that he knows the meanings of ancient mythology without her help, but he is forced to accept her explanations after she finds him raving "like a mad poet," making awful verses in his sleep. Boethius' prisoner will also be found in bed, composing bad poetry; he too will need to be told that he does not understand, and needs the professional instruction of a higher power.

The most important link between Boethius' *Consolation* and these Menippean satires is the presentation of the narrator of the work engaging in a debate with his Muse about what form the following work should take. For in *Consolation*, Philosophy is not just Wisdom, but the embodiment of the philosophical tradition; the allegorical components of her appearance and her dress at I.1.1–6 identify her as the summation of Platonic wisdom, late antiquity's "accumulated deposit of truth."[10] When she dismisses the pagan Muses who had been dictating to the bedridden prisoner (I.1.7–12), and substitutes Muses of her own, and her own rhetoric

---

[8] See my discussion in Relihan 1993, 137–51; for Fulgentius, see pp. 152–63 and Appendix B (pp. 203–10), a translation of the Prologue of the *Mythologies*.

[9] It is not without interest that this knowledge is what Philology herself had to vomit forth and thus rid herself of in order to make herself capable of the flight to heaven (2.135–39).

[10] Dillon 1999, 642.

and music (II.1.7–8), she becomes both the Platonic tradition itself and a structural principle of the composition of *Consolation*.

Therefore, in a way, *Consolation* does come back into the fold of commentary. What can the prisoner say in the presence of Philosophy that would identify him as a philosopher? For this is one of the key actions of *Consolation*, just as it is in the one Platonic dialogue that provides a strong structural model for it: *Crito*, in which Socrates argues with the embodiment of the Laws of Athens, and proves that he is a true philosopher by refusing to escape from his prison. There is a good deal of Boethius' pride built into *Consolation*, for he presents himself through the prisoner as the last philosopher (as well as the last of the Roman poets), and between the era of Socrates and Plato and his own time there can be found only the heresies of Hellenistic philosophy and the virtuous examples of Romans who were put to death for their philosophical resistance to tyranny (cf. I.3.6–10); the authors of the Neo-Platonist tradition find no place at all in the history of philosophy that is sketched out in *Consolation*. Philosophy does not only want to inspire the prisoner; she has come to him in order to find a champion, one to defend *her*. Despite her commanding size and piercing gaze, despite her scepter and her books, she comes on stage disheveled, her robes torn and covered in soot (I.1.3–5); the problem, she says, is that schismatic philosophers, the Epicureans in particular, did not understand her integrity, tore off scraps of her, and carried her away "kicking and screaming" (I.3.6–8). I would say that she has been in the Land of the Dead; the example of Boethius, imprisoned philosopher, is sufficient to bring her out of retirement—she is not obsolete; there is one who understands her as the entirety that she is. His knowledge and his willingness to die for her will vindicate her and prove her continued relevance; she has come to take him away with her, back to the Land of the Dead.[11]

In this light, Philosophy's surprise at discovering that the prisoner is mute, taking dictation from whorish Muses and unable to speak on his own, expresses not only her concern for the child that she had raised (cf. I.2) but for herself as well. In his current condition he is of no use to her; his reeducation will be to his benefit, to be sure, but also to hers. The pris-

---

[11] This is explored further in Relihan 1990. The personified genre who appears in rags to protest her treatment at the hands of moderns is a motif of Old Comedy (a good source of plots for Menippean satire, and probably transmitted to Boethius through the medium of Varro's *Menippean Satires*). In the fragments of Cratinus' *Pytine*, Comedy complains about the author's drunkenness; in Pherecrates' *Chiron*, Music complains about modern musicians; a similar action is at work in Aristophanes' *Frogs*, in which Dionysus goes to the Land of the Dead to find a worthy author for degenerate modern times.

oner's reeducation is in fact presented as a recapitulation of the whole of ancient philosophy: popular moralizing, Stoic self-examination, Platonic spirituality, Aristotelian logic, Augustinian psychology. Inspired by his Muse, the prisoner gains strength as he moves through these stages. But the prisoner is not merely acquiescent; as he regains his voice, he becomes bold enough to ask Philosophy to consider questions that she did not want to raise. Both Book IV, on the coexistence of the goodness of God and the evil of mortals, and Book V, on the coexistence of divine foreknowledge and mortal free will, are topics that Philosophy did not intend to discuss. She speaks of taking the prisoner to his fatherland (cf. IV.1.8–9, V.1.4–5), which clearly is the language of flight out of the prison, of a journey to supernatural realms, of the satisfaction of the promise of the title of the work; the bitter cup that she frequently alludes to (cf. I.5.11–12, I.6.21, II.1.7), which she wants him to drink after he has had his honeyed cups of gentler instruction, is Socrates' cup of hemlock.[12] She is eager to have the prisoner forget his earthly condition and earthly concerns and come away with her; he, by keeping her talking, grounds her; she does not fly out of this prison with him. At the end, when he turns the conversation toward questions of Aristotelian logic, we have the substitution of God's view of the world below for the expected description of the mortal view of the world above. In other words, *Consolation* is a debate between the author and his Muse; it creates a work that neither one could have predicted at the beginning of their conversation; it has surprising twists and turns, as the prisoner, to the frustration of his Muse, keeps looking back to the earth instead of raising his head up toward the heavens. He confronts Death and the world beyond but, like many a character in a Menippean satire, he comes back to earth to tell us of his adventures.[13]

The Philosophical Content of Consolation

Various philosophical systems and schools are sheltered under the umbrella of *Consolation of Philosophy*. There is the moral exhortation of the

---

[12] A point well made by Shanzer; see note 5, above.

[13] As the character Menippus does in two of the Menippean satires of Lucian, *Icaromenippus* and *Necyomantia*, though not in the famous *Dialogues of the Dead*, in which our mocker is not allowed to return from the Land of the Dead to the world above. While Seneca's *Apocolocyntosis* ultimately traps the buffoon Claudius in Hades, he too has a chance to see the world above and then escape from it. See Relihan 1993, 103–18 (Lucian), 75–90 (Seneca).

Cynic diatribe, the call to personal introspection of Stoic meditation, the Augustinian understanding of time, the Aristotelian analysis of the concluding book. The content is no less than the nature of the world and of the God who controls it. In Book II, the reality of Fortune, a principle of disorder, asserts the value of changelessness; in Book III, what is One is claimed to be the universal Good; in Book IV, goodness is a problem, the relation of God's goodness to temporal evil; in Book V, oneness is a solution, God's eternity allowing the coexistence of human free will and divine foreknowledge. The concepts involved are of varying complexity; a reader coming to them for the first time will find help in the Notes to this volume. But what is clearly at the heart of *Consolation* is Platonism: the dialogue form, the influence of *Crito*, the appropriation of the arguments of *Gorgias* and *Timaeus*. Most important, the Platonic structure of the world—the world of universal ideas and the forms, as it has been reinterpreted in Late Antiquity—is present here; the underlying philosophical principles of *Consolation* are Neo-Platonic. Now this is not as daunting as it seems, and an appreciation of *Consolation* does not require that one master Plotinus first. For in fact the Neo-Platonic content of *Consolation*, while thematically important, is really quite small, and can be explained as follows.

At the heart of the Platonic view of the world, and of Greek philosophy in general, is this: What is, is One. In the world that can be perceived by the senses, things come into being and pass away; they change, and because they change they cannot be said to exist in a real and absolute sense. The things of this world can be thought of as existing only because they participate in the One. Another fundamental principle of Greek and Platonic philosophy is that the structure of the individual is equivalent to the structure of the universe: The microcosm allows one to understand the macrocosm, and vice versa. As an individual has mind and soul, so does the universe. The One, that which truly is, is responsible for the world of sense because other levels of reality emanate from it: From the One comes the World Mind; from the World Mind comes the World Soul; from the World Soul come the individual souls that live their lives in the world of matter, the lowest level of reality.

There is much Neo-Platonic elaboration on this scheme, much that does not find its way into Boethius. The system is pruned back for two reasons: one, there is practically nothing that is Neo-Platonic in *Consolation* that is not Christian as well; two, *Consolation* is primarily concerned with the myth of the descent and return of the soul. Simply put, the individual soul descends from the One and would be severed from it were it not for the fact that the One, by its nature, so sets everything in circular motion that the straight-line descent of the soul is bent back toward its source: All created things by their nature are separated from but are also drawn back toward the One (see most particularly the central and epic poem of *Consolation*, III.m.9). This longing to return is the life of the soul. The language of descent and return, which seems to imply life in time, is in fact only a metaphor; this life of the soul is an eternal and timeless reality; return is a way of thinking about the relation between the individual in the world of change and its true existence as a changeless unity by virtue of its natural connection to that which is unity itself and the source of all unity. Philosophy is in the prisoner's cell to encourage the prisoner to return to his source.

But this is the problem of *Consolation*. The Neo-Platonic myth has little room for ethics. It is not suited for discussions of how best to live within this world; its focus is the atemporal world outside of the world of change. If the soul naturally longs for return to the One, there is no need for Philosophy to encourage the prisoner to come away with her to where the One may be found. Her function should be only to remind him of this reality; it is Platonic dogma that all true knowledge comes from the soul's memory of the eternal world that it had lived in before it came to be in a body (see III.m.11 and V.m.4). It is of crucial importance to our understanding of *Consolation* that the prisoner refuses to forget his earthly life, to let go of that kind of memory, even though, alone and within his cell, he has no real scope for ethical action either.[14] When he keeps Philosophy from pursuing her own agenda at the beginnings of Books IV and V, he is still keenly aware of his sorrow within this world; he is upset that the wicked prosper and the good are trampled underfoot. Book V ends by dealing explicitly with the moral question of whether individuals have responsibility for their actions in a world in which God sees all; the conclusion, that individuals must *of necessity* behave well before the eyes of an all-seeing judge, is far from the transcendent view of the world that Philosophy had hoped for. The prisoner, offered the path of transcendence, takes instead the path of humble access to God through prayer; he refuses to travel Philosophy's path. The ultimate ethical choice made by the prisoner in *Consolation* is to stay alive.

The Plot Lines of Consolation

If the reader is prepared to find in *Consolation* a debate between an author and his Muse, in the traditions of Menippean satire; if the central Neo-Platonic myth of *Consolation*, the soul's return to its source, is made

---

[14] Olmstead 1989, 34–35: "Boethius's text . . . offers a way for the solitary individual to overcome his isolation and understand himself to be in relation to all else that is."

problematic by the work's end; then the translator's efforts may be best employed, not in identifying where particular Neo-Platonic doctrines may be paralleled in other Neo-Platonic commentators, but in providing frameworks for understanding the action of the work. It may seem odd to ask what is the action of *Consolation*, as there is physically no action at all, and we are unaccustomed to viewing the progression of an argument as a plot. But *Consolation* is not just the demonstration of certain truths; if it were, the work would be of very limited value, especially if one did not share the presuppositions of the speakers. There are certain arguments designed to be productive of certain ends (again, I would refer the reader to the Notes), but the succession of these arguments, the changes in the methods of the arguments as well as their goals, the use of arguments in different meters to advance different goals—all of these suggest that "plot outlines" may be ultimately a more useful term for approaching *Consolation* than "outline of argument." As one critic puts it: "Boethius does not believe that philosophy's proper medium is a succession of simple declarative sentences but a highly wrought text, the many voices and tones of which interact so as to produce a pattern mirroring the complexity of the cosmos."[15] In what follows, I suggest avenues of approach and lines of argument (some of them contradictory), and pose a series of questions (not all of which I would claim to have an absolute answer for), which may help prepare the reader's mind for the appreciation of the text.

The Prisoner's Search for a Voice   The first poem seems to be the heartfelt outcry of an old man on the verge of death. We then discover that its author is taking dictation and going over these words in silence; his problem will prove to be not premature old age but false imprisonment and impending death. The confused prisoner must be forced to speak, but after he does so (I.4 and I.m.5) Philosophy takes over so completely that he is reduced to merely answering questions at I.6, providing simple interrogative or assentive noises through Book II and then, when eager to go on to the bitter cup at the beginning of Book III, told to listen again as Philosophy goes over her arguments against Fortune in a different way, this time involving him more closely as a partner. After III.m.9 he is confident enough to ask good questions; at IV.1, and again at V.1, he redirects Philosophy's arguments; at V.m.3 he speaks in verse for the fourth and last time (I.m.1, I.m.3, and I.m.5), yet he falls silent at the end of *Consolation*, Philosophy putting words in his mouth (cf. "you say"

---

[15] Curley 1986, 253. I would qualify this by saying that Boethius does believe elsewhere that philosophy is a series of declarative sentences; and by saying that this attempt to mirror the cosmos is a Menippean desire, one that cannot be flawlessly coherent, because it is a human cosmos.

and "you will say" at V.4.10, V.4.21, V.6.37 and 39). Famously, there is no concluding poem. What is the meaning of this rise and fall?

The Search for an Epic Voice   The opening poem is an elegiac couplet; that is to say, its first line is in the meter of epic, while its second line, composed of two separate but shorter units in the same meter, fails to live up to the expectations created by the first line.[16] The second word of the second line, which I translate as "Woe is me!" is designed to be bathetic; Philosophy makes fun of the prisoner for speaking this way in the first word of her first poem. But *Consolation* builds to a dramatic climax in the epic hexameters of III.m.9, and I argue that other poems, written in various poetic forms that suggest the epic meter, prepare us for this climax at various points along the way. But this central poem is embedded in patterns of other meters, and there would seem to be a falling away from its structure and its sublimity. What patterns do the meters themselves suggest?

The Progression of Philosophical Systems   After Philosophy takes a case history of her patient in I.6 and makes her diagnosis, she proceeds to speak to the prisoner in several different voices. Book II is the voice of popular philosophy, or what is called the diatribe, popular moral haranguing that involves such rhetorical flourishes as imagining that Fortune herself were present and putting words into her mouth. In Book III, the structure is Platonic, as the prisoner speaks and there is dialogue, but the tone is Stoic, as the topic turns to the true goods and how they are to be sought. Things change at III.m.9, which relies heavily on *Timaeus* for a treatment of the nature of the soul in relation to the created universe; the end of Book III is also Platonic, treating the nature of the One, and how it is the true Good. This Platonic line of argument continues in Book IV, which derives from *Gorgias* a discussion of the justice of all punishments, and how the wicked are improved by punishment. But in Book V things take an Aristotelian turn, as the arguments on the relation between chance and Providence, and between foreknowledge and free will, return the prisoner happily to the world of his own Aristotelian studies, and he is glad to have a chance to go over things that he had written in his commentaries on Aristotle's *On Interpretation*. However, at V.3 and V.m.3, practically the prisoner's last words, he speaks in Augustinian terms about the relation between the mind and the objects of its thought, how it can seek what it does not already know. The book ends on questions of prayer and humble access to God, in what seem to be Christian concerns, not the transcendental Platonism or logical

---

[16] See Notes on the meter of I.m.1 for further details.

Aristotelianism of the previous books.[17] What is the significance of this progression?

The Unfulfilled Promises Both the author, through his use of the word "consolation," and Philosophy, by means of promises made, which are never kept, involve the reader in a search for certain answers that do not explicitly come. Philosophy says (I.6.17) that the prisoner must learn what he has forgotten, what a human being is, so that he may be cured and see that there is order in the human realm as well as in the world of nature. There are teasing references to what mortals are, and to the need for self-discovery, later on in the text (cf. IV.6.41, V.4.35); may there be some implicit answer to this question, so that *Consolation* is truly about self-discovery and self-definition?

Philosophy says often that the narrator is not yet ready for the bitter cup and that he needs milder treatments before she can apply that one (cf. I.5.11–12, I.6.21, II.1.7, II.3.3, III.1.2, IV.6.5). The bitter cup is Socrates's cup of hemlock, and it is never literally given—does *Consolation* show that the cup is offered in some other sense, or offered and declined? If the bitter cup is the offer of death, of course it does not come, as the narrator reasonably does not describe his own death, but could it be argued that Death has been avoided?

Philosophy promises to take the prisoner to his true fatherland (IV.1.8–9. IV.m.1, V.1.4), but does not literally do so. The appeal to the genre of the consolation in the title suggests a vision of the abode of the blessed, which also does not come. I would argue that at the end *Consolation* substitutes God's vision of the world below for the promised human vision of the world above; if this is true, what has accounted for, or prepared the reader for, this change in perspective?

The Struggle for Control of the Work At the beginning of *Consolation*, the narrator takes dictation from the pagan Muses. Philosophy, in her role as Muse of the philosopher, banishes these Muses in an attempt to take over his work and redirect it. She is successful, but at the beginnings of Books IV and V the narrator interrupts Philosophy in order to make her

---

[17] Payne 1981, 69, speaks of the sections of the argument as Cynic (Book II–III.9), Platonic (III.m.9–IV.5), Aristotelian (IV.6–V.m.1), and Augustinian (V.2–V.6). This understates the Aristotelian portion and overstates the Augustinian one, but she offers the intriguing argument that Philosophy goes from one system to another, solving one problem while reducing the possible freedom remaining for the prisoner in the process. The prisoner's attempt to make sense out of all of her answers is the focus of our attention (cf. p. 85: "The befuddled 'I' embodies the human awareness of the inescapability of chaos").

answer questions that evidently she never considered to be part of her healing regimen. The last two books are digressions as far as Philosophy is concerned; do they represent the prisoner's attempt to reassert control over his own work? She says that she is afraid that if she answers his questions, he will never reach his fatherland (V.1.4–5), and she answers his question only to humor him (V.1.8); if the reader feels that the prisoner does not reach his fatherland, is it as a result of these demands? Is the result intended or unintended?

The Myth of Return Central to *Consolation* is the Neo-Platonic myth of the life of the soul, that it descends from its source, falls away from it, turns around again, and seeks to be reunited with it. This is a timeless reality: All souls are engaged in this process, and Philosophy has as one of her goals to make the individual aware of this truth. Crucial to the story is the point of remembering, described by Philosophy at III.m.11 and alluded to by the prisoner at V.m.3. Is the pattern of *Consolation* a falling away from the truth (the prisoner's lethargic and forgetful state in Book I), a turning point (III.m.9), and then a return upward? Does the structure of *Consolation* mirror the life of the soul?

The Mythological World It is curious that, as the material of *Consolation* becomes increasingly philosophically abstract, traditional mythology makes its presence felt more and more. In the opening books, the mythological apparatus is confined to Phoebus and Phoebe, Bacchus' wine, the Golden Age, the brawling winds. But the Orpheus and Eurydice story of III.m.12, the Ulysses and Circe story of IV.m.3, the heroic tales of IV.m.7 (Agamemnon, Ulysses and, most important, Hercules) must be more than mere poetic adornment. Astell sees in their themes a tacit answer to the otherwise unanswered question "What is a human being?"[18] In other words, there seems to be movement away from depicting the natural world (and the prisoner and Philosophy take various positions at various times as to whether the events observable in the natural world represent order or violence) to depicting the epic world. Does this suggest that human beings do not really find their place in the natural order, but rather in mythical struggles to overcome the world? Yet the poems of Book V are aggressively non-mythological.

The Particular Prisoner and the Universal Everyman Philosophy struggles to get the prisoner to leave behind his earthly concerns (the injustices

---

[18] Astell 1994, 11–12, argues that the tale of Orpheus depicts mortality; that of Ulysses and Circe emphasizes that morality and choice separate mortals from animals; that of Agamemnon, Ulysses, and Hercules describes the return of the philosophical soul to the heavenly fatherland.

that were done him, the family that is his pride; cf. I.4, I.5) and come away with her to the true fatherland, which is to die. If the prisoner chooses to live, does he do so as the prisoner, or as Everyman? Is the prisoner willing to become an abstract human being? After all, the author never names his prisoner Boethius, even though there can be no doubt of his identity. But the questions raised and emotions revealed in I.4 never go away, and at the end of the work we are still talking about the justice of earthly punishments and the need to behave well in this world. The reader could perhaps take this as a sign that the prisoner is unwilling to let go of his particular and temporal situation, which would be a frustration to Philosophy.

Consolation *as Autobiography*   It is always fair to wonder whether our appreciation of an author's text would be in any way affected if it were only known to us anonymously. In the case of *Consolation*, the fact that Boethius is the author makes a considerable difference. This is so not just because of the political realities that led to his downfall, the false accusations against him and his ultimate execution for treason at the command of Theoderic;[19] note also that the prisoner speaks to Philosophy as one who knows from personal experience about the difficulty of talking about free will and foreknowledge (cf. V.1.2). Philosophy will go on to borrow from the work done in Boethius' commentaries on Aristotle; Boethius the author presents himself as a man who, while never forgetting his family and his misfortunes, is glad to return to his books. We see the author's former studies transferred to a higher plane as the prisoner, following the example of Augustine's autobiographical *Confessions*, caps the story of his life with a theoretical discussion of the nature of time and his place in a world defined by God.

Looking Up and Looking Down   Closely related to this are the shifting perspectives offered by *Consolation*. Philosophy wants the prisoner, as she would want any soul, to look up; from the vantage point of the eternal realm, the world below may be despised, and its masters may be laughed at as cruel but powerless tyrants (cf. IV.m.1). But there never is a flight out of the labyrinth (cf. III.12.30), and the question addressed by Philosophy at the end of *Consolation*—How can God observe human actions and know our future actions without imposing necessity on them and thus depriving them of their free will?—in effect entails a description of the eternal gaze of God; it describes how he sees us, what is the

---

[19] The sad story is well known. The reader is told all that needs to be known in I.4; a full discussion in its historical context may be found in Chadwick 1981, 46–68, and in Barnish 1990.

nature of his knowledge when we are the objects of his knowledge. *Consolation* had promised a looking up by mortals into the realm of God, but ends with a looking down (or looking out, Philosophy would say, etymologizing the word "providence" at V.6.17) by God into the realm of human actions. What importance should the reader attach to this change of perspective?

Defining Philosophy   Are Philosophy's history and character slowly revealed to the reader? She first appears with torn robes, and complains at I.3.7 of the philosophers who divided up her integral self; when she describes at III.9.16 how human perversity divides up true happiness, which is a unity, into component members, is she intimating that philosophy is true happiness? In her torn robes, is she emblematic of the mendicant philosopher? Yet her robes resemble the smoke-covered death masks that aristocratic families would keep of their ancestors; she may in fact come from the Land of the Dead. If there have been no true philosophers in the eight hundred years that separate the Hellenistic philosophers from Boethius except for the martyred Romans Seneca, Canius, and Soranus (I.3.9), where has she been all this time? When she says at the end of III.m.9 that God is the soul's source, conveyance, leader, path, and haven, and goes on to say soon after at IV.1.9 that she will direct the prisoner to his fatherland by her own leadership, path, and conveyance, is she being arrogant, usurping the prerogatives of God? Or are we to think that Philosophy is God? And if so, what are we to make at V.6.46–48 of her advocacy of humble prayer as access to God?

Inner Dialogue and Self-Definition   Since *Consolation* is a fiction, the example of Augustine's *Soliloquies* as well as of his *Confessions* can embolden us to see in the dialogue between the prisoner and Philosophy an inner dialogue of the two halves of the author's own self, designed to be overheard by the reader. Just as Augustine realizes through self-examination that he has two selves, and that they do not always coincide with each other, so too may these participants function as not-quite-integratable halves of a single person. In a fascinating essay, Chadwick describes how the focus of much literature in many cultures in late antiquity is a search for an answer to the question of the relationship between body and soul; can this be made to coincide with a general critical belief that *Consolation* aims to show a reconciliation of the claims of philosophy and poetry?[20] It is a convention of consolatory literature that an equality of mourner and comforter is achieved: Philosophy and the prisoner may be equals as well.

---

[20] Chadwick 1999; Curley 1986, 255; Curley 1987, 366–67.

The Prison Document   It is often claimed that a model for *Consolation* is Plato's *Phaedo*, with its depiction of Socrates in prison, discoursing on the immortal nature of the soul and composing hymns in his cell. But I would argue that the more important Platonic parallel is Plato's *Crito*. In it, the Spirit of the Laws of Athens is imagined to come to Socrates in his cell and argue how it would be hypocritical of him to escape from prison now, as he had always accepted the rule of Athenian law before. In other words, Socrates proves that he is a true philosopher by refusing to escape from the prison. Philosophy wants the prisoner to escape with her, but he does not; his willingness to stay behind in his cell may be read in a very Socratic light; he may be the true philosopher by refusing to escape with Philosophy.

But other parts of the discussion and its progress may suggest a connection with prison literature in more general terms. The lack of final reconciliation at the end of *Consolation* may be appropriate to the condition of a prisoner who does not want the end of his story written yet;[21] what may be considered an obsession with time in *Consolation* may be plausibly related to the experience of exile.[22]

Christian versus Neo-Platonic Thought   Perhaps the most notorious fact about *Consolation* is that its author, a professing Christian and the author of five brief theological works, at the end of his life, arguably at the point of death, seems to turn for solace not to his religion but to pagan philosophy. There is no reference either to the Jesus of history or the Christ of faith; the resurrection of the dead makes no appearance; the sacraments are ignored. On the other hand, very few components of the Neo-Platonic synthesis that are incompatible with Christianity make their appearance here either: There are no henads, no decan gods, no theurgy. While there is an occasional Neo-Platonic lapse (a reference to First Mind, the possible preexistence of souls), it is generally agreed that *Consolation* represents Neo-Platonism as it may be accommodated to Christianity.[23]

---

[21] Davies 1990, 40: "As in any posthumous biography (or autobiography) I move from the presentation of self to the secrets of the self. I reveal the hidden self and utimately the hidden god. . . . The closure of the debate is a recognition of a future of which I will not be a part."

[22] Claassen 1999, 185: "The 'timeless now' of exile is most intimately involved with the 'terrible here' of the place of exile." Claassen speaks specifically of Ovid here, but it seems an elegant description of the anxieties of the prisoner of *Consolation*.

[23] For details of what is Neo-Platonic that is not in *Consolation*, see Gersh 1986, 2.655-64; for a more general account of *Consolation*'s accommodation of Christianity and Neo-Platonism, see Chadwick 1981, 247–53, "The Religion of Boethius."

But Christianity does make its appearance between the lines, so to speak: The prisoner expresses the wish that the same peace rule on earth as in heaven, echoing the language of the Lord's Prayer (I.m.5.46–48); the conclusion of III.m.9 speaks of God in language not incompatible with Trinitarian beliefs; Philosophy herself quotes from the book of Wisdom, to the prisoner's surprise, at III.12.22; *Consolation* concludes with an important allusion to Esther, speaking of the necessity laid on all people to act with righteousness, because they act before the eyes of the all-seeing God; at V.3.33–36, the prisoner speaks not of the transcendent approach to God that Philosophy had offered but of humble access to God through prayer and of the meriting of divine grace, and he speaks of God as "the inapproachable light" in language that echoes that of 1 Timothy 6:16. The question is clearly complex; but if the prisoner has been keeping Philosophy from achieving her program of reeducation by redirecting her argument away from escape from his prison, has he not elected to keep himself alive? If he is, like Socrates, the true philosopher because he does not escape from the prison, has the prisoner shown that he is a different kind of philosopher? Menippean satire is a medium in which the author's true convictions are frequently hidden by his text; the genre has a Platonic reluctance to believe that what is true can be adequately represented by words.[24]

The Acceptance of the World of Time   *Consolation* ends by defining God's knowledge; this turns on the nature of God's timelessness as opposed to the time-bound human world. In effect, *Consolation* ends by defining the world of human experience and human action; this stands in opposition to the expressed desire of Philosophy that the prisoner transcend the world of time in order to rise and come away with her to eternal realms. Can this be read as an Aristotelian (or a Christian) assertion of the value of the physical world, and has this been prepared for all along by the prisoner's extreme reluctance to dismiss his concern for his earthly life, for his family, his friends, and the very real wrongs done to him? The prisoner, and through him the author, struggles to locate himself within the world of time, and not outside of it.

---

[24] I argue, for example, that the Emperor Julian's Menippean satire *The Caesars* depicts a comic Olympus in which his predecessors are ridiculed, while a special heaven and a special fate is reserved for him at the end of the work (Relihan 1993, 119–34). Wherever we can compare a Menippean satire of a given author to his other works (Seneca, for example, or the Christian Fulgentius), we see a discrepancy between the other world created for the sake of the satire and what may be plausibly imputed to the author's personal beliefs.

Suggestions for Further Reading

The arguments that I would put forward for reading *Consolation* within the context of Menippean satire as a work that is essentially Christian are controversial; they are argued at length elsewhere.[25] But the best course for readers who wish to achieve a better understanding of *Consolation* is to immerse themselves in primary literature. The works that have the greatest claim on being models, parallels, or analogues to *Consolation* may be read with the greatest profit; so too are the other works of Boethius, which suggest the strangeness and fullness of *Consolation* by their great distance from it.

Boethius: *On Music* (with translation and notes of Bower 1989), *Institutes of Arithmetic* (with translation and notes of Masi 1983), *Commentaries on Aristotle, On Interpretation* (selections in Blank and Kretzmann 1998).

Plato: *Phaedo* (Socrates composing hymns in prison), *Crito* (Socrates refusing to leave his cell), *Timaeus* (the structure of the universe; cf. *Consolation*, III.m.9), *Gorgias* (on the value of punishment; cf. *Consolation*, Book IV).

Aristotle: *On Interpretation* (especially Chapter 9; see also Boethius' commentaries on it in Blank and Kretzmann 1998).

Augustine: *Confessions* (especially Book 10; cf. *Consolation* V.3 and V.m.3), *Soliloquies* (dialogues between Self and Reason).

Consolatory literature: pseudo-Plato, *Axiochus* (Socrates speaking to an invalid on his bed; the vision of the other world, in the form of a Platonic myth); pseudo-Plutarch, *To Apollonius*; Dio Chrysostom, *Charidemus*; Cicero, *Tusculan Disputations* (also in five books: philosophy as the medicine for the fear of death in Books I–IV; a protreptic portion on virtue as the only necessity for a happy life in Book V).

Menippean satire: Petronius, *Satyricon*; Martianus Capella, *The Marriage of Philology and Mercury* (especially the allegorical Books I and II, describing Philology's preparations for and ascent to Olympus); Fulgentius, *Mythologies* (the prologue is translated in Relihan 1993, 203–10).

Philosophical poetry: The tragedies of Seneca, particularly the *Hippolytus* and the *Hercules Furens (Mad Hercules)*; see Lerer 1985, 237–50.

Other classical works: Lucian, *The Fisherman* (the author's fictional self stands trial before Philosophy for having insulted her), *Zeus Catechized* (one Cyniscus travels to Olympus to embarrass Zeus by asking him hard questions about human free will and the relation of that to

---

[25] *The Prisoner's Philosophy: On the limitations of pagan thought in Boethius's Consolation*, forthcoming from University of Notre Dame Press.

Fate and divine foreknowledge; cf. *Consolation*, Books IV and V); Marcus Aurelius, *Meditations* (spiritual exercises on the value of retreating within yourself and debating within yourself).

There is a wealth of secondary literature. To speak only of recent works in English, pride of place goes to Chadwick 1981, for a full treatment of all necessary aspects of Boethius' life, times, and work. However, I would recommend that the reader start out small.

Brief introductions to Boethius: Chadwick 1998, Minio-Paluello 1970.

Introductions to Late Antiquity: Bowersock, et al. 1999 offers many riches to anyone who browses through its articles and essays (see especially Dillon, "Philosophy," and O'Donnell, "Boethius"); most important for *Consolation* is the essay of Chadwick 1999, "Philosophical Traditions and the Self," which, though never mentioning Boethius once, is nevertheless an accurate description of the intellectual world in which *Consolation* takes shape, in which the relation of body and soul is a question of paramount importance.

Further works on the historical background: Chadwick 1981, 1–68 ("Romans and Goths"), is a good starting point; Barnish 1990, on politics and literature; Moorhead 1992, on Theoderic, to be read in conjunction with the review of O'Donnell 1993.

The best introduction to Boethius' relation to Neo-Platonism, and the ways in which *Consolation* avoids those aspects of Neo-Platonism that are contradictory to Christian belief, is Gersh 1986, 2.647–718. Sharples 1991, both in its introduction and in its commentary, is an invaluable guide to the content of the last third of *Consolation*.

For *Consolation* as a religious text, see the essay of Olmstead 1989 and the concluding chapter of Pelikan 1997.

Literary studies: Crabbe 1981 is a long and detailed essay; Curley 1986 and 1987 may now seem the more sophisticated analysis. Boethius the poet is the subject of O'Daly 1991; Boethius the writer of dialogue is treated by Lerer 1985. For *Consolation* as a Menippean satire, see Relihan 1993; see also Payne 1981 and Dronke 1994. Claassen 1999 offers useful insight into *Consolation* within the traditions of the literature of exile; Davies 1900 and Scott 1995 address the traditions of prison literature; Astell 1994 profitably connects *Consolation* and Job and shows their influence in the creation of secondary epics in the Middle Ages.

Bibliographies: The medieval Boethius is well documented in the annotated bibliography of Kaylor 1992. Gruber 1997 offers a detailed bibliography of all Boethian studies up to the year 1998; unfortunately, this is only the first volume, and the second, which contains the bibliography concerning *Consolation*, is only forthcoming at this writing.

PRINCIPLES OF TRANSLATION

Latin poetry does not rhyme; its rhythms, far more complex than those of English, are not related to the accents of the words themselves but to the succession of long and short syllables; that is to say, they depend upon the length of time that it takes to pronounce each syllable. The music of Latin poetry is accordingly quite polyphonic; sometimes word accent agrees with verse accent, and sometimes conflicts with it. Within this rhythmic environment is found a highly artificial poetic language: The great Latin poets (Vergil, Horace, Ovid) did not just write memorable works in verse but, for each writer who came after them, offered new solutions to the old problem of how to fit the Latin language into the shapes of Greek verse. Consequently, every Latin poem is a mosaic of phrases learned from earlier poems; the reading of any Latin poem is a complicated intertextual game, as even a lone word in a given place in a line of a certain rhythm may evoke associations with an earlier poem that then becomes part of the context in which the new poem is meant to be read.

There are thiry-nine poems in *Consolation*, written in a wide range of meters and combinations of meters. The poetic nature of the text cannot be ignored; only *Satyricon* and Martianus Capella's *Marriage* come close to the richness of its mixture of prose and verse. No English translation of a Latin poem can hope to mirror the music of these Latin originals, or the complexities of their associations with the whole of Latin literature. That is for specialists; students curious to see Boethius the poet in his workshop, adapting the themes and language of his originals, may be referred to the study of O'Daly 1991. What I have done here, and what has not been done before in the long history of translation of *Consolation* into English, is reproduce through English accents the rhythms and meters of the original poems. I have thought it important to do so in order to make the reader stop and take the poems seriously; there is a tendency to take the poems as mere metrical restatements of the arguments of the preceding prose sections. I would claim that in fact the poems often shift the focus of arguments, or redirect them in surprising ways; the reader needs to linger on them. The rhythms of the Latin will for the most part not be familiar; I have included accent marks to show where the stresses should fall, and have added in the notes to each poem a brief discussion of the meter and its associations. The reader needs to know only that the stress marks are intended to have their Latin force: That is, they show where the syllables should be dragged out a bit, pronounced more slowly, given more time.[1] It is possible for other English accents to be heard against this background, and I flatter myself in thinking that the resulting synthesis of these two competing rhythms, while not the equivalent of the Latin complexity, makes a worthy music of its own.

The language of poetry is not the language of prose. I have tried to represent the prose speeches of the participants in this dialogue with full respect for what may be called their pedanticisms and niceties: And so it is for this very reason that . . . ; it cannot in any way be doubted . . . ; I see that that is indeed the logical consequence. . . . *Consolation* tells of the worlds of God and of mortals, of timeless reality and physical things, and I have not tried to substitute, as would be the standard translation practice, more elegant English abstract nouns for these crucial "things."[2] I have often used the plural for the singular when the discussion turns on the nature or the actions of an abstract individual, so as to avoid sexist language or the cumbersome he/she; but when the prisioner's own experience lies clearly below the surface of such generalized argument, I have used "he" (e.g., lawless men) and have retained the crucial religious term "fatherland" as a literal translation of *patria*. Philosophy often switches back and forth in addressing a singular and a plural "you"; I have not hesitated to clarify the plural as "you mortals" or "you people"; at times the vehemence of her address justifies the exclamation "Mortal men!" The apparatus also makes clear the difference between you singular and you plural: You singular is sometimes in italics. The contrast to the poems, at least in terms of fullness and movement, is absolute; but the same vocabulary can be found in both prose and verse. I have tried

---

[1] Stress marks fall on the second element of a diphthong (e.g., eách). When on the first element, they help suggest a polysyllabic pronunciation (e.g., concéaled is trisyllabic at IV.m.5.9.).

[2] For example, IV.6.9: "Should one look at the force of these two terms in one's own mind, it will appear quite easily that they are different; for Providence is the divine reason itself, established in the highest ruler of all things, which arranges all things; Fate is the arrangement that inheres in the things that have motion, the arrangement through which Providence weaves all things together in their proper orders." In the verse sections, necessities of meter at times force me to exploit a fuller range of translation options.

to make the language consistent in both key terms and conversational turns of phrase, and it is the function of the apparatus at the bottom of each page to make the reader see that the highly repetitive language of *Consolation* makes its own intertextual realities. The prisoner says "Woe is me!" in the second line of his first poem, and Philosophy mocks him by repeating it in her first poem; she makes fun of him again at I.6.6, "But fancy that!", and the prisoner returns the taunt at IV.2.1. These complexities are not to be missed; and if at times the size of the apparatus seems oppressive, it is to be remembered that I offer it in the hopes that the reader may thus see things that I have not; it has been created not as a concordance to *Consolation* but as a key for the further unlocking of the mysteries of the text. Not all parallels are given at each place, but if each is pursued most parallels can be discovered quickly. The running heads offer another index to the text, for rapid reference; the Glossary is yet another avenue to the content of *Consolation*.

I hope that the contrast in the forms of expression in prose and verse is heightened by my choices, and that the reader will take into consideration these shifts in tone when evaluating the plot and the argument. Latin poetry does not have the length and leisure of prose; one of the curious facts of the history of Latin verse is that prepositions are used less and less, and the case endings of nouns are pressed into service more and more, to establish the relations between nouns; another fact is that elision (the process by which two words are allowed to run together, when one ends with a vowel and the next begins with one, so that only a single syllable is accounted for in the rhythm) is also less and less frequent. Boethius can write entire poems without prepositions and without elision; what results is an almost mortarless masonry in which words are piled on top of each other in elegant structures. English with its wealth of monosyllables cannot do without *a, an, in, of, the, from, by, to, that*: in these necessary little words English finds the ability to translate Latin verse in meter, because here is often where the unaccented syllables will be found to correspond to the Latin short syllables. To give a brief example, a simple, complete sentence (I.m.7.1–4):

> nubibus atris
> condita nullum
> fundere possunt
> sidera lumen

To translate in order: clouds black / hid no / shed can / stars light; or: Stars hidden by black clouds can shed no light. As a prose translation, this would adequately express the meaning of these words as a string of vocabulary items, but no more. The rhythm requires that something be added:

> Stárs that lie hídden
> Báck of the bláck cloúds
> Cánnot províde us
> Líght we can seé by.

What has been added? The first person pronoun, and the phrase "we can see by"; the justification is that the phrase "to shed light" actually has the verb that means "pour out," "pour over," and the image is of light flooding the landscape. This is in fact a bold image, given how little light stars actually provide, whether or not there are clouds; Philosophy exaggerates. But what has been retained is the forcefulness of expression; the marching rhythm of these verses cannot be missed; just as important, these brief metrical units (technically called adonics) represent the last two units of a line of epic verse. I argue that the initial poem gives a promise of epic that is quickly denied, and that the movement of the first half of *Consolation* is toward the regaining of the epic voice, achieved in the pivotal poem III.m.9. The combinations of philosophical material and lyric structures found in between these two poems is intended to be striking, with sometimes the one, sometimes the other, gaining the upper hand. This is a part of the meaning of the piece that I try to bring out in translation.

These methods and devices require a certain amount of patience on the reader's part, but I believe that Boethius the poet seems more respectable this way. He is usually seen as more of a versifier than a poet, but I come away from these efforts with great respect for his innovations and his skill; the sheer hard work of respecting his images and his meters simultaneously has kept me, I hope, from merely representing his poetry as trivialities; and while I cannot hope that all the poems are contributions to the history of English versification, I take some pride in believing that doggerel has been for the most part avoided.

A Note on the Text and the Apparatus

The Latin text of *Consolation of Philosophy* is sound. There are only a few passages that present any textual difficulty: Angle brackets (<>) enclose a few editorial additions. I have generally used Bieler's second edition (1984) as the basis of my translation, but often have incorporated the emendations suggested by the commentary of Gruber 1978. The effect on the translation is often quite minor, and I have not thought it necessary to record all the divergences in detail. I have had the advantage of consulting the new edition of Moreschini 2000; but this is a conservative text, more concerned with establishing the state of the manuscripts in the ninth century than to try to establish what Boethius wrote in the sixth.[1] An English reader curious about the Latin text should consult the editions of O'Donnell 1984 and Sharples 1991; the *Concordance* of Cooper 1928, without which this sort of translation could never have been attempted, is invaluable.

It is traditional to label the various parts of *Consolation* with the words "meter" and "prose." For example, Book I Meter 4 (or I.m.4) identifies the fourth poem of the first book; Book I Prose 4 (abbreviated with numbers only: I.4) identifies the fourth prose section. The notes use these designations, as does the apparatus, but with this simplification: In the apparatus, after the first entry for any section (I.4.1, for example), the book number is omitted to save space (4.2); so too will I.m.4.2 be

---

[1] One mistake of Bieler's is corrected: At I.5.4, Moreschini restores the word *summa* ("the highest") that had slipped out of Bieler's text, though he had printed it in his apparatus: *cuius agi frenis atque obtemperare iustitiae summa libertas est.* Curiously, Bieler has *summa* in angle brackets in the lemma in the textual apparatus, as if the word were to be added by emendation; Moreschini reports that the word is found in all manuscripts. Some later translations have followed Bieler's error. However, Moreschini makes two mistakes of his own in Book I. The word *residens* ("dwelling") disappears from I.4.3; at I.1.1, a curious typo appears, *adtitisse* for *astitisse*. Such is the nature of textual progress.

truncated to 4.2, as there can be no confusion as to the reference, given the fact that the actual text stands above it. In any other place (in the Introduction or Notes, for example), a reference of the form I.4 refers to the entirety of the fourth prose section of the first book. Further, all passages referred to in the apparatus for a given line of verse or sentence of prose contain the full designation, even if it is to a passage within the same prose or verse section being catalogued. When a string of references are given in parentheses after an entry in the apparatus, the semicolon separates direct parallels from more general parallels (these latter also marked by "cf."); when a number of parallels are given to a single meter or prose, commas separate the sentence or line numbers, and then a semicolon intervenes before the next parallel. Where I have not been able to preserve an identical English translation or use a closely related root for the Latin word in question, I often place the word that is to be found in the parallel passage in parentheses. An example from Book IV may make all of this clear:

6.9 ruler (III.10.7, 9, 14; V.3.35; cf. III.m.9.28 (leader)).

No doubt there are inconsistencies within the details compiled in the apparatus, but I do not think that they will detract from its usefulness.

NOTE TO THE SECOND PRINTING

The occasion of the second printing has presented a welcome opportunity to correct some typographical errors and minor inconsistencies, and to rethink a passage or two (cf. I.m.7.23–24). Some early reviewers have prompted other revisions. To John Marenbon of Trinity College, Cambridge (*The Medieval Review* 02.09.22), I owe the important revision at V.3.9, as well as the regularization of the terminology surrounding recuperation (*sospitas:* cf. IV.1.9). To Daniel Sheerin (*The Classical Review* 53 [2003]: 255–56) I owe the rewriting of IV.m.7.6–7; a few other poetic passages have been modified through suggestions which he graciously communicated to me privately.

The second installment in Gruber's bibliography of Boethian studies (see p. xxvii) has now appeared: *Lustrum* 40 (1998): 199–259. John Marenbon's important new study (*Boethius* [Oxford 2003]) must now be consulted by all serious readers of *Consolation.*

NOTE TO THE THIRD PRINTING

The third printing sees mostly minor changes: a comma added, a simple typo corrected; *sea-swell* is now properly compounded, and some adjustments have been made to the accents in the poems; there are two additions in the cross-references. More important is the change from *function* to *obligation* at IV.6.1 (see my *The Prisoner's Philosophy* [Notre Dame 2007] 194 n.11); and from *act* to *plead your case* in the very last line, an improvement I owe to Danuta Shanzer.

Of the most recent Boethian publications, I recommend John Marenbon, ed., *The Cambridge Companion to Boethius* (2009); Antonio Donato, *Boethius'* Consolation of Philosophy *as a Product of Late Antiquity* (Bloomsbury Academic 2013) and my review (*Bryn Mawr Classical Review* 2014.06.20); and Stephen Blackwood, *The Consolation of Boethius as Poetic Liturgy* (Oxford 2015).

CONSOLATION OF PHILOSOPHY

Book I

Meter 1

Í who was ónce at the heíght of my pówers a máster of vérsecraft—
    Woé is me!—weéping, coérced, énter the gríef-ridden móde.
Ló! Their cheeks hárrowed, the Múses come téll me the wórds I must
                                        táke down,
    Ánd they now dámpen my fáce with láchrymose élegy's trúth.
Thém, and them ónly, no pánic could vánquish or fríghten from cóming   5
    Ás my compánions alóne óver the páth I must treád.
Théy who were ónce the delíght of a yoúth that was prósperous and
                                          háppy
    Ín my misfórtunes consóle mé, now a griéving old mán.
For nów has arríved, unexpécted and hástened by évils, my óld age—
    Paín gave the órder; its yeárs nów must be be ádded to míne.   10
Nów from the tóp of my heád flows down snów-white hair, quíte out of
                                          seáson;
    Bárren, my bódy is sheáthed, in shívering, límp, nerveless skín.
Háppy the deáth of a mán that would thrúst itself nót in the sweét years!
    Bút, when incéssantly cálled, cómes to those strícken with gríef.
Woé is them! Wíth a deaf eár she rejécts all pleás of the wrétched—   15
    Mérciless, shé will not clóse éyes that are brímming with téars.

Meter 1 I.m.1.2 woe (I.m.2.1, I.m.2.17, II.m.6.16, III.m.12.49), coerced
(I.m.2.27), grief-stricken (I.m.1.14; I.5.2; cf. III.9.14, III.12.1).   1.3 harrowed
(cf. I.1.5).   1.4 elegy (cf. II.1.8).   1.6 companions (IV.m.1.11, IV.3.14).
1.12 barren (I.m.2.24).   1.13 thrust (V.m.4.22).   1.15–16 (cf. II.m.1.5–6).
1.16 eyes . . . tears (I.2.7).

Whíle faithless Fórtune was pártial to mé with ephémeral fávors,
    A síngle, deplórable hoúr neárly plunged mé in my gráve.
Nów that she's dárkly transfórmed her appeárances, éver deceítful,
20   Múst then my únholy lífe drág out this ghástly deláy?
Téll me, my friénds, why you boásted so óften that Í was so bléssèd—
    Sóldiers who féll never hád stáble ground ón which to stánd.

Prose 1

As I was conning these words over within myself in silence, and putting
my seal on this tearful complaint with the aid of my pen, there appeared
to me a woman who had taken her stand directly above my head. Her
countenance demanded absolute reverence: Her eyes glowed like fire,
penetrating far beyond the common capability of mortals; her color was
intense, her strength inexhaustible, even though she was so full of eternity that it was impossible to believe that she was of my own generation;
2   and her height was of a measure hard to fix. For at one time she would
keep herself within common mortal limits, but at another she would
seem to strike at the heavens with the crown of the top of her head—
and whenever she stuck her head up still higher she would pierce
heaven itself and disappoint the vision of those mortals who tried to
contemplate her.

3   And her robes: They were perfectly finished of the most microscopic threads, of cunning manufacture and of indecomposable material. As I learned later (she herself offered the information) she had
woven them herself, with her own hands; but their appearance was
obscured by a sort of gloom of untended antiquity, such as is found on
4   the smoke-covered death masks of one's ancestors. On the hem at the
bottom it could be made out that the Greek letter pi had been woven

---

1.17 Fortune (I.4.2, I.5.10, II.1.2 ff., III.2.2 ff.), ephemeral (III.m.3.6).
1.18 hour (II.m.1.8–9), plunged (I.m.2.1, III.m.11.14 (buried)), grave
(I.4.36).   1.19 deceitful (I.6.21, III.6.1).   1.20 unholy (I.4.28, I.4.36; cf.
III.m.9.27 (holy)), drag out (II.m.7.24 (protracts)).   1.21 friends (II.8.6,
II.m.8.26–7, III.2.9).   1.22 stable (I.4.16, II.m.8.1, III.m.2.38, III.m.9.3)

Prose 1 1.1.1 silence (I.2.4, II.7.20), pen (I.4.25, V.m.4.6), reverence (I.4.40, cf.
IV.1.1), penetrating (III.3.1, IV.4.22, V.2.7), strength (V.m.4.10, 35), inexhaustible (II.7.18).   1.2 (cf. V.m.4.20–25) head (III.10.31), vision (I.3.2), contemplate (III.8.8).   1.3 microscopic (III.9.3), indecomposable (IV.6.19), learned
later (at I.3.7), woven (I.3.7, III.12.30, IV.6.6, 9), antiquity (II.7.13, III.5.2),
masks (II.m.7.12).   1.4 climb up (II.2.10).

in, and at the top a theta; between the two letters, after the fashion of a
ladder, it could be made out that certain steps had been emblazoned, so
that there could be by their means a way to climb up from the lower letter to the upper. Nevertheless, the hands of certain violent men had   5
torn this same robe and had carried off such scraps as each one could.
But her right hand held her books, and her left her scepter.   6

And then, when she saw that the women who were sitting at my bed-   7
side were the Muses of poetry, dictating words to my tears, she was upset
for a time. Who, she said, her pitiless eyes ablaze, let these little stage   8
whores come visit this invalid? They do not tend to his pains with any sort
of a remedy; not only that, but they actually encourage them, adding their
own sweet poisons. For these are the women who choke out the rich fields   9
of reason's fruits; theirs are the barren brambles of the passions; they accli-
matize the mortal mind to disease, and do not liberate it. Now, if it were   10
some unhallowed man that your sweet nothings were leading astray, as is
your all-too-common custom, I'd think that this could be tolerated with
less annoyance—after all, my efforts would not be under attack in such a
one as that. But him! Raised in the disciplines of the followers of Parmenides and Plato—But no; just you get out of here, you Sirens, sweet   11
unto shipwreck; leave him to my Muses for his convalescence and his cure.

This tragic chorus, thus scolded, stared down at the ground in sorrow;   12
by their blushing they revealed their disgrace and they went out the
door, depressed. But I—my eyes had been awash in tears and darkened   13
over, and so could not make out who was this woman with such over-
mastering authority—I was dumbfounded. I kept my eyes fixed on the
earth, and began to wait silently for whatever she was going to do next.
Then she came closer; she sat on the very edge of my bed; she stared at   14
my face, burdened with grief and staring down at the ground in sorrow;
and in these verses she complained about the confusion of my mind:

1.5 torn (I.3.7, III.12.23; cf. IV.6.49), scraps (I.3.7; cf. III.9.16).   *1.6* books
(I.5.6), scepter (IV.m.1.19).   *1.7* dictating (cf. I.m.1.3), for a time (I.2.6,
II.7.20, IV.6.2).   *1.8* pitiless (IV.m.1.29, IV.m.2.3), stage (II.3.12), tend to
(III.m.6.9 (embraces)), pains (I.m.1.10), remedy (I.5.11–12, I.6.21), poisons
(II.m.6.17, IV.m.2.6; cf. II.5.16).   *1.9* fruits (IV.6.51), passions (I.5.11, IV.4.27),
disease (I.2.5, III.7.2).   *1.10* leading astray (I.4.10), annoyance (IV.7.17), Plato
(I.3.6, I.4.5).   *1.11* Muses (I.5.10; cf. II.1.8).   *1.12* down . . . sorrow
(I.1.14; cf. I.m.2.27), depressed (cf. I.3.1 (depression)).   *1.13* eyes (I.m.3.9–
10), darkened (I.6.21, III.2.13), fixed (III.2.1, III.m.9.24), earth (I.m.2.27),
silently (I.1.1).   *1.14* staring . . . sorrow (I.1.12), complained (II.2.7), confusion (IV.1.9, IV.6.1, 21; cf. I.5.12, I.6.9, 13, 21).

Meter 2

Woé is him! Plúnged to the dépths, súnk to the bóttom,
Mínd loses áll of its édge, cásts off its ówn light,
Tákes itself óff to the gloóm, álien dárkness,
Whén deletérious cáre, fánned by the stórm winds,
5   Bórn of the phýsical wórld, gróws past all meásure.
Tíme was when hé would ascénd to heáven unboúnded,
Freé to proceéd in the tráck of stárs in their coúrses.
Hé would obsérve at the dáwn the sún's constellátions,
Wátch for the Zódiac sígn óf the cold néw moon;
10 Áll the recúrsions of áll wándering plánets,
Bént and constraíned into shápe, várious órbits,
Hé as a víctor posséssed boúnded by númber.
Nó, there is móre—every caúse: whý in their blúster
Stórmwinds can teáse and excíte ócean's calm súrface;
15 Whát spirit rótates the eárth, stáble, unmóving;
Hów can the stárs that will fáll ín the Atlántic
Ríse up agaín in the Eást, rádiant-dáwning;
Whát renders tránquil and cálm the hoúrs of the spríng day,
Só to adórn all the eárth with róse-colored flówers;
20 Whó was the reáson that Fáll ín the year's fúllness,
Fértile and rích, overflóws, grápes full to búrsting—
Ít was his hábit to próbe áll of these quéstions,
Náture's root caúses to sólve, áll of them hídden.
Nów here he liés, and his mínd's bríghtness is bárren;
25 Weíghed down, draped óver his néck pónderous sháckles,
Weáring a fáce that looks dówn, bént by the deád weight—
Woé is him! trúly coérced he stáres at the hárd earth.

Meter 2 I.m.2.1–5 (cf. III.m.11.1–5).   2.1 woe (I.m.1.2, 16, I.m.2.27,
II.m.5.27), sunk (III.m. 8.18).   2.2 light (III.m.11.3).   2.3 alien
(III.m.9.4).   2.4 care (III.2.2) winds (I.m.3.3–8).   2.6–12 (cf. IV.m.1.5–
14).   2.9 cold moon (IV.m.6.7).   2.10 recursions (cf. IV.m.1.14).
2.14 surface (I.m.7.5–12, III.m.10.13).   2.15 fixed and unmoving (= stable:
I.m.1.22; cf. III.12.14).   2.18–21 (seasons; cf. I.m.5.14–22, I.m.6.1–17).
2.23 root causes (cf. IV.m.5.18), hidden (I.4.4).   2.24 barren (I.m.1.12,
III.10.5 (exhausted)).   2.25 weighed down (cf. IV.m.2.10), neck (III.m.2.14,
III.m.3.3), shackles (I.m.4.18, III.m.10.3, III.m.12.4).
2.26 face . . . down (cf. I.1.12–14), bent (III.m.2.27–30).   2.27 coerced
(I.m.1.2), earth (I.1.13).

Prose 2

But it's time, she said, for medicine, not for complaint.

Then, staring at me with the full force of her eyes, she said: Are you 2
really the same man who, once upon a time, nursed with my milk,
raised on my food, emerged into the strength and vigor of a mature
mind? Yet we had supplied you with such weapons as would still be pro- 3
tecting you now, unconquered and unshakable, if you hadn't cast them
away beforehand. Do you know me? Why don't you say something? Is it 4
from shame or from incomprehension that you have fallen silent? I'd
prefer shame, but it's obvious to me that incomprehension has had its
way with you.

Because she saw that I was not merely silent but dumb, completely 5
without a tongue, she gently put her hand upon my chest. There's no
danger here, she said; he's suffering from lethargy, a disease common in
abused minds. He has forgotten himself for a time, but he'll remember 6
easily enough, since he knew us once before. And so that he can remember, let us just wipe his eyes for a time, eyes clouded with the cataracts of
the human world.

That's what she said; and then she began to dry my eyes, tearful and 7
overflowing, by gathering the cloth of her robe into a twist.

Meter 3

Thén was night's dárkness dispélled and its shádows releásed me
　　　　　　　　　　　　　　　　　　　　　enlíghtened,
　　　Thén to my éyes came their úsual pótency.
Júst as when másses of cloúds are compácted by squálls of the Wést Wind,
　　　Fírmament sólid and thíck with the thúnderstorm,
When sún is in híding though nó stars retúrn to their pláce in the 5
　　　　　　　　　　　　　　　　　　　　　heávens,

Prose 2 I.2.1 medicine (I.6.17–21, IV.6.5).　　2.2 nursed (cf. I.3.2, 4;
III.9.28).　　2.3 unshakable (IV.2.3 (stability)), cast away (I.m.4.17,
I.6.21).　　2.4 incomprehension (IV.5.5), silent (I.1.1, I.1.13).　　2.5 dumb
(cf. I.1.13), tongue (I.4.36), lethargy (cf. III.1.2), disease (I.1.9).　　2.6 forgotten
(cf. I.6.10, III.2.13, III.m.11.10–16, IV.1.1, IV.4.31), for a time (I.1.7, II.7.20),
knew (cf. III.1.7), eyes (I.m.3.2, 10), clouded (cf. III.m.11.7, V.2.10).
2.7 dry . . . eyes (cf. II.4.9), tearful (I.1.13; cf. I.m.1.2)

Meter 3 I.m.3.1 night (IV.m.1.28).　　3.2 eyes (I.1.7, I.2.2, 7, I.m.3.10).
3.3–10 (cf. III.m.1.7–8).　　3.3 West Wind (IV.m.5.13).

And dówn from on hígh on the eárth is the níght-time spilled—
Thén should the Nórth Wind, reléased from its bóndage in Thrácian ..
                                                                          cáverns,
   Sháke out the níght and unbár captive dáy again,
Ít flashes fórth and, with líght unexpéctéd, shímmering Phoébus
10   Bátters our éyes with his ráys in our wónderment.

Prose 3

It was in no other manner that the clouds of my depression were sent in
2   tatters away. I took the daylight deep into myself and recovered my mental senses, so that I could recognize the face of my doctor. And so, when
I directed my eyes toward her and fixed my vision on her I recognized my
nurse, in whose house and in whose presence I had dwelt since I was a
child—Philosophy.
3   I said: Why have you come to this, the solitude of our exile, leaping
down from the center point of heaven? You are the teacher of every virtue; can it be that you too, my codefendant, are here to be tried on
trumped-up charges?
4   But she said: I nursed you; did you think I'd abandon you? That I
wouldn't share with you in collaborative effort the burden that you
5   have come under because of the hatred of my name? No; it was forbidden that Philosophy leave unaccompanied any innocent's path. But
evidently you thought that I'd be afraid of an accusation against myself,
6   and be terrified that something unexpected would happen. Surely you
don't think that now is the first time that wisdom has been attacked
and imperiled in the court of unrighteous custom? Surely in the court of
the ancients as well, even before the era of our beloved Plato, we often

---

3.5–6 (cf. I.m.7.1–4).   3.7 North Wind (I.m.5.19).   3.9–10 (cf.
III.m.11.7–8).   3.9 Phoebus (I.m.5.9, III.m.2.31).   3.10 batters ... eyes
(V.m.4.33)

Prose 3 I.3.1 depression (cf. I.1.12 (depressed)), doctor (I.4.1, IV.2.25, IV.4.38,
IV.6.28).   3.2 vision (I.1.2, I.6.21, III.9.24), nurse (I.2.2).   3.3 exile (I.5.2,
II.4.17), center point (III.10.38, IV.6.15, 22), codefendant (cf. I.4.41–42).
3.4 nursed (III.9.28).   3.5 forbidden (I.3.14, I.4.38, I.5.3, IV.6.54), unaccompanied ... path (cf. I.m.1.6), unexpected (II.1.9).   3.6 think (I.4.22),
attacked (III.12.24), ancients (IV.6.8), Plato (I.4.5), insolence (I.6.4 (randomness)), stupidity (I.3.14, III.12.23), Socrates (I.3.9, I.4.24), victory (cf. 1 John 5:4,
Apoc. 17:14), death (cf. IV.6.42).

fought the great fight against the insolence of stupidity; and though he himself survived, his teacher Socrates won the victory of an unjust death while I stood at his side. And afterward, when the herds of the Epicureans and Stoics and the others, each after its own fashion, were attempting to go and steal his legacy and were dragging me off kicking and screaming as if I were to be a part of their ill-gotten gains, they ripped apart the robe that I had woven with my own hands; they tore scraps from it and went away, each of them believing that I had gone off with them in my entirety.

Now since a few traces of my real appearance could be seen in these scraps, their temerity led them to believe that they were my kinsmen, and it even led astray not a few of them in the aimless miscalculation of the unhallowed mob. But if, because they happened in a foreign land, you don't know of the exile of Anaxagoras, the poison of Socrates, or the torture of Zeno, still you could have known about Canius, Seneca, Soranus, and others like them—their memory is neither very old nor very obscure. What dragged them down to disaster was nothing other than the fact that, because they were established in our ways, they were seen to be utterly unlike the unrighteous and their enthusiasms. So there is no reason why you should be amazed if, on the high seas of this life, storm winds from all directions buffet us about, for this in particular has been our guiding principle, that we be displeasing to those who are most despicable. And even though their army is great in sheer numbers, it must be dismissed all the same, for it is not led by any general but is only yanked this way and that, at random, by a berserk aimlessness. And if this army should ever array itself against us and attack us with all its might, our leader withdraws all her forces into her own citadel, leaving the others to occupy themselves with the plundering of useless baggage. But we laugh at them from on high as they snatch at each and every

7

8

9

10

11

12

13

14

3.7 herds (cf. IV.4.30, IV.m.5.20), Epicureans (cf. III.2.12), steal (III.6.2), ripped (I.1.5; cf. I.4.42, III.12.23, IV.6.49), robe (I.1.3–5), woven . . . hands (I.1.3), scraps (I.1.5; cf. III.9.16).   3.8 temerity (I.4.24), kinsmen (IV.6.33), miscalculation (III.2.4), unhallowed (I.1.10).   3.9 Socrates (I.3.6), torture (II.4.29), Seneca (III.5.10).   3.10 established . . . ways (I.4.41), wicked (III.4.9). 3.11 no . . . amazed (III.12.38), seas (I.m.5.45), despicable (II.5.33, II.6.13, IV.6.51).   3.12 army (cf. IV.2.27, IV.m.4.8), dismissed (II.1.12, II.7.23; cf. II.1.5).   3.13 citadel (I.5.5, IV.m.3.34, IV.6.8).   3.14 laugh (cf. II.m.4.22, II.6.4), worthless thing (II.5.28, III.2.15, III.9.17), maddened riot (IV.7.17), wall (I.6.9, II.m.4.20), stupidity (I.3.6, III.12.23), forbidden (I.3.5), assault (II.4.25 (aim at), V.5.7).

worthless thing—we are safe from all their maddened riot, protected by
a wall that marauding stupidity is forbidden to assault.

Meter 4

Ín tránquíllity, lífe secúre and séttled,
Úpríght, feét on the néck of peácock Fórtune,
Loókíng squárely at fáte, benígn or brútal—
Hé, úncónquered, who képt his beárings, dreáds not
5   Thé ínsánity óf the ócean's ménace,
When ít chúrns up the wáves from dépths abýssal;
Nór Vésúvius, whén from fráctured chímneys
Fíre fliés spíraling úp with smóke at rándom;
Nór bríght traíls of the líghtning bólts, accústomed
10   Tó démólish the lófty tówers of prínces.
Téll mé, whý are the weák in áwe of týrants,
Férál, víolent, bút withoút true pówer?
Íf yóu hópe for and feár for nóthing éver
Thén yoú've bróken the swórd of the mádman's ánger.
15   Bút á cóward who dreáds or lóngs for sómething,
Whó cánnót stand his groúnd upón his ówn rights,
Hás díscárded his shiéld; out óf posítion,
Hé hás fáshioned the chaín he'll weár in slávery.

Prose 4

She said: Do you understand this? Does it work its way into your mind?
Or are you like the ass at the lyre? Why are you crying? Why do your
cheeks run with tears? As Homer says,

> Oút with it, dón't keep it lócked in your mínd!

Meter 4 I.m.4.2 Fortune (I.m.1.18, I.5.10).   4.5–6 (I.m.7.5–13).   4.6
abyssal (II.m.2.1).   4.7 Vesuvius (cf. II.m.5.25–6 (Aetna)).   4.10 towers
(I.3.13), princes (I.m.5.39–41).   4.11 tyrants (II.6.8, IV.m.1.29–30, IV.m.2.9;
cf. Nero II.m.6, III.m.4).   4.12 violent (II.6.9).   4.13 hope, fear (cf. I.m.7.
25–28).   4.16 stand (I.m.1.22), own rights (II.2.14).   4.17 discarded
(I.2.3).   4.18 fashioned (cf. III.10.27), chain (I.m.2.25, III.m.2.8).

Prose 4 I.4.1 understand (III.1.3; cf. I.2.4), tears (I.m.1.2, I.1.13), Homer (Iliad
1.363, . . . so that we both may know), doctor (I.3.1).

If you are anticipating the doctor's attentions, you need to uncover your wound.

I gathered up my courage to its full strength: The bitterness of the   2
Fortune that wildly rages against me—does it still need to be called to mind? Doesn't it sufficiently stand out on its own? Does the appearance of this place move you not at all? Is this the library which you yourself   3
had chosen in my house to be your ever-fixèd dwelling place, in which you often stayed with me and would discourse upon knowledge of things both human and divine? Was this my appearance, was this my counte-   4
nance, when I would investigate with you the hidden things of nature, when you would with your measuring rod plot out for me the paths of the stars, when you would mold both my actions and the principles of life in general in accordance with the model of the heavenly order? Are these the rewards that I bring back as your faithful follower?

Yet you were the one who through the mouth of Plato decreed this   5
inviolable axiom, that states would be happy and prosperous if either those devoted to wisdom should rule them, or if it were to happen that those who did rule them devoted themselves to wisdom. And it was   6
through the mouth of this same man that you warned that this was the compelling reason for the wise to enter into political life, that the rud-ders of the state not be handed over to its unrighteous and criminal citi-zens and so bring their disease and disaster upon the good. So it was in   7
accordance with this authoritative pronouncement that I desired to put into action what I learned from you in the course of our private and lei-surely sessions—that is, the action of public service.

You and the God who planted you in the minds of the wise are my   8
witnesses that no enthusiasm brought me to high office other than the enthusiasm for the community of all good people. From this sprang for-   9
midable and relentless conflicts with the unrighteous and, a thing that freedom of conscience entails, the perpetual displeasure of those in greater power; this I despised because of my safeguarding of the law.

4.2 Fortune (I.m.1.17, I.m.4.3 (fate), I.4.19, 35, 43–44), wildly rages (II.6.8), call to mind (cf. III.7.5), stand out (IV.2.28), appearance (I.5.6).
4.3 library (I.5.6), dwelling place (I.5.5, 6; II.m.4.2 (foundations)), discourse (II.6.1, III.6.5).   4.4 hidden (I.m.2.22–23, IV.6.1), nature (I.m.2.6–23), stars (I.m.2.10–11, I.m.3.3–4, I.m.5.3–4; cf. II.7.3), rewards (I.4.34), bring rewards (IV.4.28).   4.5 Plato (*Republic* 473d, 487e; I.3.6, III.m.11.15, III.12.1, 38), decreed (III.12.38, IV.4.28).   4.6 disease (cf. III.5.14, III.7.2).
4.7 desired (II.7.1).   4.8 planted (I.4.38, II.4.28, III.2.4), enthusiasm (I.3.10).   4.9 relentless (II.8.1), unrighteous (I.3.10, I.4.6), displeasure (I.3.11).

10 How often I put myself between Conigastus and the assault he was making on some defenseless man's goods! How often I forced Trigguilla, who
was in charge of the royal household, to abandon some outrage that he
had undertaken, or that he had in fact accomplished! How often I
placed my own authority in the line of fire to protect the weak whom the
barbarians' greed, perpetually unpunished, would constantly harass with
infinite indignities! Never did anyone lead me astray from the law to any
unlawful thing.

11   When the affairs in the provinces were going to ruin through private
larcenies and public confiscations, I was no less distressed than were the
12 people who were sustaining them. When, at a time of acute famine, it
seemed that an inexplicably onerous forced sale of grain would lay waste
the province of Campania through sheer deprivation, I entered into battle with the praetorian prefect out of consideration for the good of all
the state, I argued my case (the king himself presiding), and I won—and
13 so that forced sale was not demanded. When the court dogs had already
consumed his wealth, at least in their expectations and ambitions, I
snatched the ex-consul Paulinus from the very jaws of those who would
14 devour him. To keep Albinus, that ex-consul, from being robbed by pen-
alties imposed through partisan accusations, I stood up to the hatred of
the informer Cyprianus.

15   Does it seem to you that I have provoked sufficiently powerful ani-
mosities against myself? And surely among the rest of the senators I
ought to have been more secure, I who through my love of justice stored
up for myself nothing that would make me more secure among the men
16 of the imperial court. Yet who were the informers who threw me down?
One was Basilius—formerly dismissed from royal office, he was driven by
17 the exigencies of debt to bring my name forward. Then there were
Opilio and Gaudentius. When it was decreed by royal pronouncement
that they should go into exile because of their countless and multifarious
double-dealings, they did not want to submit and so sought to protect
themselves by right of holy sanctuary. When the king found out about it,
he decreed that if they did not leave Ravenna before the appointed day
18 they would be driven out with brands burned into their foreheads. You
could not possibly top such severity! Yet on that very day these same
men informed against me and the denunciation of my name was offi-

---

4.10 lead astray (I.1.10).   4.12 king (Theoderic).   4.14 Albinus (I.4.32),
informer (I.4.21, 22, III.4.4), Cyprianus (brother of Opilio at I.4.17).
4.15 provoked (IV.6.45), secure (III.5.12 (relax)), courtiers (III.5.10).
4.16 Basilius (father-in-law of Opilio, I.4.17).   4.17 exile (I.3.3, I.5.2),
sanctuary (I.4.36).

cially accepted. So what does this mean? Did my efforts deserve *this*? Or 19
did the condemnation that preceded them make such accusers just? Was
Fortune so unashamed, if not of innocence accused, at least of the
depravity of its accusers?

But you will ask for the crux of the charge of which I stand accused: It 20
is said that I desired the safety of the Senate. Do you want to know how? I 21
am accused of blocking an informer from bringing documents by which he
would have it that the Senate was guilty of treason. So, my teacher, what 22
do you think? Shall I deny the charge, so as not to be an embarrassment to
you? But I did want the Senate's safety, nor will I ever cease to want it.
Shall I admit to it? But there was no effort to block the informer. Or shall I 23
call the desire for the safety of the senatorial order a crime? To be sure, by
its decrees against me the Senate has brought it about that this is a crime.
But such temerity, which always lies to itself, cannot change the merits of 24
things, and I do not think, in accordance with the decree of Socrates, that
it is right for me either to hide the truth or to connive at lies. But I leave it 25
to your judgment, and to the judgment of the wise, to determine just however this may be. A continuous account of this affair and the truth of the
matter I have entrusted to my pen and so to public memory, so that it cannot be hidden from those who come after me. For what good does it do 26
now to speak of the forged letters, the evidence by which I am accused of
desiring Roman liberty? This fabrication would have been laid wide open
if I had been given the opportunity to avail myself of the confession of the
informers themselves—confession, which has the greatest validity in all
legal proceedings. For what liberty is left that can be hoped for now? How 27
I wish that there were some! I would have made my defense in the words
of Canius. When he was accused by Gaius Caesar, the son of Germanicus—by Caligula!—of having been an accomplice to a conspiracy made
against him, he said, "If I had known, you never would have."

In all this affair my grief has not so dulled my sensibilities as to make 28
me complain that sacrilegious men have undertaken lawless efforts
against virtue. No; what utterly amazes me is that they have accomplished the things that they hoped for. For we may grant that a desire for 29
what is inferior comes from common human failing, but that the designs

---

4.19 deserve (I.5.5), innocence (IV.6.35; cf. I.3.5).   *4.21, 22* informer
(I.4.14).   *4.24* temerity (I.3.8), merits (I.4.43, II.7.2, III.6.3, IV.5.1), Socrates
(I.3.6, 9; Plato, *Theaetetus* 151d).   *4.25* judgment (III.6.6, V.6.2), pen (I.1.1).
·4.26 informers (I.4.14, 21, 22), confession (I.4.35).   *4.27* Canius (I.3.9).
4.28 (cf. IV.4.24).   *4.28* sacrilegious (I.m.1.20 (unholy), I.4.36), lawless
(I.4.46), utterly amazes (I.6.6, II.5.8, IV.5.4).   *4.29* inferior (IV.4.29), god
watching (cf. V.2.11, V.m.2.9–14, V.6.48), monstrosity (IV.1.6).

that the lawless entertain are powerful against innocence while God is
30   watching over it—this is like some monstrosity. And so it is hardly without cause that one of your intimates made this inquiry: "If there really is
a God," he said, "what is the source of evil? But what is the source of
31   good if there is not?" Now we may grant that it is proper for improper
men, who seek the blood of all good men and of the entire Senate, to
have desired to encompass my destruction as well, for they had seen me
32   fighting on behalf of the good and the Senate. But surely I did not
deserve the same treatment from the senators as well? You do remember,
I think—after all you were yourself constantly at my side, steering me
whenever I was going to say something or do something—as I was saying, you do remember that time at Verona: With what bold disregard for
my own peril I stood up for the innocence of that entire body when the
king, who was impatient for our universal downfall, tried to turn the
charge of treason that had been made against Albinus against the entire
senatorial order.

33   You know that the claims that I have made here are true, and that I
have not ever made boast of them for any selfish praise. Somehow or
other one diminishes the reward of a conscience that approves of itself
whenever one makes a display of a secret deed and receives the reward
34   of praise. But you see what was the outcome that awaited my innocence:
In place of reward for true virtue I have incurred punishment for a
35   trumped-up charge. Tell me: For what sort of a crime did even a full and
open confession ever produce judges so unanimous in their merciless-
ness that neither the fallibility of human intelligence nor the universal
unpredictability of human fortune and circumstance could make some
36   of them bend? Were I accused of having wanted to torch the holy temples, to cut the throats of priests with a sacrilegious sword, to engineer
the slaughter of all the good citizens—for all that, sentence would have
been passed for my punishment while I stood before the court; for all
that, after I had confessed and been convicted! But now! At a remove of
nearly five hundred miles, without voice and without defense, I am condemned to death and confiscation because of my overzealous concern

---

4.30 hardly without cause (III.6.1, IV.4.1), intimates (I.3.8 (kinsmen)), inquiry
(IV.1.3).   4.32 remember (I.6.10), I think (II.3.9, V.4.9), at my side (I.3.6,
II.1.5), steering (IV.6.21, 55), Albinus (I.4.14).   4.33 conscience (I.4.37,
II.7.19, IV.6.46, 49), reward of praise (cf. II.7.20).   4.34 reward (I.4.4, I.4.34,
cf. I.m.5.29–36), trumped-up (I.3.3).   4.35 confession (I.4.26), fallibility of
human intelligence (cf. IV.6.24–25).   4.36 temples (I.4.17), sacrilegious
(I.4.28; cf. III.m.9.27 (holy)), without voice (I.2.5).

for the Senate. Would that no one could be convicted of such a crime ever again, Senators—you have earned it!

Even those who informed against me have seen the dignity of this 37 criminal standing, and in order to stain it by the admixture of some illegality or other they lied that I had defiled my own conscience by unholy arts in my pursuit of the dignity of high office. No! You were 38 planted within me; you would drive every desire for mortal things out of the dwelling place of my mind; it was forbidden that there be any place for unholy arts before your eyes. Why? Because every day you would make that Pythagorean maxim flow into my ears and into my thoughts: FOLLOW GOD. I had no interest in trying to secure the assis- 39 tance of the basest of spirits, I whom you tried to raise up to this superiority, that you would make me similar to God. And besides, the guiltless 40 inner recesses of my home, the circle of my most honorable friends, my father-in-law too (a holy man, as worthy of reverence as you are)—all these defend me from any possible suspicion of this charge. And yet— 41 abomination!—they gain approval for their incredible charge because of you. It is for this very reason that it will appear that we have been partakers in evil deeds, because we had been steeped in your studies and established in your ways! And so it is not enough that my reverence for 42 you has done me no good; no, rather you must on your own account be torn because of the wrong done to me.

But it is this that makes the full measure of my disasters overflow, that 43 the opinions of most people look not to the merits of things but only to the outcome of Fortune, and that their judgment is that only the things that good Fortune has endorsed have been in the care of Providence. So it is that the good opinion they once enjoyed is the first thing of all that forsakes the unfortunate. It disgusts me to bring to mind what the gossip 44 is now, how discordant and how diverse are the popular beliefs. I would only say this: The terminal burden of contrary Fortune is the fact that everyone believes that unfortunate people deserve what they suffer

---

4.37 stain (IV.3.10), admixture (IV.4.16), conscience (I.4.33, IV.4.49).
4.38 planted (I.4.8, cf. III.m.11.11), dwelling place (I.5.6, III.2.1, III.9.32), forbidden (I.3.5, I.3.14, IV.6.54).   4.39 assistance (III.3.16, III.9.5, 32), superiority (II.5.10), similar to God (cf. II.5.26), God (III.10.23, III.12.32; cf. IV.6.37).   4.40 most honorable (III.7.5), father-in-law (Symmachus; cf. II.3.5, II.4.5).   4.41–42 (cf. I.3.3, II.2.2).   4.41 studies (cf. I.4.4), established (I.3.10).   4.42 torn (I.1.5, I.3.7).   4.43 full measure (II.3.7), opinions (cf. IV.6.24), merits (I.4.24), Providence (III.11.33, IV.6.8).   4.44 bring to mind (III.3.6, III.7.3), gossip (II.7.19, III.6.3), discordant (V.4.21; cf. V.m.3.1, 6), contrary Fortune (II.1.9, II.4.2).

45 whenever some accusation attaches to them. Look at me! Forcibly
    removed from my possessions, stripped of the dignity of political office,
    disgraced in public opinion—instead of promotion I have received pun-
46 ishment. And here is what I seem to see: the wicked workshops of law-
    less men overflowing in joy and jubilation; every last degenerate making
    threats with brand-new deceptions and denunciations; good men fallen,
    laid low by their fear of this crisis of mine; every last criminal encouraged
    to dare a crime because he will go unpunished, and to commit it because
    he will be rewarded; and the guiltless deprived not only of their safety
    but even of their defense. And so I will cry out:

Meter 5

Creátór of the sphére beáring the fíxed stars,
Yoú whó on a thróne everlásting resíde,
Cónfoúnding the ský with the swíft stórm wínd,
Cómpélling the stárs to submít tó láw—
5   Thus, with líght in her hórns fúll now and brílliant,
Cátchíng fúll fórce fíre from her bróther,
Does the moón put to béd dím constelláations;
Thus, with hórns in a shroúd, dárk now and ghástly,
Phoébús hárd bý, does she lóse all her líght;
10 Thús, at first twílight Vésper is síghted,
Eárlý shépherding frígid moon-rísings;
Thén ás Lúcifer, pále at the súnrise,
Hé chánges agaín hís reíns and his páth—
Yoú whó in the chíll of the leáf-shedding fróst
15 Make the dáy cóntráct, brief in durátion;
Yoú whó púnctuate níght's fleeting hóurs
Whén súmmer appeárs íncándéscént;
Yoú whose strength bálances múltiform seásons,
So the leáves caúght úp bý the sharp Nórth Wind

4.46 (cf. IV.34, I.m.5.29–36, IV.5.4).   4.46 lawless (I.4.28, 29; IV.2.28,
IV.4.1), cry out (III.6.1).

Meter 5 I.m.5.1–13 (cf. I.m.2.8–17, I.m.5.1–14, II.m.8.1–15, IV.m.6.1–18).
5.1 creator (I.6.4, IV.m.6.34, V.m.2.7, V.6.9).   5.2 throne (I.m.5.31, IV.m.2.1).
5.5–9 (cf. IV.m.5.7–10).   5.5 full moon (II.m.2.6), horns (I.m.5.8, III.m.6.3).
5.9 Phoebus (I.m.3.9, III.m.6.3).   5.10 Vesper (IV.m.6.13).   5.12 Lucifer
(III.m.1.9, IV.m.6.15), sun (= Phoebus).   5.14–22 (seasons: cf. I.m.2.18–21,
I.m.6.1–17).   5.17 incandescent (IV.m.5.16, IV.m.6.27).   5.18 balances
(IV.5.7, IV.6.18).

Thé Wést Wind brings báck plíant and súpple;   20
Só seéds ónce sówn únder Arctúrus
Wíll Sírius sínge as ácres of rípe grain—
There is nóthing dischárged fróm the old órders,
Désérting its póst and próper posítion.
Cóntrólling all thíngs towárd their set óbject,   25
Only húmán deéds you disdaín to rein ín
In the wáy they desérve— yoú, theír hélmsmán.
So it ís; whý cán slíppery Fórtune
Cause such chánge and such spórt? Hárd púnishment dué
For the breách of the láw quáshes the guíltless;   30
Dégénerate wáys on a lóftý thróne
Crush beneáth theír heél, guílty and sínful,
Thé nécks of the goód in hórrid revérsal.
Ánd glórious ríght is shroúded in shádow,
Búried in dárkness; thé júst man accépts   35
Bláme for the wícked.
Nó, nót pérjury, nó proud impósture
Hárms ór húrts thém, dréssed in false cólors;
Bút whén they delíght in fléxing their múscles,
Gládly they óverthrow próminent prínces,   40
Thóse whó térrorize númberless nátions.
Nów, nów have regárd for pítiful nátions,
Whóéver you áre who bínd the world's cóncord.
We are nó poór párt óf thís vást wórld,
Wé mórtals, storm-tóssed on Fórtune's salt ócean—   45
Ó hélmsman, make cálm the swíft-running seá-swell,
Máke stáble the eárth in the sáme cóncórd
Wíth which you pílot the límitless heávens.

5.20 West Wind (II.m.3.5).   5.21 Arcturus (cf. IV.m.5.1 (Great Bear)).
5.23–24 (cf. IV.6.53).   5.24 post (I.m.1.22, I.m.4.16–18).   5.25 set object
(II.m.2.16).   5.26–27 (cf. I.6.5).   5.26 disdain (II.6.13), rein in
(I.m.6.16–19).   5.27 helmsman (I.m.5.46, I.6.7, 19).   5.29–42 (cf. I.4.34,
IV.5.4).   5.31 degenerate ways (cf. IV.3.4), throne (I.m.5.2, IV.m.2.1).
5.32 heel (IV.1.4).   5.35 darkness (I.m.2.3).   5.36 blame (I.4.4, I.4.42).
5.38 dressed (III.m.4.1).   5.40 overthrow . . . princes (cf. I.m.4.9–10, II.m.1.3).
5.41 terrorize . . . nations (cf. I.m.4.11–14, IV.m.1.29).   5.42–48 (cf. V.m.3.1–5).
5.43 bind (III.12.6), concord (IV.m.6.4, V.m.3.1).   5.45 Fortune's ocean (cf.
I.3.11).   5.46–48 (cf. I.5.10, cf. Matthew 6:10).   5.46 helmsman
(I.m.5.27).   5.47 stable (II.6.7, III.6.6), concord (cf. I.m.5.43).   5.48 pilot
(cf. III.8.8, III.m.10.15), heavens (II.m.8.28–30).

Prose 5

When I was through barking all this out in my protracted lamentation, Philosophy maintained her serene expression and was in no way moved
2   by all my complaining. She said: When I saw you grief-stricken and in tears I knew on the spot that you were a man to be pitied, an exile; but I would have had no idea just how far away your place of exile was had
3   your set speech not given it away. How great the distance is! Yet you have not been driven out of your fatherland; no, you have wandered away on your own or, if you prefer to think of yourself as driven out, it is rather you yourself who have done the driving—for such a power over
4   you could never have been granted to anyone else. But perhaps you remember what fatherland is yours by birth? Power is not wielded there as it once was by legions of Athenians but, as Homer says,

> Thére is one rúlér, thére is one kíng

who takes delight not in the expulsion but in the congregation of his citizens. To be driven by his reins, and to submit yourself to his justice—
5   that is the highest freedom. Or don't you know that law of your city, the most primordial one by which it is established that there is no prescription of exile for anyone who has determined to establish his dwelling place within it? True; for no one who is kept within its walls and battlements need ever be afraid of meriting to be an exile, while anyone who ceases to desire to dwell within it ceases at the same time to merit it.
6   And so it is not the appearance of this place that moves me so much as your own appearance; and I am not so much looking for library walls polished in ivory and glass as for the dwelling place of your own mind, in which I have stored up not books but that which makes books worth their
7   price, the axioms of books that used to be mine. To be sure, what you said about your merits for the common good was true enough, but in proportion to the great number of your good deeds it was not extensive enough.
8   You have brought to mind things that everyone knows concerning the integrity (or rather the illegitimacy) of the charges made against you. You were quite right to decide that you only needed to touch briefly on the

---

Prose 5 1.5.1 barking (cf. II.7.20).   *5.2* grief-ridden (I.m.1.3), tears (I.1.13, I.2.6–7), exile (I.3.3, II.4.17, III.m.11.10, IV.1.9), far away (I.m.2.1–5).
5.3 fatherland (III.12.9, IV.1.9), forbidden (I.3.5, 14, IV.6.54).   *5.4* Homer (*Iliad* II.204), reins (I.m.7.31, V.m.1.12), justice (IV.4.13).   *5.5* city (cf. IV.5.2), dwelling place (I.4.3, I.5.6), battlements (I.3.13–14, II.m.4.17–22), merit (I.4.4, 34, 43, I.5.7).   *5.6* library (I.4.3), books (I.1.6), axioms (I.4.5).
5.8 charges (I.4.20–23), denounced (I.4.15–19), common people (III.6.2, IV.7.7).

crimes and perjuries of those who denounced you, for such things are better (and more fully) recounted on the lips of the common people, who stick their noses into everything. Further, you railed passionately against 9 what the Senate did unjustly; still further, you lamented the charges made against me, and you wept as well for the loss of my damaged reputation.

But ultimately it was your lamentation against Fortune that glowed 10 white-hot; you complained, in the last lines of your delirious Muse, that rewards are not paid out that are equal to merits, and you made a wish that the peace that rules the heavens rule the earth as well. But since a 11 full-scale rebellion of the passions has besieged you; since depression, anger, and sorrow drag you off in different directions—in your present state of mind, the more caustic remedies are not yet appropriate. So let 12 me use the gentler ones for a time, so that what has grown into a hard tumor from the inrush of confusing emotions may, by my gentle caress, become more yielding to and susceptible of the strength of a more bitter-tasting medicine.

Meter 6

Whén hígh búrdensome Cáncer, hót
Wíth thé bríght rays of Phoébus, búrns,
Thén áll thóse who entrúst their seéds
Tó drý róws that refúse their grówth,
Dísáppoínted of Céres' gíft,   5
Táke ácórns from the treés for food.
Tó píck víolets, néver trý
Púrplé fórests and gróves, not whén
Nórth Wínds, whípping through fiélds, full fórce,
Máke thé brístling fúrrows moán.   10

5.9 passionately (III.1.2, III.9.31); Senate (I.4.35–37), reputation (I.4.41–42).
5.10 Fortune (I.4.19, 43–44), last lines (I.m.5.44–48), Muse (I.1.7), rewards
(I.4.43–46).   5.11 passions (I.1.9, IV.4.27), depression, anger, and sorrow (cf.
I.m.7.25–31), drag . . . directions (III.8.5), caustic (II.5.1; cf. II.1.7), remedies
(II.3.3, III.1.2).   5.12 gentle/bitter (cf. IV.6.27), gentler (I.6.21), for a time
(I.1.7, I.2.6, II.7.20), confusing emotions (I.6.9, 13, 21), caress (I.2.5), bitter
(III.1.2).

Meter 6 I.m.6.1–6 summer (cf. I.m.5.16–17, 22).   6.1 burdensome (III.m.8.21).
6.2 Phoebus (I.m.3.9, I.m.5.9, 13 (sunrise); II.m.3.1, 9; II.m.6.10, II.m.8.5).
6.5 Ceres (III.m.1.4, IV.m.3.23, IV.m.6.27).   6.6 acorns (II.m.5.5).
6.9 North Winds (II.m.3.11), whipping (II.2.8).   6.7–10 winter
(cf. I.m.5.14–15, 21).

Nór woúld yoú, with a greédy hánd,
Rúsh tó prúne back the vínes in spríng,
Íf yoú wánt to enjóy their grápes—
Nó, bút Bácchus in aútumn bríngs
15   Hís pártícular gífts to ús.
Gód gíves sígns for the seásons, fít
Fór eách óne to its próper tásks.
Ín thé cýcles he képt in boúnds
Nó cónfúsion does hé allów.
20   Só, déféction from fíxed desígns,
Dówn á réckless and heádstrong páth,
Fínds nó prófitablé resúlt.

Prose 6

So will you first allow me, with just a few little questions, to take the pulse of your mental state, to get the feel of it, so I can understand what is to be the manner of your cure?

2   As you think best, I said; just ask me whatever you want, and I will answer you.

3   Then she said: Do you think that this world is moved by random and chance occurrences, or do you believe that there is some guidance of reason present within it?

4   There is no way, I said, that I would ever think that things so well-defined move by chance randomness; no, I know that God the creator presides over his own creation, nor could there ever come a day that would drive me away from the truth of this belief.

5   And so it is, she said; for just a little while ago you proclaimed it in verse and you lamented the fact that mortals alone have no share in the guidance of the divine. As for the rest, you were not budging from the

---

6.11–13 spring (cf. I.m.5.20, III.8.9).   6.14–15 autumn (cf. I.m.5.18–19).
6.14 Bacchus (II.m.5.6).   6.18 kept (IV.6.20, V.1.8).   6.19 confusion
(IV.5.5).   6.20 defection (II.3.14, III.m.6.9; cf. I.m.4.15–18).   6.21 down . . .
path (cf. I.m.2.1–5).   6.22 result (III.7.3; = success, III.12.20).

Prose 6 I.6.1 take the pulse (cf. I.2.5), state (cf. II.1.2, III.1.3).   6.2 think best
(III.12.25; cf. IV.6.6).   6.3 random (IV.5.5, 7), chance occurrences (IV.5.5–6,
IV.6.4), reason (III.8.8).   6.4 well-defined (I.m.5.25 (set)), randomness
(I.6.20, IV.6.53, V.1.8), creator (I.m.5.1, II.5.26), presides (II.6.4), drive away
(III.m.11.9).   6.5 a little while ago (II.2.11, III.9.25), in verse (i.e., I.m.5),
mortals alone (cf. I.m.5.26–27).

position that they were controlled by reason. But fancy that! What　6
utterly amazes me is why you're sick at all, given your solid grounding in
such a healthy belief. But let's look a little more deeply; I can guess that
there is something missing. So tell me this: Since you have no doubt that　7
the world is controlled by God, do you understand what are the rudders
by which it is governed?

I said: I can hardly understand the meaning of your question, let　8
alone venture to respond to the matter at issue.

She said: So, I wasn't deceived, was I? There is something missing, like a　9
gaping hole in the masonry of a wall, and through it the disease of confusing emotions has crept into your mind. But tell me this: Do you remember　10
what is the goal of things, or to what end the striving of all nature strives?

I said: I had heard it once, but grief has blunted my memory.

But surely you know the source from which all things have proceeded?　11
I said: I do know; and I answered that it was God.

So how can it happen that, if you understand the origin of things, you　12
do not know what is their goal? But such are the habits of confusing　13
emotions—while they have the power to move a man from his position,
they do not have the power to pluck him out completely and uproot him
from himself. But I would like you to answer this as well: Do you remem-　14
ber that you are a human being?

I said: Well of course I remember.

So will you be able to define for me what a human being is?　15

Are you asking me this, whether I know that I am a rational and mortal animal? I do know it, and I admit that that is what I am.

She said: And you've learned that you are nothing other than that?　16
Nothing.

She said: Now I know that there is another, and it is possibly the great-　17
est, cause of your disease—you have ceased to know who you yourself
are. And it is for this reason that I have discovered fully and absolutely

---

6.6 fancy that (IV.2.1), utterly amazes (I.4.28), can guess (IV.2.18, V.3.2).
6.7 doubt (III.12.26, IV.2.22), rudders (I.6.19, III.12.3).　　6.8 can hardly
understand (cf. II.8.2).　　6.9 wall (I.3.14), confusing emotions (I.1.9, I.5.11,
I.6.13).　　6.10 remember (I.2.6, I.4.32), goal (I.m.5.25 (set object), III.m.9.27,
III.11.41), striving (III.2.9, 15), memory (I.2.6, III.2.13; referred to at III.11.40).
6.11 proceeded (III.10.5).　　6.12 origin (III.3.1).　　6.13 habits (II.1.10–12,
18), confusing emotions (I.6.9, 21; IV.4.27), position (I.m.1.22).　　6.14–17 (cf.
II.5.29).　　6.14 well of course (III.3.10, 13).　　6.15 rational animal (cf.
II.5.25, V.2.3, V.6.27), animal (II.5.25).　　6.17 greatest cause (IV.1.3), disease
(I.1.9, I.2.5, III.7.2), know (I.2.6, II.5.29; cf. IV.6.41, V.4.35), recuperation
(I.6.19, III.12.9, IV.1.9).

the explanation for your sickness, and the entryway for winning back
18   your recuperation. Consider: Since you are dazed by self-forgetfulness,
you lamented that you were an exile and that you were deprived of
19   goods rightfully yours; further, since you do not know what is the goal of
things, you think that wicked and worthless men are truly powerful and
prosperous; still further, since you have forgotten what are the rudders
by which the world is governed, you reckon that the vicissitudes of individual fortunes bob up and down without a helmsman. All these are
huge causes that lead not only to disease, but to death as well. But you
may thank the sponsor of your recuperation that your nature has not yet
abandoned you completely.

20   We have as the most efficient kindling for your well-being your true
conclusion about the governance of the world, the fact that you believe
that it is not subject to the randomness of chance occurrences but to
divine reason. So you need not be afraid; from this very tiny spark a life-
21   giving heat shall soon burst into flame. But as it is not yet the right time
for stronger cures, and as it is common knowledge that the nature of
individual minds is such that they clothe themselves in false opinions
whenever they cast off true ones, I shall try for a time, by means of gentle
and routine poultices, to dispel this darkness of confusing emotions,
which arises from these false opinions and which dazes the true vision;
thus you may be able to recognize the glory of the true light, after the
shadows of these deceitful external influences have been parted.

Meter 7

Stárs that lie hídden
Báck of the bláck clouds

6.18 dazed (I.6.21), lamented . . . exile (at I.3.3, I.4.36), deprived of goods (at
I.4.45).   6.19 think . . . prosperous (at I.4.28–29, 46), governed (I.6.7, III.8.8,
III.12.3), fortunes (I.m.1.17–20), bob . . . helmsman (III.11.39), bob (IV.6.20,
V.m.1.11), helmsman (I.m.5.27), lead . . . to death (cf. I.1.11), sponsor
(III.5.3).   6.20 kindling (III.m.11.14), conclusion (III.1.2), the fact . . . reason
(at I.6.3–4), spark (III.12.25; cf. IV.6.3).   6.21 time (II.1.7), stronger
(III.10.18, IV.6.57, V.5.7; cf. I.5.11, II.5.1), cures (I.5.11–12; cf. IV.6.5 (medicine)), false opinions (II.4.3, III.6.2, III.4.13, V.3.18), for a time (I.2.6, I.5.12),
gentle (II.1.7), poultices (II.3.3, II.5.1), darkness (I.1.13, III.2.13), confusing
emotions (I.6.9, 13), dazes (I.6.18, IVm.5.9–10), vision (I.1.2, I.3.2, III.9.24),
true light (III.m.9.26; cf. I.m.3), shadows (I.m.2.3), deceitful (I.m.1.19, III.4.13),
external influences (V.5.1)

Meter 7 I.m.7.1 stars (I.m.3.5–6).   7.2 black clouds (V.m.2.10).

Cánnot províde us
Líght we can seé by.
Shoúld the mad Soúth Wind   5
Roíling the wáters
Stír up the témpest—
Ócean's glass súrface,
Cleár as the cloúdless
Ský in the heávens,   10
We'd soón see befóre us
Foúled and fílthy,
Sédiments chúrned up.
The streám that leaps dównward,
Dówn the high moúntains,   15
Choósing its coúrses,
Óften is coúntered
By rócky obstrúctions,
Boúlders fresh-loósened.
Só with you álso,   20
Desíring to seé truth
Ín the light's bríghtness—
Stárting your joúrney
Ón the straight páthway—
Drive away pleásure,   25
Drive away térror,
Exíle expectátion,
Make nó room for sórrow.
Where thése have domínion,
Mínd is becloúded,   30
Reíned in, imprísoned.

7.5–13 (I.m.4.5–6).   7.5 South Wind (II.m.3.7, II.m.4.9).   7.6 roiling
(II.m.4.17).   7.7 stir up (I.m.2.13–14, I.m.4.4–6).   7.8 surface
(I.m.2.14).   7.12 fouled (cf. IV.4.29).   7.14 leaps downward (cf.
V.m.1.9–10).   7.22 (true) light (III.m.9.23).   7.23 pathway (cf. I.m.1.6,
I.3.5, III.2.13, III.m.11.2, IV.1.8, V.1.5).   7.25–31 (cf. I.m.4.13, III.m.5,
IV.m.2.5–10).   7.27 exile (cf. I.5.2–3).   7.30 beclouded (cf. I.m.3, I.3.1),
reined in (I.5.4), imprisoned (I.m.2.25).

Book II

Prose 1

After this she fell silent for a while and then, when she had focused my concentration by means of her own unassuming silence, she began as follows:

2   If I have understood the past causes and current condition of your illness completely, you are wasting away from a desire and a longing for your former good Fortune; after it changed (or so you pretend to yourself that it had) it led so much of your mind astray. I understand the ever-shifting deceits and disguises of that monster; I understand too her sweet-talking intimacy with those whom she strives to seduce, continuing all the way to the point at which she abandons them against their expectations and bewilders them with grief that they cannot endure. But should you remember her nature, her behavior, and her true worth, you will realize that in her you neither possessed nor lost anything that was beautiful; in fact, I think that I will not need to work very hard to recall these facts to your memory.

5   After all, even when she stood before you, even when she talked sweetly to you, it was your practiced habit to attack her with courageous words; you would put her to flight with axioms brought forth from my holy chamber. But every sudden change in things happens with its own kind of, shall we say mental, turbulence; and so it happened that you too for a while deserted your post, which is your mental serenity. But it is time for you to take in and taste something mild and agreeable; this will then prepare a way for the stronger potions after it has been conveyed

---

Prose 1 II.1.1 for a while (I.2.6), focused (I.4.2), silence (cf. I.1.1), concentration/silence (III.1.3).   *1.2* causes (I.6.17), condition (III.1.3, V.m.3.26), wasting away (II.4.6), desire (V.5.3), pretend (cf. II.1.9; cf. III.10.4 (imagine)).   *1.3* disguises (II.8.1), monster (I.4.29), sweet-talking (II.1.5, 10; II.8.3), seduce (cf. II.1.10 (deceive)), bewilders (I.6.21 (dazes)).   *1.4* (cf. III.12.9), remember (I.5.4), work (II.7.9).   *1.5* stood before (I.4.32, II.1.13, II.4.29; cf. I.3.6), talked sweetly (II.1.3, 10; cf. II.2.8), attack (cf. II.3.9), chamber (cf. I.3.13).   *1.6* for a while (II.1.1), deserted (cf. I.m.4.15–18), serenity (I.m.4.1, II.1.12, II.m.4.21, II.6.7, III.m.9.27).   *1.7* it is time (I.2.1), take in (I.3.1, 3), taste (III.1.3), stronger potions (I.5.11–12, I.6.21), inner depths (cf. II.3.4, II.6.5).

into your inner depths. So let the persuasive power of the sweetness of   8
rhetoric assist us, that power that only travels the straight path when it
does not abandon what I have instructed her; and along with her let this
musical handmaiden from our own house sing in accompaniment, now
the more lilting measures, now the more solemn ones.

So what is it, mortal man, that has cast you down into sorrow and   9
grief? You have seen something new, I suppose, something out of the
ordinary. You think that Fortune changed in her relation to you; you are
wrong. These are always her habits, this is always her nature. She has   10
maintained her characteristic steadfastness toward you by her very ability to change; this is the sort of thing that she was both when she would
sweet-talk you and when she would deceive you with her enticements of
false happiness. You have discovered the fluctuating features of this   11
blind goddess; she who up to now has hidden herself from the others has
made herself completely and utterly known to you. If you approve of her,   12
take advantage of her and her habits, don't complain about them. But if
you shudder at her faithlessness, dismiss her; push her away, playing her
games of destruction. The same one who for you is now the cause of so
much sorrow ought to have been the cause of just as much serenity.
Why? Because she has abandoned you, and what mortals can ever be
free from the anxiety that she will not abandon them?

Or do you reckon that a happiness that will withdraw is valuable? Is   13
Fortune your treasured possession if when she stands before you she cannot be relied on to stay, and when she leaves she brings on sorrow? And   14
if she cannot be kept back by the exercise of the will, and when she runs
away she makes people catastrophic, what else is she but a kind of har-
binger of future catastrophe? After all, it is not enough to stare at what   15
has been placed before your eyes; forethought measures the end results
of things, and the same ability to change in either direction means both

---

1.8 sweetness (II.1.3, II.4.20, III.1.1, IV.1.1), travels (III.2.2, IV.2.4), straight path
(I.m.7.23, V.1.5), instructed (I,3.10, I.4.41), house (II.3.6), measures (I.m.1.2; cf.
IV.6.6).   *1.9* mortal man (II.2.2), cast down (IV.3.16; cf. I.m.2.1); changed
(I.m.1.19, I.4.44).   *1.10* steadfastness (II.3.12; cf. II.8.3), ability to change
(II.1.15, II.8.3, III.8.9), deceive (cf. II.1.3 (seduce)), false happiness (II.8.3–4).
1.11 discovered (III.3.4, III.9.2, IV.5.6), fluctuating (I.m.1.19), blind (II.4.26,
III.m.8.15–16, IV.2.31), made herself known (II.8.1).   *1.12* habits (II.1.18,
II.2.9–11), dismiss/push (III.8.6), dismiss (I.3.12, II.7.23), playing (II.m.1.7),
destruction (II.5.18, IV.5.3; cf. IV.4.1), serenity (II.1.6), free . . . abandon them (cf.
II.4.26, III.5.7, III.8.5).   *1.13* stands before (II.1.3), stay (II.3.13), leaves
(II.2.6, II.8.6).   *1.14* kept back (II.4.20).   *1.15* before your eyes (V.6.48),
forethought (cf. IV.6.8), ability to change (II.1.10), sweet-talk (II.1.3).

that you should not fear Fortune's threats and that you should not covet
16 Fortune's sweet-talk. Lastly, it is only reasonable that you endure with
detachment whatever happens within Fortune's playground once you've
17 bent your neck beneath her yoke. You have freely chosen her to be your
mistress; if you should then want to prescribe for her a law for staying
and going, wouldn't you be acting unjustly yourself? Wouldn't you be
making your own lot worse by your frustration, your lot that you cannot
change?

18   If you were to raise your sails to the winds, you would head not to
where your will intended but to where the winds would drive you; were
you to trust your seeds to plowed fields, you would balance the fruitful
and the barren years against each other. You have handed yourself over
to Fortune to be ruled by her; it is only reasonable that you yield to your
19 mistress's habits. Or are you trying to hold back the force of a rolling
wheel? Of all mortals you are the most obtuse: Once it starts to stand
still it ceases to be chance.

Meter 1

When wíth a haúghty hánd she túrns things úpsíde-dówn,
Like the wíld Boeótian straíts swift-rúshing báck ánd fórth,
Then shé, inhúman, tópples ónetime feársóme kíngs,
And slýly lífts the lówly heád of the dówncást mán.
5   She doés not heár the wrétched bút rejécts theír teárs;
She laúghs to scórn the waíling thát her hárd heárt bríngs.
These áre the gámes she pláys, the wáys she shóws hér stréngth.
Thus tó her ówn she shóws a wóndrous sígn, óne hoúr
Reveáling óne man bóth unhórsed and rídíng táll.

1.16 detachment (II.4.18), neck (I.m.2.25), neck/yoke (II.m.7.7–8, III.m.1.12).
1.17 freely (II.2.3), staying and going (cf. II.1.13), frustration (II.4.19).
1.18 winds (I.3.11, II.8.4), seeds (I.m.6.1–6), plowed fields (V.1.13 ff.), mistress
(II.1.17), habits (II.1.10–12).   1.19 wheel (II.2.9), obtuse (I.m.2.27 (hard),
III.m.8.19), ceases (II.5.35, III.8.5), chance (V.m.1.12).

Meter 1 II.m.1.1 haughty (I.m.4.2), upside-down (I.m.5.28–29, II.m.7.13–14; cf.
II.2.9).   1.3 topples kings (I.m.5.39–41), kings (II.2.11–12).   1.4 slyly
(II.8.1), downcast (III.m.5.4 (conquered)).   1.5–6 (cf. I.m.1.16–20).
1.6 hard heart (II.8.6).   1.7 plays (II.1.12, II.2.9–10).   1.8–9 (cf.
I.m.1.17–22).   1.8 her own (II.8.6), one hour (I.m.1.18, II.3.12).
1.9 unhorsed (cf. II.4.16 (knocked flat)).

Prose 2

But I would like to go over a few things with you in the words of Fortune herself; you just consider whether she claims what is within her rights.

"Mortal man! Why do you put me on trial with your sorrowful com- 2
plaints, day in, day out? What injustice have we ever done to you? What goods of yours have we ever taken away from you? You can fight me in 3
court before any judge you please about the ownership of wealth and resources, of high offices. If you can show that any one of them properly belongs to any one mortal, then certainly I will freely grant that the things that you are trying to recover once were yours.

"When nature brought you forth from your mother's womb, I took 4
you, naked, resourceless, lacking in every thing, into my arms; I nurtured you from my own wealth and resources and (this is the thing that makes you impatient with us now) I pampered you and raised you, excessive in my blessings; in the radiance and in the abundance of all those things that were within my power I surrounded you. Now it pleases 5
me to draw my hand back: You have the benefit, the use of things that belong to someone else; you do not have the right to complain as if you have lost things truly your own. So why are you moaning? There was no 6
violence done to you at our hands. Wealth and resources, honors, all other such things: They are within my power. These servants recognize their mistress; they come with me, and when I go they leave. I would 7
assert this with complete confidence: If the things whose loss you complain of had ever been yours, there would have been no way you could have lost them.

"Or shall I alone be kept from exercising my rights? The sky can bring 8
forth splendid days and then hide those days in the shadows of night; the year can wreathe the face of earth with fruit and flower and then disfigure it with cloud and cold; the sea is within its rights to entice with its

---

Prose 2 II.2.1 I would like (III.10.29), rights (II.2.8).   2.2 mortal man (II.1.9), on trial (cf. I.3.3, I.4.41–42), complaints (II.m.2.8, II.3.1).   2.3 judge (cf. I.4.35), wealth (cf. II.5), high offices (cf. II.6), freely (II.1.17).   2.4 nurtured (II.3.9, II.4.1; cf. I.3.4), wealth and resources (II.2.3, 6), raised (I.2.2), radiance (II.5.8, 12), abundance (II.5.15, III.2.5), my power (II.2.6).   2.5 hand back (II.m.2.5–6).   2.6 moaning (II.4.5), wealth and resources (II.2.4, II.5.18, 20), mistress (II.1.17, 18), leave (II.1.13, II.8.6).   2.7 complain (I.1.14), yours (II.1.4), no way (I.5.3).   2.8 rights (II.2.1, II.4.4), days/night (cf. I.m.3), hide (I.m.7.1–4, II.m.8.5–8), year (= seasons; cf. I.m.5, I.m.6), sea (I.m.4.5–6, I.m.5.44–48, I.m.7.5–13), rights (II.2.2), entice (cf. II.1.5 (sweet-talk)), whipped up (I.m.6.9–10), greed (cf. II.m.2.13–14, II.6.18), habits (II.1.10, 12; II.1.17, II.2.11).

calmed, smooth surface and then to be whipped up in storm and swell—
will insatiable human greed bind us to a fidelity that is alien to our hab-
9   its? This is our strength, and this is the endless game we play: We spin a
wheel in an ever-turning circle, and it is our delight to change the bot-
10 tom for the top and the top for the bottom. You may climb up if you
wish, but on this condition: Don't think it an injustice when the rules of
my game require that you go back down.

11   "Could it be you did not know my habits? You didn't know about
Croesus, king of Lydia? How he who had just a little earlier been Cyrus'
formidable opponent was next in an instant a man to be pitied, was
handed over to be burned on a pyre, and then was protected by rain sent
12 down from heaven? Surely you haven't forgotten that Lucius Aemilius
Paullus wept holy tears for the disasters that befell king Perseus of Macedonia, his captive? What else is it that the cries of tragedy bewail if it is
not Fortune, overturning prosperous kingdoms by her indiscriminate
13 blows? And surely you learned as a boy what Homer says lies on Jupiter's
threshold?

       Twó járs, óne full of goód things and óne full of évil.

14 So what if you have drawn too abundantly from the jar of the good
things; so what if I did not completely abandon you; so what if this very
ability of mine to change is an appropriate basis for your hoping for yet
better things—would you for all that just waste away in your own mind?
When you have taken your place within the kingdom that all people
have in common, would you then long to live according to private rights
of your own?

Meter 2

"Coúnt thé sánds that the seá chúrns from abýssal dépths,
      Láshed bý swíft-footed stórm winds;
Coúnt thé líghts in a ský cárpeted thíck with stárs,
      Níght-bégótten in spléndor.

2.9 game/play (II.1.12, III.12.36), wheel (II.1.19), change (III.5.2), bottom to top
(II.m.7.14; cf. II.m.1.1).   2.10 climb up (I.1.4).   2.11 Croesus (cf. Hero-
dotus 1.86 ff., esp. 1.207.2), pitied (I.5.2).   2.12 (cf. III.3.13), L. Aemilius
Paulus (cf. Livy 45.8.6), kingdoms (II.m.1.3, III.2.19, III.5.1), indiscriminate
(IV.2.12), blows (III.1.2).   2.13 Homer (Iliad 24.527–28; V.m.2.1–3; cf. I.4.1,
I.5.4).   2.14 ability to change (II.1.10, 15), better things (II.4.9), waste away
(II.1.2), rights (II.2.1, 8), private rights (cf. I.m.4.16).

Meter 2 II.m.2.1 abyssal (I.m.4.6).   2.3 stars (I.m.7.1–4).

Íf Ábúndance's hórn poúred out such weálth, if shé   5
    Névér dréw her own hánd back,
Stíll nót reáson enoúgh fór humankínd to quít
    Whíníng désolate sórrows.
Íf thé gód would receíve wíllingly áll your práyers,
    Freé ánd lávish with fíne gold;   10
Íf hé crówned with high ránk heáds of ambítious mén—
    Ónce gaíned, thése would seem wórthless.
Brúte vórácity gúlps dówn what it ónce desíred,
    Ónce móre ópens its jáws wide.
Áre thére reíns that can chéck précipitáte desíre,   15
    Guíde ít towárd a set óbject,
Whén, déspíte ample gífts, óverabúndant, stíll
    Búrns thát thírst for posséssion?
Hé cán néver be rích whó in despaír and feár
    Thínks thát hé is a paúper."   20

Prose 3

So, if Fortune were to speak with you in her own behalf, using these words, you really would have nothing that would let you even open your mouth in response. But if there is some way you could rightly bolster your sorrowful complaint, then out with it! I will give you the opportunity to speak.

    Then I said: Yes, all this is very pretty. Yet, though it is smeared with   2 the honey of rhetorical and musical sweetness, it is delightful only while it is being heard. But in us poor, pitiable people there is a more deep-seated capacity for the perception of evils; and so, now that these words have stopped ringing in my ears, the sorrow that is planted in my spirit weighs it down.

2.5 Abundance (II.4.3).   2.6 hand back (II.2.5).   2.8 sorrows (II.2.2, II.3.1), desolate sorrows (III.m.5.9).   2.9 prayers (V.3.33, V.6.46). 2.10 gold (III.m.3.1, III.m.8.3).   2.11 rank (II.2.6).   2.13 voracity (cf. II.2.8, II.6.18).   2.15 reins (I.5.4), precipitate (II.m.7.1 (downhill): cf. I.m.2.1).   2.16 set object (I.m.5.26).   2.18 burns . . . possession (cf. II.m.5.26, III.3.18–19).   2.19 despair and fear (cf. I.m.7.25–28), despair (II.2.6 (moaning)).   2.20 pauper (cf. II.5.6, III.2.14).

Prose 3 II.3.1 sorrowful complaint (II.2.2).   3.2 honey (cf. III.m.7.3–4), rhetorical . . . sweetness (II.1.8), heard (II.5.6), pitiable (I.5.2, II.3.4, 11), sorrow (IV.1.1), planted (I.4.8, IV.1.1; cf. II.4.22).

3   So it is, she said: Such things are not yet the remedies for your disease, but they are a kind of poultice for the grief that has stubbornly
4   resisted your cure up to now. When the time is right I will apply such
medicines as will work themselves deep within you. But please: I don't
want you to think of yourself as pitiable. Have you really forgotten the
5   measure and the manner of your happiness? I'll say nothing of the fact
that after you lost your father you were taken up to be raised by the
watchful concern of men in the highest circles; that, though bound by
ties of marriage to the leaders of the state—the most valuable form of
family tie—you became their dear friend before you became their
6   closest relation. Who was there who did not call you the happiest
·man alive, for the glory of your in-laws, the modesty of your wife, the
7   advantage of your children, your sons, as well? I'll pass over—for I'd
prefer to pass over what everyone knows—the high offices that you
entered into in your youth, offices denied to older men; it is my pleasure to come now to that one thing which constitutes the full measure
of your happiness.
8   If there is any enjoyment to be derived from mortal things, one that
bears any stamp of true bliss, could the memory of that one shining
moment ever be annihilated by any juggernaut of invading evils, when
you saw your two sons, each of them now a consul, set forth from your
home accompanied by a throng of senators, and by the enthusiasm of
the common people? When they sat in the consular chairs in the Senate
House and you delivered your oration in praise of the king and earned
your glorious reputation for intelligence and elegance? When, in the
Circus, an ex-consul flanked by two consuls, you more than met the
expectations of the crowd that ringed you round with a distribution of
9   gifts on a triumphal scale? You told lies to Fortune, I think, all the time
that she was caressing you, all the time that she held you in her lap as
her favorite. You stole from her a gift that she had never before given to
a private individual; and now you demand to see Fortune's balance
10 sheet? Only now and for the first time has she made her envious eye pass

---

3.3 remedies (I.5.11–12, I.6.21; cf. II.5.11), disease (I.1.9, I.2.5, III.5.14, III.7.2),
poultice (I.6.21, I.5.1).   3.4 deep within (II.1.7, II.6.5), pitiable (II.3.2), measure and manner (II.3.10).   3.5 (cf. I.4.40, II.4.5), form (III.2.9 (category)).
3.6 happiest (cf. I.m.1.21), wife (cf. II.4.6), sons (II.3.8, II.4.7).   3.7 pass
over . . . knows (cf. I.5.8), high offices (cf. I.4.8 ff., I.4.1), full measure (I.4.43).
3.8 common people (I.5.4), chairs (cf. III.4.2, III.m.4.6), distribution (II.5.4).
3.9 told lies (cf. II.1.5), I think (I.4.32, V.4.9), caressing (II.1.10, II.2.4).
3.10 now . . . first time (II.3.12), measure and maner (II.3.4), happy . . . now
(II.4.11).

over you; were you to look carefully at the measure and manner of your joys and sorrows, you could not deny that you were happy up until now. Therefore, even if you do not reckon that you are fortunate for *this* reason, because these things that seemed to be joys have gone away, there is still no reason for you to consider yourself pitiable, because the things that are now thought to be sorrows also pass away.   11

Or have you only now, unexpected and for the first time, walked onto   12 this stage which is life as a guest? Do you think that any ability to stand unchanged is a property of the mortal condition, when one swift hour often reduces the mortals themselves to nothing? Surely not; even if, in   13 exceptional instances, the gifts of Fortune can be relied on to stay, all the same, the last day of life is a sort of death even for the Fortune that does stay. So what difference do you think it makes, whether you abandon her   14 by dying or she abandons you by running away?

Meter 3

Whén in heávén, dríving his dáwn-hued hórses,
    Phoébús scátters the líght of dáy,
Thén the stárs grów dím, and their áshen fáces
    Fáde oút, dúlled by the fórce of fláme.
Whén a greén gróve, wármed by the breáthing Wést Wind,   5
    Glóws bríght réd with the róse of spríng,
Cómes the mád Soúth Wínd with a rúsh of stórm clouds,
    Thórns áre strípped of their órnaménts.
Óften úndér cloúdless and wíndless dáylight
    Shínes thé seá with its wáves becálmed;   10
Óften boísteroús blásts are kicked úp by Nórth Winds,
    Whén thé seá is turned úpside-dówn.

3.11 fortunate (I.4.16), pitiable (II.3.2, 4), joys/sorrows (cf. II.2.13–14).
3.12 stage (I.1.8), unchanged (II.1.10), one swift hour (II.m.1.8–9).
3.13 stay (II.1.13), death (cf. II.7.21–23, II.m.7).   3.14 abandon (I.m.6.20 (defection), III.m.6.9, III.9.18).

Meter 3 II.m.3.1–12 (cf. II.2.8).   3.1 horses (III.m.1.10; cf. II.m.8.6).
3.2 Phoebus (I.m.3.9, I.m.5.9, I.m.6.2, II.m.6.9, II.m.8.5, III.m.2.31).
3.3–4 (cf. I.m.5.5–13).   3.5 West Wind (I.m.5.20).   3.6 rose of spring (cf. III.8.9).   3.7 South Wind (I.m.7.6).   3.9 daylight (cf. III.m.9.26).
3.10 becalmed (II.5.12).   3.11–12 (cf. I.m.2.13–14).   3.11 North Winds (I.m.6.9–10).   3.12 upside-down (II.m.1.1; cf. II.2.9).

Ráre the shápes óf thíngs that stand fíxed in thís world,
    Greátlý ránge their vicíssitúdes—
15 Trúst the fállíng fórtunes of mórtal mánkind!
    Trúst pósséssions that túrn their bácks!
Thís is súre, stánds fíxed by etérnal státute:
    Naúght stánds fíxed that was éver bórn.

Prose 4

Then I said: You are the nourisher of every virtue; what you bring to mind is true, and I cannot deny the amazingly swift course of my success.

2 But that's the thing that burns me so painfully as I recall it: I mean, in all of Fortune's adversities the most unhappy sort of misfortune is that one was happy once.

3 · But, she said, this is a punishment that you suffer because of your false opinions about things; you cannot in justice blame the things themselves for it. After all, if it is this empty name of Fortune-born happiness that excites you so, you may now go over with me just how multiform

4 and magnificent is your abundance still. Then, if that which was your most valuable possession in every register of your good fortune is still kept for you by the powers above intact and safe from harm, will you be within your rights to bring a complaint about your misfortune when you

5 still possess all the better part? To be sure, Symmachus, your father-in-law, still thrives unharmed, that most valuable ornament of the human race. He is a man entirely compounded of wisdom and virtue—such a thing you would eagerly buy at the cost of your own life. He has no con-

6 cern for injuries of his own, but he moans for yours. Your wife still lives: by nature, retiring; in modesty and chastity, most excellent. To summarize all the dowry of her gifts in a word, she is like her father. She lives, I say; she hates this life but for you alone she still draws breath, and even I

3.14 vicissitudes (I.m.5.28–29, II.m.8.2).   3.15 falling (II.5.2, II.4.26, III.9.29).   3.16 trust (II.5.35, II.8.7).   3.17 eternal statute (IV.4.28; cf. I.m.5.23).   3.18 fixed (cf. I.m.1.22).

Prose 4 II.4.1 nourisher (II.2.4), swift (cf. II.6.16, III.8.7).   4.2 adversities (II.4.16, II.8.4), misfortune (II.4.4, IV.4.5).   4.3 false opinions (I.6.21), empty name (II.m.7.17, III.4.15, III.6.7), Fortune-born (I.4.24, 28), abundance (II.m.2.5, III.3.5).   4.4 intact (III.5.9), rights (II.2.1, 8), bring a complaint (II.2.3).   4.5 Symmachus (I.4.40, II.4.6, 7; cf. II.3.5), wisdom (III.4.6), buy (II.8.7), life (II.4.8), moans (II.2.6).   4.6 wife (II.3.6; cf. III.2.9), modesty (II.3.6), chastity (II.m.8.25), hates (II.4.9), wastes away (II.1.2, II.2.14).

would allow that your happiness is diminished by this one thing alone, that she wastes away in longing for you, in sorrow and in tears.

What can I say about your children, the consuls? Already there is in them the shining reflection of the talents of their father, and of their grandfather, as you would expect in boys that age. So, since the primary concern that mortals have is for the preservation of their lives, how happy you are, if you would only recognize the goods that you have! Even now you have at your disposal things that are, beyond anyone's doubt, dearer than life itself. So you can dry your tears now. Fortune has not yet hated all of them, to the last one, nor has an overpowering storm laid into you, given that your anchors are still in place and holding firm. Such anchors will not have it that either your consolation in the present time or your hope for the future is nowhere to be found.

And I pray that they may long hold firm, I said; so long as they are in place, however things may stand, I will safely swim to shore. But you do see how much has been lost from what I prided myself on.

She said: We have made some little progress then if you are not now disgusted with all of your lot in life. But what I cannot tolerate is your delight in complaining so mournfully, so fretfully, that something is missing from your happiness. I mean, what man was ever possessed of a joy so secure and settled as never to complain to some degree about the quality of his condition? For the condition of mortal goods is a fretful thing, and by their nature they are neither completely beneficent nor perpetually present. One man's estate is more than ample, but his ignoble ancestors are a source of embarrassment; another's noble lineage makes him a celebrity, but because he is cramped by the severe limitations of his property he would prefer to remain anonymous. One man, luxuriating in his wealth and pedigree, weeps for his unmarried life; another, happily married but childless, fattens his estate for some unrelated heir; a third, blessed with children, still weeps in dejection for the failings of his son or daughter. And that's why no one is in simple harmony with the condition of his own Fortune, for in every single Fortune there is something present that the outsider has no knowledge of, but that the insider shrinks from in horror.

7

8

9

10

11

12

13

14

15

4.7 children (II.3.6, 8), grandfather (= Symmachus).   4.8 recognize (I.2.6), life (II.4.5).   4.9 dry your tears (cf. I.2.7, II.8.7), hated (II.4.6), in place/firm (cf. III.11.28), consolation (III.1.2), future (II.2.14).   4.10 prided (II.5.26, 30).   4.11 lot (II.1.17), fretfully (II.1.12, II.4.21, III.3.5).   4.12 what man (cf. II.1.12), secure/settled (I.m.4.1; cf. IV.6.8), condition (V.6.1).   4.13 ignoble (cf. III.m.6.8), lineage (I.1.3, II.m.7.11, III.2.9, III.6.7), limitations/property (cf. IV.6.45).   4.14 children (III.7.5).

16   And another thing: in all who are extravagantly happy there are
extravagantly refined sensibilities. If everything does not respond to
their beck and call, then they, because they have no experience of any
adversity, are knocked flat by each and every little thing—that's how
insubstantial are the things that decrease the sum total of true happiness
17   for those who are extravagantly fortunate! How many people would you
guess there are who would think themselves next door to the heavens if
they could get only the smallest part of the leftovers of your Fortune?
This place that you call exile is itself the fatherland of those who dwell
within it.

18   To be sure, nothing is pitiable except when you think it is; conversely,
every lot in life is delightful for one who endures it with detachment.
19   Who is the man who is so happy that he would not want to change his
20   standing, if once he gave free rein to his frustration? How many are the
bitternesses with which the sweetness of human happiness is stippled!
And though it may seem delightful as one enjoys it, nevertheless it can-
21   not be kept from going when it wants to. So it is clear just how pitiable is
the happiness that consists of mortal things: it does not persist in perpetuity for those who are detached, nor does it perfectly please those who
are fretful.

22   Mortal men! Why do you mortals look outside yourselves for the happiness that has been placed within you? Miscalculation and lack of
23   awareness have dazed you all. But to *you* I will reveal in brief what the
highest happiness hinges on. Is there anything more valuable to you
than yourself? You will say, Nothing. Therefore, if you have mastery over
yourself, you will possess a thing that you yourself would never want to
24   lose and that Fortune could not ever take away from you. Consider this,
so that you may realize that true happiness cannot consist of these For-
25   tune-born things. If happiness is the highest good of a nature that lives
in accordance with reason; and if the highest good is that which cannot

---

4.16 another thing (II.7.7), adversity (II.4.2, II.8.3–5), knocked flat (II.m.1.9
(unhorsed)), fortunate (II.3.11, II.8.7).   4.17 exile (I.3.3, I.5.3, IV.5.2).
4.18 pitiable (II.3.2, 3, 11), conversely (II.5.23), detachment (II.1.16, II.4.21,
27).   4.19 frustration (II.1.17).   4.20 sweetness (II.1.8), delightful
(IV.5.6), kept (II.1.14, II.5.19).   4.21 pitiable (II.4.18), perpetuity (II.4.12),
fretful (II.4.11).   4.22 mortal men (cf. II.1.9), outside (III.3.14, III.11.15),
within (II.3.2, II.5.14), miscalculation (II.5.30), lack of awareness (IV.2.31; cf.
II.4.26, III.m.8.1–2), dazed (I.6.22, III.3.5).   4.23 you will say (II.5.32,
III.3.18, IV.2.37, IV.6.23, V.4.10, V.6.37, 39), mastery (II.6.18, III.12.9).
4.24 consider this (IV.3.8), Fortune-born (II.4.3, 28).   4.25 happiness
(III.5.1), accordance with reason (V.6.2), stolen (III.3.13, III.8.3), obvious (cf.
III.10.19), instability (II.8.3), aim at (I.3.14).

be stolen away in any way at all, given that only that thing is most excellent that cannot be taken away; therefore, it is obvious that the instability of Fortune cannot aim at the acquisition of true happiness.

Further: Anyone whom this falling happiness promotes either knows   26
or does not know that it is inconstant. If he does not know, what sort of
lot in life can be truly happy when accompanied by the blindness of ignorance? If he knows, then he must necessarily fear for the loss of what he
does not doubt can be lost; consequently, everlasting fear does not allow
him to be happy. Or perhaps he thinks it an insignificant thing if he does 27
lose it? In this way too it is a very meager good whose loss can be borne
with such detachment. And since you are the same man who I know was   28
persuaded of this by many arguments, in whom I know that this has been
planted, that the minds of mortals are not in any way mortal; and since it
is perfectly clear that Fortune-born happiness ends with the death of the
body; it cannot therefore be doubted that, if this Fortune-born happiness
can confer true happiness, every single instance of mortality would lapse
into desolation at the end, which is death. Yet since we know that many   29
have sought the enjoyment of true happiness not only through death but
even through hardship and torture, how can Fortune-born happiness
ever make people truly happy when it stands before them if it does not
make them desolate once it has been dispatched?

Meter 4

Who wánts to buíld in prúdence
    Évérlásting foundátions,
Sure-foóted, nót to be léveled
    Bý thé loúd-moaning Eást Wind;
Who lóngs to scórn the deép sea,   5
    Wáves thát threáten disáster—

4.26 falling (II.m.3.15, II.5.2), blindness (II.1.11, III.m.8.15, IV.2.31), ignorance
(III.m.8.1–2; cf. II.4.22), fear (I.m.7.25–28), fear . . . happy (cf. II.1.12).
4.27 detachment (II.1.16, II.4.18, 21).   4.28 planted (I.4.8, III.m.11.11),
minds . . . mortal (cf. II.5.25), Fortune-born (II.4.24, 29), death (cf. I.3.12–14,
II.7.21–23, II.m.7), confer (III.2.12, III.9.29), desolation (III.m.4.8, III.5.3).
4.29 torture (I.3.9, II.6.8), stands before (II.1.5), desolate (III.m.4.8).

Meter 4 *II.m.4.1–2* build . . . foundations (cf. II.m.4.15–16).   4.1 who wants
(I.m.4.1).   4.2 foundations (= dwelling-place; I.4.3, I.5.5, 6).   4.3 sure-
footed (= stable ground; I.m.1.22), leveled (II.m.1.9 (unhorsed), II.4.16
(knocked flat)).   4.4 East Wind (IV.m.3.3).   4.6 threaten (I.m.4.5).

He múst rejéct the súmmits
    And the párched sánds of the seáshore.
The óne the bráwling Soúth Wind
10   Smáshés wíth all its fórces;
The óther, nóncohésive,
    Wón't beár séttling strúctures.
Run awáy from áll these dángers,
    Fátál, pleásant locátions;
15 On húmble róck, remémber,
    Buíld yoúr hóme in compléte trust.
Though wínds may roíl the óceans,
    Thúndér, raín down destrúction—
Still yoú, conceáled in sílence,
20   Bléssed wíth pówerful rámparts,
Will páss a tránquil lífetime,
    Wíll déríde the air's ánger.

Prose 5

But since the warmth of the poultices of my arguments is now working its way into you, I think I now need to apply ones that are a little more caustic.

2   So come now—even if these gifts of Fortune were not merely of the moment and doomed to fall away, what is there in them that could ever truly belong to you mortals, or that would not become worthless upon 3 close inspection and careful consideration? Take riches. Are they valuable by their own nature, or because they are yours? What sort of riches 4 is superior? Gold perhaps, and the stockpiled strength of coined money? And yet these shine brighter when they are poured out, not when they are heaped up, given that greed makes people despised, while generous 5 distribution makes them renowned. And since that which is handed over to someone else cannot stay with anyone, coined money is only

---

4.9 South Wind (I.m.7.6, II.m.3.7).   4.11–16 (cf. Matthew 7:26).
4.14 pleasant locations (II.5.11).   4.16 home (I.4.40, II.5.18, IV.1.8).
4.17 roil (I.m.7.7).   4.19 silence (I.1.1, I.2.4, II.7.20).   4.20 ramparts
(I.3.13–14; cf. I.5.5).   4.21 tranquil (I.m.4.1).   4.22 deride (cf. I.3.14).

Prose 5 II.5.1 poultices (I.6.21), more caustic (cf. I.5.11, I.6.21).   5.2 fall
away (II.m.3.15, II.4.26), belong (II.2.2–3, II.4.25), worthless (I.3.14, III.4.17,
III.8.3).   5.3 riches (cf. III.3).   5.4 gold (II.m.5.29, III.m.3.1, V.1.13), distribution (II.3.8).   5.5 cannot stay (cf. III.8.3).

valuable at the time at which it is handed over to others and ceases, by
the very act of distribution, to be possessed. Yet this same money, should   6
it be heaped up in one man's house, as much as there is anywhere in the
world, would only make all the rest impoverished of itself. Now a sound
fills the ears of many people equally, completely present for each; but
your riches cannot pass on to more than one except by being divided,
and when this happens they must necessarily turn those whom they
leave behind into paupers. O what a narrowly limited and impoverished   7
thing is riches! The many cannot have them entire, and they do not
come to any one person without the impoverishment of the rest.

    Or does the brilliance of jewels attract your eye? But whatever excel-   8
lence does exist in this radiance, the light belongs to the jewels, not to
people; and it utterly amazes me that people are amazed at them. I   9
mean, what is there, lacking the soul's self-motion and indivisibility, that
can rightly seem beautiful to a rational nature that has a soul? Even if, by   10
their Creator's efforts and by their own play of colors, they draw to
themselves something of the Beautiful at the farthest remove, they are
all the same placed far below your own superiority and are in no way
deserving of your amazement.

    Or does the beauty of tilled fields delight you? Well of course it   11
does—it is a beautiful part of an exceedingly beautiful creation. Just so it   12
is that we are sometimes gladdened by the appearance of a calm sea, and
so do we admire the heavens and the stars, the sun and the moon. But
surely none of these belongs to you, sir; surely you would not dare to
take pride in the radiance of any one of them. Or do you yourself display   13
the play of colors of the flowers in springtime? Is it your fertile abundance that makes the fruits of the summer swell? Why are you carried   14
away by empty joys? Why do you embrace goods that are external to you
as if they were your own? What the nature of things has caused to be
external to you Fortune will never cause to be your own. To be sure, the   15
fruits of the earth are beyond any doubt set aside for the nourishment of

---

5.6 sound (II.3.2), paupers (cf. II.m.2.20).   5.7 impoverished . . . wealth (cf.
II.5.35).   5.8 jewels (II.5.33, II.m.5.30, III.m.8.4, 11), radiance (II.2.4,
II.5.12), utterly amazes (I.4.28, I.6.6).   5.9 what . . . indivisibility (cf. II.5.25),
self-motion (II.m.8.21), motion (III.11.30, V.m.4.11).   5.10 Creator (I.m.5.1,
II.5.26), play of colors (II.5.13), superiority (I.4.39, III.2.17).   5.11 tilled
fields (II.m.4.13–14; cf. II.m.5.2, 18), delight (III.12.23), well of course (I.6.14,
III.3.10, 13).   5.12 calm sea (I.m.7.8–10, II.2.8), radiance (II.5.25).
5.13 flowers (I.m.6.7–10).   5.14 external (II.4.22; cf. III.6.7).
5.15 beyond any doubt (III.11.13); animate (II.5.29), need (II.5.22),
abundance (II.2.4).

animate beings; but if you only want to fill your need up again (and that
is what is enough for Nature's needs), then there is no reason for you to
16   beg for the abundance of Fortune. For Nature is satisfied with things few
in number and very small in extent; and if you try to overwhelm
Nature's simple satisfaction with superfluous things, you'll find that what
you pour over it will be either disagreeable or actually poisonous.

17   But now you think it a beautiful thing to be resplendent in clothes of all
different sorts. If their appearance is pleasing to the eye, then I will admire
18   either the nature of the material or the skill of its maker. Or is it the long
procession of your servants that makes you happy? If they are themselves
corrupt in their habits, then they are a destructive burden to the house and
are utterly opposed to the master himself. But if they are righteous—how
can the righteousness of another ever be counted among your wealth and
19   resources? From all these considerations it is clearly shown that not a single
thing of what you reckon to be your own possessions is your own possession. If they do not have within themselves any beauty worth craving, why
20   would you ever weep for them if lost or take delight in them if kept? And if
they are beautiful by their own nature, what bearing does that have on
you? For they still would have pleased you in and of themselves, even when
21   separated from your wealth and resources. Nor are they valuable by the
fact that they added themselves to your riches; rather, it was because they
seemed valuable that you preferred to count them among your riches.

22   What is it then that all of you are looking for in all of Fortune's noise
and excitement? You're trying, I think, by means of your abundance, to
23   rout your feeling of need. But for all of you this turns out exactly the
opposite; in fact, you need many things to assist you in protecting the
multiplicity of your valuable possessions. But what this means is that
those who own very many things need very many things; conversely,
those who measure their abundance not by the superfluity of their greed
24   but by the necessity of their nature need only a very little. So is it really
the case that there is no possession planted within you and truly your

5.16 satisfied (II.5.26, II.7.12), overwhelm (IV.4.5, 25, 42), superfluous (II.5.23),
disagreeable/poisonous (cf. I.1.8).   5.17 resplendent (III.8.3), material (cf.
I.1.3), maker (IV.6.12) (artisan).   5.18 destructive (II.1.12, IV.5.3), house
(II.m.4.16), utterly (II.5.8), righteous (II.6.3, IV.3.1 ff.).   5.19 clearly (III.3.4,
III.10.42), not . . . your own (II.2.7), beauty worth craving (III.4.17), craving
(III.7.10), take delight in (I.5.4), kept (II.4.20).   5.20 separated (III.2.17),
wealth and resources (II.2.3, 4, 6; II.5.18).   5.21 (cf. II.6.3).   5.22 feeling
of need (III.3.16–19).   5.23 turns . . . opposite (III.3.16), conversely (II.4.18,
III.11.32), abundance (II.m.2.5, III.3.5), superfluity (II.5.16), greed (= ambition;
I.4.13, II.7.2).   5.24 planted (I.4.8, III.m.11.11), external (II.5.22).

own, so that you all must look for your possessions in things external to
you and separate from you? Is the order of things so upside-down that an 25
animal that is divine by virtue of its reason never seems to itself to be
radiant except by the possession of its inanimate possessions? Everything 26
else is satisfied with its own, but you mortals!—though you are like God
by virtue of your minds you try to acquire from what is bottommost
things on which to pride your superior nature; you do not realize just
how great an insult you offer to your Creator. It was his desire that the 27
human race stand above all earthly things, but you trample your honor
underfoot, below each and every bottommost thing.

Why? Because if it is agreed that any possession of any thing is more 28
valuable than the thing to which it belongs, then you in your own valua-
tion place yourselves beneath them when you determine that these most
worthless objects are your possessions. This happens deservedly, for this 29
is the condition of human nature: only then does it surpass all other
things, when it knows itself; but that same nature is degraded, brought
lower than the dumb animals, if it ceases to know itself. It is merely a
part of their nature that other animate creatures are unaware of themselves, but for human beings this is morally reprehensible. O how widely 30
does this error of yours extend, all of you who think that anything can be
truly adorned with objects of pride that are external to it! This can never 31
be; should any light shine from what has been attached, the attachments
themselves receive the praise; but that which has been covered by them,
been hidden by them, persists all the same in its deformity.

But I say that there is no possession, no good, that harms its possessor. 32
I'm not lying, am I? Hardly, you say. Yet riches have often harmed those 33
who possessed them, when all the most despicable people (and for that
reason all the more eager for what is external to them) think that they
alone are most worthy to possess whatever gold or whatever jewels there
may be. And so you, who are now so anxious and fear the spear and the 34
sword, would whistle your way past the robber if you had set out on the

---

5.25 order of things (II.4.12), animal (I.6.15), virtue (IV.4.20), radiant (II.5.12),
inanimate (III.11.17, 25; cf. II.5.9).   5.26 satisfied (II.5.16), like God (I.4.39),
acquire (I.4.39), bottommost (V.6.17), pride (II.4.10, II.5.30), Creator (I.m.5.1,
II.5.10, V.6.9).   5.27 trample (IV.3.16, IV.4.29).   5.28 worthless (I.3.14).
5.29 condition of human nature (IV.3.15–16), surpass (I.4.39), knows itself (cf.
I.2.6, I.6.14–17), animals (cf. III.7.4), animate (II.5.15, II.7.4).   5.30 error
(II.4.22), objects of pride (II.4.10, II.5.26).   5.31 light (II.5.8).   5.32 hardly
(III.3.9), you say (singular: II.4.23).   5.33 despicable (I.3.11, IV.6.51), gold
(II.5.4–7), jewels (II.5.8–10).   5.34 whistle . . . robber (cf. Juvenal, *Satire*
10.20–22).

35   path of this life as an empty-handed traveler. How magnificent is the
      true happiness found in mortal wealth and resources! Once you have
      secured it, you all cease to be free from anxiety.

Meter 5

Hów háppy, that eárlier éra,
Satisfiéd with relíable graín fields,
Nót wásted in slóthful excésses
Bút eásing its slów-to-come húnger
5   With the núts that were eásy to gáther;
Never knówing the boúnty of Bácchus
Could be míxed with the freé-flowing hóney,
Nor that snów-whíte sílk cloth from Chína
Could be taínted with Týrian púrple.
10 Beds of gráss gáve whólesome soft slúmber;
Theír drínk came from fást-flowing wáters,
Theír sháde from the heíghts of the píne trees.
Nó mérchant ship clóve the deep ócean;
Nóne tráded the goóds of all nátions
15 On the loókout for únexplored shórelines.
Nó trúmpets blared mádly in báttle;
Nó bloód spilled in víolent hátred
Hád yét staíned réd the grim graín fields.
Fór whý would an énemy's ánger
20 Choóse fírst to arm sóldiers for báttle,
Fóreseéing the woúnds would be mádness,
Wíthoút any príze for the bloódshed?
O if ónly our wórld could retúrn now
To the ágeléss wáys of the áncients!
25 Nó; mádder than Aétna's erúptions
Úp blázes the hót lust for háving.

―――――――――――――

5.35 how (II.m.3.15–16), true happiness (III.9.22), cease . . . anxiety (III.8.5),
free from anxiety (II.1.12).

Meter 5 II.m.5.1 happy (II.m.8.28, III.m.12.1, 3).   *5.2* grain fields
(II.m.5.18).   *5.5* nuts (= acorns; IV.m.3.24; cf. I.m.6.6).   *5.6* Bacchus
(I.m.6.14–15).   *5.9* Tyrian (III.m.4.1).   *5.15* shorelines (V.m.5.14).
5.16–22 (cf. IV.m.4.7–10).   *5.16* madly (II.m.5.21, 25).   *5.17–18* blood . . .
stained (cf. III.m.2.11).   *5.18* grain fields (II.m.5.2; cf. I.1.9).   *5.21* madness (II.m.5.16, 25).   *5.25* Aetna (cf. I.m.4.7 (Vesuvius), II.6.1).   *5.26*
blazes . . . having (II.m.2.18 (burns . . . possession)).

Woe is hím! Whó wás that invéntor
Who uneárthed thése treácherous treásures,
Thé deád weight of góld covered óver,
Thé jéwels that lónged to lie hídden?   30

Prose 6

For all that, what can my discourse be about positions of honor and
power, positions that all of you, who know nothing about true honor and
true power, raise to the level of the heavens? If your honors and power
fell to each and every one of the most unrighteous of men, what Aetnas
with torrents of flame, what universal flood could wreak such destruction? As a matter of fact—and I believe that you remember this—the   2
ancestors of all you Romans wanted to do away with the consular power,
the thing that was the very fountainhead of liberty, because of the arrogance of the consuls themselves; earlier, these same ancestors had vio-
lently taken the name of king away from the state, because of the same
sort of arrogance. But should your positions of honor and power ever be 3
conferred upon righteous people—an extremely infrequent occurrence—
what is there in such positions that is found pleasing other than the righteousness of those who exercise them? And so it is that true honor
attaches itself not to one's innate virtues because of one's position, but
to one's position because of one's innate virtues.

But what is this power of yours, so glorious, so desirable? You crea-   4
tures of the earth! You seem to preside over creation, but surely you
think about those over whom you seem to preside? And you: Were you
to catch sight of a nest of mice and one among them claiming power and
authority for himself in preference to all the rest, what laughter would
split your sides! But if you were to look only to the body, what could you 5
find more frail than human beings, who are often killed even by the bites
of flies or by their creeping insinuation into the recesses of the body! Yet 6
how can anyone assert any right over any other individual except over

---

5.27 woe (I.m.1.2, I.m.2.1, 27).   5.29 dead weight (III.m.9.25), gold (II.5.4–7),
gold covered over (cf. V.1.13).   5.30 jewels (II.5.8–10), hidden (I.m.2.22–23,
I.4.4, IV.6.1).

Prose 6 II.6.1 discourse (I.4.3, III.6.5), power (II.6.18, III.2.19, III.9.2), each . . .
men (II.6.15), Aetna (II.m.5.25), destruction (II.m.6.1).   6.2 you (singular),
arrogance (= pride; II.7.20).   6.3 righteous (II.5.18), virtues/position (cf.
II.5.21).   6.4 creatures (III.3.1, V.m.5.12), preside (I.6.4), and you (singular),
laughter (cf. I.3.14).   6.5 body (III.8.6), recesses (II.1.7, II.3.4).

the body alone and that which is lower than the body, by which I mean
7   the individual's Fortune? Surely you will give no orders to a spirit that is
    free? Surely you will not dislodge a mind, tightly compacted in immov-
8   able reason, from the state of quiet peace that is its proper place? Once a
    tyrant thought that he would by torture compel a free man to betray his
    partners in a conspiracy formed against him; but that man bit his own
    tongue and cut it off and spat it out in the face of that infuriated tyrant.
    And that was how a wise man made his tortures an opportunity for vir-
    tue, when the tyrant had thought that they were an opportunity for
    bloodletting.
9   In fact, what is there that a person can do to someone else that can-
10 not be done to him by someone else? We have all heard the story of
    Busiris, how it was his habit to slaughter his guests and how he was him-
11 self put to death by Hercules, when he was a guest. And Regulus—he
    had many Carthaginians put in chains whom he had captured in war,
    but he soon held out his own hands for the chains of those who captured
12 him. So: Do you think that a man's power amounts to anything if he can-
    not ensure that what he can do to someone else someone else cannot do
    to him in turn?
13   Add to this the fact that if there were present in these positions of
    honor and power any measure of a good that belonged to them by their
    own nature, they would never become the possessions of those who are
    most despicable. For it is not the habit of opposites to join themselves
14 together; Nature disdains the conjunction of pairs of opposites. There-
    fore, since there can be no doubt that the most despicable people are
    commonly installed in positions of power, this then is clear: Those things
    are not good in their own nature that allow themselves to attach to des-
15 picable people. Indeed, one may entertain the same ideas in still more
    compelling terms about all of the gifts of Fortune, which arrive in still
    greater abundance for each and every one of the most unrighteous of
16 men. And this too is a point that I think needs to be taken into consider-
    ation in these matters, that people do not doubt that a man is brave if

---

6.7 spirit (cf. IV.m.3.27 (mind)), immovable (III.6.6), quiet peace (II.1.6,
III.m.9.27, III.m.10.4–5).   6.8 (cf. IV.6.42), free man (Zeno? cf. I.3.9), infuri-
ated tyrant (I.m.4.11–12, II.m.6.16–17; cf. I.4.2 (raging Fortune)), wise man
(IV.7.17), tortures (IV.4.40; cf. IV.5.3), opportunity (II.7.1, IV.7.18).
6.10 heard (II.7.3, III.12.24), Hercules (IV.m.7.13–35).   6.11 captured (cf.
IV.m.2.8).   6.13 own nature (II.6.20, III.4.12), despicable (I.3.11), disdains
(I.m.5.26), opposites (cf. II.2.8–14, II.6.17, IV.2.3).   6.14 be no doubt
(III.10.35).   6.15 gifts (I.m.6.15, II.m.2.17, II.m.5.6), Fortune (cf. II.2.4),
wickedest (II.6.1).   6.16 swiftness (III.8.7).

they catch sight of bravery within him; it is perfectly clear that a man is
swift if swiftness is present within him; in just the same way, musical　17
training makes musicians, medical training makes doctors, rhetorical
training makes rhetoricians. The nature of each particular skill effects
what is appropriate to it; it does not combine itself with the effects of
opposite skills; it drives from itself things that are beyond its scope.

And yet wealth and resources cannot extinguish insatiable greed, nor　18
can power make a man master of himself if corrupt acts of lust hold him
bound in chains he cannot break. Rank, when conferred upon unrighteous men, not only does not make them honorable but, more than this,
it betrays them and shows them up as dishonorable. Why does it work　19
out this way? Because you all so happily conjure up under false names
things that have quite a different nature, names that are readily contra-
dicted by the effects of the things themselves. And so it is that those
riches cannot rightly be called riches, nor that power power, nor that
rank rank. Ultimately, one may draw the same conclusion about Fortune　20
in its entirety—it's perfectly clear that there is present in Fortune nothing worth pursuing, nothing that has a goodness that belongs to its own
nature. Fortune does not always ally herself with good people, nor does
she make good those with whom she has allied herself.

Meter 6

Yés, we knów whát dreádful disásters hé caused—
Róme in flámes, hér sénators crúelly slaúghtered,
Bróther pút tó deáth—how he ónce, a sávage,
Drípped the spílled réd bloód of his véry móther,
Cást his éyes fúll-léngth on her cóld dead bódy,　　　　　　　　　5
Néver lét hís fáce run with teárs, but cálmly
Dáred appréciáte her depárted beaúty.
Nónetheléss hé góverned the dístant peóples
Phoébus seés whén sheáthing his líght in Ócean,

6.17 musical, rhetorical (cf. II.1.8), drives (I.6.4, III.m.11.9).　　6.18 wealth and
resources (II.5.20, 35), greed (II.2.8, II.m.2.13–14), power (II.6.1), master (II.4.23),
lust (III.m.5.3, III.7.3, III.m.10.2), chains (I.m.4.18, I.m.2.25, II.6.11, III.m.10.2,
V.2.2), dishonorable (cf. III.4.1–2).　　6.19 false names (cf. III.6.2, V.6.14), con-
tradicted (V.m.4.25).　　6.20 goodness (III.10.38), own nature (II.6.13).

Meter 6　II.m.6.1 disaster (II.6.1).　　6.2 senators (III.4.15; cf. III.m.4.5
(Fathers)).　　6.3 savage (IV.m.7.9–10).　　6.6 tears (cf. III.m.12.33).
6.9 Phoebus (I.m.3.9, II.m.3.2, II.m.8.5, III.m.2.31, III.m.6.3).

10   Whén he cómes ágaín from his dístant rísing,
      Whóm the pólár stárs overheád see snów-bound,
      Whóm the mád Soúth Wínd with its árid stórm blast
      Blísters ás ít fórges the búrning sánd dunes.
      Nó; his lóftý pówer could nót at lóng last
15   Rédiréct thé frénzy of twísted Néro.
      Woé the hárd mísfórtune, whenéver mádness
      Ádds the únjúst swórd to its stóre of poíson!

Prose 7

Then I said: You know that this ambition for mortal things has hardly
had any power over me; but I did desire the opportunity for doing things,
to keep my virtue from growing old along with me in silence.

2   And she said: But this is the one thing that does have the power to
seduce minds that, though unquestionably excellent in their nature,
have not yet been given the finishing touches by the perfection of the
virtues—I mean, the desire for glory and the reputation for the excel-

3   lence of one's merits on behalf of the state. Just look at it this way, how
paltry such reputation is, how utterly devoid of weight. As you have
heard from the demonstrations of the astronomers, in comparison to the
vastness of the heavens, it is agreed that the whole extent of the earth
has the value of a mere point; that is to say, were the earth to be compared to the vastness of the heavenly sphere, it would be judged to have

4   no volume at all. Further, as you have learned from the authority of
Ptolemy, only about one-fourth of this so minuscule spot in the universe

5   is the portion inhabited by animate creatures known to us. And if in
your calculations you subtract from this quarter-portion the amount that
seas and swamps wash over and the amount over which that desert
region, boundless in its desiccation, extends, scarcely will even the most

6.11 polar stars (cf. IV.m.5.1–6).   6.12 South Wind (III.m.1.7–8).
6.13 sand dunes (III.11.18, IV.m.7.25).   6.15 twisted (= perverse; cf.
III.9.16), Nero (III.m.4.4, III.5.10–11)).   6.16 woe (I.m.1.2, I.m.2.1, 27),
madness (II.6.8).   6.17 sword (II.5.34).

Prose 7 II.7.1 ambition (cf. I.4.8), opportunity (II.6.8, IV.7.18), silence (I.1.1,
I.2.4, II.7.20).   7.2 excellent (II.7.19), perfection (III.8.12, III.9.26), merits
(I.4.24, 43; III.6.3).   7.3 look (III.3.2, III.9.10, III.10.7, IV.2.28), heard
(III.12.24), astronomers (cf. I.4.4; cf. III.10.22 (geometers), vastness/heavens
(III.8.8), extent of the earth (II.m.7.4–6, V.4.30)).   7.4 Ptolemy (Almagest
2.1), minuscule (II.7.6, III.8.7), animate creatures (II.5.15, 29).   7.5 desert
(cf. II.m.6.12–23), circumscribed (II.7.6, IV.6.5).

circumscribed area be left for mortals to dwell in. So—do all of you who 6
are hemmed in and bounded by this infinitesimal point as it were on a
point make calculations about publicizing your reputations and promulgating your names, that your glory may be abundant and monumental
when it is compressed within such minuscule and circumscribed limits?

And another thing: There are many peoples who inhabit the enclosure 7
that is this truncated dwelling place. They differ from each other in language, in customs, in their entire way of life; and because of the difficulty
of land travel, the mutual incomprehensibility of languages, and the infre-
quency of trade, the reputation of individuals cannot reach them all; and
not only that, not even the reputation of cities can. A last point: In 8
Cicero's time, as he himself records somewhere or other, the reputation of
the Roman state had not yet crossed over the Hindu Kush, though it was
at that time a fully mature nation, inspiring terror in the Parthians and the
other peoples in that region. So do *you* see how circumscribed, how strait- 9
ened is the glory for whose expansion and prolongation you all work so?
Or will the glory of one Roman man advance through places into which
the reputation of the name of Rome could not pass? And what of the 10
fact that the customs and institutions of different peoples are at odds
with one another, so that what some deem worthy of reward others deem
worthy of punishment? And so it is that it would in no way profit a man 11
to promulgate his name among many peoples even if the proclamation of
his reputation were dear to his heart. Therefore, each man will be happily 12
constrained by a glory that has made the rounds of his own people only,
and the magnificent immortality that comes from reputation will be compressed along with it within the boundaries of a single people.

Yet how many men, highly esteemed in their own day, have been 13
erased by that amnesia which is the scarcity of historians for them! And
all the same, what good would such histories do if dark and distant antiquity suppresses them along with those who wrote them? Yet you all, when 14
you think about the times to come, seem to yourselves to be prolonging

---

7.6 hemmed in (IV.6.5), promulgating (II.7.11, III.2.6, 8), compressed (II.7.12).
7.7 another thing (II.4.16), peoples (II.7.10, III.6.5), differ . . . customs (cf.
IV.m.4.7), languages (II.m.7.10), trade (cf. II.m.5.13–15).   7.8 (cf. III.5.3–5,
III.6.4–6), Cicero (*Republic* 6.2).   7.9 do you see (IV.3.1, V.4.38), prolongation (II.7.14, III.2.6, IV.7.18), work (II.1.4).   7.10 (cf. IV.6.25), peoples
(II.7.7), reward/punishment (IV.3.1, IV.6.25).   7.11 promulgate (II.7.6),
name (III.2.6, IV.6.42).   7.12 happily constrained (= satisfied; II.5.16, 26),
magnificent (II.5.35, III.5.2; cf. II.m.3.15), compressed (II.7.6).   7.13 amnesia (cf. I.2.6, III.m.11.9, 16), antiquity (I.1.3, III.5.2).   7.14 prolonging
(II.7.9).

15 your reputation into immortality. But if *you* were to take its measure in
comparison to the infinite reaches of eternity, what would you have to
16 rejoice at in the perpetuation of your name? Compare the pause of a single moment to ten thousand years: Since each of them is a limited dura-
tion, even though it is very small the one does nevertheless have a
certain ratio to the other. But even this number of years, or any multiple
17 of it, cannot even be set next to an extent of time that has no end. For
while there would be some comparison among themselves one to the
other for finite terms, there could never be any comparison of the finite
18 to the infinite. And so it is that a reputation, lasting for however drawn-
out a time, would seem not to be insignificant but actually nonexistent
should it be thought of alongside of the inexhaustibility of eternity.
19   But you mortals—you do not know how to act honorably except in
response to flitting vulgar favors and empty gossip; you have abandoned
the excellence of your conscience and your virtue and demand your
20 rewards from the idle chatter of outsiders. Hear now how wittily someone mocked the shallowness of this sort of presumption. Once one man
upbraided and insulted another because the latter had clothed himself
in the name of philosopher falsely: not because of his practice of true virtue but because of vainglory and pride. The one added, "Now I will
know whether or not you are a philosopher if you endure the injustice
I've done you mildly and with forbearance." The other played at forbearance for a time, took the insult, then said with a taunt, "Now do you
know that I am a philosopher?" The first snapped viciously and said, "I
would have known it, had you kept your silence."
21   But what is there that the most excellent of men—and it is these men
that we are talking about, men who strive for glory through virtue—I
repeat, what is there that they get from their reputations after their bod-
22 ies have been broken by the death that comes at the end? For if people
die completely (something that our arguments forbid us to believe), then
glory is absolutely nothing, since the person to whom it is said to belong
23 absolutely does not exist. But on the other hand, if a mind conscious of

7.15 you (singular), infinite reaches (V.6.15), eternity (V.6.4 ff.), perpetuation
(III.11.32).   7.16 no end (V.6.4).   7.18 inexhaustibility (I.1.1).
7.19 flitting favors (II.m.7.23; cf. III.2.9), vulgar (III.4.8, III.6.3, 6), gossip
(I.4.44), conscience (II.7.23).   7.20 hear (singular; II.7.3), falsely (II.6.19),
true (II.6.1), pride (II.6.2, II.m.7.7), injustice done (cf. IV.4.36), forbearance
(IV.6.40), for a time (I.2.6, IV.6.2), snapped (cf. I.5.1 (barking); III.m.3.5, III.5.7,
III.7.5 (gnawing)), silence (I.1.1, II.7.1).   7.21 death (IV.4.9, IV.m.6.33).
7.22 our arguments (IV.4.26, 32).   7.23 conscious (II.7.19), released (cf.
III.m.6.5), prison (IV.5.3), fly (cf. IV.1.9, IV.m.1, V.m.5.13), dismiss (I.3.12,
III.8.6; cf. IV.m.1.4)

its own excellence, released from its earthly prison, is free to fly to the heavens, wouldn't it dismiss every earthly entanglement, glad to be delivered from the things of earth?

Meter 7

Let thóse who ónly stríve for glóry with dównhill mínds,
  Embrácing ít as híghest goód,
Come cóntempláte the vást horízons óf the ský,
  The nárrow cónfines óf the eárth,
And théy will bé ashámed of theír much-vaúnted námes   5
  That cánnot fíll so smáll a spáce.
Why dó the proúd attémpt to raíse their nécks, bowed dówn
  By Deáth's own yóke, and áll in vaín?
Though réputátion, pássing tó far-dístant lánds,
  May spreád and loósen fóreign tóngues;   10
Though a hoúse may shíne with pórtraits óf its nóble deád—
  High glóry ís despísed by Deáth.
Death cóvers óver poór and míghty skúlls alíke
  And lévels lów and lófty thíngs.
Where rést the bónes now óf Fabrícius, tríed and trué?   15
  What is Brútus ór stern Cáto nów?
Thin réputátion leáves its márk, an émpty náme,
  In spáre inscríptions língers ón.
But wé who cóme to knów the námes so shárply cárved
  Can súrely néver knów the deád.   20
You mórtals áll die útterlý withoút a náme!
  No réputátions máke you greát.
Do you thínk the flítting fávor óf a mórtal náme
  Protrácts your lífe a líttle móre?
A dáy will cóme at lást to táke this toó from yoú—   25
  For yoú a sécond Deáth awaíts.

Meter 7 II.m.7.1 downhill (I.m.2.1, II.m.2.15).   *7.3–6* (cf. III.8.8).
7.3 contemplate (I.m.2.8), horizons (cf. II.7.3–5).   *7.4* narrow confines
(II.7.6, 12).   *7.5* names (II.7.6, 9, 11).   *7.6* small space (II.7.3).
7.7 necks (I.m.2.25).   *7.8* Death (II.7.21–23), in vain (V.4.16).   *7.9* far-
distant (II.7.8–9).   *7.10* tongues (II.7.7).   *7.11* portraits (cf. I.1.3), noble
(cf. III.m.6.6–7).   *7.14* low/lofty (II.m.1.4, II.2.9).   *7.17* empty names
(II.4.3, III.4.15, III.6.7, V.1.8).   *7.23* flitting favor (II.7.19).   *7.24* protracts (I.m.1.20 (drags out)).

Prose 8

But I do not want *you* to think that I am waging relentless war against
Fortune. There is a time when that deceitful goddess deserves respect
from mortals; I mean, at the time when she reveals herself, when she
2 takes off her mask and makes her habits plain. Perhaps you do not understand yet what I am saying; what I am trying to say is paradoxical, and for
3 that reason I can hardly explain my meaning in words. You see, I think
that Adverse Fortune does more good for mortals than Favorable Fortune
does. The latter, in the guise of happiness, always lies when she seems to
be sweet-talking; the former is always true, when she reveals her instabil-
4 ity by her ability to change. The latter deceives, the former instructs; the
latter, in the guise of false goods, binds tight the minds of those who enjoy
them; the former frees those minds through their realization of the fragility of their happiness. And so you see the one, irresponsible, her clothes
loose about her, always unaware of herself; the other sober, dressed for the
5 journey, and wise through the practice of adversity itself. Lastly, Happy
Fortune by her sweet-talking drags people off the path, away from the
true good; time and again Adverse Fortune drags them back again with
her hook, and they return to the true goods.
6   Or do you think that this is to be reckoned an insignificant thing, the
fact that this cruel, this bitter Fortune has revealed the minds of the
friends that are still loyal to you? This was the Fortune that separated
those whose faces were ever toward you from those who temporized;
when she left she took her own with her, and left yours behind with you.
7 When you were all in one piece and, as it seemed to you, a fortunate
man, how much would you have paid for this? Go on, complain about
the wealth and resources that you've lost; you have found what is the
most valuable kind of riches, your friends.

Prose 8 II.8.1–5 (cf. IV.6.23).   8.1 you (singular), relentless (I.4.9), deceitful
(II.m.1.4, II.8.4, III.4.13; cf. II.1.11), mask (II.1.3; cf. II.1.11), habits (II.2.8, 11).
8.2 paradoxical (IV.2.33), hardly explain (cf. I.6.8).   8.3 sweet-talking (II.1.3,
5, 10), instability (II.4.25), ability to change (II.1.10, 15).   8.4 binds tight
(II.m.8.13), minds (cf. II.6.7), realization (cf. I.2.6), fragility (III.8.6, III.10.6),
clothes (cf. I.1.3–5), adversity (II.4.2, 16).   8.5 drags (cf. III.2.4, III.m.8.1–2,
III.9.4), path (I.m.4.17, I.5.3, III.9.28, IV.1.9, V.1.5; cf. II.2.4, III.m.11.2).
8.6 cruel/bitter (I.4.2, II.m.1.6), friends (I.m.1.21, II.m.8.26–27, III.2.9), temporized (cf. III.5.13), took/left (II.2.6).   8.7 seemed to you (cf. II.1.2), fortunate
(II.3.11, II.4.16), paid (II.4.5; cf. III.11.2–3), wealth and resources (II.5.18, 20,
35; cf. II.m.3.15–16), friends (I.m.1.22, II.m.8.26).

Meter 8

A steádfást, trústworthy únivérse
Mákes hármónious, órdered chánge;
Pácts étérnal restraín and cúrb
Wárríng phýsical eleménts.
Phoébús bríngs forth the róse-red dáy   5
Fróm á chárjot máde of góld;
Stárs thát Hésperus úshers ín
Phoébé góverns in deád of níght;
Seás ímmóderate keép in chéck
Róllíng wáves in detérmined boúnds;   10
Drý lánd, shápeless and próteán,
Máy nót strétch out beyónd its póle.
What bínds thís séquence of thíngs so tíght,
Whát ís kíng over lánd and seá,
Whát thé heávens obéy, is Lóve.   15
Shoúld hé slácken or dróp his reíns,
Thíngs thát nów love each óther wéll
Wíll dó báttle foréver móre,
Ánd wíll vénture to teár apárt
Whát théy faíthfully nów impél   20
Wíth Lóve's mótion—the wórld machíne.
Hé hólds nátions togéther toó
Wíth ínvíolate treáties bound;
Hé joíns márriage's sácred rítes
Ín ímmáculate bónds of lóve;   25

Meter 8 II.m.8.1–4 (cf. III.m.9.10–12, IV.m.6.16–24).   *8.1* steadfast
(I.m.1.22, I.m.4.16, I.m.5.47).   *8.3* pacts (I.m.5.43, 48; cf. II.m.8.23,
III.m.2.5, IV.m.6.4, V.m.3.1).   *8.4* elements (III.m.9.10), warring elements
(IV.m.6.20).   *8.5* Phoebus (II.m.6.9).   *8.6* chariot (II.m.3.1).   *8.7* Hesperus (I.m.5.11).   *8.8* Phoebe (IV.m.5.10, IV.m.6.7).   *8.10* bounds
(I.m.5.25, II.m.2.16).   *8.13* binds (II.8.4, III.m.2.4–5), sequence of things
(IV.6.4, 14, 17).   *8.14–15* king . . . Love (cf. II.m.8.29).   *8.14* land and sea
(cf. V.m.2.5–6).   *8.15* heavens (II.m.8.30), Love (IV.m.6.16, 44–48).
8.16 reins (I.5.4).   *8.17* each other (IV.m.6.17).   *8.21* motion (II.5.9),
machine (III.11.24, III.12.14, IV.6.54).   *8.22* nations (II.7.7,10; III.6.5).
8.25 bonds of love (cf. II.4.6).   *8.26* friends (II.8.6).

Fór thé lóyal and faíthful friénds
Hé láys dówn what is ríght and wróng.
Ó hów háppy the mórtal ráce,
Wére Lóve kíng over áll your heárts,
30 Lóve thát heáven accépts as kíng!

8.26 friends (II.8.6).   8.28 happy (I.5.46–48, II.5.1, III.m.12.1).
8.29 Love king (II.m.8.14–15); heaven (II.m.8.15).   8.30 king (= is governed; cf. I.m.5.48, I.6.19).

Book III

Prose 1

She had put an end to her singing just when the soothing sweetness of her song held me spellbound, eager to hear more, my mouth hanging open, my ears still pricked. And so, after just a little space, I said: Yes, you are the greatest consolation for worn-out hearts. How you have brought the warmth back to me, by the gravity of your conclusions and even more by the delightfulness of your singing! Yes, so much so that even now I would not think myself to be less than a match for the blows of Fortune from this point on. Accordingly, those remedies that you said were more bitter-tasting—I'm not only not afraid of them, but I demand them passionately, eager to hear more.

Then she said: So I understood, when in silence and concentration you grabbed hold of my every word; I have been waiting for this condition of mind in you or, what would be more honest, I have myself brought it about. In fact, this is the nature of the remedies that remain: When tasted, they certainly bite; but when taken deep inside, they turn sweet. But as to the fact that you say that you are eager to hear more—if you only realized just where I am trying to lead you, what fever you would burn with then!

I said: Where?

She said: To true happiness. Your heart also dreams of it, but as your vision has been directed only toward images, it is not able to look on it directly.

2

3

4

5

Prose 1 III.1.1 sweetness (II.1.8), spellbound (cf. I.1.13), mouth . . . open (cf. III.3.19). 1.2 (cf. III.12.23) yes, you are (IV.1.2), consolation (II.4.9, III.3.18; cf. I.m.1.8), worn-out (cf. I.2.5), hearts (II.m.8.29), warmth (II.5.1) conclusions (I.6.20), delightfulness (III.7.3), blows (II.2.12), bitter-tasting (I.5.12, I.6.21), passionately (III.9.31, III.12.1, 15 (utter)), eager (III.1.1). 1.3 understood (I.4.1, III.12.9), silence (I.1.1), concentration (II.1.1), condition (II.1.2; cf. I.6.1, V.m.3.26), brought about (III.2.3, III.9.26), remedies (I.5.11, II.3.3, III.1.2), tasted (II.1.7), bite (II.7.20, III.9.20 (gnawed)), inside (II.1.7, III.3.4, III.9.27), sweet (cf. III.1.1). 1.4 eager (III.1.1, III.1.2), if you only (III.9.28), realized (IV.2.2), lead (I.3.4–5, IV.1.9), fever (cf. III.m.12.14), burn (IV.6.51, V.m.3.11). 1.5 true happiness (III.9.26), dreams (III.3.1), images (III.3.1, III.9.30), look on (III.9.3; cf. I.1.13, III.9.1).

6   Then I said: Do this, I beg you! No delay! Show me what this true happiness is.

7   She said: I will do it, for your sake and gladly. But I will first attempt to sketch and outline in words the happiness that is more-than-well-known to you; after you have seen it clearly you will thus be able to know the appearance of true and real happiness as soon as you direct your eyes to the opposite side.

Meter 1

Whó would sow seéds in the soíl for a great cróp
Fírst must remóve from the fiéld bramble and brúsh,
Múst cut the brácken awáy with the sharp hoók;
Só will rise Céres agaín, pregnant with graín.
5 Só too the lábor of beés, sweeter by fár
Íf an unsávory táste first stings the moúth;
Áfter the Soúth Wind falls stíll, after the raíns,
Lóvelier shímmer the stárs in the night ský.
Lúcifer scátters the dárk; beautiful dáy
10 Láshes its dáwn-colored teám into the líght.
Loók at the fálse good things fírst! And so you wíll
Stárt at remóving your néck out from the yóke;
Thén shall the trué good things páss into your heárt.

Prose 2

She kept her eyes fixed on the ground for some little time. And then, as if she had first withdrawn into the holy foundations of her mind, she began:

2   All anxieties of mortal men, driven on by the exertions of uncountably diverse pursuits, travel along paths that are, to be sure, quite differ-

---

1.7 seen (III.9.1), know (I.2.6), appearance (III.3.4), true happiness (IV.1.8), direct your eyes (III.9.24, III.12.16).

Meter 1 III.m.1.1 seeds (cf. III.11.23–24).   1.3 cut away (cf. IV.4.38).
1.4 Ceres (I.m.6.5, IV.m.6.27).   1.5 bees (III.m.7.3), sweeter (cf. III.1.3).
1.6 stings (bites: III.1.3, III.m.7.5).   1.7–10 (cf. I.m.3).   1.7 South Wind
(II.m.6.12).   1.9 Lucifer (I.m.5.10–13, IV.m.6.15).   1.10 dawn-colored
(II.m.3.1), team (cf. IV.m.4.4).   1.11 look (I.m.7.20).   1.12 yoke (II.1.16,
II.m.7.7–8, III.12.18).   1.13 true (cf. III.1.7).

Prose 2 III.2.1 eyes fixed (I.1.13, II.m.9.24), foundations (= dwelling place:
I.4.38, III.m.9.22, III.9.32, III.11.22).   2.2 pursuits (III.2.13), travel/paths
(II.1.8; cf. I.m.7.23–24, IV.2.4; cf. I.m.1.6).

ent; yet they all strive to reach only one single goal: true happiness. And that is *the* good thing: Once people have secured it they cannot desire anything beyond it. It is in fact the highest of all good things and it contains all good things within itself; if anything could be added to it, it could not be the highest good, since there would remain something external to it that could still be hoped for. It is therefore clear that happiness is a state brought about by the convergence of all good things. As I have said, all mortals try to secure this state by different routes, for the desire for the true good has been naturally planted in the minds of human beings, but miscalculation drags them off the path and toward false goods. Now some of these people think that the highest good is to want for nothing, and they work hard to have riches in abundance; but others reckon as the good whatever is most worthy of esteem, and they strive to secure political honors and so be preeminent among their fellow citizens. There are those who place the highest good in the highest position of power; such people either wish to be kings themselves or try to stick by the side of those who are kings. And those who decide that renown is best hurry to prolong their glorious names by the arts of war or peace. But most people gauge the fruits of a good thing by joy and delight, and these think it the happiest thing of all to dissipate themselves in physical pleasure. There are even those who switch the causes and goals of these pursuits reciprocally: for example, those who desire wealth for reasons of power or physical pleasures, or those who try to gain power for the sake of money or of promulgating their names.

And so, it is in these and all other such pursuits that the striving of human actions and human wishes is to be found: for example, noble birth and the goodwill of the people, which seem to get for one a certain renown; or wife and children, whom they seek to gain for the sake of

---

2.3 highest good (III.2.11, III.11.39), external (III.3.14), brought about (III.1.3, III.2.14), convergence (III.8.12).   2.4 secure (III.2.19), different (III.9.15), different routes (III.2.2), planted (I.4.8, I.4.38, II.4.28, II.5.24; cf. III.m.11.11), miscalculation (I.3.8, II.4.22, III.3.1, III.9.4, IV.6.22, V.3.28), drags (III.m.8.2), off the path (II.8.5, III.m.8.2).   2.5 want for nothing (III.2.14), work hard (III.11.20), riches in abundance (III.3.5; cf. II.2.4), esteem (III.2.15), political honors (cf. II.6), preeminent (IV.5.2).   2.6 position of power (cf. II.6), renown (cf. III.2.9), prolong (II.7.9, 14), names (II.7.11).   2.7 most people (III.11.5), gauge (III.6.3), fruits (I.1.9), dissipate (IV.6.15, IV.7.19), joy (= pleasure; I.m.7.25), physical pleasure (cf. III.7).   2.8 promulgating (II.7.6). 2.9 striving (III.2.15, III.11.30), human actions (IV.2.5), noble birth (II.4.13, III.6.7), goodwill (cf. II.7.19, III.6.6), renown (III.2.6, III.6.7), wife (cf. II.4.6), children (cf. II.3.6, 8; II.4.7, III.7.5–6), decent delight (III.2.12, III.7.3; cf. III.1.2), category (cf. II.3.5), friends (II.8.6), assigned (III.2.16).

decent delight. But the category of friends, which is truly the most holy category of desirable things—this is not assigned to Fortune's list but to Virtue's, while every other category is adopted for the sake of power or
10   delight. Now as for the goods of the body, they too are readily referred to the higher categories: Muscles and size seem to offer strength; beauty
11   and swiftness of foot, acclamation; health, physical pleasure. In all of these things it is clear that true happiness alone is the thing that is desired; for any person, seeking to gain something in preference to all others, judges that it is the highest good. But we have defined true happiness as the highest Good; and for this reason a person, desiring one state in preference to all others, judges that *it* is the truly happy state.
12·   Therefore you have it, set before your eyes, what is practically the essence of human happiness: wealth and resources, political honors, power, glory, physical pleasure. Consequently Epicurus, looking at these things alone, determined for himself that the highest good is physical pleasure, because all of the other goods seem to confer this decent delight to the mind.
13   But now I return to the pursuits of mortals. The mortal heart, even if its memory is darkened over, seeks to regain what is its own good but, like a drunken man, it does not know by what path it can return home.
14   Surely those who strive to want for nothing do not seem to wander from the path? What is more, there is no other thing that is equally capable of bringing about true happiness than a state replete with all good things, which does not need any outside thing but is sufficient unto itself. Surely
15   those who think that what is best is what is most worthy of the careful cultivation of preeminence do not slip and fall? Hardly; nor is it a worthless and despicable thing that practically all mortals in their striving
16   work at securing for themselves. Or is power not to be assigned to the

---

2.10 goods of the body (III.8.7; cf. III.7), swiftness (II.6.16, III.8.7), health (cf. III.10.39).   2.11 true happiness alone (III.1.2), defined (at III.2.3; cf. III.10.2, IV.2.40).   2.12 there you have it (III.9.24), you (singular), essence (III.9.1, 24), wealth . . . pleasure (cf. III.2.19), Epicurus (cf. I.3.7), confer (II.4.28, III.9.29), decent delight (III.2.9).   2.13 pursuits (III.2.2, 20), memory (cf. I.2.6, I.6.10, III.12.1, IV.1.1), darkened over (I.1.13, I.6.21), seeks to regain (cf. IV.m.6.45), path (I.m.7.23, III.m.9.28, IV.1.9), return home (I.5.3, III.12.9, IV.1.9).   2.14 want for nothing (III.2.5), bringing about (III.1.3, III.2.3, III.8.12), sufficient (III.2.19).   2.15 preeminence (III.2.5, 19; III.4.5), hardly (II.5.32, III.3.9), worthless (I.3.14), despicable (III.4.9), striving (I.6.10, III.2.9, III.11.30), works at (III.11.16; cf. III.2.5, III.11.20), securing (III.2.4, 19; III.9.16). 2.16 assigned (III.2.9), well then (III.9.22, V.1.11, V.3.22, V.5.5), unable . . . itself (III.5.9, III.9.5).

list of goods? Well then! What everyone agrees is more excellent than all
other things can hardly be reckoned to be enervated and unable to sustain itself. Is renown to be valued not at all? But this fact cannot be set   17
aside: Anything that is most superior can't help but be seen as most
renowned as well. And what good does it do to say that true happiness is   18
not fretful or depressed, that it is not subject to sorrows and physical
afflictions? After all, even in the least significant things one only craves
what it is a joy to possess and derive benefit from. What is more, these   19
are the things that mortals want to secure for themselves, and it is for
this reason that they long for riches, positions of honor, kingdoms, glory,
and physical pleasures, because they believe that self-sufficiency, preeminence, power, acclamation, and delight will come to them by these
means. Therefore it is the Good that mortals seek to gain by such diverse   20
pursuits; and it is easily shown just how great is the force of Nature in
their pursuit of the Good, because, despite the fact that their opinions
are different and incompatible, they still concur in their loving choice of
the Good as their goal.

Meter 2

Whát are the reíns of pówerful Náture,
Guíding the úniverse? Bý whát státútes
Does her Próvidence hóld thé ínfinite sphére,
Bínding and keéping thís wórld óf thíngs
In unbreákable bónds? Ít is my pleásure   5
That my sóng síng oút tó the soft lýre.
Álthoúgh líóns cáptured in Líbya
Carry beaútiful chaíns, eát the food gíven
In the mástér's hánd, feáring his ánger,

2.17 renown (III.2.6), set aside (= separated; II.5.20), superior (I.4.39, II.5.10).
2.18 fretful (III.3.5), craves (III.10.38, III.11.5, 14).   2.19 (cf. III.9.2), secure
(III.2.4, 15), riches . . . pleasures (cf. III.2.12), kingdoms (II.2.12, III.5.1), self-
sufficiency (III.2.14, III.3.9–10), preeminence (III.2.15), acclamation (III.2.10),
delight (III.2.7).   2.20 diverse pursuits (III.2.2; cf. III.2.13, IV.2.10), force of
nature (cf. III.m.2.1), incompatible (IV.3.11), concur (III.11.37), the Good
(III.2.2).

Meter 2 III.m.2.1 reins (II.m.2.15, II.m.8.16, IV.m.6.35), Nature (III.2.20).
2.3 Providence (III.11.33).   *2.4* binding (II.m.8.13).   *2.6* lyre (cf.
III.m.12.20 ff.).   *2.7* lions (III.m.12.11, IV.3.18, IV.m.4.5).   *2.8* chains
(I.m.2.25, I.m.4.18), food (III.m.2.24, III.11.30).

10 Ínúred to the stróke óf his hard láshings—
Staín the wild múzzle wíth hót réd bloód,
Stréngth lóng dórmánt soón reappeáring
Gives the térrible roár of sélf-recognítion.
As their loóséned bónds slíp from their freé nécks,
15 Theír traíner first tórn by góry incísors
Ínstrúcts by his bloód theír mád ángér.
Thé cháttering bírd ín the high bránches
Nów is imprísoned in the vaúlt of a cáge;
Mórtal atténtions, playful, may óffer
20 Wíth sweét cóncérn cúps rimmed with hóney,
Éxtrávagant feásts fór this perfórmer.
Flúttering úpward in her clóse-woven cáge,
Cátchíng síght óf gróves and fair shádows,
Scrátching she scátters all the foód at her feét,
25 Ánd moúrning her lóss seéks the woods ónly,
Only coós "Thé woóds!" ín her soft sínging.
Thé trúnk of a treé, únder compúlsion
Óf mórtál stréngth, bénds its head dównward;
When the hánd léts gó whích once had wárped it,
30 Ít raíses its crówn, gázing at heáven.
Phoébús wíll sét Wést, in the Ócean;
By invísible wáys, éver and éver,
Hís cháriot cómes báck to its rísing.
Áll seék out their ówn páths of reéntry,
35 Réjoíce in their ówn prívate retúrnings.
There is hándéd dówn nó lasting órder,
Éxcépt that each joín énd and begínning
Ánd máke for itsélf óne stable círcle.

2.11 stain (II.m.5.18).   *2.12* reappearing (cf. I.m.3.2, III.m.2.35).   *2.13* self-recognition (I.2.6, III.2.13).   *2.14* necks (I.m.2.25, III.m.3.3, III.m.5.4).
2.20 cups (IV.m.3.7, 22), honey (II.3.2, III.m.7.3–4).   *2.23* catching sight (cf. III.9.3, III.12.3, 15).   *2.24* food (III.m.2.8).   *2.27* trunk of a tree (cf. III.11.21–22).   *2.28* of a downward (I.m.2.26).   *2.30* gazing at heaven (cf. III.m.12.52–58, V.m.5.13).   *2.31* Phoebus (I.m.3.9, III.m.10.18, III.m.11.8).   *2.32* ways (cf. III.2.13).   *2.33* chariot (II.m.3.1–2, II.m.8.5–6, IV.m.1.21), rising (I.m.2.16–17).   *2.34–38* (cf. IV.m.1.23–26).
2.35 returnings (III.2.13, III.m.9.20–21; cf. III.12.30, 37–38).   *2.37* end and beginning (cf. III.m.9.15–17), beginning (III.3.1, III.m.6.9, IV.m.1.26).
2.38 stable (I.m.1.22, II.m.8.1, III.m.9.3 (unmoved)), circle (III.m.9.13–17).

Prose 3

And you, you creatures of the earth! Even though it is an insubstantial image, you do dream all the same of your origins, and all the same you do discern that true goal of happiness by some kind of thought, even though it is of the least penetrating kind. It is for this reason both that your natural striving leads you toward the true good and that your uncountably diverse miscalculations drag you away from it. Look at it this way: Have people the ability to reach the goal they have decided to pursue by means of the things that they thought would secure them true happiness? For if coined money or political honors or the others do confer something in which none of the good things seems to be missing, we too would admit that some people *do* become happy by the securing of such things. But if these things are not able to accomplish what they promise, if they lack many of the good things, then surely it is clearly discovered that the appearance of true happiness in them is a false one.

Therefore, I ask this question first of you, who just a little while ago had riches overflowing: In the midst of all your extravagantly abundant wealth and resources, was your mind never dazed by a fretfulness born of some insult or other?

I said: In fact, I cannot remember that my mind was ever free from being fretted by something.

Because something was absent that you did not want to be absent, or because something was present that you had not wanted to be present—right?

I said: It is as you say.

You desired the presence of one thing and the absence of another?
I said: I admit it.

But, she said, the thing that one desires is a thing that one lacks?
I said: Yes, that one lacks.

Prose 3 III.3.1 creatures (II.6.4; cf. V.m.5.12), insubstantial (III.9.3), image (III.1.5, III.9.30, III.10.2), dream (III.1.5), origins (I.6.12, III.m.2.37, III.m.6.7), happiness (III.2.2), penetrating (I.1.1), striving (III.2.9, IV.2.26), diverse (III.2.2), miscalculation (II.4.22, II.5.30, III.2.4, III.m.11.7); drags away (III.2.4). *3.2* look (singular), look . . . way (II.7.3), ability . . . goal (cf. III.8.1), secure (III.2.4).   *3.3* the others (cf. III.2.12, 19), confer (III.2.12), securing (III.10.23–25).   *3.4* promise (III.3.11, III.8.1), discovered (II.1.11), appearance (III.1.7).   *3.5–19* (cf. II.5).   *3.5* just . . . ago (I.6.5, II.2.4, III.9.25), riches (III.2.5), fretfulness (III.2.18, III.m.3.5 (cares), III.7.1), daze (I.6.22, II.4.22). *3.6* I cannot (I.6.8, III.9.14), remember (I.4.44, III.7.3).   *3.7* it . . . say (III.3.13).   *3.8* desired (III.8.4).   *3.9* self-sufficient (III.2.19), hardly (II.5.32, III.2.15, III.9.23).

But one who lacks something is not self-sufficient in every respect?
I said: Hardly.

10   And so you put up with this lack of self-sufficiency even when you
were brimming with wealth?
I said: Well, of course I did.

11   Therefore, wealth is not able to make a person lack for nothing and
12   be self-sufficient, yet this is what it seemed to promise. And yet, I think
that this further and most important point also needs to be looked at,
the fact that money has in and of its own nature nothing that can keep it
from being taken away from those who possess it against their will.
I said: I admit that.

13   Well, of course you admit it, since every day some stronger man steals
it from someone else against his will. For where do the grievances brought
before the courts come from, if not from monies stolen by force or fraud
from people against their will, monies that they now try to regain?
I said: It is as you say.

14   Therefore, she said, all individuals will be in need of some externally
sought assistance in order to protect their money.
Who could deny it? I said.

15   And yet they would not need this if they did not possess money that
they could lose.
I said: That cannot be doubted.

16   So it has fallen out that the situation is just the opposite: The wealth
that is thought to make people self-sufficient makes them feel the need
17   of some assistance outside of themselves instead. But what are these
means by which the feeling of need is dispelled by riches? Surely it is not
the case that the rich cannot be hungry and cannot be thirsty? Or that
18   the limbs of people with money do not feel the winter's chill? But, you
will say, the wealthy have the wherewithal to satisfy their hunger, to satisfy their thirst, to dispel winter's chill. But while the feeling of need can
indeed be consoled in this way by riches, it cannot be taken away from

---

3.10 brimming (cf. III.3.5), well, of course (II.5.11, III.3.13, IV.4.17).
3.11 promise (III.3.4).   3.12 further point (cf. III.4.9), looked at (III.3.2),
own nature (V.5.4).   3.13 steals (III.8.3), for where (cf. II.2.12), it . . . say
(III.3.7).   3.14 externally (II.4.22, III.10.12, III.12.11, V.4.13), assistance
(III.3.16, III.9.5, III.9.32); who . . . it (IV.4.18).   3.15 cannot be doubted
(III.11.6).   3.16 (cf. III.3.14), fallen . . . opposite (V.3.8; cf. II.5.23).
3.17 limbs (IV.m.3.31).   3.18–19 (cf. II.m.2.17–20, II.m.5.25–30).
3.18 you will say (singular: II.4.23), feeling of need (III.3.17), consoled
(III.1.2), mouth . . . open (III.1.1 (different terms)), demanding (cf. III.m.2.17–
26), filled . . . wealth (III.m.3.2).

deep within. Why? Because this feeling of need, always with its mouth wide open, always demanding something—even if it is filled full by wealth, there must still remain another need that needs to be filled. I say 19 nothing of the fact that the least is enough for Nature, and that nothing is enough for greed. Therefore: If wealth cannot eliminate the feeling of need and creates its own feeling of need instead, what reason is there for you mortals to think that it can offer you self-sufficiency?

Meter 3

Although the rích man máy draw óff from floóds of góld
    Weálth overflówing, his greéd cánnot be fílled to the brím;
Although he máy weigh dówn his néck with Índian peárls,
    Óne hundred óxen may plów hís fertile coúntry estátes,
His gnáwing cáres do nót forsáke him whíle he líves;   5
    Deád, his ephémeral weálth cánnot atténd to his neéds.

Prose 4

But high offices make the man to whom they come honorable and preem-inent. Surely this is not the strength of administrative offices, that they plant virtues in the minds of those who occupy them, and drive vices out? In fact, they are more likely to reveal gross wickedness than to put it to 2 flight. And so it is that we take it as dishonorable that these positions so often fall to grossly wicked men; and it is for this reason that Catullus called Nonius a wart, even though he sat in a curule chair. So do you see 3 what disgrace high offices award to evil men? And yet the lack of honor in such men would be less obvious, if they did not gain recognition by their political honors. And in your own experience—ultimately, you 4 could not be compelled by all those threats, now could you, to be willing

---

3.19 least . . . Nature (II.5.16), self-sufficiency (III.2.14, III.2.19, III.3.9–10).

Meter 3 III.m.3.1 gold (II.m.2.10, II.m.5.29; cf. III.m.10.7–8).   *3.2* overflow-ing (III.3.5), filled (III.3.18).   *3.3* neck (I.m.2.25, III.m.2.14, III.m.5.4), pearls (cf. III.m.4.2, III.m.8.11, III.m.10.10).   *3.4* estates (cf. II.5.11).
3.5 gnawing (III.5.7, III.7.5), cares (III.3.5).   *3.6* ephemeral (I.m.1.17).

Prose 4 III.4.1 high offices (cf. II.6), plant (III.2.4), vices (III.m.6.9, IV.2.31).
4.2 reveal (cf. II.6.18), gross wickedness (III.7.2), Catullus (poem 52.2), curule chair (II.3.8; cf. III.m.4.6).   *4.3* do you see (singular: II.7.9, IV.3.1).
4.4 administrative duties (III.4.1), informer (I.4.14, 22).

to undertake administrative duties alongside of Decoratus, since you saw
in him the sensibilities of a grossly wicked man, an insolent idler, an
5   informer? Why? Because we cannot judge people to be worthy of preeminence because of their political honors if we judge them to be unworthy
6   of the honors themselves. But were you to see someone who was endowed
with wisdom, you could not think him unworthy of preeminence, could
you, or unworthy of the wisdom with which he is endowed?
     Hardly.
7   And that is because there is present within it a real rank that belongs
to virtue, and virtue pours this rank directly into those to whom it has
8   attached itself. And because popular honors cannot do this, it is clear
9   that they do not have the beauty that belongs to real rank. Now in this
there is another matter even more worthy of notice: I mean, if people
are the more disreputable as they are the more despised by more people,
then, since rank cannot make preeminent those whom it puts on display
before more people, rank actually makes unrighteous people more con-
10   temptible. But it does not do so without paying a price: The wicked
return an equal favor to their high offices, which they stain by their own
11   foul contact with them. And just so that you may understand that true
preeminence cannot be the product of these shadowy high offices—if a
man who has been consul many times turns up by some chance in bar-
barian nations, will his political honor cause him to be esteemed by
12   these barbarians? And yet, if high offices had by nature this gift to
bestow, they would in no way fail to discharge their duties in any nation,
just as fire never fails to be warm, regardless of where in the world it is.
13   But since it is the deceitful opinion of mortals, and not their own natural
force, that attaches this gift to high offices, they vanish into thin air just
as soon as they come into the presence of those who do not reckon them
to be high offices.
14   Now this is about foreign nations only; but high offices don't last for-
15   ever, do they, among those people with whom they had their origin? In
fact, the praetorship was once a great office, but it is now an empty name
and a heavy burden for a senator's resources. Once, if a man had control

4.6 wisdom (II.4.5).   4.7 pours into (IV.5.3).   4.8 popular honors (cf.
II.7.19), beauty (III.4.17, III.10.26).   4.9 another matter (cf. III.3.11), disrep-
utable (III.4.15, III.9.10, IV.1.7), despised (III.2.15), unrighteous (I.4.6, 9;
IV.2.39, 45).   4.10 return . . . favor (cf. IV.m.4.11), stain (cf. I.4.37,
III.m.2.11), contact (III.4.17, III.12.1).   4.11 preeminence (III.4.5), barbar-
ian nations (cf. II.7.7–12).   4.13 deceitful (I.6.21, III.6.1, V.3.18), attaches
(III.10.27).   4.14 last forever (III.5.1; cf. II.4.21).   4.15 empty name
(II.4.3, II.m.7.17), grain (cf. I.4.12), disreputable (III.4.9).

of the public grain supply he was called The Great; now, what is more disreputable than that particular prefecture? For as I said just a little   16 while ago, a thing that has nothing of its own to distinguish it, now acquires and now loses its brilliance according to the opinion of those who seek to exploit it. Therefore, if high offices are unable to make peo-   17 ple preeminent; if, beyond that, these positions are defiled by the foul contact of the unrighteous; if they cease to be brilliant because of the passage of the time; if they are worthless in the reckoning of other nations—to say nothing of what they can offer to others, what is the beauty that they have within themselves that is worth craving?

Meter 4

Dréssed ín Týrian púrple róbes, disdaínful,
    Décked in the nácreous príde of fíne stones,
Stíll hé thríved, univérsallý detésted
    Néro, a mán of sadístic pleásures.
Ín hís dáy, out of spíte, he gáve the Fáthers,   5
    Wórthy men, únworthy seáts of óffice.
Téll mé: Whó could thus thínk themsélves ennóbled?
    Gífts of such désolate mén are hónors?

Prose 5

Or do kingdoms and intimacy with kings have the ability to make one powerful? Well, of course they do, when their happiness lasts forever. And   2 yet antiquity is full of examples, and the present age is full of them as well, of kings who changed their happiness for disaster. How magnificent is

---

4.16 just . . . ago (at III.4.12–13).   4.17 defiled (IV.1.6), foul contact (III.4.10), worthless (II.5.2), beauty (III.4.8), craving (II.5.19, III.7.1, III.10.26).

Meter 4 III.m.4.1 dressed (I.m.5.38), Tyrian (II.m.5.9), purple/purple robes (III.m.8.12, IV.m.2.2).   4.2 nacreous stones (cf. III.m.3.3, III.m.8.11, III.m.10.10).   4.3 Nero (II.m.6, III.5.10–11).   4.6 seats (III.4.2). 4.8 desolate (II.4.29, III.5.3).

Prose 5 III.5 (cf. II.6).   5.1 kingdoms (II.2.12, III.2.19), intimacy (II.1.3; cf. III.5.9), ability (III.3.2, III.8.1), well of course (I.6.14, II.5.11, III.3.10, III.3.13), lasts forever (III.4.14, III.6.6).   5.2 antiquity (I.1.3, II.7.13), full (III.5.9), changed (II.2.9; cf. II.2.11–12), how magnificent (II.5.35, II.7.12), preservation (III.11.27, III.12.37, V.2.8).

that power, which is found out to be not even sufficiently capable of its own self-preservation!

3   Now if this power that exists in kingdoms is the sponsor of true happiness, would it not be the case that, if it were deficient in any point, it

4   would diminish that happiness and bring in desolation? But however widely the domains of mortals may spread, there must remain any num-

5   ber of peoples over whom none of these kings rules. But it is just at this point that power ceases to make people truly happy and that powerlessness enters in in consequence; this makes them desolate, and so it is in this way that kings necessarily have within them a greater portion of deso-

6   lation. A tyrant who knew well the dangers attendant upon his lot in life represented the fears inherent in royal rule by the threat of a sword hang-

7   ing over his head. So tell me: What is this power that cannot banish the gnawing of their anxieties, that cannot avoid the stings and barbs of their fears? To be sure, they would themselves wish to live without such anxieties, but they cannot; and thereupon they boast about their power.

8   Or do you think that a man is powerful when you observe him longing for what he cannot accomplish? Do you think a man is powerful when he travels in the company of bodyguards, when he is more afraid of those whom he intimidates than they are of him, when the appearance

9   of his power is placed in the hands of those who serve him? And why should I tell you stories about the intimates of kings, now that I've shown you that their kingdoms themselves are full of such an inability to sustain themselves? But kingly power, sometimes when still intact, sometimes in the course of its own destruction, has often brought such people

10   low. Nero forced Seneca, his intimate and his own teacher, to the decision that he would choose how he would die; Caracalla threw Papinianus to the swords of his soldiers—Papinianus, long a powerful man in

11   the imperial court! And yet each of these two wanted to forsake the power he had, and Seneca even tried to sign his wealth over to Nero and to go into retirement; but neither accomplished what he wanted, and the very weight of their collapse dragged them down to destruction.

5.3 sponsor (I.6.19), bring in (V.4.20), desolation (II.4.28, III.5.4; cf. II.7.7–9, III.6.4).   5.4 (cf. II.7.7–9, III.6.4).   5.5 powerlessness (IV.2.28).
5.6 tyrant (I.m.4.11, II.6.8, IV.m.1.30, IV.m.2.9).   5.7 so tell me (III.5.12), gnawing (III.m.3.5, III.7.5), without anxieties (cf. II.1.12).   5.8 do you think (singular: I.3.6, I.4.22, III.5.8; cf. III.8.4–6), placed . . . hands (IV.7.22).
5.9 intimates (III.5.1), full (III.5.2), inability to sustain (III.2.16, III.9.5, IV.1.7), intact (II.4.5).   5.10 Nero (cf. II.m.6, III.m.4), Seneca (I.3.9), choose . . . die (cf. III.11.32), imperial court (I.4.15).   5.11 accomplished (III.5.8).

So tell me: What is this power? Those who have it, dread it; and 12
when *you* want to have it you cannot relax; when you want to set it aside
you cannot get out of its way. Or can friends serve as your protection if it 13
was not your virtue but your fortune that drew them to your side? The
man whom your happiness has made your friend your punishment will
make your enemy. Indeed: What plague is there more able to accomplish 14
its goals of destruction than the intimate enemy?

Meter 5

Lét thóse who would wísh to have pówer
Fírst cónquer their béstial ánger,
Nor submít to lust's foúl reins and brídle
Nécks cónquered and bént down in báttle.
Even thoúgh distant Índia trémbles   5
At your fíats and greát proclamátions,
Though the nórthernmost ícefields obeý you—
If you cánnot dispél dark forebóding,
Nór roút all your désolate sórrow,
Thén yoúrs is not pówer, not éver.   10

Prose 6

And glory! How deceitful it often is, and how shameful! And so it is not
without cause that Euripides, *the* tragic poet, cries out:

O glóry, glóry, fór ten thoúsand wórthless mén
You háve amássed a lívelihoód unlímitéd!

5.12 so tell me (III.5.7), you (singular), relax (I.4.15 (secure)).   5.13 friends
(II.8.6, III.2.9), punishment (IV.4.5; cf. II.8.6, III.7.6).   5.14 plague (cf.
III.7.2, IVm.3.20 (curse)).

Meter 5 III.m.5.2 bestial anger (IV.3.18).   5.3 foul lust (II.6.18, III.m.10.2,
IV.3.20).   5.4 necks (I.m.2.25, III.m.2.14, III.m.3.3), conquered (II.m.1.4
(downcast), III.m.12.56; cf. II.6.11).   5.5 India (III.m.3.3, IV.m.3.15).
5.6 your (Nero's?).   5.8 foreboding (= care: I.m.2.4).   5.9 desolate sorrow
(II.m.2.7–8).

Prose 6 III.6 (cf. II.7).   6.1 deceitful (I.m.1.19, III.4.13, III.m.10.3), shameful
(III.6.2, III.8.10, IV.4.37), without cause (I.4.30), Euripides (*Andromache* 319–20;
cf. III.7.6).

2   Why? Because many have stolen this great name, through the false opinions of the common people. What can be imagined that is more shameful than that? For those who falsely receive this attribution must themselves necessarily be embarrassed by their own praises.

3   And even if such praise has been gained by his merits, nevertheless, what can it add to the conscience of a wise man, who gauges his own
4   good not by popular gossip but by the truth of his conscience? And even if it is only the prolongation of one's name that seems so beautiful, the logical consequence is that not protracting it is judged to be disgraceful.
5   But as was my discourse a little while ago: Since there must necessarily be many peoples whom the reputation of a single man cannot reach, it is then the case that the man whom *you* reckon to be glorious seems inglo-
6   rious in that part of the earth that borders your own. In light of these considerations I don't think that the appreciation of the people is even worthy of notice; it does not come about through sound judgment and it never lasts immovably forever.

7   Furthermore: Who is there who does not see how empty and how insubstantial is the very name of noble birth? If it assigned to the category of renown, noble birth is outside of it, for it seems to be a kind of
8   praise that comes from the merits of one's parents. But if it is the attribution of glory that creates this renown, then people must necessarily be renowned who have glory attributed to them, and for this reason a renown that is external to you does not make you glorious if you do not
9   have a renown of your own. But if there is some real good in noble birth, I would consider it to be this alone: that a necessity seems to be imposed on those of noble birth not to fall away from the virtue of their ancestors.

6.2 stolen (I.3.7), name (II.6.19; cf. II.7.20), false opinions (I.6.21), common people (I.5.8, IV.7.7), imagined (III.10.7, III.11.39, V.3.32), shameful (III.6.1), attribution (III.6.8).   6.3 merits (cf. I.4.24, 43; II.7.2), conscience (I.4.33, 37; II.7.19, IV.6.46, 49), wise man (cf. III.4.6), gauges (III.2.7), popular gossip (I.4.44, II.7.19).   6.4 prolongation (II.7.9, 14), beautiful (cf. III.4.8, 17), logical consequence (III.9.12, IV.2.12).   6.5 discourse (I.4.3, II.6.1, III.12.32), little while ago (cf. II.7.7–9, III.5.4), you (singular), borders (II.7.12).
6.6 appreciation (III.2.9), judgment (I.4.25, V.6.2), lasts forever (III.4.14, III.5.1), immovably (I.m.5.47, II.6.7, V.3.6).   6.7 empty (II.4.3, II.m.7.17, III.4.15), noble birth (II.4.13, III.2.9, III.m.6.6), renown (III.2.6, 9), external (II.5.14).   6.8 attribution of glory (cf. III.6.2), you (singular).
6.9 necessity imposed (V.6.48), fall (cf. III.m.6.8).

Meter 6

Thére is but óne race of mórtals on eárth,
　　　　　　　and they áll spríng from the sáme soúrce;
Thére is one Fáther alóne for the wórld,
　　　　　　　and alóne hé tends to áll thíngs.
Hé gave to Phoébus his beáms óf líght,
　　　　　　　gave the cúrved hórns to the moónlíght;
Yés, and he gáve to the eárth mortal mén
　　　　　　　as he gáve stárs to bright heávén.
Hére he enclósed ín límbs óf flésh　　　　　　　　　　　　　5
　　　　　　　human soúls soúght from their hígh hóme—
Thús does a nóble descént prodúce
　　　　　　　every mórtál man and wómán.
Whý do you boást of your fámily and líne?
　　　　　　　If you loók tó your begínníngs,
Ánd to the Gód who creáted you áll,
　　　　　　　there is júst óne who has fállén—
Hé who embráces by více what is wórse
　　　　　　　and abándóns what he róse fróm.

Prose 7

But what can I say about the pleasures of the body? On the one hand,
the craving for them is a thing full of fretfulness; on the other, their satisfaction is full of remorse. What great diseases, what unbearable grief　　2
these pleasures bring to the bodies of those who enjoy them—a kind of

---

Meter 6 III.m.6.1 source (III.m.6.9, III.m.9.23, 28).　　6.2 Father (III.9.33,
III.m.9.22, IV.1.6).　　6.3 Phoebus (I.m.3.9, I.m.5.9, III.m.10.18), horns (I.m.5.8,
IV.m.5.7).　　6.5 enclosed (cf. II.7.23), limbs (V.m.3.22), home (cf. I.5.3–5,
III.2.13, IV.1.9, IV.m.1.25–26).　　6.6 noble (III.6.7–9), descent (cf. IV.m.3.5).
6.7 family/line (cf. I.1.3, II.7.12), beginnings (III.3.1).　　6.8 created (= author;
cf. V.3.32), fallen (cf. II.4.13, III.6.9).　　6.9 vice (III.4.1, IV.2.31–32), embraces
(I.1.8 (tend to)), worse (IV.4.29), abandons (I.m.6.20, II.3.14), rose (III.m.2.37
(beginning), IV.m.1.26 (born); cf. III.3.1).

Prose 7 III.7.1 pleasures of the body (III.2.7, 10; III.8.6–7), craving (II.5.19),
fretfulness (cf. III.2.18), remorse (cf. III.7.3).　　7.2 diseases (I.1.9, I.2.5,
III.5.14, IV.4.38), enjoy (III.m.7.2), fruit (cf. I.1.9), gross wickedness (III.4.2,
IV.3.12–13).

3   fruit, as it were, of gross wickedness! I have no idea myself what delight-
     fulness the excitement of these pleasures may possess; but any man will-
     ing to call his acts of lust to mind will understand that the end results of
4   such pleasures are sorrowful. If these pleasures can create truly happy
     people, then there is no reason why herd animals can't be called happy
     as well, for all of their striving is similarly eagerly directed toward filling
     their bodily cavities full.
5   Now a decent delight in one's spouse or one's children may be a very
     honorable thing; but it has been said, a thing drawn too truly from nature,
     that someone invented children to be tormentors. And it is hardly neces-
     sary to remind *you*, who know this from earlier experience and who are
     fretful about them even now, just how your children's state of affairs
6   gnaws at you, whatever it may be. In this I approve of the conclusion of
     my good Euripides, who says that a man who lacks children is happy in
     his punishment.

Meter 7

Every pleásure knóws this óne thíng:
Goading ón those whó enjóy ít,
. Like the hóneybeés that hóvér.
Once it poúrs its pleásing néctár,
5   It is góne, and pángs the bruísed heárt
With a stíng that cán't be dráwn oút.

7.3 delightfulness (III.1.2, III.2.9, 12), call to mind (I.4.44, III.3.6), acts of lust
(II.6.18, III.m.5.3, III.m.10.2; cf. III.11.32), end results (I.m.6.22), sorrowful
(II.3.10).   7.4 create (III.12.7, IV.2.5), herd animals (cf. II.5.29), striving
(I.6.10, III.2.9, 15; III.11.15), eagerly directed (III.11.39, IV.2.10), filling full
(III.3.18, III.m.3.2).   7.5 decent delight (III.2.9), very honorable (I.4.40), too
truly (cf. IV.7.4), remind (cf. I.4.2), you (singular), gnaws (III.m.3.5).
7.6 conclusion (cf. IV.7.4), my good (V.1.12 (Aristotle)), Euripides (cf. III.6.1;
= *Andromache* 418–20), man . . . children (cf. II.4.14), punishment (II.5.13,
IV.4.17).

Meter 7 III.m.7.2 enjoy (III.7.2).   7.3 bees (III.m.1.5), honey (II.3.2,
II.m.5.6–7, III.m.2.20).   7.4 pours (cf. II.5.16, III.4.7).   7.5 heart
(IV.m.2.6).   7.6 sting (= bite: III.m.1.6, III.m.3.5, III.5.7, III.7.5).

Prose 8

It is therefore not at all to be doubted that these paths to true happiness are detours of one sort or another and that they do not have the ability to lead any people all the way to the goal to which they promise they will lead them. But I shall point out in very brief compass all of the evils in which they are entangled. 2

Well, what would *you* prefer? Will you strive to heap up money? But you will steal it from the one who has it. Would you wish to be resplendent in high offices? You will play the suppliant to the one who grants them to you, and so you who want to outdistance all others in honor will become worthless through the humiliation of having to beg for it. Do you desire power? You will be exposed to the plots of your subjects, and will subject yourself to risks and hazards. Should you seek glory? But you are dragged in all directions then, on each and every rough road, and so cease to be free from anxiety. Would you lead a life of pleasure? But who would not dismiss and push away what is the slave of this most worthless and fragile thing, the body? 3 4 5 6

Furthermore: Those who make display of the goods of the body— what a minuscule, what a fragile possession they rely on! Surely you mortals will not surpass the elephant in bulk or the bull in strength? Or will you outdistance the tiger in swiftness of foot? Contemplate the vastness, the mightiness, and the swiftness of the heavens and now, at last, stop admiring worthless things. And make no mistake: The heavens are less to be admired for these things than for the reason by which they are governed. And the fair sheen of beauty—how fugitive it is, how swift, 7 8 9

Prose 8 *III.8.1* these (cf. III.2.4–7), paths (IV.1.8, IV.m.1.23, IV.m.7.33), true happiness (cf. II.4, III.2, III.10), detours (V.1.5), ability (III.3.2, III.5.1), promise (III.3.4, 11; IV.2.1).   *8.2* point out (III.9.25, IV.1.8), entangled (IV.6.15, V.1.2, V.m.1.8).   *8.3* you (singular), money (cf. II.5, III.3), steal (III.3.13), who has it (II.5.5–6), resplendent (II.5.17), high offices (II.6, III.4), outdistance (III.8.7), worthless (I.3.14, II.5.2, III.4.17), humiliation (V.3.34), beg (cf. V.3.34). *8.4* desire (III.3.8–9), power (cf. II.6, III.5), subjects (cf. III.5.8).   *8.5* glory (cf. II.7, III.6), dragged (I.5.11), cease (II.1.19), cease . . . anxiety (II.5.35). *8.6* pleasure (cf. III.7), dismiss (I.3.12, II.1.12, II.7.23), push away (II.1.12), worthless (III.8.3), fragile (II.8.4, III.8.7, III.10.6), body (II.6.5).   *8.7* goods of the body (III.2.10, III.8.11; cf. III.7), minuscule (II.7.4, 6), bulk (III.m.8.21), outdistance (III.8.3), tiger (IV.m.3.15–16, IV.m.4.5).   *8.8* (cf. II.m.7.3–6, IV.4.29), contemplate (cf. I.1.2), vastness (II.7.3; cf. I.m.5.48), admired (cf. III.m.8.17), reason (I.6.3), governed (I.m.5.48, I.6.19, II.m.8.30, III.12.3). *8.9* ever-changing (II.1.10, 15; II.8.3), flowers of spring (II.m.3.6).

10 more fleeting than the ever-changing flowers of spring! For if, as Aristotle says, people had the eyes of Lynceus, so that their vision could pene-
trate any barriers, wouldn't the body of Alcibiades, proverbially so
beautiful on its surface, seem utterly shameful after they had peered at
the guts within? And so it is not *your* nature that makes you seem beau-
11 tiful, but only the weakness of the eyes of those who look upon you. Go
ahead, mortals, reckon the goods of the body as highly as you like, so
long as you realize that this little something that you admire can be done
away with by the paltry flame of a three-day fever.
12   From all of these considerations, this is the sum total that it may be
reduced to: These things, which cannot offer the goods that they promise, and which have not themselves been brought about by the convergence of all good things, do not lead to true happiness as if they were
various true paths, nor do they themselves bring it about that people are
perfectly happy.

Meter 8

Woé! Hów ígnorance leáds désolate mén astraý,
    And drágs them óff the próper páth!
Mórtál mén! Do you míne góld in the leáves of treés
    Or hárvest jéwels from óff the víne?
5 Woúld yoú sét out your tráps, húnt on the moúntaintóp,
    To máke a cóstly feást of físh?
Ín púrsuít of the deér, whý would you wánt to trý
    The wáters óff the Wéstern coást?
Ánglérs knów them all wéll: hídden beneáth the wáves,
10   The sánctuáries óf the seá,
Whát thé deép waters whére nácreous jéwels aboúnd,
    Or mýrex ánd its púrple dyé;

8.10 Aristotle (V.1.12, V.6.6; = *Protrepticus*, frag. 59), barriers (cf. I.m.7.13),
peered within (cf. IV.m.2.5, IV.6.26), guts (V.m.2.5), you (singular), weakness
(IV.2.45).   8.11 (cf. II.6.5), reckon (III.6.5, IV.1.6), goods of the body
(III.8.7).   8.12 (referred to at III.9.22), sum total (III.10.37), promise
(III.8.1), brought about (cf. II.7.2, III.9.26), convergence . . . things (III.2.3),
true happiness (III.8.1), paths (II.1.8, III.2.2, III.8.1), truly happy (cf. III.2.14).

Meter 8 *III.m.8.1* woe (I.m.1.2, 16; I.m.2.1, 27; II.m.5.27), ignorance (II.4.22,
26; cf. I.3.8, III.2.4).   8.2 drags . . . path (II.8.5, III.2.4).   8.3 gold (II.5.4,
III.m.3.1).   8.4 jewels (II.5.8–10, III.m.8.11).   8.11 nacreous jewels
(III.m.4.2, III.m.10.10; cf. III.m.3.3).   8.12 purple (III.m.4.1, IV.m.2.2).

Whát bést shóres for the spíked seá urchin cán be foúnd,
    Or peérless físh with ténder flésh.
Yét mén, steádfastly blínd, éver refúse to leárn   15
    The pláce where hídes the goód they seék,
Ánd thé thíng that transcénds stár-bearing heáven's póle
    They seék when súnk in dépths of eárth.
Téll mé: hów may I cúrse mínds so obtúse as thése?
    Let them stríve for hónors, stríve for weálth—   20
Thén, whén theý have amássed the búrdensome búlk they cráve,
    The fálse goods, lét them knów the trué.

Prose 9

Let this demonstration of the essence of deceitful happiness suffice, this far and no farther; if you give it a penetrating look, next in logical progression is to point out what true happiness is.

And I do see it, I said; self-sufficiency can't possibly be a property of   2
wealth and resources, nor can power be a property of kingdoms, nor preeminence of high offices, nor acclamation of glory, nor delight of physical pleasures.

And have you discovered the reasons why this is so?

I seem to myself to be looking on them as if through some microscopic   3
crack, but I would prefer to know them from you, in a more open way.

And the explanation for this is very near to hand. What is simple and   4
indivisible in its own nature, human miscalculation divides and drags away from the true and the perfect to the false and the imperfect. Or do you think that what has need of nothing lacks power?

8.15 blind (II.1.11, II.4.26, IV.2.31, V.m.3.15).   *8.16* place where (III.10.1), the good they seek (III.2.2).   *8.17* transcends . . . pole (cf. III.8.8). *8.18* sunk (I.m.2.1), earth (I.m.2.27, III.m.10.14).   *8.19* obtuse (II.1.9; cf. I.m.2.27).   *8.21* amassed (III.9.17), burdensome (I.m.6.1), bulk (III.8.7).

Prose 9 III.9.1 essence (III.2.12, III.9.12, III.10.1), deceitful happiness (III.9.24, 31; cf. III.10.1), look (III.1.5, 7; III.11.18), penetrating (I.1.1, III.3.1; cf. III.8.10).   *9.2* (cf. III.2.19, III.9.15), self-sufficiency (III.2.14, III.3.9, 10), kingdoms (III.5.1), preeminence (III.9.9), acclamation (III.2.10, 19), delight (III.2.7), physical pleasures (III.7.1), discovered (II.1.11, IV.5.6).   *9.3* (cf. III.10.32, III.12.3, 15), look on (III.1.5), microscopic (I.1.3, III.12.15), crack (IV.4.10), know (III.9.27), open way (cf. III.9.27, III.12.3).   *9.4* (referred to at III.9.15 and 25), simple (III.9.16), miscalculation (II.4.22, II.5.30; cf. II.4.26, III.m.8.1–2), drags away (II.8.5, III.m.8.1–2, III.2.4), true/perfect (III.11.5), hardly (III.3.9, III.4.6, III.9.23).

I said: Hardly.

5   And you're right; for if anything exists that is possessed of a strength that is unable to sustain itself in any way, it must necessarily need some assistance outside of itself in this regard.

I said: It is as you say.

6   Therefore the nature of self-sufficiency and the nature of power are one and the same.

So it seems.

7   Now do you think that a thing that is of this sort should be dismissed or, conversely, do you think that beyond all other things it is worthy of the highest esteem?

The latter, I said; it cannot even be doubted.

8   So let us add preeminence to self-sufficiency and power, so that we may determine that these three are one.

Yes, let's add it, so long as it is our wish to agree on what is true.

9   Well then, what's next? she said. Do you think that such a unity is veiled in darkness and undistinguished in character? Or is it the most

10   renowned thing of all, possessed of every acclamation? It is conceded that it lacks nothing, that it is both most powerful and most worthy of honor; but look at it carefully, to make sure that it does not want for a renown that it cannot provide for itself and for that reason seem disreputable in some particular.

11   I cannot help but agree with you, I said; this thing, just as it is, is just so the most acclaimed thing of all.

12   Therefore, the logical consequence is that we must admit that renown differs in no way from the above three categories.

I said: That is the consequence.

13   Therefore, a thing that needs nothing that is outside of itself, which is capable of all things by its own strength, which is renowned and preeminent—surely it is agreed that this is most full of delight?

14   In fact, I cannot even think, I said, of a place from where any grief could steal up on any such thing as this. And for this reason, so long as

---

9.5 unable to sustain (III.2.16, III.5.9, IV.1.7), assistance (III.3.16, III.9.32), outside (III.3.16), it is . . . say (III.3.7, 13; III.10.17, IV.7.8).   9.6 self-sufficiency/ power (cf. III.9.2).   9.7 dismissed (III.8.6), esteem (III.2.5, III.4.11, IV.6.42). 9.9 veiled in darkness (III.9.17; cf. II.7.13).   9.10 conceded (III.10.17), look (II.7.3, III.10.7), disreputable (III.4.9).   9.11 agree with you (III.9.14). 9.12 logical consequence (III.6.4, IV.2.12), above (cf. III.9.14), consequence (IV.4.36).   9.13 delight (III.2.7).   9.14 I . . . think (cf. I.6.8, III.3.6), grief (I.m.1.2, III.12.1), the above (III.2.10, III.9.12), remain unchanged (III.11.4, V.4.9, V.6.44, 45).

the above conclusions shall remain unchanged, I must agree with you that it is full of delight.

And so that earlier point is also necessary, and for the same reasons: 15
To be sure, the names self-sufficiency, power, renown, preeminence, and delight are different, but their substance is not different in any way.

I said: Yes, it is necessary.

Therefore it is human perversity that has divided this thing up, which 16
is one and simple by nature; and while this perversity strives to secure a part of a thing which has no parts, it neither acquires this portion, that is a nonentity, nor the whole itself, which it tries very ineffectually to win.

I said: And how is that? 17 .

A man who seeks riches in a flight from poverty makes no efforts as regards power, prefers to be worthless and veiled in darkness, and even deprives himself of many natural pleasures as well, all so that he may not lose the money he has amassed. Yet in this way not even self-sufficiency 18
is in his possession, as his bodily strength abandons him, his troubles annoy him, his worthlessness casts him aside, and his darkness surrounds him. And a man who longs for power alone wastes his wealth, despises 19
physical pleasures, despises the honor that has no power, and considers glory a thing without value as well. But you see how many things let this 20
man down as well, for it happens at various times that he lacks the necessities of life or that he is gnawed by fretfulness; and when he cannot drive these things away, he ceases even to be that one thing that he most particularly sought, to be powerful. One may use a similar line of 21
reasoning about honors, glory, and physical pleasures; as each one of them is the same as the others, whoever seeks one of them without the others does not even gain that one thing that he longs for.

Well then! I said. What if someone wants to secure all of them for . 22
himself simultaneously?

Then such a man would be wishing for the sum total of true happiness; but he will not find it, will he, in those things that we have shown to be incapable of bestowing what they promise?

9.15 earlier point (at III.9.4), different (III.2.4). 9.16 perversity (II.m.6.15, IV.4.4, 9), divided up (cf. I.1.5, I.3.7), simple (III.9.4), secure (III.2.4, 5, 15, 19), no parts (cf. I.1.5, I.3.7). 9.17 worthless (I.3.14, II.5.28, III.2.15), veiled in darkness (II.7.13, III.9.9), amassed (III.m.8.21). 9.18 abandons (I.m.6.20, II.3.14, III.m.6.9), worthlessness (III.4.9, III.8.3, 6), casts aside (I.2.3, I.m.4.17 (discarded), I.6.21). 9.20 you (singular), gnawed (III.5.7, III.7.5).
9.21 line of reasoning (III.10.21, IV.6.17, V.3.14, V.5.5, 7). 9.22 well then (III.2.16, III.11.14, V.1.11), simultaneously (V.6.4, 7, 22; cf. V.6.8, 12), true happiness (II.5.35, III.9.1; cf. III.10), we have shown (at III.8.12), bestowing (III.9.30).

23   I said: Hardly.

Therefore: True happiness is not to be tracked down in these things that are believed to offer one-at-a-time the objects that must be sought.

I said: I admit it; nothing can be said that is truer than this.

24   So there you have it, she said: Both the essence and the causes of false happiness. Now direct the gaze of your mind to the opposite side, for there you shall see immediately the true happiness that we have promised.

25   But this is quite obvious, I said, even to a blind man, and you pointed it out just a little while ago when you were attempting to reveal the
26   causes of false happiness. For unless I am mistaken, *that* is the true and perfect happiness which brings it about that a person is perfectly self-suf-
27   ficient, powerful, preeminent, acclaimed, and full of delight. And, just so that you may know that I have learned these things deep inside: Since all of these things are the same, the happiness that can truly offer any one of them I know without a doubt is happiness full and true.

28   O my son, you whom I have nursed! How happy you would be in this opinion, if you would only add this one thing to it!

I said: Tell me, what?

29   Do you think that there is anything in the world of mortal and falling things that is able to confer a status of this sort?

Hardly, I said; and I think that this was already shown by you, to the point that no more proof was desired.

30   Therefore, these things *seem* to give to mortals images of the true good, perhaps, or some imperfect goods, but the true and perfect good they cannot bestow.

I said: I agree.

31   Therefore, since you have come to know what true happiness is, and what are the things that counterfeit happiness, it only remains that you come to know the source from which you can seek this true happiness.

9.23 hardly (III.3.9), tracked down (III.10.32, III.m.11.1), sought (III.10.37, IV.2.29), I admit (III.3.12, IV.2.9).   9.24 (resumes from III.8.8), you (singular), essence (III.2.12, III.9.1), direct (III.1.7), gaze (I.6.21 (vision), V.2.11, V.6.23), gaze/mind (V.6.22).   9.25 quite obvious (IV.2.7, 39; IV.3.1), blind (II.1.11, II.4.26, III.m.8.15, IV.2.31), just . . . ago (I.6.5, II.2.11, III.3.5, III.10.2), when (at III.9.4).   9.26 (referred to at III.10.2), perfect happiness (III.1.5), perfectly (II.7.2, III.8.12).   9.27 just . . . know (cf. IV.2.40), deep inside (III.1.3), the same (cf. III.9.16), doubt (V.3.1).   9.28 nursed (I.3.4, III.m.10.14, III.11.40), if only (III.1.4), tell what (IV.4.12, IV.7.1).   9.29 falling (II.m.3.15, II.5.2), confer (II.4.28, III.2.12).   9.30 images (III.1.5, III.3.1; cf. V.6.12), bestow (III.9.22), I agree (III.11.1, III.12.1, 15).   9.31 (cf. III.9.1), counterfeit (II.8.3 (lies); cf. V.6.12), source (III.m.9.23, 28), passionately (III.12.1, 15).

I said: That's the very thing that I have been so long and so passion-ately expecting.

She said: But since, just as our Plato in *Timaeus* would have it, one 32
ought to invoke divine assistance even in the smallest matters, what do
you think we ought to do now so as to merit the discovery of the dwell-ing place of that highest good?

I said: We must invoke the Father of all things; were he to be omitted, 33
there could be no starting point that is properly grounded.

She said: Correctly so! 34

And with that word she began to sing as follows:

Meter 9

Yoú who contról all the wórld everlástingly bý your own reáson,
Sówing the seéds of the eárth and the heávens, commánding the éons
To róll from etérnity; résting unmóved, you put áll things in mótion,
Yoú whom no álien caúses demánded to fáshion creátion
From mútable mátter, but ónly the únstinting éssence of trué good   5
Plánted withín you; and fróm their celéstial exémplar you leád things,
Áll of them, oút and, most spléndid yoursélf, in your ówn mind you cárry
Thís splendid wórld and you shápe it to mírror your ímage and líkeness,
Ánd you commánd that its pérfect compónents accómplish perféction.
Yoú bind in númber and rátio the élements, íce and flame mátching,   10
Drý matching moíst, so there ís no flight úp for the rárified fíre,
Eárth is not drágged by its weíght to sink dówn to the dépths of the wáters.
Yoú center Soúl: It unítes threefold Náture, sets áll things in mótion;

9.32 our (IV.6.33), Plato (I.3.6, I.4.5, III.12.1, 38; III.m.11.15, IV.2.45, V.6.9, 10,
14), *Timaeus* (*Timaeus* 27c), assistance (III.3.16, III.9.5), merit (I.5.5, 7), dwell-ing place (I.4.38, I.5.6, III.2.1, III.m.9.22 (foundations)). 9.33 invoke (cf.
III.12.36), Father (III.m.6.2, III.m.9.22), starting point (IV.6.22, V.4.37; cf.
IV.6.19 (loom)). 9.34 correctly so (III.10.16), began to sing (cf. I.1.14,
III.2.1).

Meter 9 III.m.9.1 world everlastingly (cf. V.6.14). 9.2 sowing (cf. III.m.9.6,
20), commanding (III.m.9.9). 9.3 resting unmoved (I.m.1.22, III.12.7–8,
IV.m.1.21), all . . . motion (III.m.9.13). 9.4 alien (I.m.2.3). 9.5 essence
(III.9.1). 9.6 planted (I.4.8, III.m.9.2). 9.8 image and likeness
(III.m.9.17, IV.6.55). 9.9 command (III.m.9.2; III.8.8), perfect (I.1.3,
III.9.4). 9.10–12 (cf. II.m.8.1–4, IV.m.6.19–24). 9.10 number
(I.m.2.12), elements (II.m.8.3, IV.6.18), matching (cf. III.11.18). 9.11 flight
up (III.m.9.21; cf. IV.1.9). 9.11–12 fire/earth (III.11.26). 9.13 all . . .
motion (III.m.9.3).

Yoú divide Soúl and appórtion it ínto harmónious mémbers;

15   Soúl, once divíded, collécted its mótion in twó equal órbits,
Móving so ás to retúrn to itsélf, and complétely encírcling
Mínd at the córe, so the úniverse wheéls in its ímage and líkeness.
Yoú by like caúses bring fórth lesser soúls; for these lésser creátions
Yoú fashion nímble convéyances fít for a heávenly joúrney.

20   Yoú plant these soúls in the heávens, in eárth; by your génerous státutes
Yoú make them túrn back toward yoú and retúrn—a regréssion of fíre.
Gránt to the mínd, Father, thát it may ríse to your hóly foundátions;
Gránt it may ríng round the soúrce of the Goód, may discóver the trué
light,
Ánd fix the soúl's vision fírmly on yoú, vision keén and clear-síghted.

25   Scátter these shádows, dissólve the dead weíght of this eárthly concrétion,
Shíne in the spléndor that ís yours alóne: only yoú are the bríght sky,
Yoú are serénity, peáce for the hóly; their goál is to seé you;
Yoú are their soúrce, their convéyance, their leáder, their páth, and their
háven.

Prose 10

Therefore, since you have now seen what is the essence of the imperfect good, and the essence of the perfect good as well, I believe that I now must show you where the perfection of this happiness has been estab-

2   lished. So that no empty image of thought may confuse us, taking us

---

9.14 members (III.m.6.5, III.10.31–34).   9.16 return to itself (III.m.11.3; cf. III.12.37, IV.6.15).   9.17 mind . . . core (III.m.11.1 (mind's great depth); cf. IV.6.32), image and likeness (III.m.9.8).   9.19 conveyances (III.m.9.28, IV.1.9).   9.20 plant (III.m.9.2, 6), generous (III.12.24), statutes (V.m.1.12 (law)).   9.21 fire (III.m.9.11).   9.22 Father (III.m.6.2, III.10.12; cf. I.m.5.46–48), rise (IV.m.1.2), foundations (= dwelling place: III.9.32, III.11.22). 9.23 source of the Good (III.10.3, III.m.12.1–2), true light (I.m.7.20–22; cf. V.3.34).   9.24 fix firmly (cf. I.1.3, III.2.1).   9.25 (cf. V.m.2.8–10), scatter shadows (cf. I.m.3), dead weight (II.m.5.28; cf. III.m.12.3–4).   9.26–28 (cf. V.m.2.13–14).   9.26 splendor (III.m.10.15), bright sky (cf. I.m.7.9, II.m.3.9–10).   9.27 serenity (= peace: II.1.6, 12; II.6.7, III.m.10.4), holy (cf. I.m.1.20).   9.28 (cf. IV.1.9), source (III.10.16), leader (IV.6.9 (ruler)), haven (III.m.10.5).

Prose 10 III.10.1 (cf. IV.5.1), essence (III.9.1, 24; III.11.5), imperfect good (in Book II), perfect good (in Book III) where (III.m.8.16), established (IV.5.1).   10.2 empty image (V.m.4.15; cf. III.3.1), nature of the universe (III.10.5), defined (IV.2.20), just . . . ago (at III.9.26).

beyond the truth of the matter before us, in this investigation I think that *this* question needs to be asked first, whether there can possibly exist in the nature of the universe any good of the sort that you defined just a little while ago. But it can't be denied that it does exist and that this is, as it were, a sort of source of all good things; for everything that is said to be imperfect is held to be imperfect by reason of its distance from what is perfect. And so it is that, if there seems to be anything imperfect in any class of objects, there must necessarily be something perfect in it as well; after all, once perfection has been removed, one can't even imagine a source from which a thing that is held to be imperfect could have arisen. No; for the nature of the universe has not taken its starting point from diminished and incomplete things, but, in procession from what is whole and absolute, it disintegrates into these exhausted things at the furthest remove. Therefore if, as we have shown just a little while ago, there does exist some imperfect happiness in some fragile good, it cannot be doubted that there also exists a steadfast and perfect good.

I said: This conclusion has been drawn most unshakably and most truly.

She said: But as to where it dwells, look at it this way: the common conception of human minds grants that God, the ruler of all things, is good; since nothing can be imagined that is better than God, who could doubt that that thing is good, than which nothing is better? But reason shows that God is good in such a way that it also proves that the perfect Good exists within him. For if the good in him were not of this sort, he could not be the ruler of all things; for there would then be something more excellent than God, possessing the perfect Good, a thing that would seem to be prior to and more ancient than God; for it has been made clear that all things that are perfect are prior to things that are less whole. And for this reason we must agree, to keep this line of reasoning

3

4

5

6

7

8

9

10

10.3 denied (III.11.9, III.12.12, IV.7.10), source (III.m.9.23, 28; III.12.1–2) held to be (III.10.4, 12; V.6.8).   10.4 imagine (III.10.14).   10.5 (cf. III.9.4), nature of the universe (III.10.2), starting point (III.9.33, V.4.37), in procession (I.6.11, III.12.7, V.1.19), whole and absolute (V.4.9), whole (III.10.9), disintegrates (III.12.37, V.2.8), exhausted (cf. I.m.2.24 (gone out)).   10.6 just . . . ago (cf. III.8), fragile (II.8.4, III.8.6, IV.2.3), conclusion (III.10.16), steadfast (cf. IV.1.7, V.6.25), unshakably (IV.2.4), truly (cf. III.10.16).   10.7 look . . . way (II.7.3, III.9.10), common conception (cf. III.6.2, III.12.8), minds (III.1.2, 5), ruler of all things (III.10.9), imagined (III.6.2, III.11.39).   10.9 prior/ancient (cf. III.10.13), ancient (V.6.11), made clear (cf. III.10.5), whole (III.10.5).   10.10 line of reasoning (III.10.24), regressing (lit., progressing), established (III.2.3, III.2.11, III.10.17), I accept (III.10.37).

from regressing to infinity, that God is highest and is most full of the Good that is highest and perfect; but we have established that true happiness is the highest Good; therefore, it is necessary that true happiness is located in this highest God.

I said: I accept that, and there is nothing that can in any way be said against it.

11   She said: You do grant what we said, that the highest God is most full of the highest Good, but I beg you please observe in what a holy way you do so, a way not to be transgressed.

I said: What way is this?

12   So that you do not assume that this Father of all things perhaps took to himself from something external to himself that highest Good that he is held to be full of, or that he possesses it by his nature in such a way that you think that the substance of the God who possesses it and the

13   substance of the true happiness that is possessed are different. For if you think that it has been taken in from something external to himself, you could reckon that what gave it is more excellent than what took it; but we very appropriately agree that this God is the most surpassing of all

14   things. On the other hand, if it is present in God according to its own nature, but is present as a thing different in principle—since we are talking about the God who is ruler of all things, let anyone who is able to

15   just imagine who it was who joined these different things together. A last point: That which is different from any other thing is not itself the same as what it is understood to be different from. Consequently, that which is by its own nature different from the highest Good is not the highest Good; this is a wicked thing to think about God, as we have agreed that

16   there is nothing more excellent than he is. For as a rule there cannot exist a nature in any thing that is better than its source; and for this reason I would conclude, by the truest possible line of argument, that a thing that is the source of all things is also in its own substance the highest Good.

I said: Indeed, most correctly so.

10.11 observe (IV.2.26, IV.4.28), beg . . . please (IV.4.22, IV.6.1).   10.12 Father
(III.m.6.2, III.m.9.22, IV.1.6), external (III.3.14, III.12.37), substance
(cf. V.6.1 ff.).   10.13 taken in (III.12.37), more excellent (III.10.9).
10.14 ruler (III.10.7, 9; V.3.35), imagine (III.10.4).   10.15 wicked/think
(V.3.6, 23), agreed (at III.10.10).   10.16 source (III.m.9.28), conclude/truest
(III.10.6), line of argument (III.11.4), own substance (III.10.15 (own nature);
cf. III.9.15), correctly so (III.9.33).

But it has been conceded that the highest Good is happiness.   17
I said: It is as you say.

She said: Therefore it is necessary that we agree as well that God is
happiness itself.

I said: I cannot speak against your prior propositions, and I see that
this inference is their logical consequence.

She said: Now contemplate whether the same conclusion can be   18
assented to more strongly from this angle as well, from the fact that there
cannot exist two highest goods that are different from each other. For it is 19
clear that of two goods which are not the same the one is not what the
other one is; and for this reason neither of them can be perfect, because
either one of them lacks the other. But it is obvious that what is not perfect is not the highest thing; therefore, there is no way in which goods
that are highest goods can be different from each other. And yet we have   20
deduced that both happiness and God are each a highest good; for this
reason, what is the highest divinity is necessarily the highest happiness.

I said: No conclusion can be drawn that is more true in reality, more   21
strong in rational argument, or more worthy of God.

She said: It is the practice of geometers, after they have demonstrated   22
their propositions, to draw an additional conclusion; such things they
call in Greek *porismata*, or bonuses. Therefore I shall, like them, give to
you too in Latin a corollary, or gift, in addition to these conclusions of
ours. Since people become happy by securing happiness for themselves,   23
yet true happiness is divinity itself, it is obvious that they become happy
by securing divinity for themselves. But, as people become just by the   24
securing of justice and wise by the securing of wisdom, it is necessary, by
a similar line of reasoning, that those who have secured divinity for
themselves become gods. Therefore, every truly happy person is God.   25
But, to be sure, God is one by nature; however, nothing prevents there
being as many gods as you please by participation.

10.17 (referred to at III.10.43), conceded (III.9.10), conceded (at III.2.3), Good
is happiness (cf. III.10.10), it is . . . say (III.3.7, 13), God . . . itself (cf. III.10.43),
speak against (V.1.9), inference (IV.4.10, 11), logical consequence (III.9.12,
IV.2.12, 24).   *10.18* contemplate (III.8.8), more strongly (I.6.21, III.10.21).
10.19 (appealed to at III.11.4), not the same (III.10.33), obvious (II.4.25), not
perfect (cf. III.10.9).   *10.20* deduced (III.11.41), God . . . good (III.12.13).
10.21 conclusion (III.10.16), strong (III.10.18), rational argument (IV.6.17).
10.22 geometers (cf. II.7.3, astronomers), gift (III.12.32), corollary (IV.3.8).
10.23 securing (III.3.3).   *10.24* similar . . . reasoning (III.11.9, IV.6.15), become
gods (IV.3.10). *10.25* participation (III.11.8, IV.4.17).   *10.26 porisma* (cf. III.10.22).

26   I said: Whether you would have it called a *porisma* or a corollary, this
is indeed a beautiful and precious gift.

27   And yet there is nothing more beautiful than this additional thing
that reason convinces us must be attached to this chain.

I said: What?

28   She said: Given that true happiness seems to contain many things—
do all these things join together and make, as it were, the single body of
happiness through some sort of variety of parts, or is there among them
some one thing that consummates the substance of happiness, and all
the other parts are understood in reference to it?

29   I said: I would like you to make this question more clear by reminding
me of the things themselves.

She said: We do think that true happiness is a good, don't we?

In fact, the highest Good, I said.

30   She said: You can add that qualification to all of them. For this same
true happiness is judged to be the highest self-sufficiency, the highest
power, the highest preeminence as well, and renown and physical plea-

31   sure. Well then: Are all these things, self-sufficiency, power, and the rest,
certain kinds of limbs, as it were, of the body of happiness, or are they all
to be understood in reference to the Good, their head, as it were?

32   I said: I understand what you propose we track down here, but I long
to hear what your determination is.

33   So accept this division of the problem, as follows: If all these things were
the limbs of true happiness, they would also be different one from another;
this is the nature of parts, so that they can, as different things, compose a

34   single body. And yet all of these things have been shown to be the same.
Therefore, they are hardly limbs; otherwise, it will seem that happiness has
been joined together from a single limb, which cannot happen.

35   I said: To be sure, there can be no doubt of that; but I am waiting to
hear what comes after.

36   But it is patent that the others are to be understood in reference to
the Good. Self-sufficiency is sought for this reason, because it is judged

---

10.27 attached . . . chain (cf. I.m.4.18, III.4.13, III.11.1).   10.28 join together
(III.10.14, 34), substance (III.10.12), reference (III.2.10, III.10.30, V.3.32,
V.6.36).   10.29 I would like (II.2.1, IV.4.32), make clear (III.11.4, V.4.3,
V.6.3).   10.30 (cf. III.10.36), physical pleasure (III.7.1).   10.31 limbs (cf.
III.10.28), reference (III.10.28, 36; III.11.39), head (I.1.2, III.11.39, IV.2.28, 43).
10.32 (cf. III.9.3), track down (III.9.23, III.m.11.1), I long (III.11.14), determi-
nation (V.2.6).   10.33 accept (III.10.10), limbs (III.11.12), be different
(III.10.19, III.11.5), compose (III.11.11; cf. IV.6.38).   10.34 shown (at
III.9.15–16).   10.35 no doubt (II.6.14).   10.36 reference (III.10.28, 31).
10.37 sum total (III.8.12), pursued (IV.2.29).

to be good; and power for this reason, because it too is believed to be good; one may make the same supposition about preeminence, renown, and delight. Therefore, the Good is the sum total of and the cause of all 37
the things that are to be pursued; for that which has within itself no good at all, either in reality or in likeness, can in no way be pursued. Conversely, even those things that are not good by nature are neverthe- 38
less craved as if they truly were good, even if they only seem to be so. And so it happens that goodness is rightly believed to be the sum total, the center point, and the cause of all the things that are to be pursued. But the thing for whose sake something else is pursued seems to be what 39
is most particularly chosen. For example: If someone wants to ride horse- back for the sake of physical well-being, such a person longs for the effect of well-being, not the motion of horse riding. Therefore, since all 40
things are sought for the sake of the Good, it is not those things but the Good itself that all people desire. But we have conceded that happiness is 41
the reason why the other things are chosen. From this it is clearly obvious 42
that the substance of the Good itself and the substance of true happiness are one and the same.

I see no opportunity for anyone to be able to disagree.

But we have shown that God and true happiness are one and the same. 43
It is as you say.

Therefore we may confidently conclude that the substance of God is also located in the Good itself and nowhere else.

Meter 10

Cóme hére áll of you, síde by síde, you cáptives
Whóm foúl lúst, which resídes in mínds of mátter,
Bínds ín chaíns, ever fálse and éver wícked—
     Hére you wíll fínd peáce. Here is rést from lábor,

10.38 conversely (II.4.8, II.5.23), craved (III.2.18, III.11.5, 14), goodness (II.6.20, III.12.17, 33), rightly believed (III.12.17), center point (I.3.3, IV.6.15). 10.39 (cf. IV.3.2), chosen (III.10.41, V.2.4–5, V.3.33, V.m.3.16), well-being (cf. III.2.10, III.11.16, III.12.18).   10.41 conceded (at III.2).   10.42 (cf. IV.2.11), clearly obvious (II.5.19, III.3.4), one and the same (III.11.5), no oppor- tunity (III.11.15, 17).   10.43 shown (at III.10.17), substance (III.10.12, 28, 42; III.11.9).

Meter 10 III.m.10.1–4 (cf. Matthew 11:28 ff.).   10.1 captives (cf. I.m.2.25–26). 10.2 foul lust (II.6.18, III.m.5.3, III.7.3).   10.3 chains (I.m.4.18), false (= deceitful: I.m.1.19, III.6.1), wicked (= unrighteous: IV.4.18–25, 33; IV.6.24, 43–49).   10.4 peace (III.m.9.27).

5   Hére thé pórt that abídes in tránquil quíet,
        Ópen doór ánd réfuge from désolátion.
    Whát thé Tágus in Spaín with gólden sándbars,
        Whát the Lýdián Hérmus from búrnished shórelines,
    Whát thé Índus, hard bý the Eástern súnrise,
10   Júmbling greén ánd nácreous stónes, can óffer—
    Poúrs nó líght in the éyes, but wíth its dárkness
        Veíls and hídes thé mínds that are máde yet móre blind.
    Súch thíngs, whátever cálm or stír mind's súrface,
        Bórn of eárth, áre núrsed in her deépest cáverns;
15 Bút thé spléndor that guídes and móves the heávens
        Shúns the soúls thát plúnge down beneáth the shádows.
    Whó cán récognize ánd distínguish thís light
        Wíll dený trúe bríghtness to shíning Phoébus.

Prose 11

I said: I agree. All these points stand together, woven from the most solid lines of argument.

2   Then she said: If you come to know what the Good itself is, what do you think that will be worth?

3   I said: An infinite sum! Inasmuch as it will then also be my lot to know at the same time God, who is the Good.

4   And yet I will make this clear by the truest possible line of argument, provided that the conclusions drawn just a little while ago remain unchanged.

        They shall so remain.

10.5 port (III.m.9.28 (haven)); tranquil quiet (II.6.7, V.1.6; cf. III.m.9.27).
10.6 refuge (cf. I.5.3 ff.).   10.7–10 (gold and jewels: cf. II.5.4–10).
10.10 nacreous stones (III.m.3.3, III.m.4.2, III.m.8.11).   10.11 eyes (I.1.13).
10.12 veils (cf. III.9.9, 17), blind (III.m.8.15–16, III.9.25).   10.13 calm surface (I.m.2.14), stir (III.m.11.12 (aroused), IV.m.4.1).   10.14 earth
(III.m.8.18), nursed (I.3.4, III.9.28).   10.15 splendor (III.m.9.26), guides/
moves (I.m.5.46–48, III.8.8, III.m.9.3, 13).   10.16 shuns (III.11.16), plunge
down (I.m.2.1–5).   10.17 light (III.m.9.26–28).   10.18 Phoebus
(III.m.11.8).

Prose 11   III.11.1 I agree (III.9.30, III.12.1), woven (III.10.27, IV.6.6; cf. I.3.3, 7),
most solid (= unshakable: III.10.6).   11.2 worth (cf. II.4.5, II.8.7).
11.4 make clear (III.10.29), truest possible (III.10.16), just . . . ago (at III.10.19
ff.), remain unchanged (III.9.14).

She said: Have we not shown that the things that are craved by most   5
people are not true and perfect goods for this very reason, because they
are different one from another? When one is not present in another it
cannot confer the full and absolute Good, but they become the Good
when they are gathered together as it were into a single essence and
potentiality, with the result that what self-sufficiency is, power is that
same thing also, as are preeminence, renown, and decent delight. Were
all of these not one and the same thing, they would possess nothing that
would let them be counted among the things that are to be pursued.

I said: That has been shown, and it cannot in any way be doubted.   6

Therefore: Things that are hardly good things when they differ from   7
each other, but that become good when they begin to be *one*—surely it is
by their securing of unity for themselves that it happens that these
things are good?

I said: So it seems.

But you do concede that everything that is good is good by its partici-   8
pation in the Good—or is this hardly so?

Yes, it is so.

. Therefore you must concede by a similar line of reasoning that the   9
One and the Good are the same thing; for if there is by their nature no
diversity of result from things, then the same substance exists in them.

I said: I am unable to deny it.

She said: So do you know that everything that exists remains unchanged   10
and has substance only so long as it is one, but that it is destroyed and
disintegrates as soon as it ceases to be one?

How is that?

As is the case with animate beings, she said. When a soul and a body   11
come together and remain unchanged together, that is called an animate
being; but when this unity disintegrates through the separation of each
component from the whole, it is clear that it is destroyed and is no

---

11.5 craved (III.10.38, III.11.14), most people (III.2.7), true and perfect (III.9.4),
different (III.10.33), absolute (cf. III.10.5), essence (III.10.1), potentiality (= *effici-
entia*: III.12.7 (effect), IV.2.38; cf. III.11.9 (result)), self-sufficiency . . . delight
(III.2.19), one/same (III.10.42), to be pursued (III.10.37, IV.2.29).   11.6 cannot . . . doubted (III.3.15).   11.7 securing (III.3.3).   11.8 participation
(III.10.25).   11.9 similar . . . reasoning (III.10.24, IV.6.15); the one . . . same
thing (referred to at III.11.32), substance (III.9.15, III.10.16, 42, 43), diversity
(cf. I.5.11 (in different directions)), result (III.12.7; cf. III.11.5), deny (III.10.3).
11.10 remains unchanged (III.11.4), has substance (III.11.13 (subsists),
III.11.36), disintegrates (III.11.28).   11.11 component (III.10.33).
11.12 body/limbs (III.10.28, 31–34).

12   longer an animate being. The body itself likewise. While it remains unchanged in one form by the joining together of its limbs, a human appearance is there to view; but if the parts are divided up and separated and so pull apart the unity of that body, it ceases to be what it once was.

13   As you run through all the other examples in the same way it will become clear to you beyond any doubt that each and every thing has substance only so long as it is one, and that it is destroyed when it ceases to be one.

   I said: When I look at still more examples, it hardly seems otherwise to me.

14   Well then! she said. Is there anything that, insofar as it acts in accordance with its own nature, would abandon its craving for existence and long to come to destruction and decomposition?

15   I said: If I look at animate beings, which have some natural ability to want and not to want, I find no reason why they should cast aside their striving to remain unchanged and hasten of their own free will to their destruction, provided that there are no external forces compelling them.

16   For every animate being works at protecting its own physical well-being;

17   death, however, and physical dissolution it avoids. But in the case of grasses and trees and inanimate things as a whole—I am completely uncertain as to what I can say in agreement with you.

18   And yet there is no reason why you could possibly be in doubt about this matter as well. In the first place, when you take a look at grasses and trees, you see that they grow up in places that are appropriate for them, where they cannot quickly wither and perish, insofar as their nature is

19   capable. I mean, some spring up in the fields, others on the mountains; marshes bear some, others cling to rocks; the barren sands are teeming with still others; and they would all wither were someone to try to trans-

20   plant them into other environments. But Nature gives to each thing

---

11.13 beyond doubt (II.5.15, V.6.32, 35), has substance (III.11.10, 36), look at (III.3.12).   11.14 Well then (III.9.22, V.1.11), insofar . . . nature (III.11.33), craving (III.10.38, III.11.5), long to (III.10.32), decomposition (cf. III.12.14). 11.15 animate beings (III.11.11), I . . . reason (cf. III.10.42), remain unchanged (III.11.10–12, 20), external (II.4.22, III.3.14).   11.16 works at (III.2.15, V.m.3.14; cf. III.11.20), protecting (cf. III.11.27), well-being (III.10.39, III.12.18), dissolution . . . avoids (III.11.34), avoids (III.m.10.16).   11.17 inanimate (II.5.25, III.11.25), I am in doubt (IV.2.1).   11.18 there is . . . why (cf. III.10.42), be in doubt (III.12.26), appropriate (cf. I.m.6.16–19, III.m.9.10–11, III.11.20, 26), insofar . . . capable (cf. III.11.14).   11.19 cling (III.m.11.11, IV.6.16), rocks (V.5.3), sands (II.m.6.13, III.m.10.7).   11.20 appropriate (III.11.26), works hard (III.2.5; cf. III.11.16), remain unchanged (III.11.15).

what is appropriate to it, and works hard to keep them all from destruction, for as long as they are able to remain unchanged.

And what of the fact that trees, with their mouths as it were sunk   21
deep in the earth, draw up nourishment through their roots and then disperse this nourishment through their pith, their wood, and their bark? And what of the fact that whatever is the most tender part, as the pith   22
is, is always kept hidden away because of its inner foundation, and because of a certain strength of wood outside of it, while the outermost bark is positioned as if it were a guardian against the violence of the weather, enduring all hardship? And besides, just consider how far-   23
reaching is the careful attention of Nature, that all things are extended in time by their seed, endlessly repeated. Who is there who does not   24
know that all these processes are machines of a sort—not only for individuals, that they remain as they are in their own time, but also for species, that they remain unchanged in perpetuity?

And as for those other things that are believed to be inanimate—   25
surely, by a similar line of argument, each of them desires what is its own? For why are the flames carried upward by their lightness, and the earth   26
forced downward by its weight, if not for the fact that these places and these motions are appropriate to them? Further: That which is fitting for   27
each and every thing is what preserves it, just as the things that are opposed to it annihilate it. And besides, things that are hard, like rocks,   28
cohere in their constituent parts most unyieldingly and fight back against being easily disintegrated, while liquids, like air and water, do yield quite   29
easily to things that divide them, but quickly return again to the wholes from which they were cut off—fire, however, resists all division.

We are not now discussing the voluntary motions of a conscious soul,   30
but only its natural striving, as is the situation when we digest without thinking the food that is given us, or when we breathe in our sleep without knowing it. For not even in animate creatures does the desire for   31
remaining unchanged come from the acts of the soul's will, but from the

---

11.21 trees (III.m.2.27–30), disperse (IV.6.15).   *11.22* foundation (III.2.1, III.m.9.22), guardian (cf. I.3.13–14).   *11.23* extended (= prolonged: II.7.9, 14; III.2.6, III.6.4), seed (I.m.5.21, I.m.6.4, II.1.18, IV.6.18).   *11.24* machines (II.m.8.21, III.12.14), remain unchanged (III.11.20, 36).   *11.25* inanimate (II.5.25, III.11.17), similar … . argument (III.11.9, IV.6.15).   *11.26* lightness/weight (cf. III.m.9.11–12), appropriate (III.11.20).   *11.27* preserves (cf. III.11.16), annihilate (IV.7.20).   *11.28* cohere … unyieldingly (cf. II.4.9), fight back (IV.2.25), disintegrated (III.11.10).   *11.30* motions (V.2.2, V.3.30, V.m.4.10–11), striving (III.2.9, 15; III.11.33).   *11.31* desire (*amor* = love: II.m.8.15, 29; cf. III.11.33).

32 first principles of its nature. For when causes compel it, the will often embraces the death from which its nature recoils; conversely, the act of procreation (the only act by which the world of mortal things endures and is extended in time, the act that an individual's nature always craves) the

33 will represses from time to time. To such an extent, then, does this love of self proceed from its natural striving and not from the motion of its animating soul; for Providence has given this to the things that have been created by it as perhaps the greatest cause of their remaining unchanged, that they by their own nature desire to remain unchanged for as long as

34 they naturally can. Consequently, there is no reason why you could in any way doubt that all the things that exist crave by their nature the permanence of remaining unchanged and by their nature avoid dissolution.

35 I said: I agree with you, and now I see without any doubt the things that for so long seemed to me uncertain.

36 She said: But that which seeks to have substance and to remain unchanged desires to be one; for when you have taken that away from anything, not even existence itself will remain.

I said: That is true.

37 She said: Therefore, all things desire what is One.

I have concurred in this.

But we have shown that what is One is itself the Good.

Indeed we have.

38 Therefore, all things seek the Good; or you may in fact define the Good this way, as that which is desired by all things.

39 I said: Nothing can be imagined that is truer than this, for all things are either understood in reference to no Oneness at all and so, deprived of the One as of their head, will bob up and down without a helmsman; or, if there is something toward which things universally and eagerly direct themselves, that will be the highest of all goods.

11.32 (cf. IV.6.18), embraces (V.4.31, V.6.5), death (cf. I.m.1.20, III.5.10), conversely (II.5.23), procreation (cf. III.7.3–5), extended in time (= perpetuation: II.7.15–16), represses (IV.4.13, IV.7.12).   *11.33* love (= *caritas*: cf. III.11.31 (*amor*)), proceed (cf. III.10.5), natural striving (III.11.30), Providence (III.m.2.3, IV.6.4 ff.), as long . . . can (III.11.14; cf. III.11.20).   *11.34* remaining unchanged (III.11.10–12, IV.m.3.25), dissolution (III.11.16).   *11.35* agree (III.3.7), without doubt (V.1.7).   *11.36* have substance (III.11.10), remain unchanged (IV.5.2).   *11.37* concurred (III.2.20, III.12.10), shown (at III.11.9).   *11.38* you (singular).   *11.39* nothing . . . imagined (III.6.2, III.10.7), reference (III.10.31, 36), deprived (V.5.3), head (III.10.31), bob . . . helmsman (I.6.19, V.m.1.11; cf. IV.m.6.42–43), eagerly direct (III.7.4, IV.2.10), highest goods (III.2.3, 11).

And she said: I nursed you; now I take great delight in you, for you 40
have set securely in its place the very signpost of the all-central truth.
But what just a little while ago you said you did not know has become
obvious to you in this assertion.

I said: What was that?

She said: What is the goal of all things. For make no mistake—this goal 41
is what is longed for by all things; and because we have deduced that this
thing is the good, we must admit that the Good is the goal of all things.

Meter 11

Whoéver trácks the trúth from oút the mínd's greát dépth
And néver wánts to bé misléd on fálse sídetrácks,
Must túrn the líght of ínner vísion deép wíthin
And bénd and fórce intó a wheél the soúl's lóng páth,
Must teách the mínd that whát it stríves for fár oútsíde 5
It ówns alreády, hídden ín its ówn stórehoúse;
And whát the cloúds of mídnight érror lóng concealéd
Will bláze more thán the ráys of Phoébus, cleár tó vieẃ.
The bódy thát bore wíth it gróss forgétfúlnéss
Did nót from mínd then dríve out évery tráce óf líght; 10
There clíngs within the seéd of trúth—make nó místáke—
Aroúsed and fánned by próper teáching íntó fláme.
How coúld you mórtals freély thínk the trúth whén ásked
Were thére no líve coal búried deép in heárt's cóld ásh?

11.40 nursed (I.3.4, III.9.28), signpost . . . truth (V.m.3.12), just . . . ago (at
I.6.10).   11.41 what . . . goal of things (I.6.10), make no mistake (III.m.11.11,
IV.1.3), deduced (III.10.20, IV.2.39).

Meter 11 III.m.11.1 tracks (III.9.23), mind's depth (cf. I.m.2.1, III.m.9.16–17,
V.m.3.20).   11.2 false sidetracks (I.m.7.23–24, II.8.5, III.2.4, V.1.5).
11.3 light . . . vision (I.m.2.2).   11.4 bend . . . wheel (cf. III.12.30, IV.m.6.40–
41), soul's path (cf. III.m.9.15–17).   11.5 strives . . . outside (I.m.2.3).
11.6 storehouse (= thesaurus: cf. II.5.3 ff.).   11.7–8 (cf. I.m.3).   11.7 clouds
of error (cf. I.2.6); clouds (IV.m.1.6), error (miscalculation: III.3.1).
11.8 Phoebus (III.m.10.18, V.m.2.2).   11.9 body (III.12.1), bore (cf. V.2.10),
gross (cf. III.m.9.25 (dead weight)), forgetfulness (I.2.6, III.12.1).   11.10 drive
out (cf. I.6.4, II.6.7).   11.11 clings (III.11.19), within (V.m.4.39–40), seed
(I.4.8, 38; I.4.28, II.5.24, III.m.9.2, III.11.24), make no mistake (III.11.41,
IV.m.5.21).   11.12 aroused (III.m.10.13 (stir); IV.2.1).   11.14 coal
(= kindling: I.6.20), buried (= plunged: I.m.2.1), heart (IV.m.2.6, IV.m.3.32).

15   For íf the Múse of Pláto criés the trúth oút loúd,
      All thát forgétful mórtals leárn, they récólléct.

Prose 12

Then I said: I am in utter agreement with Plato. Now through you I am
reminded of these things for the second time; the first time was when I
lost my memory through contact with the body; and then again when
overwhelmed with the weight of grief.

2   Then she said: If you look back over what you conceded earlier, it will
not be very long at all until you remember what you admitted you had
long not known.

      I said: What is that?

3   She said: What are the rudders by which the world is governed.

      I said: I remember that I had admitted my lack of awareness; but,
though I can now see at a distance what you have to bestow, I am longing all the same to hear it from you more distinctly.

4   She said: Just a little while ago you were of the opinion that it could
hardly be doubted that this world is ruled by God.

      I do not think now, I said, nor shall I ever be of the opinion, that this
can be doubted, and I will briefly set out the reasons why I come to this

5   conclusion. This world could hardly have come together into a single
form out of components so different and so opposed to each other if there

6   were not one who could join together such different things. Further, this
very difference of natures, mutually inharmonious, would decompose and
tear apart what had been joined together if there were not one who could

7   constrain what had been bound together. Still further, there would be no

---

11.15 Muse (I.1.7, 11–12; I.5.10), Plato (I.3.6, I.4.5, III.12.1; cf. *Phaedo* 72e ff.,
76a; *Meno* 82c ff.).   11.16 forgetful (I.2.6, II.7.13, III.m.11.9).

Prose 12 III.12.1 utter (I.4.28, I.6.6, II.5.8, 18; III.9.31), agreement (III.11.1),
utter agreement (III.12.15), Plato (III.m.11.15), contact (III.4.10, 17; cf.
III.m.11.10), grief (I.m.1.2, III.9.14).   *12.2* earlier (at I.6.4), remember
(IV.2.11; cf. III.2.13, IV.1.1).   *12.3* rudders . . . governed (I.6.7, 19), governed
(III.8.8), I remember (but cf. III.9.3), awareness (II.4.22, IV.2.31), see at a dis-
tance (III.12.15; cf. III.10.29, III.11.4, V.4.3, V.6.3), longing . . . distinctly (cf.
IV.2.18).   *12.4* just . . . ago (at I.m.5, I.6.4), nor shall . . . doubted (cf. I.6.4).
12.5 (cf. II.6.13, II.m.8.1–4).   *12.6* (cf. III.11.11–13), inharmonious
(IV.m.6.18, V.m.3.1), tear apart (cf. I.1.5), constrain (II.7.12), bound together
(I.m.5.43).   *12.7* procession (III.10.5), create (III.7.4, III.12.35, IV.2.5), well-
arranged (III.12.12, 14, 17, 22; IV.1.6, IV.5.7, IV.6.8–9, 21), effect (III.11.5
(potentiality)).

such definite order to the procession of nature, nor would the different parts create such well-arranged motions in place, time, effect, distance, and quality if there were not one who, remaining unchanged himself, arranged these multiplicities of change. This thing, whatever it is—by which the things that have been established both remain unchanged and are set in motion—using the word that everyone habitually uses, I call God.

8

Then she said: Since such is your understanding, I think that I have only a little work remaining so that you can return to your fatherland fully recuperated, the master of your happiness. But let us look closely at the propositions we have established. Have we not counted self-sufficiency as part of true happiness, and have we not concurred that God is happiness itself?

9

10

Indeed we have.

And for governing the world, she said, he will need therefore no externally sought instruments; were it otherwise, he would not have complete self-sufficiency if he lacked anything.

11

I said: Yes, that is necessarily so.

Therefore he arranges all things by means of himself alone?

12

I said: That can't be denied.

And yet it has been shown that God is the Good itself.

13

I said: I remember.

Therefore he arranges all things by means of the Good, inasmuch as he who we concur is the Good governs all things by means of himself; this is as it were the tiller and the rudder by which the world machine is kept fixed, secure, and undecomposed.

14

I am in utter agreement, I said, and that is what just a little while ago I saw from a distance that you were going to say, though it was only a microscopic presentiment.

15

12.8 unchanged/motion (III.m.9.3), everyone uses (cf. III.10.7, V.6.2).
12.9 understanding (III.1.3), I think . . . remaining (cf. II.1.4), return/fatherland (IV.1.9; cf. I.5.3), recuperated (I.6.17, 19; IV.1.9), master (II.4.23, II.6.18, IV.m.1.18, V.6.8).   *12.10* look closely (V.6.1), counted (II.5.18, III.11.5, IV.2.43, IV.7.5; cf. III.2.9, 16 (assigned to the list)), self-sufficiency (III.9.6 ff.), concurred (at III.10.17; III.11.37, V.2.1).   *12.11* externally sought (III.3.14, III.10.12, III.12.35), instruments (cf. III.3.14).   *12.12* arranges (III.12.7), denied (III.10.3).   *12.13* God . . . itself (III.10.43, III.11.3), I remember (III.12.3, IV.m.1.25, IV.2.10).   *12.14* tiller and rudder (III.12.3; cf. III.11.39), world machine (II.m.8.21; cf. IV.4.8), kept (III.12.37), fixed (I.m.2.15), undecomposed (cf. III.11.14).   *12.15* utter agreement (III.12.1), what . . . distance (III.12.3), microscopic (III.9.3).

16   She said: I believe you because, as I see it, you are directing your eyes
with greater watchfulness now, so that they can see the things that are
true. But what I am about to say is no less obvious to behold.

I said: What is that?

17   She said: Since God is rightly believed to pilot all things by the tiller
of Goodness, and since, as I have taught you, all these things eagerly
direct themselves toward the Good by their natural striving, then it can't
be doubted, can it, that they are governed voluntarily and that they of
their own free will turn themselves toward the beck and call of the one
who arranges them as if they were in agreement with and adapted to
their governor?

18   I said: It must be so; his governance would not seem to be truly happy
if it were a yoke for those who resist him and not the health and well-
being of those who obey him.

19   So there is nothing that can preserve its own nature and attempt to
move in opposition to God?

I said: Nothing.

20   She said: And were it to make the attempt, would it ultimately have
any success against him who is, by the principle of true happiness, as we
have conceded, most powerful as well?

I said: It would be completely incapable of it.

21   Therefore there is nothing that either desires to or is able to oppose
this highest Good?

I said: I do not think so.

22   It is therefore the highest Good, she said, that governs all things
forcefully and arranges all things sweetly.

23   Then I said: It is not only the summary of your arguments, which you
have just completed, that delights me; what delight me much more are
the words themselves that you have used! Now at long last they make
the stupidity that rips great things apart ashamed of itself.

24   She said: You have heard in myths of the Giants attacking heaven;
but it was a generous forcefulness that put them in their proper place as

---

12.16 directing/eyes (cf. III.m.1.7), see (III.m.9.27).   12.17 rightly believed
(III.10.38, V.6.6), Goodness (III.10.38, III.12.33), taught (at III.11.30–41),
eagerly direct (III.7.4, IV.2.10), natural striving (III.7.4), free will (III.11.15).
12.18 yoke (II.1.16, II.m.7.7–8, III.m.1.12), health/well-being (III.10.39, III.11.16,
IV.6.29).   12.20 success (cf. I.m.6.20–22), conceded (at III.10.29–31).
12.21 able to . . . good (IV.2.20).   12.22 (cf. Wisdom 8:1).   12.23 delights
(II.5.11), stupidity (I.3.6), rips apart (I.1.5, I.3.7; cf. IV.1.7).   12.24 you (singular), attacking (I.3.6), generous (III.m.9.20), forcefulness (III.12.22), put . . .
place (= arranged: cf. III.12.7).

well, just as they deserved. But do you want us to smash the arguments 25
themselves into each other? Perhaps from a striking of this sort some
beautiful spark of truth may fly out.

I said: As you think best.

She said: No one can doubt that God has the power to do all things. 26

I said: Provided that he is in his right mind, there is absolutely no one
who is in doubt of this.

She said: But he who has the power to do all things—there is nothing 27
that such a one cannot do?

I said: Nothing.

Now God is not able to do that which is evil, is he? 28

I said: Hardly.

She said: Therefore, evil is nothing, since he cannot do what is evil, 29
and there is nothing that he cannot do.

I said: Are you playing with me, weaving with your arguments a laby- 30
rinth from which I cannot find the path that leads out? Now you go in
where you just went out, and now you come out where you just went
in—or are you joining together the ends of some marvelous circle of
divine simplicity? For just a little while ago you started with happiness 31
and said that it was the highest Good, and you said that it was located in
the highest God. Then your discourse was that this God is the highest 32
Good himself, and complete and true happiness; from this you gave me
as a little gift that no one would be truly happy except by being God at
the same time. Furthermore, you said that the essence of the Good is the 33
substance of God and of true happiness, and you taught me that Oneness itself is the very Goodness itself that is sought by every nature of
every thing. You also argued that God governs the universe by the rud- 34
ders of Goodness, that all things willingly obey him, and that there is no
real nature of evil. And what is more, you were unfolding these argu- 35
ments by proofs located within, domestic as it were, each acquiring its

---

12.25 do you want (IV.7.7), spark (I.6.20), as . . . best (I.6.2). *12.26–29* (cf.
IV.2.40–42). *12.26* power . . . things (IV.1.5), right mind (cf. IV.2.41), in
doubt (III.11.18, IV.2.22). *12.29* evil is nothing (cf. IV.2.32, 39).
12.30 playing (III.12.36), weaving (I.1.3, 7; IV.6.13; cf. IV.6.6, 9), joining
together (cf. III.12.35 (unfolding)), circle (III.m.9.15–17, III.m.11.4, III.12.37),
divine simplicity (cf. IV.6.8). *12.31* just . . . ago (at III.10.37). *12.32* gift
(III.10.22), being God (I.4.39, III.10.23). *12.33* you said (at III.10.43), you
taught (at III.11.36–40; cf. IV.3.14), Goodness (III.12.17). *12.34* you argued
(at III.12.14–17), universe (cf. V.4.30, V.5.7). *12.35* unfolding (cf. III.12.30),
from the others (IV.2.2, IV.6.11), not . . . external (cf. III.12.38, V.4.13), adopted
(IV.4.12), external (III.3.14, III.10.12, III.12.11, V.4.13).

trustworthiness from the others, not a one of them adopted from something external to it.

36   Then she said: This is hardly a game that we are playing; this fact is
the most important one of all, and we have achieved it by the gift of
37 God, whom we prayed to just now. For such is the essence of the divine
substance: It never disintegrates into the things that are far removed
from it, nor does it take up into itself anything external to it but, just as
Parmenides says about it,

> éver resémbling the shápe of a sphére, wéll-roúnded on áll sides,

it spins the moving circle of the universe while it keeps itself unmoving.
38 And as to the fact that we have repeatedly used arguments that were not
externally sought but within the bounds of the topic we were discussing,
there is no reason for you to be amazed—after all, you have learned, as
Plato has decreed it, that discourse ought to be closely related to the
topics that it addresses.

Meter 12

Ó hów háppy the mán who viéwed
Áll thé rádiant soúrce of Goód;
Ó hów háppy the mán who bróke
Áll thé búrdensome chaíns of eárth!
5   Ónce thé póet and seér of Thráce,
Deép ín grief for his yoúng wife deád,
Throúgh hís dírges and moúrnful sóngs
Fórced thé treés to get úp and rún,
Fórced thé rívers to stóp and stáy.

12.36 game/playing (II.2.9; cf. II.1.12), prayed (at III.9.33, III.m.9).
12.37 divine substance (cf. V.2.7), disintegrates . . . from it (III.10.5), take up . . .
external (III.10.12), Parmenides (Plato, *Sophist* 244c), moving circle (I.m.2.15,
III.m.9.15–17), preserves (III.11.27, V.2.8), unmoving (III.m.9.3, III.12.14).
12.38 not externally sought (III.12.35), amazed (I.3.11), Plato (III.12.1), Plato
decreed (I.4.5, IV.4.28; at *Timaeus* 29b).

Meter 12 III.m.12.1 happy (II.m.5.1, II.m.8.28), viewed (IV.m.1.28).
12.2 source (III.m.9.23).   *12.4* chains (cf. I.m.2.24–27).   *12.5* poet
(= Orpheus), Thrace (cf. I.m.3.7).   *12.6* wife (= Eurydice).
12.7 mournful songs (I.m.1.1–2).   *12.8* trees (III.11.21–22).   *12.9* rivers
(cf. III.m.10.7–9).

Thén, íntrépid, the deér would stánd   10
Bý thé rávenous líon's síde;
Thén thé rábbit, made bóld, behéld
Dógs nów cálmed by such hármoniés.
Yét, stíll hótter the féver búrned
Deép insíde of his heárt and soúl,   15
Ánd thé sóngs that subduéd all élse
Coúld nót plácate their lórd, who criéd
Thát thé góds in the ský were cruél,
Ánd só wént to the hálls belów.
Thére hé cárefully pláys his sóngs   20
Ón hís lýre's sympathétic stríngs,
Síngs ín teárs what he ónce had drúnk
Fróm thé spríngs of his Móther Múse,
Síngs whát óbstinate griéving prómpts
Ánd thé lóve that redoúbles griéf,   25
Sénds á shúdder through Hádes' cáves,
Ánd ín géntle and lýric práyer
Ásks thé lórds of the shádes for gráce.
Nów, énthrálled by this únknown sóng,
The wátchfúl threé-headed dóg stands dúmb;   30
Nów thé góddesses whó pursué
Guíltý mén and avénge their crímes
Lét theír cheéks run with teárs, depréssed;
Nów thé swíftly-revólving wheél
Doés nót cást down Ixíon's heád;   35
Thírst-párched Tántalus, wásted lóng,
Nów dísmísses his wátercoúrse;
Nów thé vúlture, fed fúll on sóng,
Shúns thé líver of Títyús.
Nów thé júdge of the shádes is móved,   40
Criés ín sýmpathy, "Wé submít!
Nów wé gíve to this mán his máte,

12.11 lion (III.m.2.7–16, IV.m.7.15).   *12.14* fever (III.1.4), burned (cf.
II.m.5.26).   *12.16–17* songs/placate (cf. III.1.1).   *12.18* cruel (cf.
IV.m.7.20–21).   *12.23* Mother Muse (= Calliope).   *12.28* shades
(III.m.12.40).   *12.30* dog (= Cerberus: IV.m.7.19).   *12.31* goddesses
(= Furies).   *12.33* cheeks . . . tears (cf. II.m.6.6).   *12.34* wheel (II.1.19,
II.2.9).   *12.35* cast . . . head (cf. II.m.1.4).   *12.37* dismisses
(II.7.23).   *12.40* shades (III.m.12.28).   *12.41* submit (= are conquered:
cf. III.m.12.56).

Gíve thé wífe he has boúght with sóng.
But lét thís láw limit whát we gíve:
45 Hé múst nót give a báckward glánce,
Nót befóre he leaves Héll behínd."
Whó cán gíve to such lóve a láw?
Lóve ís láw to itsélf alóne.
Woé ís hím! At the édge of níght
50 Órpheús sáw his Eurýdicé,
Sáw ánd lóst her and diéd himsélf.
Mórtál mén! This tale poínts at yoú,
Yoú whó seék to condúct your mínds
Tó thé líght of the dáy abóve:
55 Lét nó mán give a báckward glánce
Ín defeát, to the cáves of Héll—
Whát hé tákes with himsélf as hís
Hé wíll lóse when he seés the deád.

12.43 song (III.m.12.29–30, IV.m.3.7).   12.45 backward glance (III.m.12.55).
12.46 Hell (= Tartarus: III.m.12.56).   12.47–48 love (= amor: II.m.8.15–30,
III.11.31, IV.m.6.16, 44).   12.49 woe (I.m.1.2).   12.52–58 (cf. IV.m.1.23–
30, V.m.4.21–25).   12.54 light (III.m.9.22–24).   12.55 backward
(III.m.12.45; cf. IV.m.1.3–6).   12.56 Hell (III.m.12.46).   12.57 as his (cf.
IV.3.8).   12.58 dead (cf. II.7.23).

Book IV

Prose 1

Philosophy had sung these words softly and sweetly, never losing the dignity of her appearance or the impressiveness of her speech, but I had not yet forgotten the sorrow that was planted within me, and so I interrupted her train of thought then, just as she was getting ready to say something else.

I said: Yes, you are the one who leads on toward the true light, and the words that flowed from your pleading were not only obviously divine, examined in themselves, but also irrefragable, according to your arguments; still, though I had recently forgotten them in my depression because of the wrongs done to me, you have spoken things that were not completely unknown to me before. But here is what is perhaps the greatest cause of my sorrow: the fact that evil things can exist at all, or that they can pass unpunished, when the helmsman of all things is good. Make no mistake: Only you can ponder this with the amazement that it deserves. No, there is another, an even greater thing connected to it: I mean, when gross wickedness thrives and has dominion, that not only does virtue go without its true rewards, but it is even forced to grovel at the feet of lawless men and to be ground beneath their heels, subjected to punishments as if for crimes committed. That such things happen in the kingdom of a God who knows all things, who is capable of all things, but who desires good things and the good alone—no one can be amazed at it, and no one can complain about it, as it deserves.

And then she said: True, it would be everlastingly incomprehensible, a thing more monstrous than all other monstrosities if, as you reckon it,

---

Prose 1 IV.1.1 (cf. II.1.1, III.1.1, V.1.1), sweetly (III.12.22; cf. II.1.8), dignity (cf. I.1.1), forgotten (I.2.6, IV.4.31), sorrow/planted (II.3.2). *1.2* yes, you are (III.1.2), true light (= God; cf. III.m.9.26, V.6.18), pleading (V.1.1), depression (cf. I.5.11). *1.3* (cf. I.4, I.m.5), greatest cause (I.6.17), helmsman (I.m.5.25, 46; IV.5.5, 7; cf. IV.6.29), make no mistake (III.11.41), outrage (cf. IV.1.5). *1.4* (cf. IV.4.1, IV.5.4), gross wickedness (IV.3.13–14), thrives (IV.5.2), virtue without rewards (cf. IV.3.1–8), heels (I.m.5.31–33). *1.5* capable of all things (III.12.26), amazed (I.4.28, IV.1.3, IV.5.4). *1.6* incomprehensible (cf. I.2.4, IV.5.5), monstrosities (I.4.29), defiled (III.4.17), master (= father of the household: cf. III.m.6.2), appointed (= arranged: cf. III.12.7).

the cheap earthenware pots were prized, and the expensive ones defiled,
7   in what I may call so great a master's perfectly appointed house. But that
is not the way it is. If the conclusions we reached a little while ago have
not been torn to pieces but still hold, then, by the agency of that same
creator of whose kingdom we now speak, you will come to see that good
people are always powerful, while evil people are always disreputable and
unable to sustain themselves; that vices are never without punishment,
and virtues never without reward; that things worthy of rejoicing always
happen to good people, and disasters always happen to the evil.

There are many other conclusions of this sort, and they can brace you
with an unshakable steadfastness, when first your complaints have been
8   laid to rest. And since you have seen the essence of true happiness
through my previous demonstrations, and have even come to recognize
where it is to be found, I will show to you the way that can carry you
back home, after we've run through all the things that I think I must
9   first set before it. In fact, I will equip your mind with wings, so that it can
raise itself on high, so that you can cast your confusion into exile and
return recuperated to your fatherland, following my lead, along my path,
by my conveyances.

Meter 1

Seé what I háve: These are swíft-beating wíngs for you,
      Alért to ríse to heáven's heíghts;
Swíft-thinking mínd, once these wíngs are attáched to it,
      Looks dówn to eárth in vást disgúst.
5   Quíckly surpássing the límitless átmosphere
      It seés the cloúds behínd its báck;

1.7 torn (cf. III.12.23), good people . . . sustain themselves (IV.2.3, 15, 24), dis-
reputable (III.4.9), vices/virtues (III.4.1, V.3.32, V.6.47), punishment/reward
(IV.3.1, IV.6.25), rejoicing . . . evil (cf. IV.4.15), steadfastness (cf. III.10.6,
V.6.25).   1.8 essence (III.9.1), previous demonstrations (at III.9–12), way
(= path: I.m.7.23, III.m.11.2), carry (V.1.4), back home (III.2.13).   1.9 wings
(IV.m.1.1), confusion (I.1.14), exile (I.5.2–5), recuperated (I.6.17, 19; III.12.9),
fatherland (I.5.3, II.4.17, III.12.9, IV.m.1.25, V.1.4), lead . . . conveyances
(III.m.9.28), conveyances (III.9.27).

Meter 1 IV.m.1.1 swift (IV.m.1.21, IV.m.4.4), wings (IV.1.9).   1.2 rise . . .
heights (cf. II.7.23, III.m.9.22, IV.m.6.1–3).   1.3 mind (cf. I.m.2.2, III.m.9.22,
29).   1.4 looks . . . earth (III.m.12.55–58, V.m.5.10–11), disgust (cf.
II.7.23).   1.5–14 (cf. I.m.2.6–12).   1.6 clouds (III.m.11.7).

Soón it transcénds fire's tápering élement
     That glóws in éther's rápid coúrse,
Vaúlts itself ínto the dwéllings that hóld the stars,
     And the wáys of Phoébus áre its ówn.   10
Ór it may fóllow the páth of the cóld old man,
     The fiéry plánet's sátellíte;
Ór on the bríght-painted cánvas of mídnight black
     May retráce the círcles óf a stár.
Thén when it hás been exhaústed in órbiting   15
     It leáves the pólestar fár behínd,
Ánd as the máster of trué light's preéminence
     It rídes on rápid éther's báck.
Hére with the scépter and reíns of the úniverse
     In hánd, is foúnd the Lórd of kíngs,   20
Ánd he, unmóving, contróls the swift chários,
     As fiéry júdge of áll the wórld.
Nów if your páth takes you báck to this pláce again,
     Which nów you loók for únrecálled,
Yoú will say, "Nów I remémber my fátherland—   25
     Here wás I bórn, here sháll I stánd."
Thén should it pleáse you to víew on the eárth below
     The níght that yoú have léft behínd—
Pítiless týrants, whom désolate peóples fear,
     You wíll behóld as éxiles thére.   30

1.7 transcends (V.4.29), fire (III.m.9.11, 21). ⎯ 1.8 ether (II.m.7.3 (sky),
IV.m.1.18; cf. V.m.5.5). ⎯ 1.10 Phoebus (III.m.10.18, III.m.11.8). ⎯ 1.11 old
man (= Saturn). ⎯ 1.12 fiery planet (= Mars). ⎯ 1.14 retrace (cf. I.m.2.10,
III.m.2.34), circles . . . star (= Zodiac?). ⎯ 1.15 orbiting (or, viewing).
1.16 polestar (III.m.8.17 (or, outermost layer of the universe)). ⎯ 1.17 master
(II.4.23, III.12.9, V.6.8), light (III.m.9.23, V.3.34), preeminence (III.4.5–6).
1.18 ether (IV.m.1.8). ⎯ 1.19 reins (III.m.2.1, IV.m.6.35). ⎯ 1.20 Lord of
kings (I.m.5, esp. 1–4, 25, 42–48). ⎯ 1.21 unmoving (III.m.9.3), chariot
(II.m.8.6, III.m.2.33; cf. IV.m.4.4). ⎯ 1.22 (cf. V.6.48). ⎯ 1.23–26 (cf.
III.m.2.34–38). ⎯ 1.23–28 (cf. IV.4.29). ⎯ 1.23 back again (cf. III.m.2.12–
13). ⎯ 1.24 unrecalled (cf. I.2.6, III.m.11.15–16, III.12.1). ⎯ 1.25 fatherland
(I.5.3–5, III.12.9, IV.1.9, V.1.4). ⎯ 1.26 born (I.5.4, III.m.6.6–9), shall stand
(cf. I.m.1.22). ⎯ 1.27–28 (cf. III.m.12.52–58, IV.m.1.4). ⎯ 1.28 night
(I.m.3.1). ⎯ 1.29 pitiless (IV.m.2.3), tyrants (I.m.4.11–12, II.6.8, IV.m.2.9; cf.
Nero, II.m.6, III.m.4), fear (I.m.5.41 (terrorize)) ⎯ 1.30 exiles (I.3.3, I.5.2–5,
I.6.18, II.4.17).

Prose 2

Then I said: Well fancy that! What great promises you make! And I have no doubt that you will fulfill them, but please, don't hold me back now that you have aroused me.

2   She said: Therefore you will first be permitted to realize that power is always the possession of good people, and that evil people are always deserted by every one of their strengths; in fact, the one proposition is

3 proved from the other. For, since good and evil are opposites, if it is established that good is powerful, then the inability of evil to sustain itself is obvious; on the other hand, if the fragility of evil is made clear,

4 then the stability of good has been recognized. However, in order to make this axiom of ours all the more abundantly trustworthy, I shall proceed along each of the two paths, making my two propositions mutually unshakable, now from the one side and now from the other.

5   There are two things on which the outcome of every human act depends: These are will and power, and if either one of the two is missing,

6 there is nothing that can then be created. After all, if the will should fail, a person does not even attempt what is not desired; but should power be

7 absent, the will would be in vain. So it is that, should you see someone desiring to secure for himself that which he does not secure for himself at all, you would not be able to doubt that he lacked the strength necessary to make what he wanted his own.

I said: This is quite obvious, and it cannot in any way be denied.

8   But should you see someone accomplish what he wanted, you would not doubt that he had the power to do so as well, would you?

Hardly.

9   Each person must be thought to be powerful in regards to that which he can do, but must be thought to be incapable in regards to that which he cannot.

I said: I admit that.

Prose 2 IV.2.1 fancy that (I.6.6), promises (III.8.1), aroused (III.m.11.12, IV.m.4.1, V.m.4.35).   2.2 realize (III.1.4), deserted (IV.2.27), every strength (IV.2.30), proved (cf. II.7.3 (demonstration), III.10.1 (show)).   2.3 opposites (II.6.13), inability to sustain (cf. III.9.5, IV.1.7, IV.2.9), fragility (III.10.6), stability (I.2.3 (unshakable)).   2.4 each . . . paths (cf. II.1.8), paths (III.2.2), unshakable (IV.1.7).   2.5 human act (III.2.9, IV.3.3), outcome/will/power (IV.4.5), created (III.7.4, III.12.35).   2.6 in vain (V.4.16).   2.7 you (singular), make . . . his own (IV.2.28), quite obvious (III.9.25, IV.2.39, IV.3.1). 2.9 incapable (= unable to sustain: cf. IV.2.3).

So do you remember, she said, that it was deduced by our previous 10 arguments that all the striving of human nature, which is driven on in diverse pursuits, directs itself eagerly toward true happiness?

I said: I remember that that has been shown as well.

You do remember, don't you, that true happiness is the Good itself, 11 and that when happiness is sought, it is in this way that the Good is longed for by all people?

I said: No, I hardly *remember* that, since I have it now fixed in my memory.

Therefore all mortals, the good and the evil alike, strive to reach the 12 Good by their indiscriminate strivings?

I said: Yes, that is the logical consequence.

But it is certain that people become good by securing the Good for 13 themselves?

It is certain.

So they are the good who secure for themselves that which they crave?

So it seems.

But if the evil secure for themselves what they crave, which is the 14 Good—then they couldn't be evil.

It is as you say.

Therefore: Since both the good and the evil seek the Good, but the 15 former do secure it while the latter do not at all, it is not a doubtful proposition, is it, that the good are powerful, while those who are evil are incapable?

I said: Whoever doubts this cannot be looking closely either at the 16 universe or at the logical consequences of rational arguments.

Or from the other angle, she said. If there are two people who have 17 the same goal in accordance with their natures, and one of these two performs it and brings it to completion in accordance with his natural functioning, while the other is not at all able to manage this natural functioning, but rather, in some manner other than what is appropriate

---

2.10 deduced (III.1.41, IV.2.39), previous arguments (at III.2), striving (I.6.10, III.2.9, 15), diverse pursuits (III.2.20; cf. III.2.2), directs itself (III.7.4, III.12.17).   2.11 true happiness . . . good itself (III.10.42), remember (cf. III.m.11.9–16), memory (III.2.13, III.12.1).   2.12 to reach (IV.2.26), indiscriminate (II.2.12, V.3.32), logical consequence (III.9.12, IV.2.24).
2.13 (cf. III.2.2, III.3.3, III.10.23, III.11.7–8).   2.15 incapable (IV.2.9, 24).
2.16 looking at (III.11.13), logical consequences (IV.2.24, IV.4.22).
2.17 brings to completion (IV.4.3), functioning (IV.5.3), manage (IV.6.12), satisfy (IV.4.3, V.6.12), judge (IV.6.1).

to his nature, does not even satisfy his goal but only imitates the one
who has satisfied it—which do you judge to be the stronger of these two?

18   Even if I can guess at what you're after, I said, I am longing all the
same to hear it more distinctly.

19   She said: You won't deny, will you, that the motion of walking is in
accordance with the nature of mortals?

      I said: Hardly.

20   You don't doubt, do you, that the functioning of the feet is the natural functioning for this?

      I don't deny this either, I said.

21   Therefore, if someone walks who has the ability to move by means of
his feet, while another man, who lacks this natural functioning of his
feet, tries to walk supporting himself with his hands—which of these can
rightly be thought to be the stronger?

22   I said: Weave in your other arguments; for there is no one who is in
doubt that the man who has the power of his natural functioning is
stronger than the man who cannot do the same.

23   But the highest Good, which is equally the goal of evil people and of
good people, good people seek to gain by the natural functioning of their
virtues while the evil try to secure the same thing for themselves
through their multiform desires, which do not constitute a natural functioning for the securing of the Good—or do you think otherwise?

24   I said: Hardly, for it is also obvious what is the logical consequence of
this; I mean, from the points that I have granted it must be the case that
the good are powerful, while the evil are incapable.

25   She said: You are hurrying on ahead of me and on the right path; this,
as is the doctors' usual expectation, is a sign of a nature that is both
26   revived and fighting back. But since I see that you are now very eager for
learning, I will pile up my arguments thick and fast; just observe how
great is the weakness of corrupt men who cannot even reach that goal
toward which their natural striving leads and practically forces them.
27   And what would happen if they were to be deserted by these reinforce-

---

2.18 (cf. III.9.3), can guess (I.6.6, V.3.2), I am longing (III.12.3, IV.5.4).
2.19 walking (IV.2.29, V.6.27–29).   2.22 weave in (IV.6.6), in doubt (I.6.6,
III.12.26).   2.23 virtues (cf. II.7.2, V.6.47), multiform desires (cf. III.2–III.8).
2.24 logical consequence (IV.2.12, IV.3.14; cf. IV.2.16), the good . . . incapable
(IV.2.2, 15).   2.25 doctor (cf. I.3.1, I.4.1, I.5.11–12, II.3.3, III.1.2, IV.4.38,
IV.6.45), revived (cf. V.5.12), fighting back (III.11.28).   2.26 observe
(III.10.11, IV.4.28), corrupt men (II.5.18, II.6.18, IV.2.35).   2.27 deserted
(IV.2.2, IV.4.6), reinforcements (military metaphors: cf. I.m.1.21–22, I.3.12–14,
IV.7.10–21).

ments (so great, practically undefeated) of a nature that would lead
them onward? Just look at what great powerlessness has lawless men in   28
its grip. For the rewards that they seek to gain and that they cannot
achieve and cannot make their own are no "trifling or trivial things."
No, but at the very height and head of things they fall away, and the outcome that is the only thing they struggle for day and night never comes
to them in their desolation; and it is in this that the strength of the good
people stands out. Take a man who, walking on foot, was able to go all   29
the way to that place beyond which there lay nothing further that was
accessible to his walking. Just as you would judge him to be the most
powerful person in terms of walking, just so must you judge that man to
be most powerful absolutely who has gained the goal of the things that
are to be sought, beyond which there is nothing else.

So it is that the opposite is true, that <those who do not achieve   30
their ultimate goals> seem to be deserted by all of their strengths. I   31
mean, why have they left their virtue behind to go chasing after vices?
Because of their lack of awareness of the things that are good? But what
is there more powerless than the blindness of ignorance? Or do they
know what they should chase after, but lust drives them headlong away,
at right angles? In this way too they are fragile in their lack of self-control, because they are unable to wrestle against vice. Or do they desert   32
the Good knowingly and willingly, and cast themselves off toward the
vices? But in this way they not only cease to be powerful, but cease even
to exist at all; after all, those who abandon the common goal of all the
things that are also quit existing as well.

Now this is a fact that may seem paradoxical to some, that we say   33
that evil men, the majority of mortals, do not exist; but that is the way it
is. To be sure, I do not reject the statement that evil men are evil men;   34
but I do deny that they exist in the pure and simple sense. For just as you   35
may call a corpse a dead human being, but cannot denominate it a

---

2.28 just look at (III.9.10, III.10.7), powerlessness (III.5.5), lawless (I.4.28, 29,
46; IV.4.1), trifling (Vergil, *Aeneid* 12.764–5), head (III.10.31, III.11.39), fall
away (IV.2.36, IV.3.15, V.6.12), outcome (IV.4.4), stands out (I.4.2).   *2.29*
walking (IV.2.19, V.6.27–29), things to be sought (III.9.23, III.10.37–38, III.11.5,
IV.2.43).   *2.30* deserted . . . strengths (IV.2.2, 27).   *2.31–32* (cf. V.m.3).
2.31 left behind (IV.4.40), vices (III.4.1), lack of awareness (II.4.22, III.12.3),
blindness of ignorance (II.4.26; cf. V.m.3.8), lust (III.m.10.2, IV.m.2.6), headlong
(I.m.2.1; cf. III.m.11.1–6), fragile (III.8.6, III.10.6, IV.2.3), lack of self-control
(IV.3.18).   *2.32* desert (IV.2.2, 27), cast off (cf. IV.4.29), quit existing
(cf. III.12.29).   *2.33* fact . . . some (cf. IV.4.3), paradoxical (II.8.2, IV.4.12,
IV.5.7), the way it is (V.3.18, V.4.23).

human being in the simple sense, so may I grant that there are corrupt
men, but I am unable to admit as well that they exist in an absolute
36 sense. For that thing exists that keeps its place in nature and preserves
its own nature; but whatever falls away from this abandons even the
37 existence that was placed within its own nature. But, you will say, evil
people have power; I wouldn't deny this either, but this power of theirs
38 derives not from their strength but from their incapability. For they have
the power to do evil things, things that they would not be able to do at
all had they been able to remain unchanged with the potentiality of
39 good people. And this false power proves even more clearly that they
have no real power; for if, as we deduced just a little while ago, evil is
nothing, then, since they only have the power to do evil things, it is clear
that the unrighteous have no power at all.

This is quite obvious.

40 And, just so you can understand exactly what the force of this power
of theirs is—just a little while ago we defined it this way: There is nothing more powerful than the highest Good.

I said: It is as you say.

But, she said, the highest Good cannot do what is evil.

Hardly.

41 So tell me, she said, is there anyone who thinks that mortals have the
power to do all things?

There is no one, except for the madman.

And yet these mortals have the power to do evil things?

And how I wish, I said, that they did not!

42 Therefore: Since he who has power only to do good things has the
power to do all things, while those who do have the power to do evil
things do not have the power to do all things, it is perfectly clear that
43 those who have the power to do evil have less power. To this is attached
the fact that we have shown that all power is to be counted among the
things that are to be sought, and that all the things that are to be sought

---

2.36 place in nature (IV.4.27), falls away (IV.2.28), placed (IV.7.22, V.6.37).
2.37 you will say (singular: cf. II.4.23).   2.38 remain unchanged (cf.
III.11.14–34), potentiality (III.11.5).   2.39 false power (cf. IV.2.44, IV.4.6),
deduced (III.11.41), a little while ago (at III.12.29, IV.2.32), unrighteous (I.4.6,
9; IV.2.25), quite obvious (III.9.25, IV.2.7, IV.3.1).   2.40 (cf. III.9.27), a little
while ago (at III.12.21), defined (V.1.8, 10, 12, 18), cannot do (cf. III.12.26–29).
2.41 anyone (cf. IV.3.7), except for (cf. IV.4.41), madman (cf. III.12.26), power
to do evil (cf. IV.1.4), how I wish (I.4.27; cf. II.m.5.23, IV.4.1).   2.43 power
(III.10.30–31), things . . . sought (IV.2.29), all the things . . . their nature (cf.
III.10.31, 38), head (V.5.12, V.6.17).

are understood in reference to the Good as if to a sort of head and summation of their nature. But this false power of committing crimes cannot   44
be referred to the Good, and is therefore not a thing to be sought. And
yet every power is to be sought; consequently, it is clear that this false
power is not true power. From all of these considerations it is the power   45
of the good people and the utterly unquestionable weakness of the evil
that is made obvious, and the truth of that opinion of Plato's is clear:
Only the wise have the power to do what they long to do, while the
unrighteous, though they may keep themselves busy at whatever they
please, do not have the power to accomplish what they long to do. For   46
they do whatever they please, thinking all the while that they will secure
for themselves the good that they long for by means of the things that
give them joy; but they secure it not at all, since wicked deeds do not
come into the realm of true happiness.

Meter 2

Hígh exálted týrants sítting on their raísed thrónes—can you seé thém,
Brílliant ín the bláze of púrple, through the hígh fénce of their grím speárs,
Gláre and threáten wíthout píty, in the hót breáth of their mád heárts?
Coúld you stríp awáy the tráppings from the príde óf their adórnmént,
Únderneáth you'd seé these másters in the tíght chaíns of their shácklés.   5
Hére is lúst with ácid poísons, discompósíng all the lífebloód;
Ánger whíps the mínd to frénzy on the hígh seás of the pássións;
Sórrow hére exhaústs her cáptives or incónstánt hope torménts thém.

2.44 (cf. V.3.32), false power (IV.2.39), crime (IV.3.1), committing crimes
(IV.4.6), false power/true power (cf. IV.4.24).   2.45 weakness (III.8.10,
IV.2.26; cf. IV.6.35), Plato (*Gorgias* 466d–e; III.12.38, V.6.9, 10,14), unrighteous
(IV.2.39, IV.3.5, 12), do not have . . . long to do (cf. IV.m.2.10).   2.46 joy
(III.2.18, V.1.6), wicked deeds (IV.3.1).

Meter 2 IV.m.2.1 tyrants (cf. I.m.5.41, II.m.1.3, II.2.11–12, III.5.1–8), raised
thrones (I.m.5.2, 31), you (singular).   2.2 purple (III.m.4.1, III.m.8.12), high
fence . . . spears (cf. III.5.8, III.8.4).   2.3 without pity (I.1.7, IV.m.1.29), mad
hearts (II.m.6.15).   2.4 strip away (IV.m.3.36).   2.5 see underneath (cf.
III.8.10), chains (I.m.2.25, III.m.12.4).   2.6 lust (II.6.18, III.2.31, III.m.5.3,
III.7.3, III.m.10.2, IV.2.31), poisons (I.1.8, II.m.6.17, IV.m.3.35–39), lifeblood
(IV.m.3.32 (heart)).   2.7 anger (I.m.4.14, I.5.11, III.m.2.15–16), mind
(IV.m.3.27), high seas (cf. I.m.2.4, II.1.6, III.m.10.13), passions (cf. I.5.11,
I.m.7.25–31).   2.8 sorrow (I.5.11), captives (II.6.11, III.m.10.1), inconstant
(I.m.5.28 (slippery)), hope (I.m.4.13).

Whén you seé one síngle pérson thus endúríng all these týránts—
10   Hé does nót do whát he wánts to, overwhélmed bý cruel mástérs.

Prose 3

So do you see what is the expanse of filth in which wicked deeds wallow,
and what is the light with which righteousness shines? From this it is
quite obvious that the good people are never without their rewards, and
2   that crimes are never without their punishments. The fact is, for all
actions that are undertaken, that particular thing for the sake of which
any individual action is undertaken can be seen, not without cause, as
the reward of the action, just as the crown for which the race is run lies
3   as the reward for running on the track. But we have shown that happiness is the Good itself; the Good is the very thing for the sake of which
all actions are undertaken; therefore it is the Good itself that has been
4   placed before human actions as if it were their common reward. And
yet, this reward cannot be separated from good people—for one would
not rightly be called good any longer if one lacked the Good—and for
5   this reason its proper rewards do not abandon righteous conduct. Therefore, no matter how brutal evil people may be, the crown shall never fall
from the head of the wise man and shall never wither; nor shall another
person's unrighteousness pluck from the souls of the righteous the distinctions that are theirs alone.
6   For were a person to take delight in a reward received from an external source, then it could be taken away, perhaps by someone different, or
even perhaps by the very person who had bestowed it; but since it is
each person's righteousness that bestows this reward on each of them,
then only when he ceases to be righteous will a righteous man be with-
7   out his reward. Finally, since every reward is craved for this reason, that

---

2.9 you (singular), tyrants (I.m.4.11, IV.m.1.29–30, IV.m.2.1).   2.10 does not
do (IV.2.45), overwhelmed (I.m.2.25 (weighed down)).

Prose 3 IV.3.1 do you see (singular: II.7.9, III.4.3, V.4.38), wicked deeds (I.2.46),
wallow (cf. IV.3.20), righteousness (II.5.18, II.6.3, IV.3.6), quite obvious (IV.2.7),
rewards . . . punishments (II.7.10, IV.6.25), crimes (IV.2.44).   3.2 (cf.
III.10.39), not without cause (III.6.1, V.4.39, V.6.36), crown (cf. IV.3.5).
3.3 we have shown (at III.2), human actions (III.2.9, IV.2.5).   3.4 separated
(IV.3.11) righteous conduct (I.3.6, I.m.5.31–32, IV.4.14).   3.5 brutal
(IV.m.3.39), crown (cf. IV.3.2), wither (III.11.18–19).   3.6 without (IV.4.7
(free of)).   3.7 craved (IV.2.13–14), who is there (cf. IV.2.41), without a
share (cf. IV.1.4).

it is believed to be good, who is there who would judge a person who is master of the Good to be without a share of its reward? But what sort of 8 a reward is it? Only the most beautiful, the greatest reward of all—please remember that corollary that I gave you just a little while ago as your very own, and consider this: Since true happiness is the Good itself, it is 9 clear that all good people, by the very fact that they are good, become truly happy. But it is agreed that those who are truly happy are gods. 10 Therefore, *this* is the reward of good people, which no future day can grind down, which no other man's power can humble, which no other man's unrighteousness can stain—to become gods.

Given that all of this is true, may the wise man never be in doubt 11 about the punishment that cannot be separated from evil people. For, since good and evil, and likewise punishments and rewards, are incompatible, their faces set against each other, the same things that we see constituting the reward of the good man must necessarily, on the opposite side, correspond to the punishment of the evil man. Therefore, just 12 as righteousness itself becomes the reward of the righteous, so too is gross wickedness itself the punishment of the unrighteous. And further, no one who has been affected by a punishment doubts that he has been affected by an evil. So tell me: Those whom this gross wickedness, this 13 farthest limit of all evil things, not only has affected, but has even passionately infected—if these people want to take their own measure, can they seem to themselves to have no share of punishment?

But as to what is the punishment that is the companion of the 14 unrighteous—take a look at it from the other side, the side of the good people. You have learned just a little while ago that everything which exists exists as one thing, and that the One itself is the Good; the logical consequence of this is that everything that exists seems in fact to be good. And so it is in this way that whatever falls away from the Good 15 ceases to exist. And so it happens that evil people cease to be what they once were. But the very appearance of a human body that remains shows them up as having been human before; and for this reason,

---

3.8 corollary (at III.10.22–26), as your very own (III.m.12.57), consider this (II.4.24).   3.10 stain (I.4.37), become gods (cf. I.4.39, III.10.24–25).
3.11 separated (IV.3.4), good and evil (cf. IV.2.3), incompatible (III.2.20, IV.m.4.7), set against each other (V.3.3), constituting (IV.6.42 (befall)), opposite side (III.1.7).   3.12 gross wickedness (III.4.2, III.7.2, IV.1.4).   3.14 companion (I.m.1.6, IV.m.1.11 (satellite)), a little while ago (at III.11.40, III.12.33), logical consequence (IV.2.12, 24).   3.15 falls away (IV.2.28), ceases (cf. II.1.19), ceases to exist (cf. IV.2.32), appearance . . . body (IV.4.1), human nature (II.5.29).

because they have turned toward evil conduct, they have lost their human nature as well.

16   But since it is righteousness alone that has the power to promote any-one beyond the realm of human beings, it is necessarily the case that unrighteousness deservedly tramples down below what a human being deserves those whom it has cast down from the human condition. And so it comes about that anyone whom you see metamorphosed by vices

17   you can no longer judge to be a human being. One man, a savage thief, pants after and is ravenous for the goods of other people—you can say that he is like a wolf. Another man, vicious, never resting, has his tongue

18   always in motion in lawsuits—you can compare him to a dog. One man, the hidden plotter, lying in wait, is glad to steal by his deceptions—he can be said to be the same as the foxes. Another roars, giving free rein to his anger—he may be believed to have within him the spirit of the lion.

19   One man, a coward, is quick to turn tail, afraid of things that he need not fear—he is thought to be like the deer. Another, indolent and slack-

20   jawed, is simply inert—he lives the life of an ass. One man, fickle and flighty, changes his interests constantly—he is not at all different from birds. Another wallows in foul and unclean lusts—he is held under by

21   the physical delights of a filthy sow. And so it is that anyone who has ceased to be a human being by deserting righteousness, since he has not the power to cross over into the divine condition, is turned into a beast.

Meter 3

Ónce, the Íthacan cáptain's shíp
Wíth his fleét that had beén adríft
Cáme by wínds from the Eást to pórt
Whére the beaútiful góddess líved,
5   Bórn the chíld of the Sún, who míxed

3.16 righteousness (IV.3.1, 6, 12; V.6.48), tramples down (II.5.27, IV.4.29), human condition (II.5.29; cf. IV.3.21).   3.17–21 (cf. wise man examples at IV.6.35–42).   3.17 wolf (IV.m.3.13), dog (III.m.12.12–13).   3.18 hidden plotter (cf. I.4.46), roars (III.m.2.13, IV.m.5.14), lion (III.m.2.7–16, IV.m.3.11–12). 3.19 deer (III.m.2.10–11), slack-jawed (III.1.1, III.3.18; cf. I.2.4 (incomprehension)), ass (I.4.1).   3.20 birds (III.m.2.17–26; cf. V.m.5.4–5), wallows (cf. IV.3.1), physical delights (III.7.1), sow (cf. IV.m.3.24).   3.21 ceased to be (cf. IV.3.15), divine condition (cf. IV.3.16).

Meter 3 IV.m.3.1 Ithacan (IV.m.7.8), captain (= Ulysses; IV.m.3.19).   3.3 East (II.m.4.4).   3.4 goddess (= Circe).   3.5 born (cf. III.m.6.6).

Fór her chánce, unsuspécting guésts
Cúps that shé had transfórmed by sóng.
Stróng in mágical hérbs, her toúch
Túrns these mén into mány shápes—
Óne is sheáthed in a boár's-head másk;   10
Óne, a líon from Líbyá,
Seés his teéth and his náils grów;
Óne is néw to the páck of wólves,
Hówling whén he inténds to waíl;
Óne, an Índian tíger, strólls   15
Úncomplaíningly throúgh her hálls.
Thoúgh Arcádia's wíngèd gód
Ín compássion for áll the ílls
Whích encómpassed the cáptain's lífe,
Sét him freé from the lády's cúrse,   20
Yét the bánd of his shípmates thén
Pút their líps to the poísoned cúps,
Chánged the foód that was Céres' gíft
Fór the ácorns they áte as pígs.
Nóthing, nóthing remaíns intáct;   25
Áll is lóst of their voíce, their shápe.
Nó; the mínd stands unchánged alóne,
Moúrns the hórrors it hás endúred.
Áh, her toúch was a wórthless thíng,
Ánd her hérbs had no stréngth at áll!   30
Théy could ónly transfórm the límbs,
Bút could néver transfórm the heárt;
Húman lífe force was képt secúre
Ín its cítadel, oút of síght.
Thére are poísons with fár more stréngth,   35

3.7 cups (III.m.2.20, IV.m.3.22), song (III.m.12.29–30, 43).   3.8 (cf. IV.m.3.29–
30).   3.11 lion (cf. III.m.2.7–16, IV.3.18).   3.13 wolves (IV.3.17).
3.15 Indian (III.m.3.3, III.m.5.5), tiger (III.8.7).   3.17 Arcadia's god (= Mercury).
3.19 captain (IV.m.3.1).   3.20 curse (III.5.14 (plague)).   3.22 cups
(IV.m.3.7).   3.23 Ceres (I.m.6.5, III.m.1.4, IV.m.6.27).   3.24 acorns (I.m.6.6,
II.m.5.5), pigs (cf. IV.3.20).   3.25 remains (cf. III.11.4, 10–12, 15, 33–34).
3.27 mind (II.6.7, III.m.9.16, 22; III.m.12.54, IV.m.2.7), stands unchanged
(I.m.1.22).   3.29–32 (cf. II.5.35, II.7.12, III.5.2).   3.29–30 touch/herbs
(IV.m.3.8).   3.31 limbs (III.3.17, III.10.31–34).   3.32 heart (III.m.11.14,
IV.m.2.6).   3.33 life force (= vigor: I.1.1; cf. IV.m.2.6).   3.34 citadel (I.3.13;
cf. I.5.5).   3.35 poisons (I.1.8, I.3.9, II.m.6.17, IV.m.7.22).

Whích can stríp from a mán his sélf,
Pássing hórribly deép withín,
Leáving bódy unhármed alóne,
Brútalízing with méntal woúnds.

Prose 4

And then I said: I admit that, and I see how it is not improperly said that corrupt men, even if they preserve the appearance of a human body, are all the same changed into beasts in the quality of their minds; but as to the fact that their minds, so abominable and so lawless, act so brutally for the destruction of good people—I would not have wanted that to be allowed them.

2   She said: But it is not allowed them, a proof that shall be made in its own proper place; but all the same, if the very thing that is thought to be allowed them should be taken away from them then, to a large extent, the

3   punishment of these lawless men would be alleviated. In fact, and this is a thing which may perhaps seem incredible to some, it is necessarily the case that evil men are less happy if they have brought to completion the things that they once desired than if they are unable to satisfy what they now

4   desire. For if it brings desolation merely to have desired immoral things, it brings even greater desolation to have had the power to do them; without

5   this power, the outcome of the desolate will would collapse. And so, since each of these things one by one has its own desolation, it is necessarily the case that those people are overwhelmed by a triple punishment, the people you see to be willing, capable of, and bringing to completion a criminal act.

6   I said: I yield that, but it is my passionate desire that these people be deserted by their false power of committing crimes and so immediately be free of this punishment.

3.36 strip (IV.m.2.4).   3.37 deep within (II.1.7, II.3.4, II.6.5).   3.39 bru-
talizing (IV.3.5, IV.4.1, IV.m.4.10), mental (IV.m.3.27).

Prose 4 IV.4.1 (cf. IV.4.42, IV.5.4).   4.1 not improperly (IV.3.2), corrupt men (IV.2.26, 35), appearance . . . body (IV.3.15), beasts (IV.3.16–21, IV.m.3, IV.4.30), quality . . . minds (IV.6.40), minds/minds (animus/mens), abominable (IV.4.42), lawless (I.4.46), brutally (IV.3.5, IV.m.3.39), I would . . . allowed them (I.4.28, IV.1.4, IV.2.41).   4.2 proof . . . place (at IV.6), alleviated (IV.4.17). 4.3 (cf. IV.2.17), a thing . . . to some (cf. IV.2.33), bring to completion (IV.2.17, V.4.39).   4.4 desolation (IV.4.9), immoral things (cf. IV.4.9), power/will/out-come (IV.2.5).   4.5 overwhelmed (II.5.16, IV.4.25, 42), punishment (III.5.13, IV.4.6).   4.6 yield (IV.4.30); passionate desire (cf. I.4.28), deserted (IV.2.27), false power (IV.2.39, 44), committing crimes (IV.2.44), free of (IV.3.6).

She said: Ah, but they will be free of it, perhaps even sooner than you   7
yourself would wish, perhaps even sooner than they would think that they
would be free of it themselves. The mind is first and foremost an immortal
thing, and within the swift circuit of this life there is nothing that comes so
late that the mind would consider the anticipation of it to be long drawn
out. The great hope of these people, the lofty siege engine of their crimes,   8
often falls to ruins in a sudden and unexpected end. In fact, this places a
limit to their desolation—for if it is gross wickedness that makes them desolate, then it is necessarily the case that, the more long-lasting is his wickedness, the more desolate a man is. And I would judge them to be   9
incalculably unhappy if that death that comes at the end did not put an
end—to say no more—to their evil conduct; for if we have drawn true
conclusions about the punishment attendant on immorality, it is clear that
a desolation that we have agreed is eternal is infinite as well.

Then I said: This is indeed a paradoxical inference, difficult to admit   10
to; but I recognize that it agrees to an incredible degree with the points
that were conceded earlier.

She said: And you are right to think so. On the other hand, it is only   11
fair that someone who thinks it difficult to accept a conclusion either
prove that some false proposition has preceded it or else show that the
ordered sequence of propositions is not productive of a necessary conclusion; otherwise, there is absolutely no reason for him to object to the
inference, if all of the preceding propositions have been conceded. For   12
this point too that I am about to make may seem no less paradoxical, but
it is no less necessary, drawn from the propositions already adopted.

I said: Tell me, what?

She said: That the unrighteous are more happy when they suffer their   13
punishments than when no penalty derived from justice represses them.
Now, I'm not laboring the point that might come into anyone's mind, that   14
immoral conduct is corrected by retribution and led back to the right path
by fear of punishment, and that for other people as well this is a deterrent

---

4.7 (cf. IV.4.24), mind (*animus*).   4.8 lofty (V.6.17, 47), siege engine
(= machine: cf. II.m.8.21, III.12.14), sudden and unexpected (cf. II.1.3, IV.6.4),
gross wickedness (IV.3.12, 13; IV.6.46), the more . . . man is (cf. IV.4.24).
4.9 death . . . end (cf. II.7.21, IV.m.6.33), immorality (cf. IV.4.4), we have agreed
(cf. IV.7.3), eternal (IV.4.24).   4.10–11 (cf. IV.7.5).   4.10 inference
(III.10.17, IV.4.11), agrees (IV.3.10), earlier (at IV.4.3–5).   4.11 accept
(IV.4.6), productive (V.4.4), absolutely (IV.4.41).   4.12 paradoxical
(IV.2.33, IV.4.10, IV.5.7; cf. IV.4.3), adopted (III.12.35), tell me, what (III.9.28,
IV.7.1).   4.13 (cf. IV.6.44), justice (I.5.4), represses (III.11.32, IV.7.12).
4.14 (but cf. IV.6.44), mind (*mens*), retribution (IV.4.21), led back . . . path
(cf. II.8.5), reproach (IV.4.38).

that they should run away from things that would bring them reproach. No; it is in another way that I think that the unrighteous are unhappier when unpunished, even if correction is not taken into account, even if there is no consideration for deterrence.

15   And what would this other way be, I said, that leaves these behind?

And she said: Have we not granted that good people are happy, and that evil people are desolate?

It is as you say.

16   She said: Therefore, if some good be added to a person's desolation, such a person surely is happier than the one whose desolation is unmixed and unaccompanied, without the admixture of any good?

I said: So it seems.

17   Now what if some evil, beyond the evils that make him desolate already, were added to this same desolate man who lacks all good things? Surely he must be judged to be much more unhappy than one whose punishment is alleviated by participation in the good?

I said: Well, of course he must.

18   But it is perfectly clear that the punishment of the unrighteous is just, and that it is not right that they make their escape unpunished?

Who could deny it?

19   But there is no one, she said, who could deny this either, that what is just is good and that, on the other hand, what is unjust is evil.

20   I answered that it was clear.

Therefore the unrighteous do indeed have some good added to them when they are punished; namely the punishment itself, which is good by reason of its justice. These same people, when they are free of punishment, have within them some further evil, which is impunity itself, a thing that you have agreed was evil by virtue of its injustice.

21   I cannot deny it.

Therefore: The unrighteous are much more unhappy when they receive the gift of unjust impunity than when they are punished in just retribution.

22   Then I said: Those are indeed the logical consequences of the conclusions that were drawn just a little while ago. But, I said, I beg you,

---

4.15 granted (cf. IV.1.7).   4.16 admixture (I.4.37).   4.17 added (IV.4.20), punishment (III.5.13), alleviated (IV.4.2), participation (III.10.25), well, of course (III.3.10, 13).   4.18 (cf. IV.4.33, IV.7.12), who could deny it (III.3.14). 4.20 (cf. I.6.11 (indirect speech)), added (IV.4.17), impunity (IV.4.27), virtue (II.5.25).   4.21 retribution (IV.4.14).   4.22 logical consequences (IV.2.16, IV.4.36, IV.7.1), beg please (III.10.11, IV.6.1).

please: Do you bequeath no punishments for souls, after the body has been extinguished by death?

I do, and they are great indeed, she said. I think that some of the pun- 23 ishments are employed in the bitterness of discipline, others in the clem- ency of purgation; but it is not now my plan to discourse upon them. We 24 have taken this discussion up to this point so that you could realize that the power of evil people, which seemed to you to be the most dishonorable thing, is no power at all; so that you could see that the people who you complained were unpunished are never free from the punishments of their own unrighteousness; so that you could learn that the license granted them, a license whose swift termination you prayed for, is not for long, and that it is the more unhappy the more long-lasting it is, and that it would be the most unhappy if it were to be eternal; and so that, after all these dem- onstrations, you could learn that the unrighteous are more desolate when let go by an unjust impunity than when punished by a just retribution. The 25 logical consequence of this conclusion is that they are overwhelmed by weightier punishments precisely when they are believed to be unpunished.

Then I said: When I look at your arguments, I think that nothing has 26 been more truly spoken; but, should I go back to the judgments of mor- tal men, who is there for whom they would seem, I won't say credible, but even worthy of a hearing?

She said: It is as you say. Once their eyes have become accustomed to 27 the darkness, people are not able to raise them up to the penetrating light of truth; they are like the birds whose vision the nighttime illu- mines though the daytime blinds them. So long as they do not look closely at their place in nature but only at their own passions, they think that the license for their crimes, or the impunity for their crimes, is a happy thing. But observe what eternal law has decreed. If you mold your 28

4.23 bitterness (cf. IV.4.38), discipline (IV.6.47), discourse (II.6.1, IV.6.7).
4.24 realize . . . no power (cf. I.4.28, IV.2.2–32), dishonorable (cf. III.4.2), no power (IV.2.44), see that . . . unrighteousness (cf. I.4.10, 46; IV.3.11–13), learn that . . . eternal (cf. IV.4.6–9), license (IV.4.27), you prayed for (at IV.4.6), learn that . . . retribution (IV.4.13–21). 4.25 logical consequence (IV.4.22), over- whelmed (IV.4.5). 4.26 look at (III.11.13, IV.6.21). 4.27 darkness/light (I.m.2.2–3, I.2.6, I.m.3, I.6.21, I.m.7, V.2.10), penetrating (I.1.1, III.3.1), birds (IV.3.20, V.m.5.4–5), blinds (II.1.11, II.4.26, III.m.8.15, III.9.25, IV.2.31, IV.4.31), look closely (III.1.5, III.12.10), place in nature (IV.2.36), passions (I.1.9, I.6.13, V.5.3), license (IV.4.24), crimes (IV.6.44), impunity (IV.4.20, 21). 4.28 observe (singular: III.10.11, IV.2.26), eternal law (II.m.3.17; cf. I.m.5.23), decreed (I.4.5, III.12.38), mold (IV.7.18 (educate)), mind (*animus*), you have (cf. II.4.22), judge (V.6.48), bring reward (I.4.4), superior things (III.2.17, IV.6.38).

mind to the shape of better things, you have no need of a judge to bring
you your reward, for you yourself have added yourself to the realm of
29   superior things; if you direct your pursuits toward the worse things, don't
look for any avenger outside of yourself, for you yourself have trampled
yourself down into the realm of inferior things. It is just this way—if you
were to contemplate now the foul earth, now the heavens, in alternation, then, if all other things were disregarded, you would seem to yourself, just by the very principle of your perception, now to dwell in the
mud, now to dwell among the stars.

30   But the common herd does not contemplate these things. Well then!
Are we to yield to those whom we have shown to be no different from
31   beasts? What if a man who had completely lost his sight were to forget
that he even had vision once, and so think that there was nothing lacking in him for human perfection—we who can see wouldn't think the
32   same things this blind man thinks, would we? People will not even yield
this point, which is supported by foundations of rational argument that
are just as strong, that those who commit an injustice are more unhappy
than those who suffer it.

I said: Myself, I would like to hear these very arguments.

33   She said: You don't deny, do you, that every unrighteous person is
worthy of punishment?

Hardly.

34   And it is clear in many ways that those who are unrighteous are
unhappy?

I said: So it is.

So you have no doubt that those who are worthy of punishment are
desolate?

I said: That is consistent.

35   So if you were sitting as magistrate, she said, to whom would you
think punishment ought to be given: to the one who committed the
injustice or to the one who endured it?

I said: There is no dispute—I would give satisfaction to the victim
through the pain of the one who committed the injustice.

4.29 direct pursuits (III.1.7, III.9.24, IV.2.32), worse things (III.m.6.9), trampled
(II.5.27, IV.3.16), inferior things (I.4.29), contemplate (III.8.8), foul (I.m.7.12),
earth/heavens (I.1.13, I.3.1, III.8.8, IV.m.1.23–28).   4.30 herd (I.3.7,
IV.m.5.20, V.1.11), well then (III.2.16, III.9.22, V.1.11, V.3.22), yield (IV.4.6),
shown (at IV.3.15–21), beasts (IV.4.1).   4.31 forget (I.2.6), blind man
(cf. IV.4.27).   4.32 supported (IV.4.37, IV.7.4), who commit . . . suffer it
(cf. Plato, *Gorgias*, 474b–475e), I would like (cf. III.10.29).   4.33 (cf. IV.4.18).
4.35 victim (IV.4.38).

Therefore, the one who does the injustice would seem to you to be   36
more desolate than the one who receives it.

I said: That is the logical consequence.

Therefore: It is for this reason, and for other reasons that all rest   37
upon this one root—that shamelessness makes people desolate by its very
nature—that this is obvious: An injustice that is done to someone is the
desolation not of the one who receives it but of the one who does it.

<I said: It is obvious.>

She said: And yet the lawyers do just the opposite. I mean, they try to   38
rouse the compassion of the judges in behalf of those who are the victims
of some serious or bitter wrong, when a more just compassion is owed to
the perpetrators instead. It is better that they be led to judgment, not by
indignant accusers, but rather by kindly and compassionate accusers, like
sick men to the doctor, so that the diseases brought on by their wrongdoing
can be cut out by their punishment. From these considerations, the efforts   39
of the defense lawyers would either be utterly superseded or, if these lawyers preferred to do some good for mortal men, they would transform
themselves for the prosecutor's role. So also the unrighteous themselves—   40
were it permitted them to gaze through some crack at the virtue that they
had left behind, and to see that they could set aside the defilement of their
vices through the tortures of their punishments, the righteousness that they
would secure for themselves would counterbalance such tortures. They
would think that those were *not* tortures; they would reject the efforts of
their defense lawyers, and they would give themselves over completely to
their accusers and to their judges. So it is that, as far as the wise are con-   41
cerned, there is absolutely no place left for anger. I mean, except for the
most utter fool, who would hate good people? And to hate evil people has
no logical defense. Just as physical collapse is a disease of bodies, so too is a   42
vice-ridden nature a sort of disease of minds. If this is the case, then, since
we certainly judge those who are sick in body to be worthy of compassion
rather than anger, it is all the more true that vice-ridden people are to be
pitied, not persecuted, since their minds are driven on by an unrighteousness that is more abominable than any physical collapse.

4.36 does injustice (II.7.20), that is ... consequence (III.9.12).   *4.37* rest upon
(IV.4.32 (supported), V.4.13), shamelessness (cf. III.6.1), by its very nature (V.5.4),
obvious (III.10.42).   *4.38* rouse (IV.m.4.1 (stir up), victims (IV.4.35), bitter (cf.
IV.4.23), doctor (IV.2.25), diseases (I.1.9, I.2.5, III.5.14, III.7.2, IV.4.42), cut out
(III.m.1.3).   *4.40* crack (III.9.3), virtue ... behind (IV.2.31), tortures (II.6.8; cf.
I.3.9, IV.5.3), defilement (III.4.17, IV.1.6).   *4.41* anger (IV.6.51 (hatred)),
except for (IV.2.41).   *4.42* collapse (cf. IV.4.4), disease (IV.4.38), vice-ridden
nature/disease (cf. IV.6.29), minds/minds (*animus/mens*), abominable (IV.4.1).

Meter 4

Whý délíght to stir úp such greát upheávals?
　　Whý would you teáse your own fáte, goád it on bý your own hánd?
Mórtál mén! Is it Deáth you seék? Behóld her
　　Hére of her ówn freé wíll, swíft horses néver held báck.
5　Snáke, beár, boár, with the líon ánd the tíger
　　Seék to kill mén with their teéth, whó seek themsélves with their
　　　　　　　　　　　　　　　　　　　　　　　　　　swórds.

Incómpátibly dífferent cústoms *fórce* them,
　　Márching to béstial wár, swélling injústice's ránks,
To lóng tó dié in the gíve-and-táke of speár-points?
10　　Nó! Where is jústice enoúgh, fít for brutálity's caúse?
Shoúld yoú wísh then to gíve their deéds their mérits—
　　Chérish in jústice the goód, shéd for the évil your teárs.

Prose 5

At this point I said: Now I see what is the happiness, and what is the
desolation, that has been established for the actual merits of the righteous and the unrighteous. But as I weigh things, there is some good and
2　evil to be found in the very Fortune of popular opinion. After all, there is
not a single wise man who would prefer to be an exile, to have no
resources and no good name rather than to remain unchanged in his
own city and to thrive as one predominant in his wealth and resources,
3　preeminent in his political honor, and strong in his power. For the proper

---

Meter 4 IV.m.4.1 stir up (III.m.10.13, V.m.4.31, 35; cf. IV.4.38 (rouse)), upheavals
(cf. V.4.37).　　*4.2* tease (I.m.2.14; cf. I.m.4.6).　　*4.3* behold (cf. I.m.1.20).
4.4 own free will (cf. IV.4.37 (own nature)), swift horses (III.m.1.10, IV.m.1.21).
4.5 (cf. IV.3.17–20), snake (cf. V.m.5.2–3), lion (III.m.2.7–16, IV.m.3.11–12), tiger
(III.8.7, IV.m.3.15–16).　　*4.6* teeth (III.m.2.15–16).　　*4.7* incompatibly
(IV.3.11), different customs (cf. II.7.7, 10).　　*4.8* ranks (I.3.13 (array)).
4.10 brutality (IV.m.3.39, IV.4.1).　　*4.11* you (singular), give . . . merits (cf.
III.4.10).

Prose 5 IV.5.1 (cf. III.10.1), merits (I.4.24, IV.m.4.11, V.2.11).　　*5.2* weigh
(IV.6.4, 56; V.4.15), Fortune (cf. II.2), popular opinion (III.2.9, III.6.3), exile
(I.3.3, I.5.2, I.m.7.24–27, II.4.17, III.m.11.10), no resources . . . name (cf. I.4.36,
45; IV.6.45), remain unchanged (III.11.36), his own city (cf. I.5.5), thrive
(IV.1.4), preeminent/honor (III.2.5).　　*5.3* functioning (IV.2.17–23), spills
over (III.4.7 (pours into)), peoples . . . borders (but cf. II.7.7–10), prison, death . . .
citizens instead (cf. IV.1.4), tortures (I.3.9; cf. II.6.8, IV.4.40), destructive
(II.1.12, II.5.18), established (III.10.1, IV.5.1).

functioning of wisdom is carried out with greater renown and to better acclaim in this way, when the true happiness of those who govern spills over somehow or other into the peoples who are at their borders, and especially when prison, death, and all the other tortures that belong to the punishments of the legal process are reserved for the destructive citizens instead, for whom they have in fact been established. Therefore I   4
am utterly amazed that these things are changed and reversed, that punishments for crimes overwhelm good people, and that evil people snatch away the rewards owed to virtues. I am longing to learn from you what seems to be the just principle for such an unjust confusion.

And in fact I would be less amazed at this were I to believe that all   5
things are confused together by chance occurrences happening at random. But as it is now, the God who is the helmsman makes my incomprehension that much greater. Given that he assigns delightful things to   6
good people and calamitous things to evil people, but on the other hand assigns harsh things to good people while granting to evil people the things that they desire—if a reason for this cannot be discovered, what is there here that differs from chance occurrences happening at random?

She said: It is not paradoxical that something is believed to be random and confused if the principle behind the order is not known. But   7
even though you do not know the cause of this great arrangement, please have no doubt that all things happen in the right way; indeed, the one who is the helmsman, who balances the world, *is* good.

Meter 5

Áre you blínd to thís? Stárs of the Greát Bear
Turn slówly néxt to heáven's high cénter;
Slów to doúse his flámes, lágging Boötes

5.4 (cf. I.m.5.29–42, IV.1.4, IV.4.1), utterly amazed (I.4.28, I.6.6, II.5.8), amazed (IV.1.3, 5), reversed (I.m.5.33), I am longing (III.12.3, IV.2.18), just (cf. IV.m.4.10), confusion (IV.6.23, 34).   5.5 confused together (I.m.6.19), chance occurrences (I.6.3, 4; IV.6.4), happening at random (V.1.8), helmsman (I.m.5.27, 46; I.6.19, III.11.39, IV.1.3, IV.5.7; cf. I.6.7, V.m.1.11), incomprehension (I.2.4).   5.6 assigns (IV.7.11), delightful (II.4.18, IV.7.3, 11), calamitous (IV.7.3), they desire (IV.6.23, 43), chance . . . random (IV.5.5).   5.7 paradoxical (IV.4.10, 12), random (I.6.3, 4), order (III.12.7), you (singular), arrangement (III.12.7; cf. IV.1.6, IV.6.9, 21), no doubt (cf. IV.6.42), helmsman (IV.5.5), balances (I.m.5.18, IV.6.18).

Meter 5 IV.m.5.1 you (= someone), Great Bear (II.m.6.11, IV.m.6.9).
5.2 center (I.3.3, III.10.38, IV.6.15, 22).

Condúcts his óxen dówn toward the Ócean.
5   Whén he soón displáys swíftness in rísing,
Then yoú'll be áwed by láws of high heáven.
Shoúld the fúll moon's hórns grów dark and ghástly,
By níght's thick shádow grímly infécted;
Shoúld dazed Phoébe shów stárs once concéaled,
10 The stárs kept hídden bý her bright súrface;
Máss delúsion dríves nátions to mádness,
Who frét brass kéttles éndlessly clánging.
Nó one stánds amázed that blásts of the Wést Wind
Can bátter shórelines, roáring with seá-swells;
15 Nór that drífts of snów, íce-hard and frígid,
Are tháwed by Phoébus, his heát incandéscent.
Thése have caúse and énd, símple to wítness,
While hídden cáuses troúble the spírit.
Áll that lápse of tíme bríngs unexpécted,
20 That áwe the brúte herd, eásily stártled:
Dríve delúsion oút, the cloúd of unknówing—
Make nó mistáke—they'd ceáse to seem wóndrous.

Prose 6

I said: It is as you say. But since it is your obligation to unfold the causes
of things that are hidden and to reveal their principles, veiled in darkness, I beg you, please explain in full what is your judgment in these matters. For this supernatural occurrence confuses me most of all.

5.6 awed (IV.m.5.20, IV.6.31).   5.7–10 (cf. I.m.5.5–9).   5.7 horns
(III.m.6.3).   5.8 infected (IV.3.13).   5.9 dazed (I.6.21), Phoebe (II.m.8.8,
IV.m.6.7).   5.11 delusion (= error: IV.m.5.21; cf. II.4.22, II.5.30, III.3.1).
5.13 West Wind (I.m.3.3).   5.14 shorelines (II.m.5.15), roaring (III.m.2.13,
IV.3.18).   5.15 frigid (I.m.5.14 (frost)).   5.16 Phoebus (I.m.6.1, II.m.8.5,
III.m.2.31, V.m.2.2), incandescent (IV.m.6.27).   5.18 hidden (IV.6.1), causes
(I.m.2.22–23, IV.6.1), trouble (IV.6.1 (confuses); V.2.10 (whirlwind)).
5.20 awe/startled (IV.6.31), herd (I.3.7, IV.4.30).   5.21 (cf. IV.m.5.11), delu-
sion (IV.m.5.11), cloud of unknowing (V.2.10).   5.22 make no mistake
(III.m.11.11), wondrous (IV.5.7 (paradoxical)).

Prose 6 IV.6.1 unfold (IV.6.10, 54; V.m.4.11), hidden (IV.m.5.18; cf. I.m.2.22–23,
1.4.4, II.m.5.27–30, V.1.13–17, V.m.3.11–12), reveal (III.7.4), darkness (V.4.23),
judgment (IV.2.17), supernatural occurrence (= miraculum: IV.6.27, 31, 50),
confuses (I.1.14, V.3.2).

Then she smiled at me for a time and said: You now summon me to a   2
matter that is, in the asking, the greatest of all and for which, in the
answering, there is hardly anything that will suffice. For its composition   3
is such that, after one source of doubt has been lopped off, others grow
up to replace it, more than you can count, like the heads of the Hydra.
There would be no limit to these doubts if one didn't keep them in check
with the mind's liveliest fire. In this matter questions are usually asked   4
about the simplicity of Providence, the sequence of fated events, unexpected chance occurrences, divine perception and divine predestination,
and the freedom of independent judgment—and just how burdensome
such things are you yourself can weigh in the balance. But since it is a   5
certain portion of your medicine that you know these things as well,
although we are hemmed in by the circumscribed limit of our time, we
shall try all the same to examine them, to some limited extent. And yet,   6
if it is the delights of music and song that you find delightful, you must
put off this physical pleasure for a time while I weave together arguments that are tightly bound to each other in sequence.

I said: As you please. Then, as if beginning from another starting   7
point, she presented the following discourse:

The coming-into-being of all things, each and every development of
natures that are subject to change, whatever is set in motion by whatever means—all these things are allotted their causes, their order, and
their appearances from the immutability of the divine mind. This divine   8
mind, securely settled in the citadel of its own simplicity, has established
for the carrying out of things a complex mode of operation. When this
mode is viewed in the unmixedness of the divine intelligence, it is called
Providence. However, when it is referred to those things that the divine

---

6.2 for a time (I.2.5).   6.3 doubt (IV.6.42), Hydra (IV.m.7.22), fire (cf.
I.6.20).   6.4 simplicity of Providence (IV.6.11, 13, 17, 20, 55; cf. II.m.8.13),
sequence of fated events (IV.6.11, 14, 55), unexpected (IV.4.8), chance occurrences (I.6.3, IV.5.5–6), perception (V.5.2, 7), predestination (cf. V.2.11), freedom of independent judgment (V.2.2, V.3.3), weigh in the balance (IV.5.2,
IV.6.56).   6.5 medicine (I.2.1, I.6.21), hemmed in (II.7.6), circumscribed
(II.7.5–6), time (cf. V.1.4).   6.6 music and song (II.1.8, III.1.1, IV.6.58), for a
time (I.2.6, IV.6.2), weave (IV.2.22), tightly bound (= woven: III.11.1, IV.6.9),
as you please (II.2.5, II.3.7 (prefer); cf. I.6.2, III.12.25).   6.7 beginning . . .
point (cf. II.1.1, III.1.1), discourse (I.4.3, II.6.1, III.6.5), development (IV.6.18),
allotted (V.6.41), divine mind (IV.6.10, 20; V.3.28, V.5.11; cf. IV.6.16).
6.8 securely settled (I.m.4.1, II.4.12), citadel (I.3.13, I.5.5, IV.m.3.34; cf. IV.6.30),
simplicity (III.12.30, IV.6.13), carrying out (IV.6.13), mode of operation
(IV.6.21), referred (III.10.28, 31, 36 (reference); V.3.32, V.6.26, 36), sets in
motion (III.m.9.3), arranges (III.12.7), ancients (I.3.6).

intelligence sets in motion and arranges, it has, according to the
9   ancients, received the name of Fate. Should one look at the force of
these two terms in one's own mind, it will appear quite easily that they
are different; for Providence is the divine reason itself, established in the
highest ruler of all things, which arranges all things; Fate is the arrangement that inheres in the things that have motion, the arrangement
through which Providence weaves all things together in their proper
10   orders. Providence embraces all things equally, despite the fact that they
are different, and despite the fact that they are infinite; Fate sets out
individual things into their motions, things that are apportioned to specific places, appearances, and times. As a result, this unfolding of the
order of things in time, which is unified according to the divine mind's
seeing of it in advance, is Providence; this same unification, when set
out and unfolded in specific times, is called Fate.

11   Though it be granted that these are different, nevertheless the one is
dependent on the other; the order of fated events proceeds from the
12   simplicity of Providence. For example: An artisan anticipates in his mind
the appearance of the thing that he is about to make, sets in motion the
process of the work's completion, and so leads through the ordered
stages of time the thing which he had seen in advance in its simplicity
and in a single moment. It is in just this way that God by his Providence
arranges the things that are to be made in a uniform and unchanging
way; by Fate he manages these very things that he has arranged in a mul-
13   tiform and temporal way. Now whether Fate is driven by certain divine
spirits that are servants of Providence; whether the sequence of fated
events is woven together by the World Soul or by all of nature in service
to it, or by the heavenly motion of the stars, the power of angels, the
multiform resourcefulness of demons, or by some of them or all of them
together; this is at any rate perfectly clear, that Providence is the
unmoving and simple form of the things that are to be carried out, and
Fate is the interweaving in motion and the ordering in time of those
things that divine simplicity arranged so that they could be carried out.

6.9 ruler (III.10.7, 9, 14; V.3.35; cf. III.m.9.28 (leader)), arranges all things
(III.12.7, 12), have motion (cf. IV.6.19), weaves (IV.6.6, 13).   6.10 embraces
all things (IV.6.53), apportioned (IV.6.40), unfolding (IV.6.1, 15), seeing in
advance (IV.6.12).   6.11 order of fated events (cf. IV.6.4), simplicity
(IV.6.15).   6.12 example (IV.6.15), artisan (II.5.17 (maker)), single moment
(= present moment: V.6.12, 15, 43), manages (IV.2.17), multiform (cf. IV.6.8
(complex)).   6.13 servants (IV.6.44), sequence (IV.6.4), woven (IV.6.6, 9),
demons (cf. I.4.39), unmoving (IV.6.19), things . . . out (IV.6.8, V.6.15).

And so it happens that all the things that are subordinated to Fate   14
have been made subject to Providence as well, and even Fate itself is subject to Providence; however, there are certain things, placed inferior to
Providence, that are superior to the sequence of Fate. These are the
things that are set firmly and unchangeably next to the first divinity and
pass beyond the realm of the ordering of motion by Fate. For example: Of   15
all the circles that turn about the same center point, the one which is
innermost approaches the simplicity of the middle, and for all of the
other circles that lie outside of it *it* exists as a kind of center point about
which they turn. However, the outermost circle, set in rotation in a
greater circumference, is unfolded in areas that are ever greater the
greater is its remove from the central indivisibility of that point. On the
other hand, if something could bind itself and join itself to that center, it
would be forced into simplicity and would cease to be dispersed and to
dissipate itself. By a similar line of reasoning, that which is at a further
remove from the first mind is entangled in greater meshes of Fate; a thing
is free from Fate to the extent that it seeks to gain ever more closely that
center point of things. And should it cling to the stability of the mind   16
that is above it, then, free from motion, it transcends the necessity of Fate
as well. Therefore: As is the relation of rational argument to knowledge;   17
of that which comes into being to that which is; of time to eternity; of the
circle to its center point—such is the relation of the moving sequence of
Fate to the unchanging simplicity of Providence.

This sequence moves heaven and the stars, balances the elements   18
among themselves one with the other, and transforms these elements in
the interchange of each with each; the same sequence renews all the
things that are born and die, through the development of their offspring
and seed, resembling each other from generation to generation. This   19
sequence also ties together the actions and the fortunes of mortal men,

---

6.14 subject (V.1.8, V.4.15), sequence of Fate (cf. IV.6.4, 11).   *6.15* example
(IV.6.12), center point (I.3.3), simplicity (IV.6.11, 13), outermost (V.m.4.5),
unfolded (IV.6.1, 10), dispersed (III.11.21), dissipate (III.2.7, IV.7.19), similar . . .
reasoning (III.10.24, III.11.9; cf. V.3.7), first mind (cf. IV.6.7, 16), entangled
(III.8.2, V.1.2, V.m.1.8), meshes (V.6.36).   *6.16* cling (III.11.19, III.m.11.11),
stability/mind (II.6.7), mind above (cf. IV.6.7, 15; V.m.3.20), transcends (V.4.30,
V.6.15), necessity (V.3–6 passim), necessity of Fate (cf. IV.6.55).   *6.17* rational argument (III.10.21, V.4.2, V.5.5), rational argument/knowledge (cf. V.4.27).
6.18 balances (I.m.5.18, IV.5.7, IV.m.6.19), among . . . other (II.7.17), seed (cf.
III.11.13–14).   *6.19* sequence (II.m.8.13, IV.6.4,14, 17, 18, 55; V.2.1), ties
together (V.2.2, V.3.28), indecomposable (I.1.3), interweaving (V.1.8, 19; cf.
V.3.33), motionless (IV.6.13, V.6.12; cf. IV.6.9), actions . . . unalterable (cf.
V.3.3–6 ff.).

in an indecomposable interweaving of causes; and since this sequence
sets out from the loom of motionless Providence, it is necessarily the
20   case that these actions and fortunes be unalterable as well. For it is in
this way that things are governed best, if the simplicity that remains
unchanged in the divine mind brings into the world an inevitable order
of causes, while here in the world this order keeps in bounds, in their
proper and mutual unalterability, the things that are alterable and other-
21   wise liable to bob up and down at random. And although you mortals
have not at all the strength to investigate this order, so that all things
seem to you confused and dislocated, nevertheless there is for all things
individually a proper mode of operation that arranges them and directs
22   them toward the Good. For there is nothing that happens for the sake of
evil, not even what the unrighteous themselves do; as has been most
abundantly shown, it is an immoral miscalculation that turns them from
the path as they seek the Good. It is hardly the case that the order that
advances from the center point of the highest Good changes course in
any direction away from its own starting point.

23   You will say: But what confusion can there be that is more unjust
than this, that good people now have adverse things as their lot, now
favorable things; while evil people too have now the things they hope
24   for, now the things they detest, as theirs? But surely people do not live
their lives with such an infallibility of mind that it is necessarily the case
that those whom they have judged to be righteous or unrighteous must
25   also actually be just as others think they are? And what is more, the
judgments of people are at odds in this matter; those whom some think
to be worthy of reward others think worthy of punishment. But let us
26   grant that someone could tell good people and evil people apart—surely
such a person could not therefore look upon, to use the term usually
27   applied to the body, the inmost constitution of the mind? For example:

6.20 simplicity (IV.6.4), divine mind (IV.6.7, V.3.28; cf. IV.6.13), order of causes
(V.3.9), keeps in bounds (I.m.6.18), bob up and down (I.6.19, III.11.39, V.m.1.11).
6.21 strength (IV.6.32), mode of operation (IV.6.8, 28; cf. V.3.4 (way)), arranges
(III.12.7, IV.6.8, 9), directs . . . Good (IV.6.55).   6.22 nothing . . . evil (cf.
III.12.34), shown (at II.5–7, III.3–9; cf. IV.2), miscalculation (III.2.4), center
point (I.3.3, III.10.38, IV.6.15), starting point (III.9.33, IV.6.19 (loom), V.4.37).
6.23 you (singular), you will say (II.4.23, II.5.32, III.3.18, IV.2.37, V.4.10, 21;
V.6.37, 39), adverse/favorable (II.8.1–5, IV.6.40; cf. IV.6.36 (adversity)), things
they hope for (IV.6.43).   6.24 (cf. I.4.35), infallibility (V.4.23), mind (*mens*),
judged (V.6.6).   6.25 judgments (cf. II.7.10), reward/punishment (IV.3.1).
6.26 tell apart (V.2.4), look upon (cf. III.8.10, IV.m.2.5), constitution (IV.m.6.30
(balance)), mind (*animus*).   6.27 sweet (cf. IV.6.57), gentle/bitter (I.5.12),
supernatural occurrence (IV.6.1, 31, 50).

someone does not know why, in the case of healthy bodies, sweet things are right for some, sour things for others; or why some sick people are helped by gentle things while others are helped by more bitter things; such would seem to be a "supernatural occurrence" that is no different. But the doctor, who can distinguish the mode of operation and the con-   28
stitution of health itself and of sickness itself, is not at all amazed. In   29
fact, what else does the health and well-being of the mind seem to be other than its righteousness; what else is its sickness other than its vices? Or who else is there who preserves what is good and drives out what is evil other than God, the helmsman and the healer of minds? When God   30
has looked down from the high watchtower of Providence, he sees what is appropriate for each person, and he supplies to each what he knows to be appropriate. And it is here that the remarkable supernatural occur-   31
rence of the order of Fate comes to be; it is a thing that holds the igno-
rant spellbound, but which is put into effect by one who knows.

For if I may touch briefly on just those few aspects of the unfathomable   32
depth of God that human reason has the strength for: To the Providence that knows all things, it seems quite otherwise concerning the man whom *you* think to be the most just and the one most devoted to the preservation of what is right. As our kinsman Lucan has warned us, it was the   33
conqueror's cause that pleased the gods, but the cause of the conquered pleased Cato. In this regard, therefore, whatever you see happening that   34
falls short of your hopes—though to your opinion it is a topsy-turvy con-
fusion, for the things themselves it is the right ordering. But let there be   35
someone of such excellent character that divine and human judgment are in complete accord about him; but he is weak as to the strength of his mind and would perhaps, if something adverse happened to him, cease to cherish the innocence that was the reason why he could not keep his fortune. And so it is a wise dispensation that spares him, a man whom   36

6.28 doctor (I.3.1, I.4.1, IV.2.25, IV.4.38), distinguish (V.2.4), mode of operation (IV.6.21), amazed (IV.6.44).   6.29 health and well-being (III.12.18), mind/minds (*animus*/*mens*), sickness/vices (cf. IV.4.42), preserves . . . evil (cf. IV.4.38), helmsman (I.m.5.27, 46; I.6.19, IV.1.3, IV.5.5, 7).   6.30 high watchtower (cf. IV.6.8, V.6.17), appropriate (IV.6.36, V.1.11, V.4.13).   6.31 remarkable (IV.6.50), supernatural occurrence (IV.6.1, 27, 50), spellbound (cf. I.1.13, III.1.1, IV.m.5.6, 20).   6.32 unfathomable depth (cf. III.m.9.16, III.m.11.1), strength (IV.6.21), you (singular).   6.33 our (III.9.32), kinsman (I.3.8), Lucan (*Pharsalia* I.128).   6.34 opinion (III.4.13, V.3.18), confusion (IV.5.4, IV.6.23, V.3.32), ordering (IV.6.20).   6.35 mind (*animus*), adverse (IV.6.23), innocence (I.4.19).   6.36 dispensation (IV.6.45, V.6.45), adversity (IV.6.35), appropriate (IV.6.30).

adversity could have made worse, and does not allow him to struggle with
37   something that is not appropriate for him. Another man is perfect in all
of his virtues, holy and next to God himself; Providence judges it wicked
that such a man have any adversity at all as his lot, so much so that it
38   does not even allow him to be hounded by diseases of the body. For as
someone who is even superior to me has said:

Heávenly pówers have fáshioned the hóly man's phýsical bódy.

39   Furthermore, it often happens that the fortunes of the state are handed
over to good men for them to control, so that unrighteousness running
40   riot can be beaten back. To others Providence apportions certain mix-
tures of the favorable and the adverse in accordance with the quality of
their minds. Some it torments to keep them from an overindulgence in
protracted happiness; others it hounds with difficulties so that they may
strengthen the virtues of their minds by the experience and the practice
41   of forbearance. Some fear more than is appropriate that which they can
endure; others disparage more than is appropriate that which they cannot endure. Such people Providence leads on, by means of disagreeable
42   measures, to discover by trial who they are. There are some who have
purchased at the price of a glorious death a name that is esteemed by the
ages; some, proved to be unconquerable by the punishments imposed
upon them, have offered an example to others, that evil people have no
victory over virtue. There is no source of doubt that these things happen
in accordance with what is right and what is the divine arrangement,
and for the good of those to whom they are seen to befall.

43   Furthermore, this too comes from the same causes, that now things that
are disagreeable, now things that they hoped for, spring up for the unrigh-
44   teous. In particular, no one is amazed at the disagreeable things, at least,
because everyone thinks that these people deserve evil. In fact, the punishments of such people both frighten others away from criminal deeds and
improve those very people to whom the punishments are applied. On the
other hand, the prosperity of evil people speaks a great argument to good

---

6.37 next to (cf. I.4.38–39), wicked (III.10.15), his lot (IV.6.23), hounded
(IV.6.40), diseases (IV.4.38, 42).   6.38 superior (IV.4.28).   6.39 handed
over (cf. IV.7.3).   6.40 apportions (IV.6.10), favorable/adverse (IV.6.23),
quality of minds (IV.4.1), minds/minds (*animus/animus*), hounds (IV.6.37), for-
bearance (II.7.20).   6.41 disagreeable (IV.6.43), who they are (cf. I.6.17).
6.42 price . . . death (cf. I.3.6, 9), name (cf. II.7.11–13, III.2.6), unconquerable
(IV.4.13 ff.; cf. II.6.8), example (IV.m.7.32), victory (I.3.6), source of doubt
(IV.6.3).   6.43 disagreeable (IV.6.41), hoped for (IV.6.23), spring up (V.1.16,
V.6.31).   6.44 amazed (IV.6.28) criminal deeds (IV.4.27), improve (but cf.
IV.4.14), servant (IV.6.13).

people as to what they ought to think about a happiness of *this* sort, which
they often observe to be the servant of the unrighteous. And I believe that   45
this prosperity falls to such a man in this case by dispensation, for a man
may be by nature so headlong and so impulsive that a lack of resources and
prosperity could actually provoke him to criminal acts; Providence cures
such a man's disease by the remedy of money conferred upon him.
Another man, contemplating a conscience befouled by immoral acts and   46
drawing the parallels between himself and his fortune, perhaps grows fear-
ful that the loss of what is for him a delightful experience would be depressing; he will therefore change his ways and will, at the same time as he fears
for the loss of his fortune, forsake his gross wickedness. A happiness that   47
has been unworthily lived has cast some down headlong into a disaster
that they deserved; others have been granted the right to administer discipline that this may be a cause of training for the good and of punishment
for the evil. After all, just as there is no eternal pact between the righteous   48
and the unrighteous, so too can the unrighteous themselves never agree
among themselves. No, of course not: The unrighteous individually are of   49
two minds within themselves, as their own vices pull their consciences to
pieces, and they often perform acts that they determine should never have
been committed after they have committed them.

And it is from this that most high Providence produces the remarkable   50
supernatural occurrence that evil people make evil people good. For while   51
some people seem to suffer what they do not deserve at the hands of those
who are most despicable, as they burn with hatred for those who are to
blame, they have returned in fact to the fruits of virtue because they strive
to make themselves unlike the people whom they hate. Indeed, the divine   52
power is the only power in respect of which even evil things are good,
when by using them in due proportion it draws forth from them the end
result of some good. For there is a certain order that embraces all things;   53
consequently, whatever has withdrawn from the principle of the order that

---

6.45 dispensation (IV.6.36), headlong (II.m.7.1, IV.6.47), lack ... prosperity (cf.
II.4.13, IV.5.2), provoke (I.4.15), cures/disease (IV.4.38; cf. IV.2.25).   6.46 conscience ... acts (cf. I.4.37), gross wickedness (III.4.2, III.7.2, IV.1.4, IV.3.12, 13;
IV.4.8).   6.47 headlong (IV.6.45), others have ... evil (cf. IV.4.23), training (cf.
II.6.8, IV.6.42).   6.48 pact (I.m.5.43, 48; II.m.8.3, 23; IV.m.6.4, V.m.3.1).
6.49 of course not (IV.4.17), pull to pieces (cf. I.1.5), consciences (I.4.37).
6.50 most high Providence (V.3.16), supernatural occurrence (IV.6.1, 27, 31).
6.51 for while ... most despicable (I.m.5.29–36, IV.1.4), most despicable
(I.3.11), burn (III.1.4, V.m.3.11), fruits (I.1.9).   6.53 embraces all things
(IV.6.10, V.6.43), withdrawn (military language: cf. IV.m.7.17–21), falls into
another order (cf. IV.3.16–21), randomness (I.6.4, 20; V.1.8), Homer (*Iliad*
12.176 (god)); cf. I.4.1, II.2.13, V.m.2.1).

has been assigned to it falls into another order, but it is an order all the same; there is therefore no room given to randomness in the kingdom of Providence. Yet, as Homer says:

Bút it is hárd to expláin all these thíngs as if Í were a góddess.

54 No, and it is forbidden to mortals either to grasp all of the machines of the divine operation in the acuity of their minds or to unfold them in the
55 words of their mouths. I hope it is enough just to have seen this, that God, who brings forth all natures, is the same one who arranges all things and directs them toward the Good; and that, inasmuch as he hastens to keep the things that he has brought forth in his own image and likeness, he banishes every evil from the boundaries of his state through
56 the agency of the sequence of fated necessity. And so it is that the evils that are thought to be present in abundance on the earth—if you should look to the Providence that arranges all things well, you would weigh in the balance that there is no evil anywhere.

57   But I see that you have been for some time now both burdened by the weight of the question and exhausted by the great length of the explanation, and so you are waiting for some sweetness that comes from song. So take a drink—once you have been refreshed, you may press forward toward the further reaches as a stronger man.

Meter 6

If you lóng tó seé, mínd pure and fácile,
The Thúnderer's státutes, lófty, exálted,
Loók to the zénith, heáven's high pláces.
Thére, constellátions keép ancient cóncords,
5 Thé wórld thús héld in bónds that are jústice,
The réd planet's fíres néver impélling

6.54 forbidden (I.3.5, 14; I.4.38, I.5.3), machines (II.m.8.21, III.11.24, III.12.14), unfold (IV.6.1, 10).   6.55 arranges (III.12.7, IV.6.12–13, V.1.19, V.2.11), directs toward the Good (IV.6.21), image and likeness (III.m.9.8, 17), state (I.4.6; cf. I.5.3–5), sequence of necessity (IV.6.4, 11, 14).   6.56 weigh in the balance (IV.5.2, IV.6.4, V.4.15).   6.57 exhausted (V.1.5), sweetness (cf. IV.6.27), song (III.1.1, III.m.12.21, 30, 48; IV.m.3.7, IV.6.6; cf. II.1.8), drink (I.5.11; cf. II.1.7), stronger (I.6.21).

Meter 6 IV.m.6.1–18 (cf. I.m.2.8–17, I.m.5.1–13, II.m.8.1–15, III.m.9). 6.1 you (singular), see . . . facile (cf. III.m.11.1, IV.6.4, V.4.30).   6.2 statutes (cf. IV.m.5.6).   6.3 heaven's high places (cf. IV.m.5.2).   6.4–5 concords/ bonds (I.m.5.43, V.m.3.1).   6.6 red planet (cf. IV.m.1.12).

The sún to block Phoébe's cóld path and órbit.
And the Beár gíves reín tó her swift coúrses
At the hínge of the wórld, híghest abóve us.
Though she seés others sínk ín Western wáters,   10
Stárs báthed in the deép, shé néver desíres
Tó doúse hér flámes in wáves of the Ócean.
Véspér broádcásts shádows at évening
In tíme's just exchánges, órdered, as álways,
Ánd now as Lúcifer bríngs back the deár day.   15
Thus, recíprocal Lóve mákes new the páthways
Étérnally sét, thús from the fíxed stars
Wár's díshármony fleés into éxile.
Thís hármony rúles élements bálanced
Ín their just meásures: Moístness and drýness,   20
Át wár back and fórth, yiéld to each óther,
Íce and flame joíning tógéther as friénds.
Thus the quívering fíre ríses to heáven
Ánd heávý eárth sínks by its ówn weight.
Fór thése reasóns ín the warm spríngtime   25
Thé yeár in its bloóm breáthes forth sweet ódors;
Summer párches the graín, íncándéscént;
Aútúmn retúrns weíghted with ápples;
Raín leaping dównward floóds through the wínter.
Thís sáme bálánce noúrishes, bríngs forth   30
Eách creáture on eárth with the breáth óf lífe;
Ít steáls them awáy, búries them, hídes them,
Sínks their begínnings ín their last éndings.
And the creátor sits stíll throúgh all, abóve all,
Guíding the reíns and contrólling the whóle world,   35
Íts kíng and its lórd, its soúrce and begínning,

6.7 Phoebe (II.m.8.8, IV.m.5.9).   6.8–12 (cf. II.m.6.11, IV.m.5.1–6).
6.8 courses (I.m.2.7, V.m.1.12).   6.13 Vesper (= Hesperus: I.m.5.10,
II.m.8.7).   6.15 Lucifer (I.m.5.12, III.m.1.9).   6.16–24 (cf. II.m.8.1–4).
6.16 reciprocal Love (cf. II.m.8.13–21, IV.m.6.44–48).   6.18 war (II.m.8.18),
exile (IV.5.2).   6.19–24 (cf. III.m.9.10–12).   6.19 rules (IV.6.18
(balances)).   6.25–29 (cf. I.m.2.18–21, I.m.5.14–22, I.m.6.1–15).
6.27 incandescent (I.m5.17, IV.m.5.16).   6.29 leaping downward (I.m.7.14–
15).   6.30 balance (IV.6.26 (constitution)).   6.33 (cf. III.m.2.34–38,
IV.m.1.23–26).   6.34 creator (I.m.5.1, V.m.2.7, V.6.9).   6.35 reins
(III.m.2.1, IV.m.1.19).   6.36–37 (cf. III.m.9.28).   6.36 king (I.5.4), lord
(IV.m.1.20), source (III.m.9.23, III.m.12.2, V.m.1.3).

Íts láw and its júdge, its wísdom and jústice.
He impéls things to móve, tó chánging of státe;
He recálls them to hált, mákes stand what wánders.
40   If he díd not recáll thése straight-line mótions
Ánd bénd thém báck ínto curved órbits,
Thíngs that are képt now ín stable órder,
Cút óff from their soúrce woúld búrst at the seáms.
Ánd thís ís Lóve cómmon to áll things:
45   Théy seék the embráce of their goál, thé Goód.
Ín nó other wáy coúld they be lásting
Únléss bý Lóve túrning them báckward
They flow báck to the caúse thát gave them beíng.

Prose 7

So do you see now what is the logical consequence of all that we have
said?
        I said: Tell me, what?
2   She said: That absolutely every fortune is good.
        And how can that be? I said.
3   She said: Concentrate. Since every fortune, be it delightful or calamitous, is handed down sometimes for the sake of rewarding or training the
good, sometimes for the sake of punishing or correcting the unrighteous,
then every fortune is good, since we have agreed that it is either just or
advantageous.
4   I said: The argument is true, too true. And if I look to the Providence
and to the Fate that you taught me about just a little while ago, it is a
5   conclusion that is supported by steadfast fighting forces. But, if you don't
mind, let's count it among those arguments that you established just a
little while ago as unexpected.

6.39 recalls/halt/stand (military language: cf. IV.2.27, IV.7.17–21, V.2.9–10).
6.40–41 (cf. III.m.2.34–38, III.m.9.13–17, III.m.11.4, IV.m.6.46–48).
6.42 stable (I.m.1.22).   6.43 (cf. V.3.36).   6.44 Love (II.m.8.15,
IV.m.6.16).   6.45 goal (III.m.9.27).   6.47 backwards (cf. IV.m.6.40–41).

Prose 7 IV.7.1 logical consequence (cf. V.4.7), tell me, what (III.9.28, IV.4.12,
V.1.3).   7.2 absolutely (IV.4.11, 41).   7.3 (cf. IV.7.22), concentrate (II.1.1,
III.1.3), handed down (cf. IV.6.39), rewarding (V.3.31), training/correcting
(IV.7.9), we have agreed (cf. IV.4.9).   7.4 too true (III.7.5), just . . . ago (at
IV.6), conclusion (III.7.6), supported (IV.4.32, IV.7.19, V.6.24), fighting forces (cf.
IV.7.21).   7.5 just . . . ago (at IV.4.10–11), unexpected (IV.7.14, V.1.14, 18).

She said: Why?

Because the everyday conversation of mortal men uses the expression, and uses it quite often, that some people have an evil fortune.   6

She said: Do you want us then to enter the realm of the conversations of the common people so that we do not seem to have withdrawn too far from the usages of humanity?   7

I said: As it pleases you.

So: you do think, don't you, that what is to someone's advantage is good?   8

I said: It is as you say.

And the fortune that trains or corrects—is it to someone's advantage?   9

I said: I admit that.

And so it is good?

Well, of course it is.

But this is perhaps the fortune of people who, standing their ground in virtue, wage war against calamities, or of those who turn aside from their vices and rapidly start down the road of virtue.   10

I said: I cannot deny it.

But what about a delightful fortune, which is granted to the good as a reward—common people don't judge that to be an evil fortune, do they?   11

No, not at all; in fact, they think that it is, just as it is, the best fortune of all.

And what about the fortune that remains which, because it is calamitous, represses the evil with a punishment that is just? The people don't think that *that* is a good fortune, do they?   12

I said: No; they judge it rather to be the most desolate of all the fortunes that can be imagined.   13

Watch out! In following the opinion of the people we may have achieved something *really* unexpected.   14

I said: What?

She said: Because from these points that have been conceded it turns out that for these people, who are in possession of, or who are making progress toward, or who are just securing, virtue for themselves, every   15

7.7 do you want us (III.12.25), common people (I.5.8, III.6.2), as it pleases you (cf. IV.6.6).   7.9 trains/corrects (IV.7.3).   7.10 standing their ground (I.m.1.22, IV.m.6.39, IV.7.19), wage war (cf. IV.7.20, IV.m.7.1–2), rapidly . . . road (V.6.13), cannot deny (III.10.3).   7.11 common people (IV.7.7), judge (V.1.8, V.3.24 (judgment)).   7.12 represses (III.11.32, IV.4.13), just (IV.4.18, 33). 7.14 unexpected (IV.7.5).   7.15 these . . . conceded (cf. IV.4.10), progress toward (IV.7.19).

fortune is good whatever it is, while for those who remain unchanged in their unrighteousness every fortune is the very worst.

16   I said: This is true, even if no one dares to agree with it.

17   She said: And for this reason the wise man ought not to take it with annoyance whenever he is drawn into a struggle with Fortune, just as it is shameful for a strong man to take offense whenever the roar of the clash

18   of battle is heard. For each of them the difficulty is itself opportunity: for the latter, for the prolongation of his glory; for the former, for the edu-

19   cation of his wisdom. Indeed, it is from this that it is called virtue, the fact that, because it is supported by its own strength, it is not overcome by adversities. No; for all of you who stand your ground in your progress toward virtue have not come this far to dissipate yourselves in self-

20   indulgences or to fade away in physical pleasures. Now with your minds you join harsh battle with every fortune, so that a depressing fortune may

21   not overwhelm you nor a delightful one annihilate you. Seize the middle ground with steadfast fighting forces; whatever halts below it, or marches beyond it, has a contempt for happiness, but not a reward for labor, to

22   show for it. For the fortune that you prefer to fashion for yourselves has been placed in your own hands; indeed, every fortune that seems calamitous *does* punish you, unless it trains you or corrects you.

Meter 7

Thé avéngíng són of Atreús for tén yeárs
Foúght and lévéled Tróy to make réparátion
Fór his bróthér's béd, for a wífe abdúcted—
Hé who lónged tó seé all the Greék fleet sét sail,
5   Paíd the príce ánd boúght off the wínds in bloódshed,
Sloúghed his fáthér's skín, for his lúckless daúghter
Hé, as priést, máde cóvenant fróm her slít throat.
Ánd the lórd óf Íthaca wépt for lóst friends—

7.17 wise man (II.6.8), annoyance (I.1.10), strong man (IV.m.7.32), roar . . . battle (cf. I.3.14).   7.18 opportunity (II.6.8, II.7.1), prolongation . . . glory (II.7.9), education (IV.4.28 (molding)).   7.19–22 you (plural throughout). 7.19 virtue/strength (Latin *virtus*, *vires*), stand your ground (IV.7.10), dissipate (III.2.7, IV.6.15), pleasures (III.m.7.1).   7.20 minds (*animus*), annihilate (III.11.27).   7.21 steadfast . . . forces (IV.7.4).   7.22 (cf. IV.7.3, V.6.44–48).

Meter 7 IV.m.7.1 son of Atreus (Agamemnon).   7.3 brother (Menelaus), wife (Helen).   7.6 daughter (Iphigenia).   7.8 lord of Ithaca (Ulysses; cf. IV.m.3.1).

Ín his vást cáve wíld Polyphémus sánk them
Deép in hís húge gút, lying át his leísure.   10
Áll the sáme hé paíd for his jóy in hót tears
Fróm his blíndéd fáce, driven nów to mádness.
Hérculés ís súng for his toíls and lábors:
Hé it wás whó beát down the haúghty Céntaurs,
Toók as spoíls thé skín of the sávage líon,   15
Shót the swíft-wínged bírds with unérring árrows,
Stóle the fruít áwáy from the wátching drágon
(Wíth a máss óf góld to weigh dówn his léft hand),
Léd on threé chaíns Cérberus oút of dárkness.
Só the stórý goés: conquered Díomédes,   20
Máde their hársh lórd foód for his sávage hórses;
Pút a tórch tó poíson and kílled the Hýdra;
Máde the rívér gód Achelóus, shámefaced,
Plúnge his défórmed brów far belów the wáters;
Laíd Antaéús lów on the sánds of Líbya;   25
Kílled, to stíll thé wráth of Evánder, Cácus;
Thén the wíld boár's fróth dripped to staín the shoúlders
Soón to bé weíghed dówn by the glóbe of heáven.
Ón his néck únbówed was his fínal lábor,
Heáven tó úphóld; his rewárd was heáven   30
Fór his fínál lábor, the príce and páyment.
Fórward, stróng mén áll, where this greát exámple,
Whére this hígh roád leáds! Shoulder nów your búrden,
Nów withoút déláy, for the eárth, once cónquered,
    Gíves you the fíxed stars.   35

7.9 wild (= savage: cf. II.m.6.3), sank (IV.m.6.33, IV.m.7.24 (plunged)).
7.12 blinded (cf. IV.4.31).   7.13 Hercules (II.6.10), labors (IV.m.7.29, 31).
7.15 lion (Nemean lion; cf. III.m.2.7–16, III.m.12.11).   7.16 birds (Stymphalian birds).   7.17 dragon (on island of the Hesperides).   7.18 gold
(= golden apple).   7.22 Hydra (IV.6.3).   7.27 boar (Erymanthian boar).
7.29 labor (IV.m.7.13).   7.32–35 you (plural; cf. IV.7.19–22, V.6.47–48).
7.32 example (IV.6.42).   7.35 stars (IV.6.18).

Book V

Prose 1

So she concluded, and she was starting to turn the direction of her pleading toward the treatment and explanation of some other things.

2   But then I said: A proper encouragement to be sure, completely and absolutely worthy of your authority! But as to what you said previously about Providence, that it is a question bound up with many other ques-
3 tions—I know that by personal experience. That is to say, I'm asking you whether you think there is such a thing as chance at all and, tell me, what sort of thing do you think it is?

4   Then she said: I'm hurrying to make good the debt of my promise, and to open up for you the path by which you may be carried back to
5 your fatherland. But these questions—even though they are quite useful to know, they are all the same a little off to one side of the path of what I had proposed. And it's reasonable for me to be afraid that you'll be exhausted on the sidetracks and won't be able to bear up for traveling the straight path through to its end.

6   I said: You must have absolutely no fear of that. For it will be like tranquil quiet for me to bring to mind the things in which I take the
7 greatest delight. And at the same time, when every side of your argument stands fixed, its trustworthiness undoubted, I want there to be no doubt at all about what follows.

8   Then she said: I'll humor you; and as she did so she began as follows.

She said: If someone were to define chance as a result that is a product of random motion, without any interweaving of causes, I would state that chance is nothing at all; my judgment is that it is a word absolutely devoid of meaning, in the absence of any signification of any underlying

---

Prose 1 V.1.1 pleading (I.5.2 (set speech), IV.1.2), explanation (V.4.3).
1.2 authority (I.1.13, I.4.7), previously (at IV.6.3–4), personal experience (III.10.37 (reality)).   *1.3* tell me (III.9.28, IV.4.12, IV.7.1).   *1.4* carried back (IV.1.8), fatherland (IV.1.9).   *1.5* path (I.m.7.23), sidetracks (III.m.11.2; cf. II.8.5).   *1.6* tranquil quiet (III.m.10.5).   *1.7* undoubted (cf. III.11.34).   *1.8* result (V.3.9, V.4.6), random motion (I.6.7), interweaving (IV.6.19, V.1.19), word . . . meaning (cf. II.4.3), devoid (V.5.6), absolutely (V.1.1), randomness (I.3.6 (insolence)), keeps in bounds (IV.6.20).

reality. I mean, what place can be left for randomness, when there is a
God who keeps all things in bounds, binding them into order? For that   9
axiom is true, which none of the old philosophers ever spoke against:
Nothing comes from nothing. (Granted, they laid this down as a sort of
foundation for all of their theories about the natural world only in consideration of the subject material, not the active first principle.) But   10
should something arise from no causes, it will seem to have arisen from
nothing; but if this can't happen, then it is impossible that there be
chance of the sort that we have just now defined.

Well then! I said. Is there really nothing that can rightly be called   11
chance or accident? Or is there something that these words are appropriate for, even if it is hidden from the common herd?

She said: It is in his *Physics* that my good Aristotle has defined it, in a 12
brief demonstration that is very near to the truth.

I said: Tell me, in what way?

She said: Whenever something is done for some one particular pur-   13
pose, and something other than what was intended occurs, from whatever
causes—this is called chance. For example: if someone plows the earth in
order to cultivate a field, and finds a mass of buried gold. And so it is that 14
this is actually believed to have happened accidentally, but it is not from
nothing, because it has its own causes, and it is the unforeseen and unexpected confluence of these causes that seems to have engineered a chance
occurrence. For if the cultivator of the field were not plowing the earth,   15
and if the one who hid the money had not hidden it in that very place, the
gold would not have been found. And so these are the causes of the acci-   16
dental profit, which arose not from the intention of the doer but from
intersecting and confluent causes. For neither the one who buried the gold   17
nor the one who worked the field intended that this money be found but,
as I've said, that the one dug where the other had buried—this is a coincidence and a confluence. We may therefore define chance as follows: In the   18
realm of things done for some particular reason, it is an unexpected outcome, deriving from confluent causes. Further, the order that makes these   19
causes coincident and confluent proceeds in an inescapable interweaving

---

1.9 spoke against (III.10.17, V.5.5), active (cf. V.1.14 (engineered)).   *1.11* well
then (III.11.14, V.3.22, V.5.5), appropriate (IV.6.30, V.4.13).   *1.12* my good
(III.7.6), Aristotle (III.8.10, V.6.6), *Physics* (*Physics* 2.4–5; cf. *Metaphysics*
4.30.1025a14 ff.).   *1.13* finds . . . gold (cf. II.m.5.27–30).   *1.14* unexpected
(IV.7.5, 14; V.1.18).   *1.16* intention (III.11.30, 33 (striving)).   *1.19* proceeds (III.10.5 (in procession)), inescapable (cf. V.3.23 (inevitable)), interweaving
(V.1.8; cf. V.3.33), Providence (V.1.2), arranges (III.12.7, 12, 22; IV.6.8–9, 21),
places/times (III.12.7).

of causes; it descends from the source of Providence and arranges all
things in their proper places and in their proper times.

Meter 1

Dówn from the crágs of the Párthian moúntains, where gálloping árchers
    Sénd arrows shót in retreát ínto the énemy's breást,
Thére the Euphrátes and Tígris, twin rívers, are freéd from the sáme
                                             source,
    Soón flowing séparate wáys, keéping their wáters apárt.
5 Shoúld they combíne and be súmmoned agaín into óne single cúrrent,
    Shoúld what the wáves of each beár meét in conflúence at ónce,
Shíps would collíde and the trúnks of the treés tórn loóse by the tórrent;
    Wáves thus confoúnded would bríng tángles of rándom evénts.
Súch chance evénts and meánders are rúled by the lándscape, the órder
10   Óf the deep éddies themsélves, fálling, down-leáping, downhíll.
Chánce then that seéms to be gíven free reín, to bob úpward and
                                  dównward—
    Ít has the bít in its moúth, ít too must rún on by láw.

Prose 2

I said: I recognize this, and I concur that things are just as you say they
2 are. But in this sequence of causes, so attached to one another—is there
any freedom of our independent judgment? Or does the chain of fate tie
together the very motions of human minds as well?
3   She said: There is; in fact, there can be no rational nature without
4 there being freedom of independent judgment in its possession. For a

---

Meter 1 V.m.1.3 source (III.m.9.23, III.10.3, III.m.12.2, IV.m.6.36, 43;
V.3.36).   *1.4* keeping apart (III.12.6 (decompose)).   *1.5* summoned
(V.6.40).   *1.6* confluence (V.1.14, 18).   *1.7* collide (V.1.17
(coincidence)).   *1.8* random (I.6.3–4, IV.5.5–6, V.1.14 (accidentally)).
1.9 order (IV.6.20, 22, 53).   *1.10* down-leaping (I.m.7.14).   *1.11* rein
(III.m.2.1, IV.m.1.19, IV.m.6.35), bob upward and downward (I.6.19, III.11.39;
cf. IV.m.6.42–43).   *1.12* bit (I.5.4, I.m.7.31), law (III.m.9.20 (statutes)).

Prose 2 V.2.1 concur (III.12.10).   *2.2* freedom of judgment (IV.6.4); chain
(I.m.2.25, II.6.11, 18; III.m.10.2, IV.m.2.5, IV.m.7.19), tie together (IV.6.19,
V.3.28), motions (cf. III.11.30), motion/minds (V.3.30), minds (*animus*).
2.3 rational nature (cf. I.6.15).   *2.4* tell apart (IV.6.26, V.6.22), distinguishes
(IV.6.28), avoid (V.5.3), choose (V.3.33).

thing that is able by its own nature to employ reason has the discrimination by which it can tell things apart; consequently, it distinguishes between things that it must avoid and things that it must choose on its own. What it judges must be chosen, it seeks to gain; what it reckons   5
must be avoided, it runs away from. For this reason, within the beings   6
that have reason present within them, a freedom to want and not to want is present as well. However, it is my determination that this freedom is not the same in all of them. For substances that are ethereal and   7
divine have at their disposal a penetrating discrimination, a will that suffers no decomposition, and a true power capable of effecting the things they have chosen.

Now it is necessarily the case that human souls are indeed at their   8
freest when they preserve themselves intact within the contemplation of the divine mind; but they are less free when they fall away toward bodies, and still less free when they are tied to limbs of earthly matter. At   9
their furthest remove there is slavery, when they have fallen away from the possession of the reason that belongs to them because they have surrendered themselves to vices. For once they have cast their eyes down   10
from the light of the highest truth to the lower and shadowy realms, they are soon darkened over by the cloud of unknowing, they are caught in the whirlwind of destructive passions. By yielding to these passions and agreeing with them they help along the slavery that they have brought down upon themselves and, in a certain sense, they are the captives of their own liberty. Nevertheless, the gaze of Providence perceives these   11
things, a gaze that from eternity looks out at all things in advance; it assigns to their merits each and every thing that has been predestined for them.

2.6 determination (III.10.32).   2.7 divine substances (cf. III.12.37), penetrating (I.1.1), discrimination (V.2.4), decomposition (III.12.14; cf. III.11.27, III.12.6, IV.7.20 (annihilation)), effecting (= productive: IV.4.11, V.2.7, V.4.4, V.m.4.26).   2.8 preserve (III.11.27, III.12.37), divine mind (IV.6.7, 10, 20; V.3.28, V.5.11, V.6.10), fall . . . bodies (cf. III.10.5 (disintegrates), III.12.1), limbs (III.m.6.5, III.m.9.14, III.10.31–34, IV.m.3.31, V.m.3.8).   2.9 slavery (cf. I.1.9, IV.3.16), surrendered (military language: cf. IV.7.17–21).   2.10 cast . . . down (I.m.2.24–27, I.6.21, III.m.12.52–58, IV.4.27), darkened over (I.2.6 (clouded)), cloud of unknowing (IV.m.5.21), whirlwind (cf. IV.m.5.18 (trouble)), passions (cf. I.6.21), brought down upon (cf. III.m.11.9–10).   2.11 from eternity (V.3.5), looks out at (V.3.4, 28; V.6.17), merits (I.4.24, 43; IV.5.1), predestined (IV.6.4).

Meter 2

Thís is the sóng of the hóney-voiced Hómer:
Glórious Phoébus, in púre líght shíning,
Loóks over áll things and lístens to áll things.
Yét he cannót, in the dím glow of súnshine,
5   Piérce to the ínnermost wómb of the hárd Earth,
Ór to the híddén dépths of the Ócean.
Bút the creátor of heáven's great círcle—
Thére is no máss óf eárth that withstánds him,
Ás he looks dówn from abóve over áll things,
10 Neíther can níght and its bláck clouds obstrúct him.
Hé, in a sínglé stróke of his ówn mind,
Seés whát ís, whát wás and what wíll be.
Thús you may cáll him the óne and the trué sun—
Hís is the vísion of éverything sólely.

Prose 3

Then I said: Now look here! Now I am confounded by a still more difficult doubt.

2   She said: Tell me—what is that? Although I can already guess at the
things that are the source of your confusion.

3   I said: That God has foreknowledge of absolutely everything and that
there is any freedom of independent judgment—these things seem to me
to be set against each other, and to be at odds with each other, far too

4   much. For if God sees all things in advance and cannot be mistaken in
any way, that thing must necessarily happen that Providence foresees

5   will happen. And for this reason, if Providence has foreknowledge from

Meter 2 V.m.2.1 Homer (cf. I.4.1, I.5.4, II.2.13, IV.6.53).   *2.2* Phoebus
(I.m.3.9, I.m.5.9, I.m.6.2, II.m.3.2, II.m.6.9, II.m.8.5, III.m.2.31, III.m.6.3,
III.m.10.18, III.m.11.8, IV.m.1.10, IV.m.5.16).   *2.3* (*Iliad* 3.277 = *Odyssey*
11.109, 12.323).   *2.5* innermost (cf. III.8.10).   *2.7* creator (I.m.5.1, I.6.4,
II.5.10, 26; IV.m.6.34, V.6.9).   *2.8–10* (cf. III.m.9.25–26).   *2.10* black
clouds (I.m.7.2; cf. III.m.11.7).   *2.11* single stroke (V.4.33, V.6.40;
cf. IV.6.12).   *2.13* you (singular).

Prose 3 V.3.1 doubt (III.9.27; cf. V.4.2; cf. IV.6.3 (the Hydra)).   *3.2* I can
guess (I.6.6, IV.2.18), confusion (I.1.14, IV.6.1).   *3.3* independent judgment
(V.2.2, V.6.31), set against each other (IV.3.11; cf. III.12.25?).   *3.4* in
advance (V.3.28).   *3.5* from eternity (V.2.11), independent judgment
(V.3.14), does not know (V.m.3.15, 17, 27).

eternity not only of the actions of mortal men but of their deliberations and of their wills as well, then there would be no freedom of independent judgment. For there could exist no action, no will of any sort, other than what divine Providence, which does not know how to be mistaken, perceives beforehand. I mean, if such things could be forcibly turned   6
aside in some other direction than they were foreseen to go, then there would now be no immovable foreknowledge of the future, but only indefinite opinion instead. And this I judge to be a wicked thing to believe about God.

Nor do I approve of the line of argument by which some people   7
believe they can untie the knot of this question. I refer to the people   8
who deny that *this* is the reason that something will happen, that Providence sees in advance that it will be so. Rather to the contrary: Because something is going to be, it cannot escape the notice of divine Providence, and in this way the necessity falls to the other side. For they say   9
that the things that are foreseen are not contingent by necessity; rather, the things that are going to be are necessarily foreseen. Ha! As if the contention were which is the cause of which—whether foreknowledge of future things is the cause of the necessity, or whether the necessity of future things is the cause of the foreseeing. *This* is what we are striving to demonstrate: Exactly how the order of causes is constituted is irrelevant—there is a necessary result of foreknown things, even if the foreknowledge does not seem to impose a necessity of resulting on future events. In fact, if someone is sitting, it is necessarily the case that the   10
opinion that conjectures that he is sitting is true; and then again, from the other side, if it is a true opinion about someone that he is sitting, it is necessarily the case that he is sitting. Consequently, necessity is present in   11
either case: in the latter, the necessity of the sitting; in the other, the necessity of the truth of the opinion. But it is not for *this* reason, that the   12
opinion is true, that someone is sitting; rather, this opinion is true because the fact of a man's sitting preceded it. Thus, even though the cause of   13
truth proceeds from only one side, there is present all the same a common necessity on both sides. A similar line of reasoning is obvious concerning   14

3.6 unshakable (III.6.6 (immovably), V.3.27), indefinite (cf. V.3.19), wicked . . . God (III.10.15), wicked (IV.6.37, V.3.23).   3.7 (cf. V.4.4, V.5.2), line of reasoning (III.10.10, 24; III.11.9, IV.6.15).   3.8 falls to the other side (cf. III.3.16).   3.9 contingent (V.4.12), constituted (cf. V.3.18, 21), order of causes (IV.6.20; cf. IV.6.19, V.1.8, 19 (interweaving)), result (V.1.8, V.4.6). 3.10 opinion (V.3.6), from the other side (cf. V.3.8).   3.12 preceded (IV.4.11).   3.14 similar line of reasoning (III.9.21, V.3.7), independent judgment (V.3.5).

Providence and future events. For even if things are foreseen because they are going to happen, and they do not happen because they are foreseen, it is nevertheless the case that things to come are foreseen by God, or that things foreseen by God happen as they were foreseen to happen. This alone is sufficient to destroy the freedom of independent judgment.

15 16   What's more, how utterly backwards it is to say that the outcome of temporal events is the cause of eternal knowledge! To judge that God foresees future things for *this* reason, that they are going to happen— what else is this but to think that things that happened at some point before are the cause of his most high Providence? In addition, just as when I know that something is, it is necessarily the case that that same thing be; similarly, when I know that something will be, it is necessarily the case that that same thing will be. And so it happens that the outcome of a foreseen event cannot be avoided. A last point. If someone were to think that something is otherwise than it is actually constituted—not only is that not knowledge, but it is a deceitful opinion, far removed from the truth of knowledge.

17

18

19   Therefore, if something is going to happen in such a way that its outcome is not a definite and necessary thing, how could it happen that its occurrence be foreknown? For true knowledge admits no admixture of falsity; in just the same way, whatever has been thought by knowledge cannot be in any way other than it was thought to be. Furthermore, the reason why such knowledge has no share of falsehood is that each action is necessarily constituted in just the same way that knowledge grasps that it is constituted. Well then! Tell me, what is the way in which God has foreknowledge that these indefinite things will occur? I mean, if he determines that things will inevitably happen that could possibly not happen, then he is mistaken, and it is wicked not only to hold this opinion but to speak it out loud as well. On the other hand, if it is his judgment that these things will be just as they are, so that he recognizes that they can just as well happen as not happen—what sort of foreknowledge

20

21

22 23

24

3.15 (answered at V.6.42–43), temporal (V.6.4, 12).   *3.16* most high Providence (IV.6.50).   *3.17* cannot be avoided (V.1.19 (inescapable), V.3.23 (inevitably)).   *3.18* constituted (V.3.9, 21), deceitful (cf. I.m.1.19, I.6.21, III.4.13, III.6.1, III.m.10.3 (false)).   *3.19* (restated at V.5.9), definite (cf. V.3.6, 24; V.m.3.7).   *3.20* falsity (V.3.28), thought (cf. V.4.36 (conception)).
3.21 constituted (V.3.18, V.4.23), grasps (IV.6.54, V.3.24, V.4.25, 26, 32).
3.22 well then (V.1.11, V.5.5), indefinite (V.3.6).   *3.23* inevitably (cf. V.1.19), mistaken (V.3.4, 5), wicked . . . as well (cf. IV.6.54), wicked (V.3.6).   *3.24* judgment (V.1.8), definite (V.3.19).

is this, which grasps nothing as definite, nothing as stable? Or in what   25
way is this different from that absurd prophecy of Tiresias in Horace?

Whatéver I sáy either wíll be or wón't be.

And really, how would divine Providence be superior to mere opinion if,   26
just as mortals do, it makes judgments about indefinite things that have
indefinite outcomes?

And yet, if within that source of all things, that most definite source,   27
there can be nothing that is indefinite, then there is a definite outcome
of those things which he, by his unshakable foreknowledge, knows will
be. So for this reason there is no freedom for human resolutions or for   28
human actions: The divine mind that sees all things in advance without
the miscalculation of falsity binds them and ties them all together for
one and only one result. And as soon as this is accepted, it is clear what   29
a great downfall of human affairs follows as its logical consequence. I   30
mean, rewards and punishments are set before good and evil people in
vain—no free and voluntary motion of their minds has deserved them.
That the righteous are rewarded and the unrighteous are punished, as is   31
now judged to be perfectly just—this will seem to be the most perfectly
unjust thing of all, for it would not be an individual will that directs
them, but the definite necessity of the future that forces them, to the
one or the other. Consequently, both virtues and vices would be noth-   32
ing; in their place would be a jumbled and indiscriminate confusion of
all merits. Nothing more wicked can be imagined than this: Since that
entire order of things is led out from Providence and since there is nothing permitted to mortal resolution, what happens is that our vices too
are to be referred to the creator of all good things.

Therefore: There is no reason to hope for something or to pray for   33
deliverance; for what would a person hope for or even pray to be delivered from if an unbendable sequence weaves together all the things that

---

3.25 (cf. V.5.12), Horace (*Satires* II.5.9).   *3.27* unshakable (V.3.6).

3.28 divine mind (*mens*: IV.6.7, 10, 20; V.5.11, V.6.10), resolutions (V.3.32), in
advance (V.3.4), miscalculation (II.4.22, II.5.30, III.2.4, III.3.1, III.9.4, IV.6.22,
V.4.24), falsity (V.3.20), binds (V.6.12), ties (IV.6.19, V.2.2).   *3.29* accepted
(V.3.35), logical consequence (IV.4.22, 25; V.4.22).   *3.30* rewards . . . set
before (V.6.44), in vain (V.4.16), voluntary (V.6.22), motion (III.11.30, V.2.2,
V.m.4.10–11), minds (*animus*).   *3.31* rewarded (IV.7.3), necessity (V.3.9, 11,
13, 35; V.4.4), forces (V.6.29).   *3.32* indiscriminate (IV.2.12), confusion
(IV.5.4, IV.6.23, 34; V.6.22), imagined (III.6.2), led out (IV.6.12), resolution
(V.3.28), what happens . . . good things (cf. IV.2.44), creator (= author:
III.m.6.8).   *3.33* no reason to hope (cf. V.6.46), weaves (cf. IV.6.19, V.1.19,
V.3.35), chosen (V.2.4).

34 could be chosen? Therefore: That one and only avenue of exchange between human beings and God will be taken away, the avenue of hope and prayer for deliverance; provided, of course, that for the price of our rightful humility we deserve the return of divine grace, which is beyond price. This is the only way by which human beings seem to be able to speak with God—by the act of supplication—and to be joined to that

35 inapproachable light even before they succeed in attaining it. Once the necessity of future events is accepted, if these hopes and prayers are then believed to have no force, what will there be by which we can be woven

36 together with and cling to that most high ruler of all things? And so it is, just as you were singing a little while ago, that it will necessarily be the case that the human race, separated and "cut off from its source, will burst at the seams."

Meter 3

Whát díscordant caúse tóre into piéces
Áll the world's cóncord? Whát gód has decreéd
Fór thése twó trúths súch bitter wárfare?
Eách stánding its groúnd séparate and équal,
5 Bút dráwing the líne at joíning togéther.
Ór coúld ít bé thére is no díscord—
Thát définite trúths ever clíng each to eách—
Bút mínd, búriéd bý body's blíndness,
Éxcépt by the fíre of líght deep-concéaled,
10 Cánnót see the wórld's bónds, microscópic?
Bút whý does it búrn wíth súch a great lóve
To discóver the trúth, trúth's hidden sígnposts?

3.34 humility (III.8.3), only way (cf. IV.6.8, 21, 28), supplication (III.8.3), inapproachable light (cf. 1 Timothy 6:16), inapproachable (cf. V.6.25), light (III.m.9.23, III.m.10.17, IV.m.1.18). 3.35 accepted (V.3.29), woven (V.3.33), cling (III.2.6, III.11.28, IV.6.16), ruler (III.10.7, 9, 14; IV.6.9). 3.36 a little while ago (at IV.m.6.40–43).

Meter 3 V.m.3.1 discordant (V.m.3.6), tore into pieces (cf. I.1.5, I.3.7, III.12.23, IV.6.49). 3.2 world's concord (I.m.5.43; cf. IV.m.6.4–5). 3.3 warfare (II.m.8.18, IV.m.6.18–24). 3.4 separate (cf. V.m.3.21, 24, 30–31 (parts)). 3.6 discord (V.m.3.1). 3.7 definite (V.3.19, 24), cling (V.3.35). 3.8 buried (V.1.15, 17), blindness (II.4.26, IV.2.31), body's blindness (cf. V.m.3.22). 3.9 light (I.m.7.20–22, III.m.9.23, V.3.34). 3.10 microscopic (I.1.3, III.9.3). 3.11 burn (III.1.4, IV.6.51), love (II.m.8.17, IV.m.6.16, 44–48). 3.12 truth's signposts (III.11.40).

Does it knów ít knóws what it frétfully seéks?
Whó strúggles to knów thát which he doés know?
Bút íf he knows nót, whý look for blínd things?   15
Whát ígnorant mán coúld máke any choíce?
Whó hás thé stréngth tó cháse the unknówn?
Whére would he fínd it? Whó then could seé it,
Its fórm thus discóvered, íf unenlíghtened?
Ór, whén it behéld the dépths of divíne mind,   20
Did it knów thése trúths, thé whóle and its párts?
Now hídden in dárk clouds, límbs of the bódy,
Ít doés not forgét sélf absolútely,
Ánd lóses the párts bút clíngs to the whóle?
Thús, whóévér seárches for trué things   25
Hás neíther condítion: for he doés nót knów,
Nór does he *nót* know, áll things complétely.
With an éye on the whóle, képt and remémbered,
Hé pónders anéw the dépths he once gázed on,
Thát he may ádd to párts that were képt safe   30
    Párts once forgótten.

Prose 4

Then she said: This is an old complaint about Providence. It was a topic
passionately discussed by Cicero when he broke divination into its constituent parts; you pursued it yourself over quite a long period of time
and at great length. However, up until now it has been in no way adequately dealt with by any one of you in a painstaking and rigorous way.
Here is the cause of all this darkness: The motion of human rational   2

3.13 fretfully (III.2.18, III.3.5).   3.14 struggles (= works at: II.7.9, III.2.5, 15;
III.11.20).   3.15 blind (V.m.3.8).   3.16 choice (V.2.4–5, V.3.33).
3.19 form (V.4.32).   3.20 depths of divine mind (cf. III.m.9.16–17, III.m.11.1,
IV.6.16, 32).   3.21 parts (V.m.3.4, 24, 30–31).   3.22 hidden in dark clouds
(cf. V.m.3.8), clouds (I.2.6, III.m.11.7, IV.m.5.21, V.2.10), limbs (III.m.6.5).
3.23 forget (cf. I.2.6, IV.4.31, V.m.3.31).   3.26 condition (II.1.2, III.1.3).
3.28 whole (V.m.3.21, 24).   3.29 depths (V.m.3.20).   3.31 parts
(V.m.3.21, 24).

Prose 4 V.4.1 complaint (I.2.1, II.2.2, 7; IV.1.7; cf. I.1.14), passionately (III.12.1,
15 (utter), IV.4.6, IV.5.4 (utterly)).   4.2 darkness (I.1.3 (gloom), I.6.21,
IV.6.1, V.4.23), rational argument (III.10.21, IV.6.17, V.5.5), simplicity (IV.6.4,
55; V.5.12, V.6.12, 15).

argument cannot set itself next to the simplicity of divine foreknowledge. If this could in any way be imagined, there would then be abso-
3   lutely no doubt about it remaining. I shall try at the end to make this
clear to you and explain it to you, provided that I can first get the heft of
4   the things that have got you upset. I want to know why you hold that
one line of reasoning offered by those who would solve this problem is
less than productive—the line of reasoning that holds that freedom of
independent judgment is not obstructed by foreknowledge, because it
thinks that foreknowledge is not a cause of necessity for future events.
5   You aren't drawing your argument about the necessity of future things
from any other source, are you, than that things that are foreseen cannot
6   *not* happen? Therefore: If foreknowledge places no necessity upon future
events—a thing that you yourself admitted a little while ago—what reason is there for the voluntary outcomes of events to be forced toward a
definite result?

7   And further, just for the sake of argument, so you can see what the
8   logical consequence is, let us claim that there is no foreknowledge. It
isn't the case then, is it, as far as this situation is concerned, that such
things as come from independent judgment are forced toward necessity?
Hardly.

9   Next, let us claim that there is foreknowledge, but that it binds no
necessity on events; there will remain unchanged, I think, that same
10 freedom of the will, whole and absolute. But foreknowledge, you will say,
even if there is no necessity of their resulting for future things, is never-
11 theless a sign that such things are necessarily going to occur. And so it is
in this way that it would be agreed that the outcomes of future things are
necessary, even if there is no cognition beforehand; the point being that
every sign merely *shows* what is, but is not *productive* of what it points to.
12 For this reason, what would have to be shown first is that there is no
contingency except through necessity, so that it may be manifest that
foreknowledge is a sign of this necessity. Otherwise, if there were no

---

4.3 make clear (III.10.29, III.11.4, V.6.3), explain (V.1.1).   4.4 line of reasoning (at V.3.7; IV.6.15, V.4.13, V.5.2), productive (IV.4.11, V.4.11, V.m.4.26), foreknowledge . . . future events (cf. V.4.20).   4.5 drawing (V.6.28), cannot not
happen (cf. V.6.25).   4.6 a little while ago (at V.3.9). result (V.1.8).
4.7 just so . . . consequence is (cf. IV.7.1).   4.8 forced (V.4.6), hardly (IV.4.33,
V.4.16, V.6.19).   4.9 I think (I.4.32, II.3.9), whole and absolute (III.10.5),
absolute (V.6.31; = divorced from: V.4.18, V.5.1).   4.10 you (singular), you
will say (IV.6.23, V.4.21, V.6.37), sign (V.4.11, 12, 13), occur (V.4.20).
4.11 cognition beforehand (V.4.19), productive (V.4.4).   4.12 contingency
(V.3.9, V.6.25), through necessity (V.5.10).

such necessity, it could not be a sign of an event that does not exist. However, it is already agreed that a proof that rests upon an unshakable 13 line of argument must be drawn neither from signs nor from arguments that are sought in what is external to it, but rather from causes that are appropriate and necessary. But how can it happen that those things do 14 not come to pass that are foreseen as things that are going to be? As if we were to believe that what Providence foreknows as things that are going to be are not going to happen! As if we were to believe this instead, that, granted that they do happen, they nevertheless had by their own nature no necessity that they happen!

Now this objection you will be able to weigh easily in the balance, from 15 this consideration. There are in fact many things that we gaze upon while they are happening, things subject to our eyes. For example, the things that charioteers are seen to do as they guide their teams and give them rein, and all the other things of this sort. Surely it is not the case here, is it, 16 that any necessity compels any of these things to happen as they do?

Hardly; if all these were forced actions that were set into motion, the effect of the driver's skill would be all in vain.

Therefore: The things that lack the necessity of their existence while 17 they are happening are things which, before they happen, are going to exist without necessity. For this reason there are certain things that will 18 happen whose outcome is divorced from all necessity. In fact, I think 19 that no one would say this, that things that are now happening were not about to result before they happened? Consequently, these things, even if there were cognition beforehand, have free outcomes. For knowledge 20 of present events brings in with it no necessity to the things that are happening; and in just the same way foreknowledge of future events brings in no necessity to the things that are going to occur.

But, you say, this is itself a source of doubt: *Can* there be any fore- 21 knowledge of those events that do not have necessary outcomes? They 22 do indeed seem to be discordant: you think that if things are foreseen

---

4.13 rests upon (IV.4.32, 37), unshakable (I.2.3, IV.1.7, IV.2.3), line of reasoning (V.4.4), sought . . . external to it (III.3.14; cf. III.10.12, III.12.11), appropriate (IV.6.30, 36; V.1.11).   4.14 come to pass (V.5.10), by their own nature (III.10.15, V.4.24).   4.15 weigh in the balance (IV.6.4, 56; V.4.29), gaze upon (V.4.26), subject (IV.6.14, V.1.8), rein (V.m.1.12).   4.16 in vain (II.m.7.8, IV.2.6, V.3.30, V.6.46).   4.18 divorced from (V.5.1; cf. V.4.9 (absolute)).   4.20 brings in (III.5.3), occur (V.4.10).   4.21 you (singular), necessary outcomes (cf. V.4.19, 23), doubt (cf. III.12.17).   4.22 discordant (I.4.44; cf. V.m.3.1, 6), logical consequence (III.9.12, IV.4.36, IV.7.1, V.4.7) grasped (V.3.21,24; V.6.7, 8, 15), knowledge (V.3.18, 20, 21; V.6.1, 15, 33, 42, 43).

then necessity is the logical consequence; you think that there can in no way be foreknowledge if necessity is absent; you think that nothing can
23   be grasped by knowledge unless it is a definite thing. For if things that are characterized by indefinite outcomes are foreseen as if they were definite, that would be the darkness of opinion and not the truth of knowledge; for you believe that it is opposed to the infallibility of knowledge to
24   think of a thing in some way other than it is constituted. The cause of this miscalculation is that it judges that all the things that a person knows are perceived only in accordance with the force and nature of the
25   things which are known themselves. But it is completely the opposite. Everything that is perceived is grasped not according to its own force but rather according to the capability of those who perceive it.

26   To make this clear with a brief example: Vision and touch, each in its distinct way, recognize the same three-dimensionality of a body. The former, at a distance, remaining itself unmoved, gazes upon the whole thing all at once by casting its rays; the latter, adhering to its curvature and joined to it, set in motion on all sides of the surface itself, grasps its
27   three-dimensionality part by part. Similarly, sense perception, imagination, reason, and understanding, each in its distinct way, view the same
28   human being. For sense perception judges the shape as it has been constituted in its subject material, while imagination judges the shape alone,
29   without its material; reason transcends this as well and from its universal point of view weighs in the balance that very appearance that is present
30   in all individuals. And the eye of understanding exists as something higher yet; for it has passed beyond what is encompassed by universality and views the one simple form itself in the pure vision of the mind.

31   In all of this, here is the one point that must be considered in particular: Namely, that the higher power of comprehension embraces the lower,
32   but in no way does the lower rise to the level of the higher. For sense perception has no power beyond what is material; imagination does not view universal appearances; reason does not grasp the simple form. Understanding, however, looking down as it were from on high, grasps the form

---

4.23 darkness (V.4.2; cf. V.m.3.8–10), infallibility (IV.6.24), constituted (V.3.9, 18, 21).   4.24 miscalculation (V.3.28).   4.25 (cf. V.4.39, V.6.1), perceived (V.6.1), grasped (V.4.22), capability (V.4.38).   4.26 gazes (V.4.15).
4.27 sense perception . . . understanding (cf. V.5.3–4).   4.28 subject material (V.1.9).   4.29 transcends (IV.m.1.8), weighs in the balance (V.4.15, V.6.26), individuals (= particulars: cf. V.5.6, V.6.36).   4.30 eye (V.6.38), exists (V.4.39), passed beyond (V.6.15), universality (V.5.7), pure (IV.m.6.1), mind (V.m.3.20).   4.31 comprehension (= grasping; cf. V.4.22, 25).   4.32 looking down (cf. V.6.45).

and then judges separately the things that are beneath it, all of them; but it does so in the way in which it comprehends the form itself, which could not be known to any of the other powers. For it perceives reason's univer- 33 sal and imagination's shape and sense perception's material, but not by using reason or imagination or the senses but by the characteristic single stroke of mind, formally, if I may use the word, seeing all things in advance. And reason similarly: When it views something universal, it com- 34 prehends the things that can be perceived by imagination and the senses, but not by using imagination or the senses. This is reason, and it defines 35 the universal of its own conception this way: A human being is a two-legged, rational animal. And although this is a universal knowledge, there 36 is no one who is unaware that its object is a thing of the imagination and a thing of sense perception as well, yet a thing that this knowledge looks at not by imagination and not by sense but in its state of rational conception.

And imagination similarly: Even if it has taken from the senses the 37 starting point of seeing and forming shapes, nevertheless it is in the absence of sense that it casts its gaze over each and every thing of the senses by a rationale of judgment that is not of the senses but of the imagi-nation. So do you see how in perception all things use their own capability 38 rather than the capability of the things that are perceived? And not with- 39 out cause: For since every judgment exists as an act of the one who judges, it is necessarily the case that all who judge bring their work to completion by their own true powers, and not by a power outside of themselves.

Meter 4

Ónce, óld Stóic philósophý
Broúght fórth ríddling, obscúre old mén:
Sénse pércéptions and ímagés,

4.33 single stroke of mind (V.m.2.11, V.6.40), seeing all things in advance (V.2.11, V.3.4, 28; V.6.17).   4.34 similarly (V.4.37), perceived by . . . the senses (V.5.6).   4.35 human being (cf. I.6.15–17, IV.6.41).   4.36 knowl-edge (*notio*: V.m.4.17, V.5.7, V.6.26, 31, 43), no one (III.12.26, IV.2.22), looks at (V.6.3, 15), conception (III.10.7, V.4.35, V.5.6).   4.37 similarly (V.4.34), starting point (III.9.33, III.10.5, IV.6.19 (loom), IV.6.22).   4.38 (cf. V.4.25), you (singular), so do you see (II.7.9, IV.3.1, IV.7.1).   4.39 not without cause (III.6.1, IV.3.2, IV.4.1 (improperly), V.6.36), for since . . . who judges (V.6.15), exists as (V.4.30), one who judges (cf. V.6.48), bring to completion (IV.2.17, IV.4.3), true powers (II.6.13).

Meter 4 V.m.4.3 (cf. V.4.28).

Théy béliéved, were impréssed on mínds
5 Fróm thé oútermost skín of thíngs.
Á swíft stýlus does múch the sáme,
Ón á páge's smooth súrface cálm,
Imprínting létters now deép-impréssed
Whére thére wére no such sígns befóre.
10 Bút íf mínd with its próper stréngth,
Própér mótions, unfólds no trúths—
Liés stíll ín its passívitý,
Júst súbjéct to the sígns of thíngs,
To réprodúce, as a mírror doés,
15 The émptý ímage of wórldly thíngs—
Whénce thís stréngth in the húman mínd?
Whénce thís knówledge that seés all thíngs?
What fórce seés séparate thíngs so cleár?
Whát fórce séparates whát is knówn?
20 Whát fórce gáthers the séparate párts?
Whát fórce choóses the twófold páth,
Thrústs íts heád in the híghest reálms,
Goés báck dówn to the dépths belów,
Thén retúrns to itsélf its sélf,
25 Thús tó cóntradict fálse with trúe?
Seé á fár more prodúctive caúse,
Móre fár-reáching, more pówerfúl,
Thán thát caúse which, as mátter doés,
Áccépts pássively sígns impréssed.
30 Nónethéléss, there is pássive fórce
Whích précédes, which excítes and stírs

4.4 impressed (V.m.4, 8, 29).   4.5 outermost (IV.6.15).   4.6 stylus
(I.1.1, I.4.25).   4.8 letters (I.1.4, II.m.7.18 (inscriptions)), impressed
(V.m.4.29).   4.9 signs (V.m.4.13, 29, 38; III.11.40, V.m.3.12 (signposts)).
4.10 strength (I.1.1, V.m.4.35).   4.11 motions (II.5.9, III.m.11.30, V.3.30),
unfolds (IV.6.1, 10, 54).   4.12 passivity (V.m.4.29, 30).   4.15 empty image
(III.10.2; cf. III.3.1).   4.16–25 (cf. V.m.3.1–24 (questions)).
4.16 strength (V.m.4.10, 35).   4.17 knowledge (V.4.36, V.5.7, V.6.26, 31, 43).
4.21–25 (cf. I.1.2, III.m.10.13–18, III.m.12.52–58, IV.m.1.23–30).
4.22 thrusts (I.m.1.13).   4.22–23 highest/depths (cf. II.2.9, II.m.7.13–14).
4.24 (cf. III.m.9.15–17).   4.25 contradict (II.6.19).   4.26 productive
(V.2.7, V.4.4).   4.29 passively (V.m.4.12, 32), signs (V.m.4.8, 13, 38),
impressed (V.m.4.8).   4.31 precedes (V.3.12, V.5.1), excites and stirs
(IV.m.4.1; cf. III.m.10.13).

Mínd's ówn stréngth in the bódy's lífe,
Ás whén líght batters át the éyes,
Ór whén voíces ring ín the eárs.
Thén thé stréngth of the mínd, aroúsed,　　　　　　　35
Dráws áppeárances képt withín,
Cálled tó mótions as líke to líke,
Poínts thém tó these extérnal sígns,
Thús tó míngle with ímagés
Thóse trué fórms that were hoúsed withín.　　　　　　40

Prose 5

When physical objects are perceived by the senses—even though their qualities, presented from the outside, exert an influence on the instruments of sense perception, even though the strength of the active mind is preceded by the passivity of the body, which calls forth an act of the mind within the body and arouses the forms that have hitherto been dormant within—when, as I was saying, physical objects are perceived by the senses, if it is the case that the mind is not in passivity impressed by a sign, but by its own strength judges the passivity to which the body is subject, well then! To an even greater extent do the things that are divorced from all of the external influences exerted on bodies set the action of their own minds free in their acts of judgment, not pursuing the things presented to them externally. And so it is, according to this　2 line of reasoning, that multiple modes of perception have been allotted to the various substances, different among themselves. For sense and　3 sense alone, deprived of all other modes of perception, has been allotted to animate creatures without self-motion (to the shellfish of the sea, for example, and to other such things as cling to rocks); while imagination

---

4.33 batters/eyes (I.m.3.10).　　4.35 strength (IV.m.3.33 (life force), V.m.4.10, 31).　　4.36 appearances (V.4.32), appearances within (cf. V.m.4.40). 4.38 signs (V.m.4.8, 13, 29).　　4.39–40 (cf. III.m.11.11–16, V.5.1). 4.39 mingle (I.m.6.19 (confusion)).

Prose 5　V.5.1 mind/mind/mind/minds (animus/mens/animus/mens), even though . . . dormant within (cf. V.m.4.30–40), strength (I.1.1, V.m.4.16), mind is not . . . by a sign (cf. V.m.4.10–15), divorced (V.4.18), external influences (I.6.21), externally (III.3.14, V.4.13).　　5.2 line of reasoning (V.3.7, V.4.4), multiple (IV.6.8 (complex)), allotted (V.5.3).　　5.3 sense (V.4.28), deprived (III.11.39), of the sea (cf. III.m.8.9–14), cling to rocks (III.11.19), imagination (V.4.28, 32), desire (II.1.2), avoided and chosen (V.2.4; cf. V.3.33).

is allotted to beasts with self-motion, who seem to have within them already some desire for what must be avoided and what must be chosen.

4   On the other hand, reason is the property of the human race only, just as understanding alone is the property of the divine; and so it is that that particular way of knowing excels all the others which, by its own nature, perceives not only what is properly subject to it, but the subjects of all the other ways of knowing as well.

5   Well then! What if sense and imagination were to speak against rational argument, and say that the universal which reason thinks it gazes

6   upon is nothing at all? After all, they could say that what can be perceived by sense or imagination cannot be universal; consequently, either reason's judgment is true and nothing that can be perceived by sense truly exists; or, since sense and imagination are well aware that there are many things subject to them, reason's conception is a thing devoid of meaning, since reason contemplates a particular thing, one that can be

7   perceived by sense, as though it were some sort of universal. Now let reason answer these arguments and counter them; let it say that it does indeed look upon what can be perceived by sense and imagination, but in accordance with the reason which is directed toward the universal, while they cannot aim at the mode of perception that is directed toward the universal; let it argue that the knowledge possessed by sense and imagination cannot go beyond the bounds of the shapes of physical bodies, whereas one should rather put one's trust in a stronger and more powerful judgment for the perception of what truly exists. So if there were to be a dispute along these lines, oughtn't we, who have within us the force of reason as well as of imagination and sense perception, give our approval rather to the case presented by reason, you and I?

8   The situation is similar with human reason: It does not think that divine intelligence gazes upon future things in any other way than it per-

9   ceives them itself. For your discourse is as follows: If there are some things that are not seen to have definite and necessary outcomes, then there

---

5.4 reason (V.4.29, 34–36), understanding (V.4.30, 32–33), particular way . . . knowing as well (cf. V.4.31), own nature (IV.4.37).   5.5 well then (V.1.11, V.3.22, V.6.18), speak against (III.10.17, V.1.9), rational argument (IV.6.17, V.4.2), gazes upon (V.5.8, 12).   5.6 perceived by sense or imagination (V.5.7; cf. V.4.34), subject (V.6.15), conception (III.10.7, V.4.35–36), devoid of meaning (V.1.8), particular/universal (cf. V.6.36).   5.7 answer (I.6.11, IV.4.20, V.6.26, 38), aim at (II.4.25; cf. I.3.14), shapes of physical bodies (cf. V.4.26–28), trust (V.6.6), stronger (I.6.21, III.10.18, IV.6.57), dispute (cf. II.2.3).   5.8 divine intelligence (cf. V.5.4, 11), gazes upon (V.5.5).   5.9 your (singular), discourse (III.6.5, IV.6.7), as follows (cf. at V.3.19), definite (I.m.6.20, V.3.19).

can be no definite foreknowledge of them as outcomes. Consequently,   10
there is *no* foreknowledge of these events; were we to believe that there is
foreknowledge in these things as well, there will then be nothing that
does not come to pass through necessity. And yet, consequently, were we   11
able to possess the judgment of the divine mind in just the same way as
we are partakers of reason, then we would think it most just that human
reason surrender to the divine mind in just the same way that we judged
that imagination and sense perception ought to yield to reason. And for   12
this reason let us raise ourselves up, if we can, into the head of that highest intelligence, for it is in that place that reason will see what it cannot
gaze upon within itself, and that is this: in just what way a fixed and definite foreknowledge can still see even those things that do not have definite outcomes, and how this is not mere conjecture but the simplicity of
the highest knowledge instead, knowledge bounded by no limits.

Meter 5

Ánimate béings in hów many shápes and forms páss acróss the
                                       lándscape!
Sóme háve bódiés strétched and elóngated, sweéping oút their dúst-
                                           trails;
Dríven by stróng désíre they léngthen out óne unbróken fúrrow.
Óthers, caprícious, take wíng in their weíghtlessness, beáting wínd and
                                     témpest,
Skímming expánses of límitless átmosphere in flúid éxaltátion.   5
Óthers delíght to set foót on the sólid earth, stríding throúgh the greén
                                        fields,
Ínto the greénwood and únder its cánopy, wíth a fírm impréssion.
Thoúgh you may wítness in thése many shápes and forms nóthing bút
                                        discórdance,

5.10 come to pass (V.4.14, V.6.21), through necessity (V.4.12, V.6.25).
5.11 human reason (V.5.8), judged (at V.5.5–7).   5.12 raise ourselves up (cf.
IV.1.9, IV.m.1.1–4, V.m.4.21–25), if we can (cf. V.6.1), head (IV.2.23; cf. I.1.2,
V.m.5.10), gaze upon (V.5.5, 8), do not have definite outcomes (cf. V.4.17–23,
V.5.9), simplicity (IV.6.17; cf. IV.6.20, V.3.28, V.4.30).

Meter 5 V.m.5.1 animate beings (cf. III.11.11–17; cf. II.6.4, III.3.1 (creatures)).
5.4–5 (birds: cf. III.m.2.17–26).   5.4 weightlessness (= lightness; cf.
V.m.5.11).   5.5 (cf. IV.m.1.1–10).   5.7 impression (V.m.4.8).   5.8 you
(singular), many shapes and forms (cf. V.m.5.1), discordance (= are different:
III.10.33, III.11.5; cf. V.4.22).

Theírs is the dówncást coúntenance, cápable of weíghing dówn dull
                                                        sénses.
10 Nót so the ráce óf·mórtál mén, who can líft their úpraised heáds high,
Stánd wíth bódy upríght and impónderous, loók to eárth belów them.
Bé not a creáture of eárth! Be not ígnorant! The pósture thús remínds
                                                            you:
Yoú whó reách for the heíghts with your úpturned gaze, poínting fáce to
                                                            heáven,
Yoú must lift spírit as wéll to such áltitude— mínd must nót be weíghed
                                                            down,
15 Múst nót sínk down belów where the bódy is, raísed to hígher státure.

Prose 6

Therefore: Since, as has been shown just a little while ago, everything that
is known is perceived not in accordance with its own nature but rather the
nature of those who grasp it—let us now look closely, as far as is allowed,
at what is the condition of the divine substance, so that we may be able to
2   recognize what its knowledge is as well. Therefore: It is the common judg-
3   ment of all who live in accordance with reason that God is eternal. Therefore, let us look at what eternity is, for this will make obvious to us the
divine nature and the divine knowledge at one and the same time.

4   Therefore: Eternity is a possession of life, a possession simultaneously
entire and perfect, which has no end. This becomes clear in a more trans-
5   parent way from a comparison with temporal things. For whatever exists
in time proceeds as a present thing from the things that have happened

---

5.9 weighing down (V.m.5.14), dull senses (cf. I.m.2.2 (loses its edge)).
5.10 lift high (cf. V.m.5.15), heads (I.1.2, V.5.12).   5.11 imponderous (cf.
V.m.5.4), look to earth (IV.m.1.4).   5.12 creature of earth (II.6.4, III.3.1), you
(singular).   5.13 (cf. III.m.12.52–58, IV.m.7.32–36).   5.14 weighed down
(V.m.5.9).   5.15 sink (IV.m.6.24).

Prose 6 V.6.1 been shown (III.12.13), little while ago (at V.4.25; cf. V.4.38), per-
ceived/grasp (V.4.25), look closely (III.12.10), allowed (cf. I.4.30, V.5.12), condi-
tion (II.4.12, V.6.15), able to recognize (I.6.21).   6.2 common judgment (cf.
III.10.7, III.12.8), accordance with reason (II.4.25), God is eternal (V.6.14).
6.3 look at (III.11.13, 15; V.4.36, V.6.15), make obvious (= make clear:
III.10.29, III.11.4, V.4.3), same time (V.6.5, 8, 10, 12, 22).   6.4 eternity
(II.7.15, 18; IV.6.17, V.6.45), entire (V.6.5), has no end (II.7.4), temporal
(V.3.15, V.6.12).   6.5 established (III.10.1, IV.6.9, V.6.43), embrace
(III.11.32, IV.6.10, 53; V.4.31, V.6.7, 13, 40), entire space . . . same time (cf.
V.6.12), gain (III.9.21, IV.2.29), you (plural), swift . . . moment (cf. V.6.12),
swift (V.6.8).

into the things that are going to happen, and there is nothing that has been established in time that is able to embrace the entire space of its own life at one and the same time. Instead, it does not yet gain what is tomorrow's, but has already lost what is yesterday's; furthermore, within the life that is today's, none of you lives to any greater extent than in that swift and passing moment. Therefore: That which endures the condition of 6 time—even granted that, as Aristotle has judged to be true about the world, it did not begin to exist at any time, nor would it cease to exist, and its life would be extended to the infinity of time—it is, for all that, not the sort of thing that can rightly be believed to be eternal. For it does not grasp 7 and embrace the entire extent of its life, even though it is infinite, simultaneously; rather, it does not yet have the future things, and the things that have been completed it has no longer. Therefore: That which grasps and 8 possesses the entire fullness of a life that has no end at one and the same time (nothing that is to come being absent to it, nothing of what has passed having flowed away from it) is rightly held to be eternal. Further, it is necessary both that, as master of itself, it always be present to itself as a present thing and that it always have the infinity of swift time as present.

There are certain people who think, when they hear that it was Plato's 9 opinion that the world neither had a beginning in time nor would it ever disappear, that in this way the created world is coeternal with its creator. But from these considerations, they do not think correctly. For it is one 10 thing to be drawn out through a life that has no end (this is what Plato assigned to the world), and quite another to have embraced the entire presentness of a life which has no end at one and the same time (this is what perfectly clearly is appropriate to the divine mind). Further, God 11 ought not to be seen as more ancient and glorious than created things by the measurement of time, but rather by the distinctive character of his own simple nature. For that infinite motion of temporal things imitates 12

6.6 endures (IV.m.3.28), condition (V.6.23, 27, 28, 29, 31, 33), Aristotle (V.1.12), judged (IV.6.24), the world (cf. Aristotle, *de Caelo* I.12, 283b26 ff.), infinity of time (V.6.8), rightly believed (III.10.38, III.12.17, V.5.7).   6.7 embrace (V.6.5). 6.8 entire fullness of life (V.6.12), has no end (V.6.4), held to be (III.10.3, 4, 12), attend to (cf. I.1.7 (sitting at)), infinity of time (V.6.6), swift (V.6.5).   6.9 Plato (I.3.6, I.4.5, III.9.32, III.m.11.15, III.12.1, 38; IV.2.45, V.6.10, 14), creator (I.m.5.1, I.6.4, IV.m.6.34, V.m.2.7), opinion (cf. *Timaeus* 28b ff.).   6.10 appropriate (II.6.17), divine mind (IV.6.7, 10, 20; V.3.28, V.5.11).   6.11 more ancient (III.10.9), distinctive character (V.6.21), simple nature (cf. III.12. 30, IV.6.8, V.6.41).   6.12 temporal things (V.6.4), motionless (IV.6.19), falls away (IV.2.28), to come/passed (V.6.8, 15), entire fullness . . . same time (cf. V.6.5, 8), fullness (V.6.8, 13), satisfy (II.2.17, IV.4.3), binding (V.3.28), minuscule (II.7.4, 6; III.8.7), swiftly (IV.m.1.1, 21; IV.m.4.4), are seen (V.5.7).

this present-moment condition of motionless life. Since the former cannot represent or equal the latter, it falls away from motionlessness into
motion and devolves from the simplicity of the present into the infinite
quantity of what is to come and what has passed; and since it is not able
to possess the entire fullness of its own life at one and the same time,
then, for this very reason, because it never ceases to be (in some way or
other) that which it cannot satisfy or express, it seems to rival it to some
small degree by binding itself to any sort of presentness it can of this
minuscule and swiftly-passing moment. Because this presentness carries
within itself a sort of image of that other, stable present, it provides *this* to
whatever things it happens to come in contact with: that is, that they are
13   seen to be. But, because such a thing could not be stable, it started rapidly down the infinite road of time and it is in this way that it happened
that it protracted its life through motion, the life whose fullness it was not
14   able to embrace by remaining unchanged. Consequently, if we want to
impose on things names that are worthy of them, let us follow Plato and
say that God is eternal, but that the world is perpetual.
15   Therefore: Since every judgment grasps the things that are subject to
it in accordance with its own nature, and since God has an ever-eternal
and ever-present-moment condition, his knowledge as well has passed
beyond all the motion of time and is stable in the simplicity of its own
present; it embraces the infinite reaches of what has passed and what is to
come and, in its own simple perception, it looks at all things as if they are
16   being carried out *now*. And so, should you want to ponder the foresight
by which God distinguishes all things, you will more accurately determine
that it is not a foreknowledge as of something that is to come, but rather
17   a knowledge of a never-failing present. From these considerations, it is not
named Previdence (foresight) but Providence (looking out), because,
established far from the bottommost things, it looks out at all things as if

---

6.13 stable (V.6.15), started . . . road (IV.7.10), protracted (I.5.1), fullness (V.6.8,
12), embrace (V.6.7), remaining unchanged (III.11.24).   6.14 want (V.6.39
(wish for)), Plato (cf. *Timaeus* 37d ff.), perpetual (II.m.8.4, III.m.9.1; cf. I.m.5.2,
III.4.14 (forever)).   6.15 every judgment . . . own nature (cf. V.4.39, 24–25;
V.6.1), eternal (V.6.14), present-moment condition (V.6.12, 43; cf. IV.6.12 (in a
single moment)), condition (V.6.1), passed beyond (V.4.30), stable (V.6.12, 13;
cf. V.6.44, 45 (remains unchanged)), simplicity . . . present (V.6.12), infinite
reaches (II.7.15), passed/to come (V.6.8, 12; cf. V.6.7), simple perception (cf.
IV.6.8), perception (IV.6.4, V.5.2, 3, 7; V.6.24), looks at (V.4.36), carried out
(IV.6.8, 13).   6.16 you (singular), foresight (cf. V.3.4, V.4.22), distinguishes
(IV.6.28, V.2.4, V.6.22).   6.17 these considerations (V.6.9), bottommost
(II.5.26, 27), lofty (V.6.47), head (I.1.2, IV.2.43, V.5.12).

from some lofty head of things. Well then! Do you demand that the   18
things that the light of the divine eye passes over come about as necessary
things, when not even human beings cause the things that they see to be
as necessary things? Why would you? Surely your gaze does not add any   19
necessity to those things that you perceive as present? Hardly. And yet, if   20
there is any worthy comparison between the divine present and the
human present—just as you humans see certain individual things in this
time-bounded present of yours, he perceives all things in his own eternal
present. And it is for this reason that this divine foreknowledge does not   21
change the nature and the distinctive character of things; it looks at such
things as are present to it just as they will eventually come to pass in time
as future things. Nor does it confuse its judgments; rather, with the single   22
gaze of its own mind, it distinguishes both what will happen of necessity
as well as what will happen, but not of necessity. Similarly, when you mortals see in the same way both a man walking upon the earth and the sun
rising in the heavens, although each of these two has been observed at
one and the same time, nevertheless you tell them apart and judge that
the former is voluntary and the latter is necessary. Therefore: The divine   23
gaze, by discerning all things in this way, does not at all confuse the quality of the things which are, to be sure, present to it but which, in respect
of their condition in time, are going to come to pass. And so it happens   24
that this is not mere opinion but rather perception supported by truth,
that the same thing which it knows will arise it does not fail to know lacks
the necessity of coming into being.

Now if you should say at this point that what God sees will happen   25
cannot *not* happen, and that what cannot not happen is contingent by
necessity, and if you bind me tight to this word "necessity," then I will
admit that it is indeed a thing of the most steadfast truth, but one that
scarcely anyone but a contemplator of the divine has approached. For I   26

6.18 well then (V.5.5, V.6.33, 39), divine eye (cf. V.4.30, V.6.38), passes over (cf.
III.m.9.23 (ring round)).   6.19 your (singular), gaze (V.2.11, V.6.22, 23), add
(cf. V.4.20, V.6.29), hardly (V.6.40).   6.20 worthy (V.6.14).   6.21 distinctive character (V.6.11), looks at . . . future things (cf. V.6.23, 31).   6.22 single
(cf. V.4.33, V.6.40 (single stroke)), gaze of its mind (III.9.24), distinguishes
(V.6.16), man walking (V.6.27; cf. V.3.10–12 (man sitting)), man/sun (cf.
V.6.34), same time (V.6.3), tell apart (IV.6.26, V.2.4), voluntary (V.3.30).
6.23 divine gaze (V.6.31), quality (V.6.45), condition in time (V.6.6).
6.24 opinion (V.3.18), perception (V.6.15).   6.25 (cf. V.3.4), you (singular),
contingent by necessity (V.3.9), steadfast (III.10.6, IV.1.7), approached (cf. V.3.34).
6.26 I shall answer (V.6.38), referred (IV.6.8), knowledge (V.6.31, 43), weighed
in the balance (V.4.15, 29).

shall answer that the same future event seems to be necessary when it is referred to divine knowledge, but completely and absolutely free when

27 weighed in the balance of its own nature. There are in fact two necessities: One is simple (for example, the fact that all human beings are mortal); the other is conditional (as when it is necessary that a man is

28 walking if you know that he *is* walking). For whatever anyone knows cannot exist in any other way than it is known to exist, but this condi-

29 tion does not at all draw along with it that other, simple necessity. For it is not the thing's own nature that makes this necessity but only the addition of condition; for no necessity compels a man to move forward who is taking a step voluntarily, even though it is a necessary thing that he

30 move forward at the point at which he takes a step. Therefore, it is in just this way that it is necessary that a thing exists if Providence sees it as

31 a present thing, even if it has no necessity in its nature. And yet, God views as present those future things that come to pass from the freedom of independent judgment. Therefore: These things, when referred to the divine gaze, come about as necessary things, because of the condition of divine knowledge; but when looked at in and of themselves they do not

32 cease from the absolute freedom of their natures. Therefore: Beyond any doubt, all the things that God foreknows as future things will come into being, but certain of these things proceed from free and independent judgment; although they do happen, nevertheless they do not lose by their existing their own proper nature, by virtue of which they could have *not* happened before they did come into being.

33 Well then! Does it make a difference that they are not necessary when, because of the condition of divine knowledge, what is in all

34 respects a facsimile of necessity will happen? Yes it does, and in this way. The examples that I proposed just a little while ago, the rising sun and the man taking a step: while they happen, they cannot *not* happen; nevertheless, it was necessary even before it happened that one of them

35 come into existence, but the other one not at all. So too the things that God possesses as present: They will beyond any doubt exist, but one descends from the necessity of things while another descends from the

---

6.27 simple (V.6.28), human beings (cf. I.6.15, V.2.3), conditional (V.6.29), walking (cf. V.6.22).   6.28 draw (III.m.12.57 (takes), V.4.5).   6.29 addition (II.7.19, III.6.3, III.9.28).   6.31 (cf. V.6.36), views (V.4.27, 30, 32), freedom of independent judgment (V.3.3, V.6.44; cf. V.6.32), divine gaze (V.6.23, 40), condition of divine knowledge (V.6.33), looked at (V.4.36, V.6.15, 36), cease (III.11.12, 13; IV.2.32, V.6.6, 12).   6.32 beyond any doubt (II.5.15, III.11.13, V.6.35).   6.34 a little while ago (at V.6.22), taking a step (V.6.29).
6.35 descends (cf. V.6.12), power (II.6.13, V.4.39, V.6.37).

power of those who do it. Therefore, it is not at all improper that we said 36
that these things are necessary if they are referred to divine knowledge,
but divorced from the meshes of necessity if they are looked at in and of
themselves. Similarly, everything that is obvious to the senses is universal
if you refer it to reason, but particular if you look to the things themselves.

But, you will say, if it has been placed within my power to change my 37
intention, then I shall gut Providence, since, perhaps, I shall have
changed the things that it has foreknowledge of. I shall answer that yes, 38
you can alter the course of your intention; however, since the present
truth of Providence observes that you can do so and whether you will do
so and to what end you will redirect it, you cannot avoid divine foreknowledge, just as you cannot escape the gaze of its present eye even
though you redirect yourself by your free will toward actions of different
sorts. Well then! you will say; will divine knowledge be changed by my 39
arrangements, with the result that, when I wish for now this thing, now
that, divine knowledge seems to switch back and forth the vicissitudes of
its foreknowing? Hardly. For the divine gaze runs on ahead of every 40
thing that will come to pass and twists it back and calls it back to the
present of its own proper perception; it does not, as you reckon it, switch
back and forth in an alternation of a foreknowledge of now this thing,
now another; rather, remaining stable, it anticipates and embraces your
changes in its single stroke. It is not from the coming to pass of future 41
events but rather from his own proper simplicity that God has been
allotted this present grasping and seeing of all things. And from this also 42
comes an answer to the problem you had posed just a little while ago,
that it is an unworthy thing that our future actions be said to provide a
cause for the foreknowledge of God. For such is the force of this knowl- 43
edge, embracing all things by its present-moment knowledge, that it has

6.36 improper . . . said (IV.4.1; cf. I.4.30, III.6.1, IV.3.2 (without cause)),
divorced (V.4.18, V.5.1), meshes (IV.6.15), obvious (V.3.14), universal/particular
(cf. V.5.6; cf. V.4.29 (individual)), you (singular).   6.37 (cf. V.3.15–16), you
will say (V.4.10, 21), you (singular), power (V.6.35).   6.38 I shall answer
(V.6.26), observes (= gazes at: V.5.5, 8; cf. V.6.19), eye (V.4.30; cf. V.6.18).
6.39 well then (V.6.33), you will say (V.6.37), you (singular), arrangements (cf.
IV.5.7, IV.6.9, 21).   6.40 hardly (V.6.19), runs on ahead (cf. V.6.45), calls
back (V.1.5), perception (V.6.15), stable (= remaining unchanged: cf. V.6.44,
45), anticipates (cf. V.6.45), embraces (V.6.5), single stroke (V.m.2.12, V.4.33; cf.
IV.6.12).   6.41 allotted (IV.6.7), present (IV.6.40).   6.42 little while ago
(at V.3.15–16; cf. V.6.37).   6.43 embracing all things (IV.6.10, 53), present-
moment (IV.6.12 (single moment), V.6.12, 15), knowledge (*notio*: V.6.26, 31).

itself established the status of all things, while it owes nothing to things that are subsequent to it.

44   And since this is the way things are, this remains unchanged for mortals: an inviolate freedom of independent judgment. Laws are not unjust, and they assign rewards and punishments to wills that are free of

45   every necessity. God also remains unchanged, looking down from on high with foreknowledge of all things; the ever-present eternity of his vision keeps pace with the future qualities of our actions, dispensing

46   rewards to good people and punishments to the bad. Nor are hopes and prayers placed in God in vain; they cannot help but be effective, pro-

47   vided that they are blameless. Therefore, all of you: Avoid vices, cherish virtues; raise up your minds to blameless hopes; extend your humble

48   prayers into the lofty heights. Unless you want to hide the truth, there *is* a great necessity imposed upon you—the necessity of righteousness, since you plead your case before the eyes of a judge who beholds all things.

6.44 remains unchanged (= stable: V.6.40), laws are not unjust (cf. V.3.31), rewards/punishments (V.3.30, V.6.45).   6.45 looking down from on high (cf. V.4.32), keeps pace with (cf. V.6.40), quality (V.6.23), dispensing (IV.6.36, 45). 6.46 hopes and prayers (cf. V.3.33–36), in vain (V.3.30, V.4.16), effective (= productive: IV.4.11, V.4.4, 11).   6.47 vices/virtues (cf. III.4.1, IV.1.7, V.3.32), raise up (cf. V.5.12), hopes (cf. IV.4.8), humble (cf. III.8.3, V.3.34), lofty (V.6.17). 6.48 necessity (V.6.25), righteousness (IV.3.1, 6, 12, 16), eyes (V.4.30), who beholds all things (Esther 16:4), beholds (V.m.3.20).

NOTES

The title, traditionally translated as *The Consolation of Philosophy*, is a provocative variation on the convention by which consolatory works are labeled by their addressee: Seneca's *Consolation to his Mother Helvia*, for example. Boethius does not name his addressee; it is therefore technically open whether the title speaks of the consolation that Boethius' Philosophy provides to one unnamed, the consolation that Philosophy provides to Boethius, or the consolation which Boethius provides to Philosophy. For the latter, see Notes to I.1.

Book I, Meter 1

The topic of this poem is how the prisoner is no longer capable of writing good poetry. It is not supposed to be a good poem, but only a good index to the state of the prisoner's mind (not that we know yet that he is a prisoner). Much is bathetic or trivial, and Philosophy soon mocks the poet and his language in I.m.2, but by its end several key themes have been announced: the unreliability of Fortune (the subject of Book II and the first half of Book III), the value of friends, the longing for stability (a cosmic principle that transcends earthly concerns), the military nature of the philosophical life (most intense at IV.7.4, 10, 17–22). The imagined presence of Death, and the fleeting thought of suicide, find their echoes later on as well (III.5.10, III.11.32; cf. IV.m.4.3–4); Philosophy too will appear as one who has been in the presence of Death (I.1.3–5).

Meter Elegiac couplets, a traditional meter both for erotic poetry and for lament; the latter is in evidence here, as the prisoner speaks in the language of Ovid's poems of exile (see Claassen 1999, 244–51, for an analysis of this poem in comparison to Ovid). The first line is a dactylic hexameter catalectic, or six dactyls with the last element missing ($- \cup \cup - \cup \cup - \cup \cup - \cup \cup - \cup \cup - -$); a spondee ($- -$) may be substituted for any dactyl in the first four feet. The second line, called a pentameter, breaks in two, each half two-and-a-half dactyls, no substitutions allowed in the last half, although spondees may appear for dactyls in the first ($- \cup \cup - \cup \cup - // - \cup \cup - \cup \cup -$). To the reader who has been puzzled by the title, the poem is an unfolding series of surprises. No one would expect a consolation to begin with a poem; the first line, which is in the meter of epic poetry, leads in one direction (one can read *Consolation* as a search for a return to this epic voice, which appears in the climactic III.m.9); the second word of the second line (*heu*, "Woe is me!") marks the descent to elegy. The appearance of prose immediately afterwards is another surprise. The first poem of Book V is also written in this meter, suggesting that Book V is to be taken as a sort of new beginning. A number of the subsequent poems in Book I are written in what I would call fragments of this crucial epic meter.

Book I, Prose 1

The epiphany of Philosophy, which may find some parallels in works as disparate as 4 Esdras and the hermetic text *Poimandres*, is firmly linked to two of *Consolation*'s Menippean predecessors, Martianus Capella's *Marriage of Philology and Mercury* and Fulgentius' *Mythologies*, because Philosophy appears as a Muse, whose first task is to change the author's genre and the topic of his writing. The silence announced at I.1.1, and diagnosed as lethargy at I.2.5, is broken when the prisoner speaks at I.3.3; the prisoner's search for a voice that will allow him to talk to Philosophy as an equal is one of the plot structures of *Consolation*. The ladder at I.1.4, suggesting the rise from practical to theoretical philosophy, hints at another plot structure: Philosophy's encouragement that the prisoner forget his earthly tribulations and escape with her, to view the world from her height, contending with the prisoner's attempt to return to questions concerning the justice of his punishment. This straight ascent is to be contrasted to the circular ascent of Fortune's wheel at II.2.10. Further, the creation of a symbol out of letters of the alphabet is essentially Christian: such things are called *gammadia*. The discussion of disease and health at I.1.9 prepares us for Philosophy the Doctor. The concluding sentences announce another key image: looking down versus looking up, most famously expressed in III.m.12 on Orpheus and Eurydice.

I.1.3 death-masks: Or busts, such as aristocrats would keep of their ancestors. Philosophy has been in the land of the dead (cf. I.3.7); she returns to the prisoner to find a champion of her ancient, integral self, to avenge her shameful treatment at the hands of moderns. If so, then the prisoner, if he proves to be a true philosopher, may in fact console Philosophy (see Relihan 1990). *I.1.5* How could the prisoner know at this point what Philosophy reveals at I.3.7, that certain philosophers had carried off scraps of her robe?   *I.1.9* passions: The Latin plural *affectus* translates the Greek *pathe*, emotions viewed as external assailants of the stable soul (I.5.11, IV.4.27, V.2.10); the singular is translated "desire" (II.1.2, V.5.3). Another term for the emotions is *perturbationes*, translated "confusing emotions" (I.5.12, I.6.9, 13, 21); the singular is "confusion" (I.1.14, IV.1.9); the verb *perturbare* is translated "confuse" (IV.6.1, IV.6.21, V.3.2, V.6.23). Boethius here, as often, maintains a poetic range of terms for the subject under discussion.   *I.1.11* shipwreck: The Latin *exitium* means only "destruction" or "death"; shipwreck, appropriate for Sirens, emphasizes the frequent nautical analogies of *Consolation*.   *I.1.12* contains the only reference to a door in this prison.

Book I, Meter 2

Philosophy here insults the narrator for his lack of vision, for his refusal to treat themes of natural history and cosmic order; the opening "Woe is him!" repeats the prisoner's self-pitying cry at I.m.1.2 and 15; it closes this poem as well. Philosophy combines two sets of images that are often later kept separate: the stability of the cosmic order (sun, moon, stars, seasons) and the violent unpredictability of the weather (winds and Ocean, storm and calm). The prisoner shows at I.m.5 that he has not forgotten the cosmic order, but cannot see how humans fit into it; Philosophy will appeal to the seasons at I.m.6 and to storms at I.m.7 for a different purpose: to convince the prisoner to accept her order of topics for his cure. The reader needs to evaluate the different uses to which the speakers put these stock descriptions. The contrasts of up and down, light and dark, remain prominent.

Meter A unique combination of a dactylic trimeter catalectic ($- \cup \cup -$ $\cup \cup -$; spondees are allowed for either or both dactyls), the equivalent of the first half of the pentameter line of an elegiac couplet, and a dactylic dimeter, or Adoneus ($- \cup \cup - -$), the equivalent of the last two feet of the hexameter line of the couplet. The translation allows itself an occasional extra short syllable. Philosophy mocks the narrator, both as thinker and as poet, by writing in these epic fragments, reinforcing the complaint that the prisoner has lost his epic/didactic voice. I.m.3, I.m.5, and I.m.7 also present such suggestions of epic.

Book I, Prose 2

Philosophy refers to herself in the singular (I.2.4: "Do you know me?") and in the plural (I.2.3: "we had supplied you with such weapons"; I.2.6: "he

knew us once before . . . let us just wipe his eyes"). The plural might suggest Philosophy and her Muses together, but Philosophy is no stranger to
the royal we. The translation tries to preserve singular and plural use
exactly. Similarly, she seems to speak to herself (I.2.5: "he's suffering from
lethargy"; cf. I.1.8: "Who . . . let these little stage whores come visit this
invalid?"), though the reader may imagine that the prisoner is the
intended audience for these words as well. At I.2.6 Philosophy first makes
her key diagnosis of self-forgetfulness, amplified later at I.6.15–17; but at
no point in *Consolation* does the conversation explicitly return to the issue
and resolve it, though Platonic doctrines of remembering are prominent in
later books (cf. III.m.11 and V.m.3), and though the lack of self-awareness
of animals is also discussed (II.5.29). This is one of *Consolation*'s crucial
unkept promises.

Book I, Meter 3

Now that the prisoner can see, he can look Philosophy in the eyes; the
power of her eyes had been stressed at I.1.7 and I.2.2. The mythical
apparatus of Classical poetry is preserved in *Consolation* and in this
translation; when the conversation turns to God and his Providence in
the later books, the reader may wonder what is the function of Phoebus
here. Curiously, this poem presents the prisoner's voice as narrator,
despite the fact that he is supposed to have fallen silent. The poem is
addressed to the reader, not to Philosophy; it is a sort of inconsistency,
unless it is to suggest to the reader even now that what is read has been
written down after the fact, retrospectively. In this light, we reread I.1
also as a narration composed after the fact of the dialogue.

Meter A dactylic hexameter alternates with a dactylic tetrameter (– ∪ ∪
– ∪ ∪ – ∪ ∪ – ∪ ∪); the combination is sometimes called an Alcmanian,
and is found only here in *Consolation*. An extra syllable appears at the
beginning of v.6 of the translation. Again, epic/didactic verse is suggested;
the tone is elevated, a near-epic description of a storm and the following
calm; the fulfillment of the promise of true epic is long delayed (to the climactic III.m.9).

Book I, Prose 3

Philosophy's message here is simple: Persecution proves the philosopher.
Philosophy is glad to see the prisoner suffer, even if he is not. The language of I.3.6, "the victory of an unjust death," has decidedly Christian

overtones; Philosophy looks for a martyr. *Consolation* offers no discussion of death, despite its title; it has no real place in the history of consolatory literature because the consolation that Philosophy wishes to offer the prisoner is the consolation that death itself provides. This will become clear as early as the end of Book II (II.7.21–23, II.m.7); Philosophy's eagerness to take the prisoner to his fatherland at the beginning of Books IV and V betrays this longing as well. At the end of this section, her imagined view from her tower down to the army of madmen below anticipates an often repeated command that the prisoner raise himself up so as to look down on and despise the world below (cf. III.m.12.52–58, IV.m.1). The prisoner is not so certain that he wishes to remove himself from this world.

1.3.9 The catalogue of persecuted philosophers: Greeks of the fifth century B.C.E.: Anaxagoras of Clazomenae, Socrates of Athens, Zeno of Elea; Romans of the time of Nero: Canius, Seneca, Soranus. Philosophy's history of philosophy is very brief; it is in fact an introduction to the use of Nero as the stereotypical tyrant (cf. II.m.6, III.m.4).   *1.3.12–14* For the use of military language, cf. IV.7.17–22.   *1.3.13* our leader: This leader is clearly feminine (*nostra dux*). Is this Boethius' slip of the pen, referring to Philosophy herself? But at IV.6.38 she refers to someone "even superior to me."

Book I, Meter 4

At I.m.2 Philosophy had spoken of the prisoner's former desire to investigate the causes of the ordered variations in nature, primarily the seasons and seasonal weather. Here she speaks of nature as an irrational force that a wise man may despise; ordered and violent nature will continue to be contrasted in *Consolation*. Here the theme of the tyrant is introduced, who will return frequently as Nero (II.m.6, III.m.4); the image of the philosopher as a soldier is here modified, as he is now the opponent of the tyrant. Boethius' conflict with Theoderic lies behind this, as I.4 will make clear. The Stoic ideal of the path to freedom through rejection of the emotions (on which note Book I ends) will be changed at the very end of *Consolation* (V.6.47), when hope and prayer are properly directed upward.

I.m.3.2–3 "Fortune" and "fate" here translate "fate" and "Fortune."

Meter This is the Phalacean hendecasyllable, or simply hendecasyllable ("with eleven syllables": – – – ∪ ∪ – ∪ – ∪ – –); I have allowed myself

an extra short syllable in v.14, and treat the poem's final word as disyllabic. The hendecasyllable reappears in three other places (III.m.4,
III.m.10, IV.m.4), but only in combination with other meters (Alcaics,
Sapphics, and pentameters, respectively). It is in essence a lyric meter,
standing in contrast to the epic fragments of the preceding poems and
the prisoner's lament that follows at I.m.5; it marks the beginning of
Philosophy's singing in her own voice, as it were.

Book I, Prose 4

For the historical matter contained in this section, consult Chadwick
1981, 1–68. This apology is a formally constructed speech, with *exordium*
(introduction, 2–7), *narratio* (narrative, 8–19), *probatio* (proof, 20–27),
exornatio (embellishment, 28–36), *refutatio* (refutation, 37–42), and *per-
oratio* (conclusion, 43–46). The reader's understanding of *Consolation*
does not require an appreciation of the truth of these events. The following point needs to be made: The emotion with which the prisoner
speaks builds to a crescendo in the poem that follows, a powerful statement of a belief in a God-ordered universe. At the beginning of I.5,
when the prisoner finally falls silent, Philosophy discounts what the prisoner says primarily because of the emotions involved, for at the end of
Book II she will deliver a poem on much the same theme as I.m.5. The
prisoner's complaints against Fortune here will inspire Philosophy's
attack on Fortune, which is the whole of Book II; the prisoner's voice
becomes a much more hesitant thing after the following poem, and Philosophy will tell him what he no doubt already knows. But Philosophy
will go on to say in I.5 that the prisoner could have done an even better
job of speaking about the wrongs done to him; and in Book II, the matter of Boethius' life and the glories of his family (distinguished father-in-
law Symmachus, modest and devoted wife, consular sons) reappear to
show that his Fortune was not so bad (II.3.3–9, II.4.3–9). What is crucial to the understanding of *Consolation* is whether Philosophy will ultimately be successful in getting the prisoner to let go of his earthly
attachments and his earthly frustrations at the injustices done to him;
Philosophy returns to the prisoner's complaints at IV.4.24 to say that his
persecutors will soon be punished; the end of Book V further suggests
that success has eluded her.

I.4.1 the ass at the lyre: Quoted in Greek, the proverb refers to those
who only seem to appreciate what they cannot understand.   I.4.1
Homer says: The quotation from Homer is, of course, given in Greek.

As such, it is set off from the Latin around it; I have added these introductory words for similar effect.   *I.4.6, 9* unrighteous: Anticipating the
return of these arguments in IV.2 and IV.3.   *I.4.22* there was no effort:
The Latin would most easily mean "the effort ceased," but this is no
argument that he could not admit to the charges against him. The interpretation of the verb *cessavit* that I have followed here is plausible
enough, but raises the suspicion that the prisoner is having a hard time
defending himself; in fact, Boethius may have been guilty of the charges
of treason (cf. O'Donnell 1993).   *I.4.25* The prisoner's reference to
the separate account of his downfall raises an interesting question: Why
is he writing down his conversation with Philosophy? At II.7.13, Philosophy will mock human efforts at the perpetuation of individual reputation through writing; at I.1.1 the prisoner seems to have put his pen
down.   *I.4.28–36* These complaints will be treated more formally at
IV.6.   *I.4.36* The prisoner's overwrought exclamation means that the
Senate, by its perfidious refusal to defend Boethius, deserves that there
never again rise up anyone who *could* be convicted of desiring the safety
of the Senate.

Book I, Meter 5

The prisoner's depiction of the ordered variations of nature, the topics
of his youthful scientific investigations (cf. I.m.2), stands here in contrast to Philosophy's violent and disordered nature in the previous
poem: The only mad storm is that of Fortune, and the Creator is called
on to sail the prisoner's ship safely through it. The poem divides neatly
in two; the second half (vv.25–48) enunciates the prisoner's prime complaint, that rewards and punishments are not apportioned acording to
justice. His complaint does not disappear; this will be the subject of
Book V. And while Philosophy will begin the next section affecting to be
shocked by the violence and illogicality of the prisoner's outburst, the
poem with which she ends Book II ends just as the prisoner's does,
though in a different meter: "O how happy the mortal race, / Were Love
king over all your hearts, / Love that heaven accepts as king!" Both echo
the Lord's Prayer; cf. Matthew 6:10.

Meter Anapestic dimeters, a meter which reappears at III.m.2,
IV.m.6, and V.m.3; these poems are thematically linked—Is there a
harmony that binds the universe together, and can we return to it?—
and each needs to be read in reference to the others. From a theoretical base of four anapests ($\cup \cup - \cup \cup - \cup \cup - \cup \cup -$), the meter

allows many variations, as spondees (– –) and dactyls (– ∪ ∪) are freely substituted. I have not attempted to reproduce the variations line for line. Each line divides in two (except for v.36, an anapestic dimeter), and the second half far more often than not mimics the end of a hexameter line (– ∪ ∪ – –), so as to return us to the epic atmosphere of the earlier poems. I have sometimes allowed an extra short syllable at the beginning of the second half of the line; at v.16, "hours" is disyllabic.

Book I, Prose 5

A simple section, with an important change of focus: The problem is not false imprisonment by temporal authorities and a temporal exile (I.3.3), but a self-willed exile from the philosopher's true homeland, which is not of this earth. Philosophy will endeavor to return the exile where he belongs at the beginnings of Book IV (IV.1.9) and Book V (V.1.4), only to have her intentions redirected by the prisoner's inquiries into other matters. The insistence on gentler remedies that closes this section, after Philosophy summarizes the prisoner's complaint, brings us back to the image of Philosophy as doctor; but Philosophy's bitter remedies can only bring to mind Socrates' cup of hemlock, especially given the parallels between *Consolation* and Plato's *Crito*. Here we see Philosophy decide that Fortune must be attacked before anything else can be accomplished, even if this makes her state her case a little too baldly at II.1.2; but there are ominous undercurrents here.

I.5.4 the highest freedom: The adjective had been accidentally dropped from Bieler's editions, and is restored by Moreschini 2000.   I.5.10 delirious Muse: a bold phrase, especially since the pagan Muses left the prisoner's cell at I.1.12.

Book I, Meter 6

This summary of the human actions that are appropriate for the various seasons is a simplified restatement of the first half of the prisoner's previous poem. The complaint there made about the free rein given to evil people is quietly suppressed here by the concluding assertion that deviation from the divine plan is profitless; Philosophy does not yet wrestle with the question of whether it is possible. But if the poem is to be taken as closely related to the prose section that precedes it (as is usual), then perhaps Philosophy implies that the exile is himself the defector; she would thus return to the image of the failed philosopher as the soldier who has run away (cf. I.m.4.15–19).

Meter Glyconics (– – – ∪ ∪ – ∪ –). This is the most common meter in *Consolation*, occuring in each of the five books as a significant punctuation of the text (see also II.m.8, III.m.12, IV.m.3, V.m.4); the hendecasyllables of I.m.4 are similar, having at the end an additional length (∪ – –). In the last line, "prófitablé" is accented to show that it is quadrisyllabic, not to suggest that the final vowel is itself long; in line 10, "brístling" is trisyllabic.

Book I, Prose 6

The beginning of the dialogue between Philosophy and the prisoner is presented as a doctor's taking of a medical history. But there will be very little dialogue in Book II (the prisoner speaks only at II.3.2, II.4.1–2, II.4.10, and II.7.1); Philosophy's program of healing will require that he be the audience of her upcoming diatribe against Fortune, and not a participant in a debate. But a number of key revelations are made here that will determine the course and the interpretation of the books that follow. The root cause of the prisoner's illness is that he has forgotten who he is (a diagnosis already made at I.2.6), but the promise to discuss what is the definition of a human being is not kept in *Consolation* (but see the hint at IV.6.41). Philosophy's interrogation in I.6.3–16 is summarized at I.6.17–19. At I.6.18, ignorance of self causes him to lament the loss of his goods (Philosophy's topic in Book II); ignorance of the goal toward which all things tend causes him to believe that evil people are prosperous (the topic of Book III); ignorance of the mechanisms of divine governance causes him to believe that individual lives are ignored in the divine order (the topic of Book IV). Book V, on the relation of human freewill to divine foreknowledge, is not related to this scheme. To what extent has the prisoner changed Philosophy's plans?

1.6.4 The prisoner expands upon this belief at III.12.4–8.   *1.6.6* But fancy that!: When the prisoner repeats these words to Philosophy at IV.2.1, he reminds her pointedly of the promises that she has made. *1.6.11* I answered that it was God: Only here and at IV.4.20 does the narrator reports his own words in conversation indirectly.   *1.6.19* your nature has not yet abandoned you: See IV.3.15 for an account of people who have lost their human nature by their evil conduct.   *1.6.21* which dazes the true vision: The prisoner has already had light dispel his darkness at I.m.3. Is Philosophy promising a sort of continuous revelation, or does she presume that the prisoner is more blind than he really is?

Book I, Meter 7

This restatement of the key image of Philosophy's truth as the light that scatters the shadows is remarkable primarily for its rhythm, but also for its conclusion. The Stoic goal of the banishment of the passions, the emotions of joy, fear, hope, and sorrow (vv.25–28), keeps the promise made at the end of the previous prose section.

Meter Adonics (– ∪ ∪ – –), which mimic the ends of the lines of the epic hexameter, so that this last poem returns us to the initial poem, and its intimations of epic denied. Philosophy here turns away from her lyric voice to a didactic voice; the marching tempo of these verses is unmistakable. This meter is used only here in *Consolation*.

Book II, Prose 1

The attack on Fortune in Book II presents Fortune as a "principle of disorder." As Frakes 1988, 63, points out, in this way "Boethius defines by contrast his view of divine order." What is more remarkable is that Boethius ultimately redefines Fortune as an agent of the divine, "God's representative in the affairs of men," much as Providence is. The form that this attack (and rehabilitation) takes is the diatribe, the language of popular moral/philosophical harangue. It does not call for the prisoner to respond; he is the audience, and Philosophy is the preacher. This is the world of rhetorical questions and dramatic flourishes (cf. II.1.9, *o homo*: "Mortal man"). It must also be noted that what Philosophy says in her own voice here she will put in the mouth of Fortune in the next prose section (cf. her opening words at II.2.2: "Mortal man!").

Book II, Meter 1

The first poem of Book II refers clearly to the prisoner's situation in the first poem of Book I. It is Philosophy's intention that Book II start from the very beginning, with reference to the most basic elements of the prisoner's condition; but note how much of what is said here is to be found in II.m.8, when the reader assumes that the whole matter of Book II has there been brought to a close.

I.m.1.2 Boeotian: The waters of the Euripus, the strait that separates Boeotia from mainland Attica, are proverbially treacherous.

Meter Choliambs, iambic trimeters that end with a spondee instead of an iamb. While some substitutions are allowed, I have simplified and regularized it ($\cup - \cup - \cup - \cup - \cup - - -$), and allowed myself an extra short syllable in v.2 and v.4. Obviously, this can be read in English as a simple iambic line; but the verse ends are to be read with a drag (the other name for this meter, scazon, means "limping"). This verse form will reappear at III.m.11, but with quite a different subject matter.

Book II, Prose 2

Fortune largely repeats what Philosophy had just said; but when she adds examples from nature of the ebb and flow of things (II.2.8), she enters into the debate on whether Nature represents order or violence. When she adds the famous image of Fortune's wheel, raising people up and bringing them back down again, she in effect anticipates by parody the action of the divine Mind, bending the path of the soul back toward it in a circle (cf. III.m.9.13–21, IV.m.6.38–48). The personification of Fortune is so vivid that the author, perhaps unintentionally, is responsible for the continued existence of the goddess Fortune in the Middle Ages; see Frakes 1988, 31–40, 63.

II.2.6 servants: The relation of Fortune to her servants is suggestive of Philosophy to her Muses.   II.2.12 Perseus: Also known as Perses. II.2.13 Homer says: These words are added to the translation, as at I.4.1 and I.5.4; Philosophy quotes Homer in Greek literally elsewhere, but only approximately here (*Iliad* 24.527–28). The words are from a speech of Achilles, attempting to console Priam for the death of his son Hector.

Book II, Meter 2

Fortune combines here a description of the abundance of Nature with a castigation of human greed. The root problem is revealed in the closing couplet: the passions (cf. I.m.7.25–28), here represented by fear and sorrow. It is not obvious whether Philosophy intends that the prisoner understand this poem as being in Fortune's mouth; I present it as Fortune's continuation of her argument, but it is remarkable just how like Philosophy she sounds here.

II.m.2.1, 3 Count: My own addition; the Latin begins "If as many grains of sand . . . ."

Meter Each couplet consists of a lesser Asclepiad ($- - - \cup \cup - - \cup \cup - \cup -$) and a pherecratic ($- - - \cup \cup - -$). Each is an Aeolic verse length, whose heart is the choriamb ($- \cup \cup -$), already seen in the Phalaceans of

I.m.4 and the glyconics of of I.m.6 (glyconics reappear at II.m.8). This particular combination does not occur again, but the lesser Asclepiad reappears at III.m.8 in combination with iambic dimeters; pherecratics reappear at II.m.4, also in combination with iambic dimeters. This translation regularizes Boethius' practice; anapests are allowed for the opening spondee at v.14 and v.18.

Book II, Prose 3

The prisoner's (bored) reaction to Philosophy's tour-de-force at II.3.2 is much the same as Philosophy's reaction to the prisoner's apology at I.5.1–2; the intransigence of the prisoner's sorrow is again an issue at the beginning of Book IV. We are entitled to question Philosophy's effectiveness. In this section, she goes beyond the topics of the prisoner's life and the wrongs done to him personally by speaking of his family as an example of the good gifts of Fortune; she will expand on this at II.4.3–10, and contrast his situation to those less fortunate in their families. Philosophy's concluding thoughts here on death are a foreshadowing of her description of death at the end of Book II, particularly II.7.21–23 and II.m.7, the latter on the theme of Death the Leveler.

II.3.8 ex-consul: Boethius had himself been consul in 510; this status is implied but not explicitly stated in the Latin.

Book II, Meter 3

As often, Philosophy appeals to Nature as a model of what is erratic and unpredictable; the prisoner has a nobler view of the divinity of Nature at I.m.5, which should be compared to this poem carefully. Philosophy here expands on Fortune's exclamation at II.2.8. It is curious that II.m.2, put in Fortune's mouth, is a more philosophical argument against Fortune; Philosophy speaking here usurps Fortune's arguments.

Meter A couplet compounded of a Sapphic ($- \cup - - - \cup \cup - \cup - -$, found alone at II.m.6 and IV.m.7 and in combination with hendecsyallables at III.m.10) and a glyconic ($- - - \cup \cup - \cup -$, found only here in combination with another meter; employed independently at I.m.6, II.m.8, III.m.12, IV.m.3, and V.m.4). As at II.m.2, both components are Aeolic; the back-and-forth of these complementary elements perhaps serves the poetic theme of the vicissitudes of Nature.

Book II, Prose 4

A curious section, and a change of opinion: Philosophy is willing to say that the prisoner actually enjoyed real goods bestowed by Fortune, but concludes with a praise of Death eagerly embraced as proof of the insignificance of the happiness brought by Fortune. At II.4.4 we return to the image of a court trial aginst Fortune (cf. II.2.3, II.3.1). At II.4.5–7 we expand on what had been said earlier about Boethius' family at II.3.4–9. At II.4.23 we switch from the plural to the singular you; the latter I have italicized whenever there is a possibility of confusion. At II.4.28, Philosophy speaks of the prisoner as one who agrees that the soul is immortal; this has not yet been stated in *Consolation*, and the prisoner's very spare definition of what a human being is at I.6.15–16 causes Philosophy no little surprise there.

II.4.2 The only passage from *Consolation* to appear in *The Oxford Dictionary of Quotations*.   II.4.12 what man: The Latin is not so sexist here, but the translation is justified by the male examples that follow.   II.4.15 outsider/insider: The Latin contrasts *inexpertus/expertus* (inexperienced and experienced).

Book II, Meter 4

Philosophy continues with images from the natural world, anticipating the picture of the ideal Nature of the Golden Age in II.m.5. The allusion to Matthew 7:26, building one's house on rock and not on sand, seems intentional; the additional injunction that this humble rock neither be on the heights of the mountains nor at the seashore suggests a concession to the Classical Golden Mean. The poem ends with an allusion to the city and citadel of Philosophy (I.3.13–14, I.5.5), and Olympian laughter at the earthly world. This concludes the first half of Book II; the second half, again in the forceful language of diatribe, will deal will Fortune's specific gifts.

Meter Couplets formed of an iambic dimeter catalectic (that is, missing its last element: $\cup - \cup - \cup - -$) and a pherecratic, last seen in II.m.2 ($- - - \cup \cup - -$). I have not thought it necessary to mark the last syllables of the iambic lines long; the two short syllables that begin v.13 are an acceptable substitution; the extra short syllable in v.3 does not follow Boethius' practice. The two short syllables that begin v.8, however, do follow his practice in the pherecratics. Iambic lengths will appear again at II.m.7 (trimeters

alternating with dimeters), III.m.3 (trimeters alternating with pentameters), III.m.8 (dimeters alternating with lesser Asclepiads), and IV.m.1
(dimeters alternating with dactylic tetrameters); they also appear in the
very unusual IV.m.5. In v.12, "settling" is trisyllabic.

Book II, Prose 5

The simple theme of this section is that wealth in all of its forms is external to a person, of no real value, and consequently incapable of producing
true happiness. Underlying the discussion is the Platonic idea that only
those things that do not change are real. But Philosophy veers off into the
moral realm, commending the simplicity of natural appetite over human
greed, and returning briefly to the idea first proposed in analysis of the
prisoner's condition that self-knowledge is the key to the realization of
these truths. The security of poverty, the theme with which she ends, is
addressed to a singular audience, not to the plural audience that she frequently imagines. Whether second person singular addresses are merely
according to the conventions of diatribe or contain some particular reference to the prisoner is always a question worth considering.

II.5.1 more caustic: The Latin is simply "more powerful"; I chose to
emphasize the contrast to the more gentle warmth of the initial poultices, as I did at I.5.11.   II.5.10 the Beautiful: The text here alludes to
the Platonic principle that good things are good by their participation in
Goodness itself, the absolute and unchanging form or idea of Goodness.
II.5.12 sir: The Latin merely switches from the plural to the singular;
while "sir" may seem overformal or even archaic, it is not inconsistent
with either Philosophy's meaning or her tone. She switches back to the
plural at II.5.22. I have resisted the urge to add "sir" elsewhere in Consolation.   II.5.16 pour over: It seems that the image here is that of a
rich sauce poured over simple fare; the translation then emphasizes the
culinary metaphor. See the similar metaphor at I.1.8.   II.5.24–29 Philosophy's appeal to the true nature of human beings and the value of
self-knowledge reminds us of the question asked of the prisoner at
I.6.15–16; however, these statements do not constitute a definition of
homo or a satisfaction of Philosophy's promise to teach the prisoner who
he truly is.   II.5.32 Hardly, you say: Philosophy now returns to the second person singular, and turns back to the plural for II.5.35. It is of
course possible that Philosophy does not intend her second person singular remarks here to be personally applicable to the prisoner before her
(and I have not used the word "sir"), but only to be part of a more

abstract address.   II.5.34 the quotation from Juvenal is not quite literal, and so is not set off; but cf. the quotation from Vergil at IV.2.28.

Book II, Meter 5

This poem on the Golden Age in some ways anticipates the crucial mythological poems of the later books (III.m.12, Orpheus; IV.m.3, Ulysses and Circe; IV.m.7, Agamemnon, Ulysses, Hercules); but by its emotion and its central position, it functions much as I.m.5 does, as a passionate cry for peace and order; a key word is *saevus*, translated as "mad, madness." Also to be noticed is the concluding curse on the man who first discovered gold hidden in the earth; at V.1.13 ff., the discovery of hidden gold is used to illustrate the nature of chance. The people of the Golden Age are not themselves engaged in the sorts of metaphysical movements that Philosophy elsewhere encourages in the mythological poems (primarily, return to one's homeland); the reader is however encouraged to return to the Golden Age. We have here a sort of secular vision of the eternal world.

Meter Anapestic dimeters catalectic (or paroemiac). From the theoretical basic form ($\cup\cup - \cup\cup - \cup\cup - -$), substitutions of spondees and dactyls for anapests make many variations possible. The translation reflects some of this range of forms, if not their exact proportions; so too in the anapestic dimeters of I.m.5. The meter appears again in the brief III.m.5.

Book II, Prose 6

The simple argument, that political rank and power are externally conferred upon a person and are not anything other than an arbitrary and transitory gift of Fortune, is considerably more interesting than it seems. Philosophy must realize how painful this is for the politically virtuous prisoner to hear. Not only does she speak at II.6.8 of real political virtue as resistance against corrupt tyrants ("tortures an opportunity for virtue"), but by twice referring to "each and every one of the most unrighteous of men" (II.6.1, 15) she implies both that evil needs resources in order to be truly evil and that the world is not as bad as it could be because not every evil person can act as badly as he might. Philosophy and the prisoner will cover the same ground in dialogue form at III.4.

II.6.13 positions of . . . power: Here the word that typically means true power (*potestas*) is used instead of the more neutral *potentia*.

Book II, Meter 6

It is not hard to see the realities of Theoderic behind the conventional por-
trait of Nero, the mad tyrant. Another poem on Nero is found in Book III,
again immediately after a discussion of the meaninglessness of rank and
political power (III.m.4). The closing lines make more clear what was implied
in the preceeding prose section: Evil (poison) only becomes true evil when
it has power and resources (sword) behind it. The poem is remarkable for
presenting a corrupt king in charge of the world of Nature, inverting the
ideals of I.m.5; and for showing power as the enemy of family, which is the
abiding source of the prisoner's good fortune (II.3.5–8, II.4.4–9)

For Nero's murder of his half-brother, Tiberius Claudius Caesar (v.3),
and of his mother Agrippina (vv.4–7), see Tacitus, *Annals* 13–14, and
Suetonius, *Nero* 33–34.

Meter Sapphics (– ∪ – – – ∪ ∪ – ∪ – –), found again independently at
IV.m.7 and in combination with glyconics at II.m.3 and with hendecasyllables at III.m.10. With its erotic associations, it offers a pointed contrast to
its subject matter.

Book II, Prose 7

Philosophy speaks both generally, in the language of diatribe, and specifically, goading the prisoner to accept the insignificance of the earth and
its glory. As I think is clear from the contempt heaped on authors concerned with their reputations and on philosophers who refuse to keep
silence, and from the concluding praise of Death (cf. II.4.28–29) as an
escape from the earthly prison, Philosophy is trying to get the prisoner to
put down his pen and fly to the heavens with her. As Book II draws to a
close, Philosophy moves from the general argument against Fortune to
the advocacy of a specific plan of action.

   Philosophy moves freely from the second person singular (II.7.3–5, 7–
9, 15–18, 20) to the second plural (II.7.6, 9–14, 19); the concluding sentences (II.7.21–23) have no particular addressee. At any given point
where there are no pronouns, it is uncertain just who is her audience; it
is also uncertain whether the singular imperatives *adde* at II.7.7 (literally,
"factor this in too"; translated as, "And another thing") and *accipe* at
II.7.20 ("hear now") really are pointed at the prisoner or are part of the
general baggage of diatribe.

II.7.8 Hindu Kush: Cicero uses the term Caucasus both in the passage Philosophy refers to (*Republic* 6.22) and elsewhere (*Tusculans* 5.77) to refer to

the Western Himalayas, spoken of in the same breath as the Ganges. *II.7.12* happily constrained: This translates both meanings of the punning *contentus* (content and contained); this translation could well be substituted for "satisfied" at II.5.16 and 26.   *II.7.13–18* To what extent is the reader to think about the fact that the very existence of the text of *Consolation* in which this argument is found is a refutation of it? Philosophy never tells the prisoner to write down what they say: Why has he? *II.7.20* The source of the anecdote is unknown, though the idea that the philosopher proves himself through silence is not unheard of (see Macrobius, *Saturnalia* 7.1.11). Again, the reader asks: What of the author of *Consolation*? He has not kept silent; is he therefore not a philosopher?

Book II, Meter 7

The Republican heroes of vv.15–16 again point to a political reference: The prisoner need not worry about his benefactions for the state. But can Philosophy consistently refer to the famous dead as an argument against fame? In conjunction with the previous prose section, this poem is not so much about Death the Leveler, who makes all distinctions meaningless, as it is about death as the proof of the true philosopher (cf. I.3.6, 9).

Meter Couplets formed of iambic trimeters with iambic dimeters. The reader may think of this as a sort of iambic version of the elegiac couplet (six dactyls plus two lengths of two-and-a-half dactyls), and compare it to the lament about Death that constitutes the opening poem of *Consolation*. The translation makes less use of substitutions of dactyls, anapests, and tribrachs (three short syllables) than does the Latin. Quatrains of pure iambic dimeters would constitute the hymn form created by St. Ambrose, never seen in *Consolation*; II.m.7 is not Christian but Horatian in form. Iambic meters were last seen with pherecratics at II.m.4, and will be seen with pentameters at III.m.3.

Book II, Prose 8

The end of Book II returns to the complaint which began Book I. The prisoner complained of faithless Fortune at I.m.1.16–17, and Philosophy now claims that the realization of the nature of Fortune is a valuable lesson learned; the prisoner addressed his friends at I.m.1.21–22, wondering why they ever called him happy, and Philosophy now claims that the friends whom he addressed constitute his true wealth. Philosophy has attempted to make the prisoner accept as good what he initially complained of as bad. But note the prisoner's longing for death at I.m.1.13–20, and Philosophy's words on the freedom that death has to offer in II.7; the acceptance of death is also part of her program of education.

II.8.1 *you*: Philosophy uses the second person singular throughout this passage.   II.8.6 *she took . . . and left*: Philosophy here repeats the senti-ment that she put in Fortune's mouth at II.2.6.

Book II, Meter 8

It is consistent with Philosophy's educational scheme that she returns to realizations that the prisoner had already made. Just as II.7 and II.8 return to the themes of I.m.1, so does the concluding poem reiterate what the prisoner had himself proclaimed in verse at I.m.5: that there is an order that governs the universe. Philosophy's addition is that this order may be called Love (the prisoner preferred to speak of a creator or a helmsman); but she too only speaks hopefully, not definitely, about the place of human beings within this world order. Both poems conclude with the sentiment of the Lord's Prayer, a wish that the same order be found on earth as there is in heaven; the two poems demand careful compari-son. And the end of Book II is also prospective: Much of the ground cov-ered here will be restated with greater sophistication at IV.6 and IV.m.6.

II.m.8.13 sequence: A key term in IV.6, referring to the ordering of tem-poral events by Fate and Providence.   *II.m.8.29–30* Literally: "If the love by which heaven is ruled (*regitur*) should rule (*regat*) your hearts." The word "king" is justified etymologically: *regere*, to rule = to be king (*rex, reg-*).

Meter Book II concludes in glyconics, the favorite meter of *Consolation* ($- - - \cup \cup - \cup -$). It was last seen at I.m.6 and will appear next at III.m.12.

Book III, Prose 1

While Philosophy keeps the promise that she makes in this preamble, to lead the prisoner to true happiness, it is a fair question why she feels the need to go again through the arguments against Fortune. To a certain extent, she casts a wider net, now including physical pleasure; and the argument is also now framed in a more abstract way, as the gifts of Fortune are not presented as impermanent or contemptible so much as false paths toward something that is truly desirable, which is the Good. Philosophy dampens the prisoner's enthusiasm, and slows him down at this point; he will return the favor at the beginnings of Books IV and V.

III.1.2 passionately: *vehementer.* It has been impossible to translate this simple adverb consistently; elsewhere, "utterly" and "utter."   *III.1.5* to true happiness: This goal is reached at III.9.26; the subsequent poem, the great III.m.9, is presented as if it were another beginning.

Book III, Meter 1

Philosophy here claims that the progression from bitter to sweet instruction will mimic the order of Nature; similar images can be found in I.m.6, where the theme was that those who abandon the order of Nature reap no rewards; but note II.1.7–8, in which mild potions are prepared before the stonger ones. Philosophy hopes to reap the harvest that she will plant in the prisoner (contrast the Muses as farmers at I.1.9); but, as will be clear at V.1.12–19, not everything that one finds in a field has one planted there.

Meter Each line consists of two halves, a pentameter or two-and-a-half dactylic feet ($-\cup\cup-\cup\cup-$) and a fourth paeon ($\cup\cup\cup-$); this is the so-called faliscan meter. It appears nowhere else in *Consolation*; in the context of the preceding poems, it can be heard as opening with epic solemnity but ending without it, keeping the promise of the epic voice alive.

Book III, Prose 2

Philosophy operates with a wide range of synonyms, but what she presents as the five gifts of Fortune, now redefined as the five false paths to happiness, are monetary wealth, social standing/political honors, kingly power, glory/noble birth, and physical pleasure. After the two introductory prose sections, these five goals are treated in order in prose sections 3 through 7; III.8 recapitulates that these cannot achieve true happiness; III.9 will assert that that only true happiness can achieve these five goals. We are prepared for this by III.2.19, when Philosophy quickly suggests what are the real goals of these five pursuits: self-sufficiency, preeminence, power, acclamation, and delight; a similar list is given at III.9.2. The reader may object that some of these distinctions are drawn too finely. It is curious that the pursuit of wisdom is never listed as a false or as a true path.

III.2.1 foundations: The word is elsewhere typically translated as "dwelling place" (but cf. III.11.22), but it is important to make the connection to III.m.9.22, which speaks of the holy foundations of the Creator.   *III.2.2* true happiness: This translates the single word *beatitudo*; mere worldy happiness is *felicitas.*   *III.2.3* brought about: *perfectum.* Implicit in the word, as in the English derivative "perfected," is the idea of turning something into what it truly should be.

Book III, Meter 2

Philosophy, who at I.6.17 ff. promised to make the prisoner remember who he is, and who will seem to be successful at jogging his memory at III.12.1, here speaks of recovery of lost identity in violent and pathetic terms, of animals once tame remembering their wild nature. The reference to the honeyed cup that would distract the bird casts Philosophy's own promise of a honeyed medicine in a strange light (as will Circe's cups in IV.m.3); the concluding lines, on the need for each individual to achieve a private return to its origins, couched in Neo-Platonic imagery, also suggest that a prisoner who recovers his true self may not be as docile and as easily led as Philosophy would wish.

III.m.2.34–39 At this point Neo-Platonic imagery makes its first substantial appearance in *Consolation*; the return of the soul to its origins by a circular route is found in III.m.9 and IV.m.1.

Meter The anapestic dimeter, last seen at I.m.5, to reappear at IV.m.6 and V.m.3. The first and last of these poems are in the prisoner's voice (his only other poems are the elegiac I.m.1 and the narrative I.m.3); does Philosophy, whose favorite meter is the glyconic, attempt to usurp the prisoner's speech here?

Book III, Prose 3

The topic here is wealth, as was handled in the previous book at II.5. The discussion is more "philosophical," treating it not so much as the gift of Fortune but as an insatiable need. But it is not certain that Philosophy is less interested in the prisoner's own circumstances; she talks about his own fretfulness about his wealth at III.3.5; and while her last exhortation is addressed to a plural audience, the reference to wide-mouthed greed draws us back precisely to where this book began (III.1.1), with the drop-jawed prisoner longing to hear more, believing that he is already Fortune's equal, but in reality needing further instruction.

Book III, Meter 3

Though Philosophy had at the end of III.m.2 raised the topic of the soul's return to its origins in Neo-Platonic terms, here she employs the simpler thought of the end of Book II: Death negates the value of human aspirations. Pearls appear here for the first time in the poetry of Book III: I suspect that they function as intimations of the one real thing of great price, the truth that the prisoner is to derive from Philosophy's teaching. On the other hand, this poem attempts to do much less than does II.m.5, the evocation of the Golden Age, which much more force-fully condemned the pursuit of wealth.

Meter These three couplets combine the iambic trimeter ($\cup - \cup - \cup - \cup$ $- \cup - \cup -$) with the pentameter; the latter, properly seen in the company of hexameters to make elegiac couplets (I.m.1, V.m.1), will be found with Phalaceans (hendecasyllables; cf. I.m.4) at IV.m.4. I have regularized Boethius' practice in both meters. The meter draws us back to I.m.1 and its complaints about ephemeral Fortune and its longing for death; Philosophy thinks she has transmuted that complaint into something new.

Book III, Prose 4

This section, on the worthlessness of political offices as a path to true happiness, reprises various of the arguments already made in II.6; the next section, on the power of kings, is also related to II.6; the concluding thoughts, on fame limited by the circumscribed boundaries of one's own culture, are first found in II.7.

III.4.1 The opening sentence is an objection put into the mouth of the fictional adversary of the diatribe, and is a rhetorical flourish, not an idea seriously imputed to the prisoner himself; a similar rhetorical gambit is used at IV.4.30.   III.4.1 administrative offices: *magistratus*, distin-guished from *honores* (political honors) and *dignitates* (high offices). III.4.2 wart: The Latin word *struma*, which technically seems to refer to a kind of tumor (a lymphoma, perhaps) might be better translated as "excrescence," except that *struma* has a nasty forceful brevity to it that is worth preserving.   III.4.3 lack of honor: A pun; *indignitas*, or lack of *dignitas* (honor), is to be referred to the technical meaning of its plural, *dignitates*, or "high offices."

Book III, Meter 4

Just as the substance of III.4 recapitulates that of II.6, so too is it fol-lowed by a poem on Nero, much in the manner of II.m.6. Surely this is a sort of political commentary, with Theoderic hiding behind Nero; can its goal just be to convince the prisoner that he was looking for happiness where it was not to be found? The true king, Love, was extolled in II.m.8, but one is entitled to ask whether such constant reference to the prisoner's own unfortunate situation is really designed to make him for-get it and so strive heavenward.

III.m.4.2 nacreous: Here and in the two following pearl passages
(III.m.8.11, III.m.10.10) I use "nacreous" (of the substance of mother-of-
pearl) rather than a more literal translation of the modifying adjective
(snowy white or bright white). Only in III.m.3.3 does the poet actually use
a noun that means pearls; here and elsewhere he makes do with poetic
synonyms; "snowy-white little stones" as the alternative may serve to
excuse the more recherché "nacreous."   *III.m.4.5* Fathers: The Roman
senators; Philosophy would seem to demean the prisoner's political
achievements directly.   *III.m.4.8* desolate: The adjective *miser*, which I
elsewhere translate as "pitiable," instead of the more expected—and out-
of-date, to my ear—"wretched" (cf. II.3.4, etc.), is here "desolate,"
because the noun *miseria* functions as "desolation" (cf. III.5.3, 5; IV.4.4, 9),
implying isolation, a state of being cut off from what is good.

Meter Four couplets compounded of a hendecasyllable (– – – ∪ ∪ – ∪
– ∪ – –; see I.m.4) and an Alcaic decasyllable (– ∪ ∪ – ∪ ∪ – ∪ – –).
The two lengths have obvious similarities.

Book III, Prose 5

Again, Philosophy is not just speaking against kings generally; by the end
of the section it is quite clear that she is upbraiding the prisoner personally
for his willing subjection of himself to the world of kings and courts.

III.5.6 tyrant: Cicero in *Tusculan Disputations* 5.61–62 means to refer the
story of the Sword of Damocles to the court of Dionysius I of Syracuse
(ca. 430–367 B.C.E.), the archetypical tyrant; Damocles was however a
member of the court of Dionysius II (367–357 B.C.E.).   *III.5.10–11* Seneca, forced to commit suicide by Nero, has already been mentioned at
I.3.9; Caracalla had Papinianus the jurist executed in 212 C.E.; this is the
latest point of historical reference, prior to the author's own time, in
Consolation.   *III.5.13* friends: Just as III.m.3 returns to the subject of
Death, brought to the fore at the end of Book II (II.7.21–23, II.m.7),
III.5 returns to the other topic of the end of Book II, the nature and
value of friends (II.8.6–7, II.m.8.26–27).

Book III, Meter 5

Philosophy returns to the four destructive passions of I.7.25–31. In the
context of the previous poem, and with the subsequent description of a
Roman Empire stretching to India, we may think of Nero here; but the
more generalized language is susceptible to a more contemporary refer-

ence. The suggestion that Theoderic has no true power, and is himself in the grip of desolate sorrow, anticipates in some ways the very end of *Consolation*: see Note at V.6.44–48.

III.m.5.6 your: singular. Just as the prose section ended with a second person singular address, so does the verse section.

Meter Anapestic dimeters catalectic ($\cup\cup - \cup\cup - \cup\cup - -$, with substitutions), last seen in the poem on the Golden Age, II.m.5. These two poems stand in stark contrast: In the one, there is peace without ambition, a world without ships and trade; in the other, corruption and greed and their extension to the ends of the earth.

Book III, Prose 6

While glory has been treated before at II.7, it is striking how many of the concerns of the prisoner's lament at I.4 appear here: merits, conscience, popular gossip. Then does Philosophy's denial of glory to noble birth attack one of the prisoner's weak spots, his pride in his family, especially in his sons (cf. II.4.3–9)? The one good thing about noble birth is that it imposes the necessity of good behavior on those who inherit it (III.6.9); the prisoner will like this phrase even less when Philosophy repeats it at the end of *Consolation*, in pointed reference to the prisoner's questions about divine foreknowledge destroying free will and imposing necessity on actions.

III.6.1 Euripides, *the* tragic poet: The Latin has simply *tragicus*. I have added the name Euripides, just as I have added the name of Homer whenever he is quoted; but the fact that *tragicus* serves to identify Euripides shows that he is taken as the tragic poet par excellence; Philosophy calls him "my good Euripides" at III.7.6.   *III.6.9* necessity . . . imposed: This will prove to be a crucial phrase, and will reappear in the last sentence of *Consolation*.

Book III, Meter 6

The poem deserves attention for the way in which Philosophy manages to intertwine questions of human biological descent and spiritual descent. Looking to one's beginnings is both a rejection of the value of particular family relations (Philosophy here is no longer interested in telling the prisoner that he is fortunate because of his father-in-law, wife, and sons) and a call to remember the origins of one's soul so as to return to it.

III.m.6.5 human souls: The preexistence of souls is Neo-Platonic, not Christian.

Meter A unique combination of dactylic tetrameters catalectic ($-\cup\cup-$ $\cup\cup-\cup\cup-$, or the first three-and-a-half feet of an epic hexameter) with an ionic dimeter ($\cup\cup--\cup\cup--$). The tetrameters allow for substitutions of spondees for dactyls, which I have also allowed; the dimeters allow a long syllable to replace the first two shorts, a variation that I have not allowed. The dimeter will reappear at III.m.7 in its anaclastic form (that is, with its fourth and fifth elements reversed ($\cup\cup-\cup-\cup--$), and in combination with trochaic dimeters at IV.m.2. The combination in III.m.6 suggests the epic hexameter, and lies along the line of epic experiments that culminates in III.m.9; perhaps the references to the world of mortals keep this from full participation in the epic voice.

Book III, Prose 7

Continuing along the path begun in the previous poem, Philosophy is not only lecturing against physical pleasure as a source of true happiness, but is trying to wean the prisoner away from his attachments to his own family. The childlesss man was an example of misfortune at II.4.14.

III.7.6 Euripides: Philosophy alludes to *Andromache* 418–20; the same play was quoted from at III.6.1.

Book III, Meter 7

An artfully complex analogy: Pleasure stings as bees do, but pleasure is sweet at first, sweet as honey is. Bees do not apply honey before they sting, but pleasure does. The sorrow that follows sweetness is reminiscent of Philosophy's promise of the bitter cup after the initial sweetness of her teachings.

Meter Anaclastic ionic dimeters ($\cup\cup-\cup-\cup--$). Otherwise known as Anacreontics, they are rare in Latin poetry; here, they represent a variation on the ionic dimeters seen in the previous poem.

Book III, Prose 8

This map of detours sums up the previous sections of Book III; III.9 will mark the beginning of the second half of Book III with a great change in tone and topic: a true dialogue between Philosophy and the prisoner on the nature of the Good, and no longer a mere diatribic condemnation of false goods. The invitation to peer up to the heavens, and to avoid the close inspection of worldly things, will be repeated in the poem on Orpheus and Eurydice which concludes Book III.

III.8.10 Lynceus and Alcibiades: Lynceus, one of the Argonauts, had inhumanly sharp sight; Alcibiades, the notorious Spartan sympathizer and traitor to the Athenians, was proverbially the most beautiful man in all of Greece.   *III.8.12* brought about . . . bring it about: Translating *perfectae sunt* and *perficiunt*. Underlying these verbs is the idea of drawing together disparate things and unifying them into the whole that is the culmination of their parts: "to perfect" in its original sense; see also III.2.3, III.9.26.

Book III, Meter 8

As in III.m.2 and III.m.6, Philosophy attempts to go beyond the castigation of a false path to happiness to hint at a transcendent truth (vv.17–18), in preparation for the arguments about the Good which are to come in III.9.

III.m.8.12 myrex, purple dye: This shellfish is highly prized for the purple dye, traditionally for royal robes, made from its crushed shell. The references to pearls and royal purple here again put us in the world of Nero and his brother tyrants; the delicacies of the sea often receive the moralists' condemnation for their extravagance, particularly for the fact that people have to go far to get them. So Pliny would say in his *Natural History*; cf. the shipless world of the Golden Age at II.m.5.13–15.

Meter A combination of the lesser Asclepiad (see before at II.m.2) and an iambic dimeter (in various combinations at II.m.4, II.m.7, and IV.m.1). I have allowed myself an extra short syllable at the beginning of v.20 and in the middle of v.21; at vv.4 and 11, "jewels" is a monosyllable. The two lengths are somewhat discordant; this is perhaps appropriate for the theme of false pursuit of real treasure.

Book III, Prose 9

By the end of this passage *Consolation* is ready for a new beginning; the search for true happiness, announced at III.1.5, is presented not so much as the next step in the prior argument (as is claimed at III.9.1) but as something new. But it is only the prisoner who uses the word "starting point" (*exordium*). The prisoner becomes more talkative now (cf. especially III.9.25–27, his longest speech since Book I), and his eagerness is plain to see. Note that the language describing how false happiness counterfeits true happiness and offers only images of it closely resembles the language of V.6.12, in which the world of time, bearing an image of the timeless world, attempts to copy and rival it, but imperfectly.

Book III, Meter 9

The gist of the Neo-Platonic myth contained in this elegant poem is simple enough: That which is emanates from the One (The Good, God, the Father) and passes through the realms of the World Mind and the World Soul to the realm of matter. It is the nature of the One that it bends back toward itself what would otherwise be a straight-line and irrevocable motion of descent toward decay; the soul is drawn by this nature back toward its source, and what is the universe is this circular motion centered around the One. A few implications are of particular interest: The prisoner is made aware by means of the last line that he is always in the presence of God by being at any point along this trajectory of descent and return. Does he need to follow Philosophy back home to his fatherland? And when Philosophy at the end of IV.1 promises to bring him there by her own conveyances, is she intimating that the natural return inspired by the nature of the One is different from that longing for return that is her own desire? Note too that here all of the language of recovery of vision after darkness, the sun after the night or the storm, familiar from Books I and II, is here recast as vision directed toward God as the blinkers, which are life in the world of matter, are taken away.

III.m.9.27–28 Philosophy avoids personal pronouns, other than when addressing the Father as "you." This complicates matters at the end of v.27 and in v.28, where I have chosen to add the pronoun "their"; "the" is also acceptable.   III.m.9.28 source, leader, haven: As is pointed out by Pelikan 1997, 131–32, at the end of a discussion of this poem, the language here reflects the Christian definition of the Trinity as source, guide, and goal.

Meter Epic hexameter, the meter that we have been anticipating since I.m.1. This is also the meter of didactic poetry; the vision of the order of nature and the transcendence of God is here at its most complete and perfect, and is accorded the most grand and respectful treatment.

Book III, Prose 10

This is a two-pronged argument: First, that God is the highest happiness; second, that two highest goods cannot exist simultaneously as different things. This is unexceptionable; however, when Philosophy goes so far as to say that each truly happy person is God, and that there can be many gods by this sort of participation in the essence of the One God (III.10.25; cf. IV.3.10), she has stretched her arguments to the absolute limit of what a Christian may also believe (see Gruber 1978 ad loc.). The prisoner calls this conclusion a precious gift; but the next time we see an explicit congruence of Christian and Neo-Platonic thought (III.12.22), the possibility of synthesis quickly breaks down. The argument reaches the conclusion that the substance of God is located in the highest Good, which is what all people seek.

III.10.27 attached to this chain: *hoc adnectendum est.* The verb usually has connotations of weaving and linking; the translation exaggerates this connection.

Book III, Meter 10

The poem speaks of the peaceful haven of the true light. The contrast between looking down to the depths of the dark earth and looking up to the brightness of the heavens is striking, but well-prepared for. What is remarkable is the new reference to the false light of gold and jewels. Also remarkable is the return, after the sublimities of III.m.9, of the imagery of descent into darkness, such as was found in I.m.2, which has a number of parallels here.

III.m.10.7–9 Tagus, Hermus, Indus: Note that these three rivers span the known world, in order from extreme West to extreme East.

Meter This is a metrically complex, possibly confused, poem. There is an alternation of two eleven syllable lengths, the Phalacean hendecasyllable (– – – ∪ ∪ – ∪ – ∪ – –, familiar from I.m.4 and III.m.4, to reappear at IV.m.4) and the Sapphic (– ∪ – – – ∪ ∪ – ∪ – –, already seen at II.m.3, to reappear at IV.m.7). But v.2 is not a Sapphic, and the regular alternation is not established until vv.5–6. It seems from the subject matter that vv.1–3 are insistent, while v.4 is calming. Perhaps an alternation of mood is to be imagined, consistent with the presentation of false light and true light. At v.8, "Lydian" is disyllabic.

Book III, Prose 11

The conclusion that the Good is the goal of all things (because all things desire to be one and the One and the Good are the same) points the end of Book III back to the end of Book I and Philosophy's initial diagnosis of the prisoner: self-forgetfulness, ignorance of the goal of things, forgetfulness of the rudders that steer the world. This latter point will be addressed when Philosophy discusses Providence in Book IV. Clearly, then, this prepares the reader for the fact that Book III is about to end and that Book IV will be like another beginning on another topic. In other words, the stage is set for large portions of *Consolation* to find their end and resolution; the fact that the next two books will in fact be presented as digressions will come as a surprise to the attentive reader.

III.11.22 pith, wood, bark: The ancients distinguish three parts of a tree trunk, as the following sentence shows; other translations speak of a tree's dispersing strength through pith and bark, misled by the fact that *robur* means both strength and wood; I notice that Chaucer understands the passage as I do.   *III.11.33* things that have been created: The word is *creatis*, and only here does *Consolation* employ *creata* in the Christian sense of "creation;" similarly, the word for love here is *caritas*, a Christian word but evidently no different in meaning here than the *amor* of III.11.31. Are these Christian slips of the tongue? An intentional blurring of the lines of argument? A subtle anticipation of Philosophy's quoting scripture at III.12.22?

Book III, Meter 11

One could say that this very dense and allusive poem represents the practical side of the theory expressed at III.m.9: The individual must bend the soul's straight-line motion of descent into the circular path that would direct it back to its origins in God. We are out of the realm of the cosmic mythology of the soul's return and into the realm of personal spiritual discipline. The Platonic doctrine of recollection has this emphasis, that each person must look deep within for the truth once known in the heavenly realms. This has two important functions: First, the prisoner is in fact being told to be less reliant on the explicit teachings of Philosophy; second, it prepares us for the last time that the prisoner will speak in verse (V.m.3) in which he expresses Augustinian anguish over his bewilderment at how the truths about God can reside in his memory. Philosophy's response to the prisoner's questioning will be to return to this matter of recollection in V.m.4. *Consolation* will make a problem of memory, as Augustine's *Confessions* does.

Meter The lines are all choliambs, the limping variation on the iambic trimeter last seen at II.m.1 (∪ – ∪ – ∪ – ∪ – ∪ – – –).

Book III, Prose 12

Plato begins and ends this section, but its center is Philosophy's surprising quotation from the Old Testament Book of Wisdom at III.12.22. The prisoner's delight is clearly derived from the sudden presence of scripture (cf. Chadwick 1981, 238: "as if he were saying to Philosophy: 'Fancy you, of all people, knowing the Bible'"); his next enigmatic comment, and Philosophy's equally enigmatic reply, need to be read closely, for Philosophy will find at the beginning of Book IV that the prisoner is no longer willing to follow the plan of treatment and enlightenment that she had in mind. Is "the stupidity that rips great things apart" the prisoner's own compartmentalization of philosophy and revelation? When Philosophy wants "to smash the arguments themselves into each other" so that a "beautiful spark of truth may fly out," which arguments does she refer to? Why are the mythical Giants the first words out of her mouth after the prisoner praises her for quoting Scripture? And does her praise of the circularity of her argument, justified (tongue-in-cheek?) by the circularity of God, intend to frustrate the prisoner? At any rate, Book IV will devote itself to the coexistence of God and evil, despite the argument here that evil is nothing; the prisoner will there admit that Philosophy has only told him what he knew before, and that he has still not forgotten his earthly sorrow, which she has been so eager to have him set aside. The end of Book III does play some subtle and labyrinthine game.

III.12.17–18 Here we finally read that human beings are part of the divine order, a conclusion that the prisoner despaired of in I.m.5. Yet the language of voluntary and unsuccessful departure from the divine will is a problem.

Book III, Meter 12

The story of Orpheus and Eurydice is best known through Ovid's *Metamorphoses* (10.1–11.66). Boethius' quite respectable treatment of it here is remarkable primarily for its insistence on the need to look up, and the dangers of looking down too soon. This theme is woven into all of *Consolation*, gaining more prominence in later books (it will be repeated with

less mythical apparatus in IV.m.1). Philosophy will encourage the prisoner to rise to the level of God so as to view the world through God's
eyes, and thus despise the world; but the book will end with God's view
of the world (and the prisoner) and the need for virtuous action within
it. The value of the phenomenal world is ultimately something that Philosophy cannot get the prisoner to negate.

Meter Glyconics, the same meter as also concluded Book II, and nearly
concluded Book I (I.m.6); it will be seen again at IV.m.3 and V.m.4.
These last three glyconic poems offer an interesting progression. III.m.12
and IV.m.3 have mythical/heroic themes, casting Platonic recollection
and return to the fatherland as epic struggles (as does IV.m.7, in a different meter); but in Book V, this approach is dropped, and the poem is
much more philosopical, much less fanciful.

Book IV, Prose 1

The contrast to the beginnings of Books II and III is striking: The prisoner is no longer the stunned and silent listener, but an active ques-
tioner who redirects the course of Philosophy's presentation, as he will
again at the beginning of Book V. We do not learn what topics Philosophy had in mind; she merely feels confident that once she gets out of the
way the question of the coexistence of the good God and human evil in
the world, she will be able to help the prisoner fly, like Icarus, out of his
labyrinth (III.12.30). Her closing words here clearly echo the last line of
III.m.9, in which God, not Philosophy, is the leader, the path, and the
conveyance. Does Philosophy arrogantly overstep her boundaries here?
Her belief that she will be able to brace the prisoner with "unshakable
steadfastness" will need to be reread in the light of the end of *Consolation* (see esp. V.6.25).

Book IV, Meter 1

The soul in its return to the One is thought of as passing through the
various levels of the universe until it passes beyond the stars, at which
point the universe itself is thought of as the outer region at a great
remove from the centrality of the One (a metaphysical architecture
familiar from Dante's *Paradiso*, into which this has been imported). The
poem represents, much as the previous poem at the end of Book III does,
a more practical sort of exhortation, corresponding to the more theoretical and abstract III.m.9. Here is Philosophy's true concern: that the

prisoner look up to the realm of God, and from there look down in safety to the contemptible world below. The prisoner, who thinks himself an exile, will see, once he willingly removes himself from the world, that his oppressors are the true exiles. Along with the insistence on the imagery of looking up and looking down, the reader notes that Philosophy is still forced to be concerned with the prisoner's political situation, the reality that she is eager to transcend.

Meter Couplets compounded of dactylic tetrameters (see I.m.3, III.m.6, V.m.2, V.m.5) and iambic dimeters (II.m.4, II.m.7, III.m.8); though the individual elements are common, the combination is found only here in *Consolation*. Just as the dactyls in III.m.6 were part of the cresendo that culminated in III.m.9, perhaps here there is a falling away from that epic voice. But when this poem is paired with III.m.12, the different metrical treatments of the same theme suggest that the dactylic meter of IV.m.1 is somehow more appropriate for the greater emphasis on the structure of the universe, the glyconics of III.m.12 more appropriate for its heroic content.

Book IV, Prose 2

The beginning of IV.1 revealed a prisoner willing to redirect Philosophy's arguments; the beginning of IV.2 shows him even willing to poke a little fun at her: "Well fancy that!" is the phrase that Philosophy used at I.6.6 to express her dismay at the prisoner's inability to draw life-giving conclusions from his basic premise that the world is governed by reason. As the concluding sentences of this section make clear, the argument here builds up to the Platonic conclusion that only the good are powerful, because of the congruence of their desire and their knowledge; they know what is to be sought, and pursue it according to the proper means. This does not, of course, directly answer the objection of IV.1.4: After all, in their improper pursuit of the Good, evil people may make good people grovel at their feet. That the good always have their rewards is an argument reserved for the next prose section.

IV.2.30 <those who do not achieve their ultimate goals>: I follow Gruber's suggestion for this corrupt passage.   *IV.2.31–32* For a similar string of impassioned rhetorical questions, see V.m.3.   *IV.2.39* false power: *possibilitas*, as contrasted to *potentia*; so also at IV.2.44, IV.4.6.   *IV.2.39* unrighteous: *improbi*. Familiar from II.6.1, 15, 18; this will become a key term in IV.3.

Book IV, Meter 2

Philosophy hopes that the prisoner has taken to heart the lesson of the end of I.m.7, and so banished from himself the four cardinal passions of joy, fear, hope, and sorrow. Thus will he be able to appreciate that tyrants (again, a specific reference to the prisoner's own situation) are themselves tyrannized. The paradox is that the wise are always free. Note too the reappearance of the military imagery of chains and captivity, last seen at IV.2.27; Philosophy is encouraging the prisoner, as she did in Book I, to stand his ground. The conflict of this image and the image of flight back to the fatherland is another paradox imbedded here.

Meter A unique combination of a trochaic dimeter and an ionic dimeter ($- \cup - \cup - \cup - \cup$ / $\cup\cup - - \cup\cup - -$). The ionic dimeter was last seen at III.m.6; trochees will reappear at IV.m.5. The conflicting rhythms of the two halves of the line, falling and rising, slow and swift, may be suggestive of the conflict between the tyrant's desires and his actual state.

Book IV, Prose 3

The righteous by their very nature become gods; the unrighteous correspondingly become animals. The argument from animals here turns itself away from any consideration of the order and harmony of the physical world, such as is found in III.m.2 (cf. 34–35: "All seek out their own paths of reentry, Rejoice in their own private returnings.") This sort of popular moralizing seems out of place this late in *Consolation*, but it will reappear in the last poem of Book V, which stresses the commonplace that only human beings can look upwards to heaven.

IV.3.12 gross wickedness: This translates the single word *nequitia* here and elsewhere.   *IV.3.13* farthest limit: I follow Gruber and the manuscripts here, reading *extrema*.   *IV.3.19* inert: This condition may be profitably compared to the "lethargy" of I.2.5 and the "worn-out hearts" of III.1.2.

Book IV, Meter 3

The story of Ulysses, or Odysseus, and Circe is well known from Book 10 of the *Odyssey*. Two points are worth special interest. First, in the Neo-Platonic readings of Homer which take the wanderings of Odysseus as an allegory for the life of the soul and its longing for homecoming and return, the gift that Hermes gives to him so that he can avoid transformation into a beast (the plant *moly*) is interpreted as divine reason. Second, the transformative cup of Circe, with its poisons that pass deep within, is clearly reminiscent of the bitter cup that Philosophy says she will offer to the prisoner; it too is a draught that will pass deep within (II.1.7, II.3.4). Are Circe and Philosophy mirror images of each other?

IV.m.3.1 Ithacan captain: Ulysses, of course (to give him his Roman name); Boethius does not use his name, but only the "captain from Neritos," the name of a mountain on Ithaca.

Meter Glyconics, the favorite meter of *Consolation* (I.m.6, II.m.8, III.m.12, V.m.4). Curiously, these glyconics begin not with a spondee but a trochee, except in the final verse; I have accented my translation accordingly. The poem is tightly bound to III.m.12, which is also a myth retold as an allegory of spiritual return to the heavens (Orpheus and Eurydice). The last poem of Book IV, the last of the mythical allegories (primarily on Hercules), also ends with a line that is metrically different from the preceding ones.

Book IV, Prose 4

This protracted argument on the nature of punishment has its origins in the *Gorgias*; but it is not here because of any purely theoretical interest. Philosophy is addressing specifically the prisoner's upset at what has happened to him at the hands of unjust men, and inviting him to consider that the fact that they have gotten away with it merely increases their own punishment and their own unhappiness. Philosophy sums up her arguments halfway through (IV.4.23–25), and then returns to her particular interest, namely, to get the prisoner to forget these injustices. He is to contemplate the heavens (IV.4.27–32); he is to imagine what he would do if he were sitting in judgment (IV.4.35), and to abandon his anger (IV.4.41–42). The torture that would be to the advantage of the unrighteous (IV.4.40) is elsewhere said to be to the advantage of the righteous person falsely accused (I.3.9 and II.6.8, both referring to the philosopher Zeno); Philosophy still has it in mind that philosophical martyrdom is a good thing. In the next section, the prisoner will still be unconvinced, longing for a society in which tortures are reserved for the unrighteous (IV.5.3).

It is difficult to see a consistent distinction in this section between the two words for mind. *Mens*, among other things, is properly applied to the metaphysical principle, the Mind as an emanation from the One; *animus*, among other things, is properly applied to internal moral characteristics, like courage and drive. I indicate in the apparatus which term is used.

IV.4.7 sooner than you yourself would wish: This enigmatic phrase seems to point to the prisoner's imminent death: They will no longer be able to do the prisoner wrong if he is put beyond their clutches.   *IV.4.7 swift circuit:* Literally, "brief boundaries." The word for boundaries is *metae*, originally the turning points for races in the Circus, and evidently used here to suggest again the myth of the descent and return of the soul. *IV.4.15 good people are happy . . . :* This is stated at IV.1.7 as a conclusion that will be achieved; it cannot be said that it has already been granted or proved.   *IV.4.20 I answered that it was clear:* Along with I.6.11, the only place at which the narrator reports his words in indirect speech.   *IV.4.23 but it is not now my plan to discourse upon them:* Another bit of unfinished business; this need not be a promise of a Christian topic, despite the word "purgation," but only a reference to the end of Plato's *Gorgias*. *IV.4.26 look at:* This verb (*considero*) will be met very frequently in Book V. *IV.4.28 you have no need of a judge:* Philosophy would seem to change her mind by the end of *Consolation* (cf. V.6.48).   *IV.4.30 But the common herd . . . :* This is an objection imagined by Philosophy; we are back in the realm of the language of diatribe, as in Book II.   *IV.4.42 pitied, not persecuted:* Philosophy had earlier followed her own advice, when she mocked the prisoner in her first poem, but calmed down when she resumed in prose (I.2.1: "But it's time, she said, for medicine, not for complaint").

Book IV, Meter 4

Philosophy speaks to a plural audience, asking them to imagine that they are in the presence of Death; she turns to the prisoner in quieter tones at the end. After all of the talk of men as beasts, this poem adopts a different tack; human actions are worse than those of beasts. Is Philosophy addressing the unrighteous, encouraging them to change their ways? If so, does Philosophy herself have the ability to rise above outrage at the deeds of evil men? A similar address to a general audience will conclude *Consolation*.

Meter Couplets composed of Phalaceans (hendecasyllables) and the dactylic pentameter. The pentameter was most recently seen at III.m.3, and will be seen again at V.m.1 in elegiac couplets (the meter of I.m.1, this will suggest that Book V is a new beginning). Phalaceans are also found in various combinations at I.m.4, III.m.4, and III.m.10. Perhaps

we see here Philosophy's attempt to make a meter worthy of lamentation, in contrast to the elegiacs of I.m.1. V.m.1 is hardly a lament.

Book IV, Prose 5

This brief section shows the prisoner unimpressed. He knows about the
real merits of good and evil people, but he wants assurance of justice in
the here and now. Not only is he still complaining about the unjust legal
procedures that encompassed his own downfall; he is even doubting
what he held at the beginning of *Consolation* to be the bedrock of his
beliefs, that no day would ever come that could force him to accept the
idea that the world was governed by chance randomness (I.6.4). For all
of what Philosophy has told him, he is still "utterly amazed" at how the
world works. What will follow is the longest prose section of *Consolation*;
Philosophy perhaps thinks that she must work especially hard to win
him over.

Book IV, Meter 5

We learned at I.m.2 that it was once the prisoner's habit to discover the
hidden causes of Nature; much of the language here can be paralleled in
I.m.5, the prisoner's own emotional statement of his belief that Nature's
regular patterns have causes, though he cannot see that humans fit into
them. Her words at v.18, "hidden causes trouble the spirit," are echoed
immediately at IV.6.1, by a prisoner who has lost the confidence he had
before (the substance of IV.5). Most curious is the fact that there is no
reference in this poem to the place of people in the divine order; Philosophy will go on to explain the order of the universe in rather abstract
terms in the coming prose section.

IV.m.5.1 Great Bear: The text actually says Arcturus, but the intention is
clear.

Meter This is a strange and complex form: The odd lines consist of two-
and-a-half trochees, followed by an adonic (see I.m.2, I.m.7); the even
lines substitute two-and-a-half iambs for the trochees. A fair number of
substitutions are allowed in the trochaic and iambic lengths; what I offer
here has been considerably regularized (trochees: $- \cup - \cup -$; iambs: $\cup$
$- \cup - \cup$). Iambs were last seen at IV.m.1, trochees at IV.m.2; neither
meter appears again. They seem to be part of the structure of Book IV,
framing most of it and isolating the last two poems: IV.m.6, in anapests,

mirroring the form and content of I.m.5; and IV.m.7, Sapphic lengths used for the last of the mythological poems.

Book IV, Prose 6

This, the longest section of *Consolation*, divides into two halves: The first speaks of the difference between the timelessness of Providence and the time-boundedness of Fate; the second, beginning at IV.6.32, is a discussion of specific human types and divine dispensations, according to which a just person might be reasonably punished or an unrighteous person prosper. Philosophy argues both theoretically and practically that the prisoner should stop thinking about the world of time and rise above it to the world of the simplicity of the divine mind; in Book V this will be recast as an exhortation to rise up to divine eternity. The prisoner has forced Philosophy into this topic—she wanted to take him straight to his fatherland—and she unflinchingly tells him that whatever is happening to him in prison expresses the divine will and is exactly as it should be. The question for the reader is not whether this argument seems personally persuasive or consoling; rather, is this what Philosophy really wanted to talk about? The section ends with Philosophy's anticipation that all of this has made the prisoner a stronger man, and ready for what she has in store for him. It is not a dialogue, but a lesson (cf. her interjection, "You will say," at IV.6.23); dialogue is reserved for the final prose section of Book IV.

IV.6.1 supernatural occurrence: The Latin word is *miraculum*. It soon becomes a key term in this section; at IV.6.27, where I have enclosed it in quotation marks, Philosophy uses it ironically.   IV.6.4 just how burdensome such things are: Philosophy is being quite specific; she is referring to Boethius' translation and commentary on the various logical works of Aristotle.   IV.6.7 immutability: The noun *stabilitas* appears only here; however, the related adjective *stabilis* has been frequently encountered as "standing one's ground, stable" or, in more metaphysical contexts, "remaining unmoved;" cf. I.m.1.22, I.m.4.16, III.m.9.3, and so forth.   IV.6.13 power of angels: Philosophy merely lists a number of the possible names and definitions of intermediary spirits; there is nothing particularly Christian about this.   IV.6.14 first divinity: A "Neo-Platonic slip," if you think that whatever Philosophy says is supposed to be something that the reader is to assent to; otherwise, it is an example of Philosophy leading into an area where the prisoner would not prefer to follow. IV.6.15 first mind: Philosophy uses many terms, seemingly interchangably, for divine mind: first mind, mind above, deep mind, and so on.

IV.6.19 loom: The Latin is *exordiis*, more often translated as "beginnings" or "origins."   *IV.6.35–39* This sequence of examples of human natures parallels the sequence of animal similes at IV.3.17–21.   *IV.6.38* someone: The riddling reference may be to the *Chaldean Oracles*, a Greek text in epic hexameters regarded as inspired in Neo-Platonist circles.   *IV.6.41* to discover by trial who they are: Latin, *in experimentum sui*. What is suggested here may be a partial answer to the question raised at I.6.17, what is a human being. Suffering may in effect reveal what a person is.   *IV.6.42* a glorious death: Philosophy seems to return, in pointed reference to the prisoner's plight, to the longing for a new martyr that she expressed at I.3.   *IV.6.53* another order: When using animal similes at IV.3.16–21, Philosophy spoke of humans falling below the human condition; now she adds the necessary qualification that such humans are still bounded by the divine order.   *IV.6.53* a goddess: Literally, "a god;" Homer himself speaks this line. I have added "as Homer says" here as elsewhere; the text is cited in Greek.   *IV.6.54* divine operation: This forbidden topic is utimately attempted in the concluding sections of *Consolation*, V.3–V.6.

Book IV, Meter 6

This poem is a climactic restatement of a number of metaphysical themes expressed in crucial earlier poems: that God does control the universe (I.m.5), that Love controls the universe (II.m. 8), that the elements of the universe are in balance, and that the return of the soul to its source is part of that balance (III.m.9). The seasons have their place in this poem too (I.m.2, I.m.5, I.m.6), as does death (vv.30–33). What is easily overlooked is that humans do not appear in this poem, except under the term of "each creature" in v.31. Their presence would be expected given the prominence of the human condition in the preceding prose section. Philosophy is still most concerned to speak of the order of the universe in impersonal terms.

Meter Anapestic dimeters, a meter familiar from I.m.5 and III.m.2; both of these poems are on the same theme as this, and the three call out to be read together. The meter will appear one final time at V.m.3, where the prisoner will speak and will not assert, but will forcefully question, the order of the universe and the possibility of human knowledge of it.

Book IV, Prose 7

After the impersonal praise of the ordered universe in IV.m.6, Philosophy returns to the language of moral exhortation, ultimately encouraging the prisoner to wage war with Fortune. This is not strictly consistent with the opinion expressed at the beginning, that every Fortune is good, a claim that rehabilitates the Fortune of Book II, a force for disorder that seems counter to Providence, as another force in the service of divine order. There is a dilemma here. The prisoner admits reluctantly that all fortunes are good; this means that his unjust punishment is good. But such things can be good only for those who are engaged in the perfection of their virtue (IV.7.15); the prisoner must then admit that he is not perfect. If not perfect, then he is not ready to return to his fatherland. Philosophy's attempt to make the prisoner forget his time-bound self and see the Providential and timeless world has not been successful; Neo-Platonism's concern with the cycle of the soul and the architecture of the divine leaves scant room for ethics. It is only within the context of time, in the world of progress toward virtue, not in the timeless myth of the soul's return to its origins, that the prisoner can accept his Fate.

IV.7.4 too true: As at III.7.5, this identifies a depressing conclusion; the prisoner sees the implications of this, that his imprisonment is good. IV.7.7–9 The series of responses given here by the prisoner resembles closely the sequence at III.3.7–10.   IV.7.17–21 The military language of these concluding sentences has been prepared for at the beginning (IV.7.4), but this passage, like IV.m.6, serves to summarize a number of motifs present from the beginning of *Consolation* (cf. I.m.1.22, I.3.12–14, I.m.4.15–18). The battle is for virtue itself or, when made less abstract, against tyrants (cf. II.6.8).

Book IV, Meter 7

The moral exhortation of this poem is tempered by the fact that Agamemnon is hardly an example of one who does what is right; the murder of his daughter is inexcusable. Ulysses is more positive but, as in IV.m.3, his experience is in stark contrast to that of his men. Hercules, despite the fact that his labors are imposed upon him (by the cowardly king Eurystheus) for a murder that he has committed, is the most positive example of the three, the one who achieves heaven by the sweat of his brow. Do all three heroes offer examples to follow? Verse 32 refers only to a single example; and it is possible that a range of Fates and Fortunes are on display here, from that of the tyrant to that of the tyrant's victim. A more hopeful analysis is offered by O'Daly 1991, 220–34.

IV.m.7.1–7 The famous story of Agamemnon's sacrifice of his daughter Iphigenia is, according to Lucretius (1.82 ff.), an example of the horrors wrought in the name of religion.   *IV.m.7.8–12* The story of Polyphemus is in the *Odyssey*, Book 9.   *IV.m.7.13–31* For the labors of Hercules, I have only supplied in the apparatus the names of the labors that are obliquely referred to; further information may be found in the glossary. There is no standard account of the labors of Hercules in antiquity.

Meter Sapphics, last seen at the beginning of III.m.10. Both in theme and in meter, this poem suggests that a large division of *Consolation*, starting after III.m.9, has come to an end. The next poem, V.m.1, is written in elegiac couplets, the meter of *Consolation*'s opening poem; this will suggest a new beginning.

Book V, Prose 1

Book V begins as Book IV did, with Philosophy wanting to go in one (undisclosed) direction, and the prisoner forcing her to consider other topics. The prisoner wants to talk about Aristotle; Philosophy wants to take him to his fatherland. She fears that he will not have the energy to follow the straight path to its end; but after all of the talk of God's bending straight-line motion into curves that lead back to himself (cf. IV.m.6.40–43, quoted by the prisoner at V.3.36), we may suspect that a circuitous route is in fact more appropriate. Could it be that the prisoner has himself discovered in Philosophy's own arguments a buried treasure that he is eager to claim for himself? By the conclusion of *Consolation*, Philosophy will no longer talk about going to the fatherland, or about becoming gods by participation; she will talk of prayer, the necessity of virtuous action in this life, and the approach to God through humility.

V.1.2 A proper encouragement: Referring specifically to the closing lines of the previous poem, IV.m.7.32–35.   *V.1.2* personal experience: Referring specifically to the prisoner's earlier work as a commentator on Aristotle; see also V.1.6. Boethius' two commentaries on Aristotle's *On Interpretation* provide much of the material that is discussed in Book V. *V.1.9* old philosophers: Referring to the Presocratics generally.   *V.1.13–17* The example of the buried treasure accidentally found, from Aristotle's *Metaphysics* 4.30.1025a14 ff., becomes standard in later philosophy. But it is worth pointing out that this is a popular example as well, and is one of the parables of the Kingdom in Matthew 13:44. The finder of buried gold is cursed by Philosophy at II.m.5.27–30.   *V.1.14–18* confluence/confluent: Many words are used for this key idea (running together, flowing together, occurring together, intersecting) and it has not been possible to distinguish all of them in translation.

Book V, Meter 1

The first poem of Book V takes water as its starting point: The separation of the Tigris and the Euphrates suggests the disposition of Providence, their recombination suggests disorder. The first poem of Book II is similar, in which the vicissitudes of Fortune are compared to the wild waters of the Euripus. The argument has progressed from Fortune to Chance, but the emphasis is on the downward motion of things. Philosophy would have preferred the upward motion of ascent to the fatherland.

Meter The elegiac couplet, the meter of the first poem of *Consolation*, reappears at the beginning of Book V to suggest yet another new beginning (cf. III.9.32–33, 4.1, IV.6.7). This time, the meter is sung by Philosophy, not the prisoner; a progression is implied from lament (for which the meter is appropriate) to philosophical instruction (for which it is not).

Book V, Prose 2

This introduction to the question of the relation between free will and divine foreknowledge relies on an argument just seen at IV.3.14–21, in which people who fall away from their divine potential are said to cease to be human beings and are thus compared to beasts. It is freely admitted to be a paradox (V.2.10, "captives of their own liberty"). It is also a moral exhortation, just as the end of Book IV was: Those who would be perfect must fight and not surrender to slavery. In a sense, this is an admission that the arguments to come will not be wholly satisfactory (cf. V.6.25). The following prose section and the poem after it are the last times that the prisoner speaks at length and in his own voice; he is full of angst, and speaks longingly of prayer (V.3.33–36).

V.2.4 choose: The verb *optare* is translated in Book V as "choose"; it was translated as "hope for" in earlier books (cf IV.6.23, 43).   V.2.7 substances that are ethereal and divine: A curious plural, as only God can satisfy this definition.   V.2.10 The language of darkness and light, of the passions and ignorance, was prominent at the beginning of the *Consolation* (cf. I.2.6, I.m.3, I.6.21).

Book V, Meter 2

The poem seems to be another exhortation to look down to the earth from above, as at IV.m.1. But the prisoner is not called on to look down here, as his vision would be inadequate. God's vision scatters the obstructions of matter; he was called on to do just this at III.m.9.25–26; God's vision of the world of matter closes *Consolation* (V.6.45–48).

V.m.2.1 Homer: For all the times that Homer is quoted, and for all of the times that Ulysses and Agamemnon are referred to, this is the only passage in which the poet is named specifically.   *V.m.2.3* Looks over all things and listens to all things: Quoted in Greek, this is actually the first line of the poem.   *V.m.2.13* Sees what is, what was and what will be: This is the boast of Homer's Sirens (*Odyssey* 12.189–91). When the Muses were expelled at I.1.11–12 Philosophy called them Sirens.   *V.m.2.14* solely: *Sol* (sun) and *solus* (alone, solely) were believed to be etymologically related.

Meter Only here do dactylic tetrameters appear in a pure form, not in combination with other meters (cf. I.m.3, III.m.6, IV.m.1, and V.m.5). This allows Boethius to quote Homeric epic in Greek. After the elegiac couplets of the previous poem, used for instruction rather than lament, this meter seems to sing appropriately in an epic and didactic voice; this is the last appearance of Phoebus and the only time that Homer is named; there are allusions to the epic III.m.9 as well. I have taken some liberties with the meter; although many substitutions of anapests and spondees are allowed, there are no third-foot spondees such as I have in v.2.

Book V, Prose 3

The prisoner has two objections to the coexistence of divine foreknowledge and human free will: One is that necessity binds God's knowledge to human actions; the other is that human actions cannot be the cause of divine knowledge, which must be eternal and not contingent. But the prisoner's fears are stated in another way at the end of his speech: If there is a fated chain or sequence of events, then there only a motion outward from God and his Providence and no returning. The line that he quotes from Philosophy's poem at IV.m.6 must be remembered in context: If God did not bend back in circles toward himself the lives that he sets in motion and keeps in balance, there could be no return of the soul. But the prisoner here imagines this return of his soul to God not in terms of the Neo-Platonic myth of return, but in terms of humility, hope, and prayer for deliverance. The prisoner does set a Christian longing against Philosophy's abstractions; the second half of Book V represents her best efforts to address his concerns in abstract rather than devotional terms.

V.3.4 foresees: Providence (*providentia*) means "looking out before," "seeing in advance." The related verb is *providere*; here a different compound verb with the same sense is used (*praeviderit*). Other verbs include *praenoscere* ("have foreknowledge") and *praesentire* ("perceive before-hand").   *V.3.6* foreknowledge: Of the many words used for this con-cept in Book V, the one used here and at V.3.9 and then frequently throughout the second half of Book V, *praescientia*, is more of an ecclesi-astical term.   *V.3.9* contingent by necessity: Contingent is a technical term, referring to things or actions that come into being in one way, but that could have happened otherwise; this possibility of happening other-wise is thought of as a function of things themselves and of the process of causation, not merely of human ignorance about it. Chadwick 1981, 157–63, is a good discussion of this.   *V.3.9* even if the foreknowledge does not seem to impose a necessity of resulting on future events: At V.4.6, Philosophy erroneously refers to this line of argument as the pris-oner's own, and not as one that he imputes to other philosophers.   *V.3.14* as they were foreseen to happen: These words are possibly a scribal addition, and are rejected by a number of editors.   *V.3.20* true knowl-edge: Translating *scientia ipsa*, "knowledge itself," "knowledge properly so called."   *V.3.21* grasps: The verb *comprehendere* will become very com-mon in the closing prose sections of Book V.   *V.3.26* opinion: The argu-ments here have been turning on the question of what sorts of intellectual activity have what sorts of objects; this is the crucial question of the sec-ond half of Book V (see V.4.24–39).   *V.3.31* necessity: This key noun, used by the prisoner in this section a few times, will become the substance of the discussion of the second half of Book V, occurring about thirty times; this does not count the various forms of adjectives meaning "neces-sary."   *V.3.32* our vices too are to be referred to the creator of all good things: This conclusion was explicitly denied at IV.2.44.   *V.3.33* to pray for deliverance: The simple word "pray" (as noun or verb) does not appear here, being replaced by hope; prayers appear at the end of *Consolation* (V.6.46). This verb is very specific: *deprecari*, to pray to avoid something. Its meaning in the prisoner's mouth is quite clear.   *V.3.34* While the phrase "inapproachable light" may not definitely point to a quite similar phrase in 1 Timothy, the combination of it with the approach to God through humility and the return of divine grace clearly suggests that what is on the prisoner's mind at this point is a Christian, and not a Neo-Pla-tonic, ascent to God. The prisoner's following poem, his last substantial expression, with all of its Augustinian echoes, suggests the same.

Book V, Meter 3

The prisoner delivers only four poems in *Consolation*: I.m.1, his pathetic attempt at elegy; I.m.3, a narrative, set to paper before his actual powers of speech return to him; I.m.5, his impassioned statement of his belief that God rules the world, and his hope that he would rule humans as well; and finally V.m.3, an equally impassioned statement of Augustinian doubts about the ability of the mind to recognize the truth. Book V therefore marks the return of the prisoner poet of Book I. In fact, much of Book V, perhaps as a structural restatement of the myth of return, finds itself covering the ground of Book I. There is the opening elegiac poem, parallel to I.m.1, to announce a new beginning; the imagery of blindness, darkness, and light, familiar from Book I, returns here; and the prisoner here uses the meter he had used before at I.m.5. The two poems need to be read in parallel: After all of his conversation with Philosophy, the prisoner is now not certain of what he knows and how he knows it. The language of V.m.3.13 ff. echoes Plato's *Meno* 80de; but see also Augustine, *Confessions*, Book 10. Note also the complete absence of mythological details and poetic conceits.

V.m.3.6–24 For a similar string of questions, cf. IV.2.31–32; cf. also V.m.4, Philosophy's answer to this poem, delivered in her favorite meter (glyconics).

Meter Anapestic dimeters (I.m.5, III.m.2, IV.m.6), with a concluding adonic (I.m.7). I have allowed myself some extra short syllables. The meter has been used for statements of the divine order, possibly because of the way in which the meter mimics some of the movement of epic verse. Note that when the prisoner quoted Philosophy's poetry at V.3.36, he quoted from her anapestic dimeters (IV.m.6.43); that poem concluded as did her other poem in this meter, stressing the return of each thing to its source (III.m.2.34–38).

Book V, Prose 4

The argument here is essentially simple: The same thing is perceived in different ways according to the nature of the perceiver; different modes of cognition create different types of knowledge; the higher the type of perception, the further removed is its knowledge from the world of sense toward the world of the Forms. The next prose section will go on to speak of the unique nature of the knowledge of God, and how God's knowledge by its very nature does not destroy free will because it does not impart necessity. But the second sentence here signals that an absolutely satisfactory logical proof of this cannot be achieved: "The motion of human rational argument cannot set itself next to the simplicity of divine foreknowledge."

V.4.1 broke divination into its constituent parts: The verb here is in doubt, and has been emended to mean "did away with divination," because Augustine (*City of God* 5.9) claims that this is what Cicero did in his *On Divination*. If Boethius is referring to Cicero directly and not to Augustine, the reference may be to *De Divinatione* II.8.   *V.4.1 you pursued it yourself:* The reference here is to Boethius' two commentaries on Aristotle's *On Interpretation*, which occupied the years between 513 and 516. See especially the *Second Commentary on Aristotle's On Interpretation* 9 (the famous chapter on tomorrow's sea battle and future contingents: *On Interpretation*, 225.9 ff., now available in translation in Blank and Kretzmann 1998, pp. 170 ff.).   *V.4.6 a thing that you yourself admitted:* The prisoner did not admit this at V.3.9, but only spoke contemptuously of others who believed it.   *V.4.14 happen:* The verb translated three times here as "happen" (*evenire*; cf. also V.4.18, 19), is related to the noun regularly translated as "result" (*eventus*: cf. V.1.8).   *V.4.16 in vain:* The phrase occurs at V.3.30, when the prisoner speaks of the worthlessness of rewards and punishments in a deterministic universe; and at the very end of *Consolation*, when Philosophy says that hopes and prayers are not in vain.   *V.4.26 casting its rays:* The common theory of sight in antiquity is that the eye sends out rays which bounce off of objects and bring back sense impressions to the eye. *V.4.27 sense perception, imagination, reason, and understanding:* The four levels of thought of Plato's Divided Line at *Republic* 511de are here only approximated; the lower levels of belief and conjecture are replaced by sense perception and imagination, a change probably of Aristotelian origin (cf. Sharples 1991 ad loc.). Boethius does not have fixed and exclusive technical terms for these modes of thought: Reason (*ratio*) is also the term for rational argument, and thus for discursive thought in general; understanding (*intelligentia*) is often represented by *scientia* (knowledge; cf. the apparatus at V.4.22).   *V.4.30 what is encompassed by universality: ambitum universitatis.* While *universitas* can mean "universe" (3.12.34), I think that it means here "universality" as it does in its only two other appearances in *Consolation* (both in V.5.7). Other translations imply that the world of the Forms is beyond "the boundaries of the universe."   *V.4.32 Understanding . . . looking down . . . from on high:* Philosophy here returns to a favorite theme, the need to look down to the earth from the highest possible vantage point. The soul can do this in IV.m.1; God can at V.6.45; see also "the eye of understanding" at V.4.30.   *V.4.35 human being:* Philosophy asked the prisoner at I.6.15 if he knew what a human being is; his unsatisfactory response made her promise that she would reveal the answer to him. It is a promise not explicitly kept in *Consolation*.

Book V, Meter 4

Philosophy here argues the Platonic position that the mind has its own powers against the Stoic position that the mind merely receives sense impressions. This is in response to the prisoner's previous poem, and procedes along the lines that the prisoner himself suggested, also without mythological apparatus; but this argument, which closely entails the Platonic theory of recollection, had been elegantly expressed earlier by Philosophy at III.m.11, which should be read in parallel with this.

V.m.4.17 knowledge: The word translated as knowledge here, *notio*, is found only in these concluding sections of *Consolation*.   V.m.4.21–25 Philosophy here ascribes to the mind's vigor the ability to rise up to the world above and to look down to the world below, which she has often encouraged the prisoner to do. The appearance of Philosophy at I.1.2 suggested at the outset that this ability to live in two worlds is her natural function.

Meter The last of Philosophy's five glyconic poems (along with I.m.6, II.m.8, III.m.12, IV.m.3). IV.m.3 also concluded with a statement of the inalienable force of the mind, not subject to Circe's poisons. Glyconic poems tend to come at the ends of books; the final poem in *Consolation*, in quite a different meter, will return to the moralist's theme that humans were designed not to be animals, and to look up, not down. Such a concluding poem may seem a bit of a descent after this more philosophical poem.

Book V, Prose 5

Philosophy begins this section by summarizing the argument of the previous poem: The activity of the mind is prior to the passivity of the body. Then different modes of perception and thought are assigned to different types of being; God, being highest, has the highest and most universal mode of perception, which humans do not have. There are many echoes in this section of III.10, in which God is established as the highest Good, which has taken to itself nothing outside of itself; but there it was allowed that humans could become gods by partcipation (III.10.35), a claim that Philosophy would not be eager to make here.

V.5.1 mind: A distinction may be intended between the mind as an agent that forms judgments about what it perceives (*mens*: an act of the mind) and the mind as a perceptive agent, actively gathering information (*animus*: strength of the active mind).   *V.5.1* well then!: Not translating the phrase *quid igitur* (V.1.11, V.3.22, V.5.5), but approximating the emotional turning point of this one long sentence.   *V.5.3* desire: See the note at I.1.9.   *V.5.12* let us raise ourselves up, if we can, into the head of that highest intelligence: As Gruber points out, Philosophy's appearance at I.1.2 suggests that she is the means by which mortals may do this, being at one moment on their level, at another with her head high above the clouds.

Book V, Meter 5

The concluding exhortation of the previous prose section, that the prisoner raise himself into the head of the highest intelligence, is here given a full treatment. It is an ancient commonplace that humans are distinguished from animals by their ability to look up and so contemplate their heavenly origins. Here, this is cleverly paralleled to the argument that each sort of creature has its own mode of perception; each has its own characteristic posture as well. Much of the language has no parallels in the rest of *Consolation*; note too the continued absence of mythical apparatus, in keeping with the sober nature of Book V (the only mythical intrusion in the poetry is the reference to Phoebus at V.m.2.2).

V.m.5.3 strong desire: So I interpret *pectus* (literally, "chest"), following Gruber. The phrase *vi pectoris* could mean "by the force of its chest"; and while this could be meaningful in reference to slithering snakes, I prefer to point the contrast to the birds of the next two lines.

Meter These long lines are composed of a dactylic tetrameter acatalectic and a trochaic length called an ithyphallic ($- \cup - \cup - -$); the combination is known as a fourth archilochean (as in Horace's *Odes*, 1.4). This is the only occurrence of this length in *Consolation*, though dactylic tetrameters have appeared frequently, in both catalectic and acatalectic forms, in combination with other meters and alone (see, most recently, IV.m.1 and V.m.2). It is hard to see why this is an appropriate final meter: It has the epic rhythm at the beginning, and a different rhythm at the end. But given the thematic change in the *Consolation*, from the desire to fly up to the exhortation only to look up to the heavens, the variation may suggest something of a synthesis.

Book V, Prose 6

Knowledge depends upon the knower, not the thing known; *Consolation* concludes with an argument for understanding the knowledge of God as outside of time, as a timeless now. It is an elegant argument, showing much original work on Boethius' part, and deriving from work that he had done earlier; cf. his *Second Commentary on Aristotle's On Interpretation*, p. 241 ff., on the two necessities; p. 224 ff., on the justice of laws given the reality of free will (translated in Blank and Kretzmann 1998, 180 ff., 170). This view holds the field until Aquinas makes the necessary modifications that are inconsistently made here: God's knowledge is not foreknowledge; to use the language of foreknowledge implies the irrevocability of human actions, instead of their simple existence (cf. Sorabji 1980, 124–25; Sharples 1991, introduction, pp. 43–46). But for the reader, this presentation is a stage in the plot of *Consolation* and not just a philosophical argument: The same Philosophy, who had urged the prisoner to fly up out of his prison so that he could look at the world below and despise it and its tyrants, ends by asking the prisoner and the world at large to imagine themselves as seen through the eyes of God, to view a world that is rational, Providential, and valuable, where righteousness is of necessity imposed upon them. This is not the language of escape from the prison, but of acceptance of the world as not a prison.

V.6.6 Lerer 1985, 230 notes that both Aristotle and Plato are mentioned by name in this last section of *Consolation*, and suggests that this is an expression of the harmony of the two authorities in the present work. V.6.11 ancient and glorious: The adjective *antiquior*, literally "more ancient," carries with it the additional idea of "more excellent" (cf. Gruber ad loc.); the translation preserves both senses.   V.6.12 falls away: The language of falling away into the temporal world of multiplicity is that of the Neo-Platonic myth of the life of the soul.   V.6.12 come in contact with: Another sense of the verb *contingere*, which elsewhere means "be contingent, exist by contingency." The word is punningly used at V.3.9 and V.6.25, "contingent by necessity."   V.6.14 names that are worthy: There are frequent references to false names: II.6.19, II.7.20, II.m.7.17, III.4.15, III.6.2.   V.6.16–17 Philosophy's distinction between what should be called God's knowledge pure and simple (sometimes the term *notio* is used for this abstraction: V.6.26, 31, 43), and what is falsely called foreknowledge, is not consistently maintained. The claim that Providentia does not literally mean foreknowledge is specious; the references to foreknowledge in V.6.16 use the verb *praevidere*, whence the invented Previdentia of V.6.17.   V.6.18 light of the divine eye: The word for eye here is *lumen*, translated in its twin senses of "light" and "eye"; the word for "eye" at V.4.30 and V.6.38 is the more literal *oculus*. V.6.19 hardly: Here and at V.6.40 Philosophy puts answers in the prisoner's mouth, rather as in her diatribes in Book II and the first half of

Book III.   V.6.25 a contemplator of the divine: A vague phrase, not
quite meaning "theologian," yet more elevated than "student." Philosophy with her head above the clouds at I.1.2 would seem to be contemplating the divine. The verb "approached" contains the stem of the word
found at V.3.34 in the reference to 1 Timothy 6:16, "inapproachable
light."   V.6.42 our future actions be said to provide a cause for the foreknowledge of God: Sharples 1991 ad loc. notes that human actions must
therefore be predestined (cf. IV.6.4), because God's knowledge *is* of our
actions, even if it is not of our actions as future actions. The next sentence, which is obscure, may even support this contention implicitly. If
"has itself established the status" means "defined them as they are," and
"owes nothing to things that are subsequent to it" refers to time itself,
"after they have been set into motion," then all is fixed from the
moment of creation. We may reasonably ask whether we are to take this
as part of Philosophy's own beliefs, or only an inconsistency unnoticed
by either character in the dialogue or by the author himself. The end of
Consolation certainly speaks of freedom of the will in problematic terms:
Necessity is imposed on all people to act with righteousness.   V.6.47
raise up your minds: This language is in contrast to the language of the
flight back to the fatherland at IV.1.8–9, though it does resemble the
ascent of the mind (*mens*) to God at III.m.9.22. The word for mind here
is *animus*, not quite as abstract as *mens*.   V.6.48 there *is* a great necessity imposed upon you: Not only does Philosophy speak in the plural, but
she echoes the words of Esther 16:4. The context of the passage in
Esther is important, I think: King Artaxerxes in his decree promises that
his unworthy ministers who have abused their powers and harmed his
subjects cannot avoid the eye of God; they will be punished. Does Philosophy turn to address the prisoner's persecutors here, even as the prisoner himself is left to contemplate the justice of his situation?

BIBLIOGRAPHY

The following is highly selective, comprising only those works that are referred to in the Notes, and those recent works in English that students may find particularly useful if they wish to deepen their understanding of Boethius and *Consolation*.

I. *Texts, Scholarly Aids, etc.*

Bieler, Ludwig, ed. 1984. *Anicii Manlii Severini Boethii Philosophiae Consolatio.* 2d ed. Corpus Christianorum, Series Latina, XCIV. Turnhout: Brepols.

Cooper, Lane. 1928. *A Concordance of Boethius: The Five Theological Tractates and The Consolation of Philosophy.* Cambridge, Mass.: The Mediaeval Academy of America.

Gruber, Joachim. 1978. *Kommentar zu Boethius De Consolatione Philosophiae.* Texte und Kommentare, Band 9. Berlin: Walter de Gruyter.

———. 1997. "Boethius 1925–1998 (1. Teil)." *Lustrum* 39: 307–83. (Part two, forthcoming).

Kaylor, Noel Harold, Jr. 1992. *The Medieval Consolation of Philosophy: An Annotated Bibliography.* New York: Garland Publishing, Inc.

Moreschini, Claudio, ed. 2000. *Boethius: De Consolatione Philosophiae, Opuscula Theologica.* Bibliotheca Teubneriana. Münich: K. G. Saur.

O'Donnell, James J., ed. 1984. *Boethius, Consolatio Philosophiae.* Bryn Mawr, Pa.: Bryn Mawr Commentaries.

Sharples, R. W., ed., trans. 1991. *Cicero: On Fate (De Fato) & Boethius: The Consolation of Philosophy (Philosophiae Consolationis) IV.5–7, V.* Warminster: Aris & Phillips, Ltd.

II. *General*

Astell, Ann W. 1994. *Job, Boethius, and Epic Truth.* Ithaca: Cornell University Press.

Asztalos, Monika. 1993. "Boethius as a Transmitter of Greek Logic to the Latin West: *The Categories.*" *Harvard Studies in Classical Philology* 95: 367–407.

Barnish, S. J. B. 1990. "Maximian, Cassiodorus, Boethius, Theodahad: Litera-ture, Philosophy and Politics in Ostrogothic Italy." *Nottingham Medieval Stud-ies* 34: 16–32.

Blank, David, and Normann Kretzmann, trans. 1998. *Ammonius: On Aristotle's On Interpretation 9; with Boethius: On Aristotle's On Interpretation 9, first and second commentaries.* Ithaca: Cornell University Press.

Bower, Calvin M., trans. 1989. *Fundamentals of Music, Anicius Manlius Severinus Boethius.* New Haven: Yale University Press.

Bowersock, G. W., Peter Brown, and Oleg Grabar, eds. 1999. *Late Antiquity: A Guide to the Postclassical World.* Cambridge, Mass.: Belknap Press.

Chadwick, Henry. 1981. *Boethius: The Consolations of Music, Logic, Theology, and Philosophy.* Oxford: Clarendon Press.

————. 1998. "Boethius, Anicius Manlius Severinus." In Edward Craig, ed., *Routledge Encyclopedia of Philosophy.* New York: Routledge, vol. I, 801–13.

————. 1999. "Philosophical Traditions and the Self." In Bowersock et al., 60–81.

Claassen, Jo-Marie. 1999. *Displaced Persons: The Literature of Exile from Cicero to Boethius.* Madison: University of Wisconsin Press.

Crabbe, Anna. 1981. "Literary Design in the *De Consolatione Philosophiae*." In Margaret Gibson, ed., *Boethius: His Life, Thought and Influence.* Oxford: Basil Blackwell, 237–74.

Curley, Thomas F., III. 1986. "How to Read the *Consolation of Philosophy*." *Interpretation* 14: 211–63.

————. 1987. "The *Consolation of Philosophy* as a Work of Literature." *The American Journal of Philology* 108: 343–67.

Davies, Ioan. 1990. *Writers in Prison.* Oxford: Basil Blackwell.

Dillon, John. 1999. "Philosophy." In Bowersock et al., 642–43.

Dronke, Peter. 1994. *Verse with Prose from Petronius to Dante: The Art and Scope of the Mixed Form.* Cambridge, Mass.: Harvard University Press.

Frakes, Jerold C. 1988. *The Fate of Fortune in the Early Middle Ages: The Boethian Tradition.* Leiden: E. J. Brill.

Gersh, Stephen. 1986. *Middle Platonism and Neoplatonism: The Latin Tradition.* 2 vols. Notre Dame: Notre Dame University Press.

Lerer, Seth. 1985. *Boethius and Dialogue. Literary Method in the Consolation of Philosophy.* Princeton: Princeton University Press.

Masi, Michael, trans. 1983. *Boethian Number Theory: A Translation of the De Institutione Arithmetica.* Amsterdam: Rodopi.

Minio-Paluello, Lorenzo. 1970. "Boethius, Anicius Manlius Severinus." In Charles Coulston Gillespie, ed., *Dictionary of Scientific Biography.* New York: Charles Scribner's Sons, vol. II, 228–36.

Moorhead, John. 1992. *Theoderic in Italy.* Oxford: Oxford University Press.

O'Daly, Gerard. 1991. *The Poetry of Boethius*. Chapel Hill: University of North Carolina Press.

O'Donnell, James J. 1993. Review of Moorhead. *Bryn Mawr Classical Review* 93: 8–10.

———. 1999. "Boethius." in Bowersock et al., 344–45.

Olmstead, Wendy Raudenbush. 1989. "Philosophical Inquiry and Religious Transformation in Boethius' *The Consolation of Philosophy* and Augustine's *Confessions*." *The Journal of Religion* 69: 14–35.

Payne, F. Anne. 1981. *Chaucer and Menippean Satire*. Madison: University of Wisconsin Press.

Pelikan, Jaroslav. 1997. *What Has Athens to Do with Jerusalem? Timaeus and Genesis in Counterpoint*. Ann Arbor: University of Michigan Press.

Relihan, Joel C. 1990. "Old Comedy, Menippean Satire, and Philosophy's Tattered Robes in Boethius' *Consolation*." *Illinois Classical Studies* 15: 183–94.

———. 1993. *Ancient Menippean Satire*. Baltimore: Johns Hopkins University Press.

———. forthcoming. *The Prisoner's Philosophy: On the Limitations of Pagan Thought in Boethius's Consolation*. Notre Dame: Notre Dame University Press.

Scott, Jamie. 1995. *Christians and Tyrants: The Prison Testimonies of Boethius, Thomas More, and Dietrich Bonhoeffer*. New York: Peter Lang.

Scourfield, J. H. D. 1993. *Consoling Heliodorus, A Commentary on Jerome, Letter 60*. Oxford: Clarendon Press.

Shanzer, Danuta. 1984. "The Death of Boethius and the *Consolation of Philosophy*." *Hermes* 112: 352–66.

Sorabji, Richard. 1980. *Necessity, Cause, and Blame: Perspectives on Aristotle's Theory*. Ithaca: Cornell University Press.

Spade, Paul Vincent, trans. 1994. *Five Texts on the Mediaeval Problem of Universals: Porphyry, Boethius, Abelard, Duns Scotus, Ockham*. Indianapolis: Hackett Publishing Company.

GLOSSARY

As the full apparatus makes unnecessary a complete listing of themes, images, and examples (animals, blindness, laws, prayer, seasons), I have compiled here only the proper names of the Latin text and the English translation, and have tried to indicate when the proper name has been imported, or changed, by the act of translation. Beyond the explanatory matter and the textual references, the glossary may prove useful to a reader who wants to see at a glance the nature of Boethius' poetic and mythological language, the rarity of contemporary reference, the paucity of cited sources. *Consolation* is in many ways a nostalgic document, written by a man who considers himself to be the last true philosopher, the last Roman poet, and the last Republican patriot; this is the world that he has preserved. For readers not instinctively familiar with the Classical mythology or ancient history embedded in this allusive text, additional useful data are given. *Consolation* is also more about God than human beings; the subdivisions created for the terms God, Father, Fortune, Providence are not exhaustive; it is hoped that the passages cited will prove to be adequate starting points. In citations of the poems, line numbers indicate those of the translation, not the Latin text.

Abundance   Latin Copia, as a goddess or mere personification, the spirit of Plenty (II.m.2.5), familiar in the term cornucopia.

Academic philosophers   The followers of Plato, named after his Academy; named along with the Eleatics (q.v.) as the philosophers on whose teachings the prisoner was raised (I.1.10); the term does not specifically refer to the Neo-Platonists of Boethius' own day.

Acheloüs   Longest river in Greece, emptying into the Gulf of Corinth; the god of this river was defeated by Hercules (IV.m.7.23–24) in a contest for the hand of Deianira, daughter of Oeneus, king of Calydon; Hercules broke off his horns, and Acheloüs give him the horn of Amalthea (the cornucopia; cf. Abundance) in exchange.

Aemilius Paullus (Lucius Aemilius Paullus Macedonicus)   Earned his name Macedonicus from his defeat of Perseus (q.v.) of Macedonia in 168 B.C.E. (II.2.12); he
retained for himself only Perseus' library from the spoils of this war.

Aetna   The volcano on the island of Sicily (II.m.5.25, II.6.1); see also Vesuvius.

Agamemnon   Son of Atreus, brother of Menelaus (qq.v.) and the leader of the
Greek forces against the city of Troy (IV.m.7.1–7); he sacrificed his daughter
Iphigenia (q.v.) so that his fleet could set sail; he was murdered by his own wife
(Clytemnestra, sister of Helen [q.v.]) upon his return home.

Albinus   A Roman senator of consular rank, accused by Cyprianus (q.v.) of
treason; when Boethius sought to defend him (I.4.14, 32), he too was accused of
treason; Boethius turned his own defense into a defense of the entire senatorial
order, a tactic that backfired (I.4.36).

Alcibiades   450–403 B.C.E., Athenian aristocrat and general in the Peloponne-
sian War, notorious both for his physical beauty and for his immorality (III.8.10);
in his complex career, a traitor to Athens.

Amor   Translated as "Love" (q.v.).

Anaxagoras   ca. 500–428 B.C.E., the first philosopher to practice in Athens, also
exiled from Athens (ca. 437) on a charge of impiety (I.3.9).

Antaeus   A giant, son of Earth, and inhabitant of Libya; Hercules wrestled with
him, defeated him and killed him (IV.m.7.25), thus doing to him what he did to
all who chanced by him; not one of Hercules' canonical twelve labors; cf. Busiris,
Diomedes.

Aquilo   North Wind (I.m.6.9, II.m.3.11); see also Boreas.

Arcadia   The central Peloponnesus; the god Hermes (Latin Mercury) is prominent there, worshipped on Mt. Cyllene, where he is supposed to have been born
(IV.m.3.17); home of monsters killed by Hercules: cf. Centaurs, Erymanthian
boar, Stymphalian birds.

Arcturus   The brightest star in the constellation Boötes (q.v.), often designating
the constellation itself, rising in November at the start of the rainy season
(I.m.5.21); confused with the Great Bear (IV.m.5.1).

Aristotle   384–322 B.C.E., pupil of Plato and founder of the Peripatetic School;
in late classical circles, the logician, the necessary first step on the way to Neo-
Platonic metaphysics; many of Boethius' works are translations of and commentaries on Aristotle's logical works; the commentaries on his *On Interpretation* lie
behind much of Book V, though he is explicitly cited in *Consolation* for other things
(III.8.10 = *Protrepticus*, frag. 59; V.1.12 = *Physics* 2.4–5, cf. *Metaphysics* 4.30,
1025a16; V.6.6 = *De caelo* 1.12, 283b26 ff.); called "my good Aristotle" at V.1.12.

Athenians   Not the inhabitants of contemporary Athens, but of the Classical
Athens of Socrates and Plato, the philosopher's true homeland (I.5.4).

Atlantic   Translation of the adjective Hesperius, "belonging to the evening star," or Hesperus (q.v.) (I.m.2.16); translated as "West" (III.m.2.31); see also Hesperides.

Atreus   The father of Agamemnon and Menelaus (qq.v.), most notorious for feeding to his brother Thyestes his brother's sons; Agamemnon is identified as the son of Atreus at IV.m.7.1.

Auster   South Wind (I.m.7.6, II.m.3.7, II.m.4.9); see also Notus.

Bacchus   Not as complex a divinity as the Greek Dionysus, Bacchus here functions as a synonym for grapes, the Fall grape harvest, and wine (I.m.6.14, II.m.5.6); cf. Ceres.

Basilius   One of Boethius' accusers (I.4.16), his daughter was married to Opilio (q.v.); his attack against Boethius served to recoup his fortunes and his status in Theoderic's court.

Bear   Ursa Major (IV.m.6.8); inaccurately referred to by the name Arcturus (q.v.) at IV.m.5.1; a sign of the Northern latitudes (cf. II.m.6.11).

the Beautiful   A Platonic synonym for the One, the Good (II.5.10).

Biblical allusions   While many passages in *Consolation* are suspected of betraying biblical language and allusions, the following seem secure and function as important parts of the progression of the argument: I.m.5.46–48 and II.m.8.28–30 (Matthew 6:10, the Lord's Prayer); III.12.22 (Wisdom 8:1); V.3.34 (1 Timothy 6:16); V.6.48 (Esther 16:4).

Boeotia   The region of mainland Greece just north of Attica; its eastern boundary is the Euripus (q.v.).

Boethius (Anicius Manlius Severinus Boethius)   ca. 480–524 C.E., the author of *Consolation* and the prisoner of its text. Roman aristocrat (consul in 510) and court official (Master of Offices in 522), orthodox Christian theologian, academic polymath, and Aristotelian commentator. His father (II.3.5); adopted by Symmachus (q.v.), his father-in-law (I.4.40, II.4.5); his (unnamed) wife, Rusticiana (II.3.6, II.4.5); his (unnamed) two sons, Symmachus and Boethius (II.3.6, II.3.8, II.4.7; cf. III.7.5–6); his friends (I.m.1.21–22, I.4.40, II.8.7; cf. II.m.8.26–27, III.2.9, III.5.13–14); his earlier poetic efforts (I.m.1.1–2); composes/speaks in verse (I.m.1, I.m.3, I.m.5, V.m.3); his earlier academic studies (I.m.2.6–23, I.4.3–4, IV.6.4, V.1.2–3, V.4.1; see Aristotle, Plato); raised by Philosophy (I.2.2–4); his library (I.4.3, I.5.6); his desire for public virtue (I.4.7–8, II.7.1–2, IV.5.2–4); his exile (I.5.2–5, I.6.18, II.4.17); cannot recognize Philosophy (I.1.13); his self-forgetfulness (I.2.5–6, I.6.14–17; cf. II.5.29); his silence (I.1.1, 13; II.2.4–5; cf. II.7.1, 20, III.1.3); needs medicine (I.2.1, I.5.11–12, I.6.19–21, II.1.7, II.3.3–4, II.5.1, III.1.2–3, IV.6.5); his complaint (I.4; cf. IV.4.1–6, IV.2.41, IV.4.29, IV.5.1–7); Senatorial conspiracy (I.4.20–36); accused of practicing unholy arts (I.4.37–42); a separate account of his trial (I.4.25); complaint analyzed by Philosophy (I.5.7–10, II.3.4–14); his good fortune (II.4.4–10).

Boötes   Also known as Arctophylax, or the Bear Warden, a northern constellation (IV.m.5.3); its brightest star is Arcturus (q.v.).

Boreas   North Wind (I.m.3.7, I.m.5.19); see also Aquilo.

Brutus (Marcus Junius Brutus)   ca. 85–42 B.C.E., Republican hero and chief of
the conspirators that assassinated Caesar (II.m.7.16); committed suicide after
defeat at Philippi during the Civil Wars; related to the Lucius Junius Brutus who
drove the last of the Etruscan kings out of Rome to usher in the Republic.

Busiris   Mythical king of Egypt who would regularly kill his guests until he was
himself killed by Hercules (II.6.10); not a labor of Hercules, nor is it mentioned
in IV.m.7; cf. Hercules and his defeat of Antaeus (q.v.).

Cacus   A fire-breathing monster who lived on the future site of Rome; killed by
Hercules when the latter was returning from the far West with the cattle of the
monster Geryon (IV.m.7.26), thus assisting Evander (q.v.).

Caligula (Gaius Julius Caesar Germanicus)   12–41 C.E., Roman emperor from 37,
whose madness and cruelty were legendary; suspecting a conspiracy against him,
he was responsible for the death of Canius (q.v.) (I.4.27).

Camenae   Latin poetic equivalent of the Greek Muses (q.v.) (I.m.1.3).

Campania   The west-central area of Italy that includes Rome and Naples; a
very fertile area, source of much agricultural wealth and home to many of the
aristocratic elite (I.4.12).

Cancer   The constellation of the Crab, a sign of summer (I.m.6.1).

Canius (Julius Canius [or Canus, or Kanus])   Executed by Caligula (q.v.) (I.3.9,
I.4.27); one of a number of Stoic martyrs celebrated in *Consolation* as opponents
of tyranny (see also Seneca and Soranus).

Caracalla (Marcus Aurelius Antoninus)   Roman Emperor from 198–217 C.E.;
among the many whom he had killed was the jurist Papinianus (q.v.) (III.5.10).

Carthage   Rome's enemy in the Punic Wars (264–146 B.C.E.), and the object of
any patriotic Roman's hatred; see Regulus (II.6.11).

Cato (Marcus Porcius Cato)   95–46 B.C.E., implacable foe of Caesar during the
Civil Wars; after Caesar's victory at Thapsus, Cato committed suicide rather than
accept the humiliation of Caesar's pardon; another example of a Stoic martyr and
enemy of tyranny (IV.6.33); the reference at II.m.7.15, coupled as it is with the
name of Fabricius (q.v.), could suggest Cato the Censor (234–149 B.C.E.).

Catullus (Gaius Valerius Catullus)   ca. 84–54 B.C.E., the neoteric Republican
poet; present in *Consolation* only for his unflattering description of a political
office holder; see Nonius (III.4.2).

Centaurs   Half human, half horse, uncivilized creatures said to be the descen-
dants of Ixion (q.v.); their defeat by Hercules shows his role as a civilizer of the
Greek world (IV.m.7.14).

Cerberus   The three-headed dog, guardian of the underworld (III.m.12.30); his abduction was one of the labors of Hercules (IV.m.7.19).

Ceres   Not as complex as the Greek Demeter, Ceres functions in *Consolation* as goddess of and as synonym for grain (III.m.1.4, IV.m.3.23); can be paired with Bacchus (q.v.) (I.m.6.5–14).

Chance   Latin *casus*, defined in the context of Providence at V.1.

China   A source of silk that can be dyed purple, and thus suggestive of extravagance and display (II.m.5.8, translating Seres, "the Chinese").

Cicero (Marcus Tullius Cicero)   106–43 B.C.E., the great Roman orator and politician, cited not as an example of a martyr to tyranny (proscribed and executed by Mark Antony's orders) but only as a source of philosophic detail (V.4.1, *De divinatione*) and moral persuasion (II.7.8, *Republic* 6.2); *Consolation* in theme and structure owes much to the five books of Cicero's *Tusculan Disputations*.

Circe   Mythical daughter of Helios (not to be confused with Phoebus), the sorceress who bewitches Ulysses' men and turns them (but not Ulysses himself) into pigs (IV.m.3, not explicitly named: "beautiful goddess," "child of the Sun").

Circus   At Rome, the Circus Maximus, the stadium for chariot racing and the scene of the apex of Boethius' political career, when he sat between his two consular sons and distributed largesse to the crowd (II.3.8).

Conigastus   A rapacious minister of Theoderic whom Boethius claims to have frequently opposed (I.4.10).

Copia   Translated as "Abundance" (q.v.).

Corus   Northwest Wind (I.m.3.3, IV.m.5.13, translated "West Wind" [q.v.]).

creator   An attribute of or a synonym for God; translating the Latin *conditor*, literally "founder" (I.m.5.1, II.5.10, 26; IV.m.6.34, V.m.2.7, V.6.9); translating the Latin *auctor*, literally "increaser, nourisher" (III.m.6.8 (translated as "God"), IV.1.7, V.3.32).

Croesus   Last king of Lydia (reigned ca. 560–546 B.C.E.), defeated by the Persian king Cyrus (q.v.); his fall from wealth and power taught him that human affairs turn like a wheel (Herodotus 1.207; cf. *Consolation* II.2.9); when about to be burned alive on a pyre, he called on the name of the Athenian Solon and was pitied by Cyrus and saved (II.2.11).

Cyprianus   A Roman of great power in Theoderic's Gothic court, he was one of the chief accusers of Boethius and Albinus (q.v.), and the older brother of Opilio (q.v.) (I.4.14).

Cyrus   Cyrus the Great, founder of the Achaemenid (Persian) empire; defeated Croesus of Lydia (q.v.) (II.2.11); proverbially a powerful and welcome conqueror.

Damocles   Friend of Dionysius (q.v.) II, tyrant of Syracuse, and member of his court; Dionysius is said to have illustrated the nature of kingship by inviting him to dine with a sword suspended over his head; the story is alluded to at III.5.6.

Death   Personified at II.m.7.8, 12, and 26, IV.m.4.3; not personified at II.3.13, II.4.28, II.7.21–23.

Decoratus   Served first as an advocate in Ravenna (q.v.), and later in Rome; died ca. 524; vilified by Philosophy as one with whom the prisoner could never serve (III.4.4), he is known elsewhere in positive terms; a pun on his named ("Glorified") may be intended.

Diomedes   A legendary king of Thrace, who supplied human victims to his team of flesh-eating mares; Hercules feeds him to his own horses as part of one of his labors (IV.m.7.20–21); cf. Antaeus, Busiris.

Dionysius (Dionysius II of Syracuse)   Reigned 367–357 B.C.E.; tyrant; under the influence of Plato (q.v.), became interested in philosophy; the famous story of Damocles (q.v.) is mistakenly attributed by Cicero (q.v.) to the court of the paradigmatic tyrant Dionysius I (*Tusculan Disputations* 5.61–62).

East Wind   Latin Eurus (II.m.4.4).

Eleatic philosophers   Followers of Parmenides and Zeno (qq.v.) (I.1.10).

Epicurus   341–270 B.C.E., founder of the Epicurean school (the Garden; cf. Porch), known for its exclusively materialist view of the universe (III.2.12); emblematic of the divisions that tore to pieces the unity of Platonic philosophy (I.3.7, "herds of Epicureans").

Erymanthian boar   Another Arcadian monster (cf. Centaurs) subdued by Hercules as one of his twelve labors (IV.m.7.27).

Euphrates   One of the two rivers of Mesopotamia, to the west of the Tigris (q.v.) (V.m.1.3).

Euripides   Athenian tragic poet, ca. 485–406 B.C.E., highly valued here for his epigrammatic moral sentiments; quoted at III.6.1 (*Andromache* 319–20), where he is called "the tragic poet"; alluded to at III.7.6 (*Andromache* 418–20), where he is called "my good Euripides."

Euripus   The strait to the east of Boeotia, separating it from the island of Euboea; proverbially wild and hard to navigate (II.m.1.2, translated "Boeotian straits"); functions as rivers do in *Consolation* to define order and disorder (cf. Euphrates, Hermus, Indus [q.v. India], Tagus, Tigris).

Eurus   East Wind (II.m.4.4).

Eurydice   Wife of the legendary Orpheus (q.v.) who dies on their wedding day; his unsuccessful attempt to bring her back is the topic of III.m.12 (III.m.12.6, 42–43, 50–51), an encouragement to look up to the heavens rather than down below the earth.

Evander   A son of Hermes who fled Arcadia (q.v.) and came to Italy and settled on the future site of Rome, on the Palatine hill (IV.m.7.26; see Cacus); in the *Aeneid*, he helps Aeneas in his fight against Turnus by sending his son Pallas to war; Pallas is killed by Turnus.

Fabricius (Gaius Fabricius Luscinus)   Consul in 282 and 278 B.C.E., censor in 275, proverbially frugal and incorruptible hero of the old Republic (II.m.7.15).

Fate   Contrasted to Providence (IV.6.8–17 and 31, IV.7.4).

Father   Not only an epithet or description of God, but also a pointed contrast to the tyrants whom philosophers must always oppose (III.m.6.2, III.9.33, III.m.9.22, III.10.12); not to be confused with Fathers (q.v.).

fatherland   Latin *patria*, not just the prisoner's homeland but where the Father is to be found, the natural goal of the journey of the soul (I.5.3–4, II.4.17) and the place to which Philosophy wants to lead the prisoner (III.12.9, IV.1.9, IV.m.1.25, V.1.4).

Fathers (= Roman senators) III.m.4.5.

Fortune   The explicit topic of Book II and Book III.1–III.8, a force in the world that seems to represent disorder but which is ultimately subordinated to God as one of his agents in the human world; habits described (II.1.9–19, II.m.1); her wheel (II.2.9–10; cf. II.1.19); speaks in her own voice (II.2.2–14); her gift of wealth (II.5, III.3); gift of honor and power (II.6, III.4, III.5); gift of glory (II.7, III.6); gift of physical pleasure (III.7); gifts summarized (III.8); Adverse and Favorable Fortune contrasted (II.8.3–6; cf. IV.7.7–22); true gift of Fortune (II.8.7); all Fortune is good (IV.7.2). See also I.m.1.17, I.m.4.2 (translating "Fate"), I.4.2, 19, 43–44; I.m.5.28, 45; I.5.10, II.1.2, II.3.1, 9–10, 13–14; II.4.2, 15, 17, 23; IV.5.2.

Furies   Spirits of the underworld who punish those who shed kindred blood, the Greek Erinyes; not named explicitly, but labeled as avenging goddesses (III.m.12.31–33).

Gaudentius   Along with Opilio (q.v.), brought accusations against Boethius (I.4.17); himself an exile, he sought to regain, as Basilius (q.v.) did, his lost wealth and status.

Germanicus (Germanicus Julius Caesar)   ca. 15 B.C.E.–19 C.E., father of Caligula (q.v.), a popular leader of some Republican sentiment under the emperor Tiberius (I.4.27).

Giants   Monstrous children of Earth, they attacked the Olympian gods and sought to depose them (III.12.24); in most versions of this Gigantomachy, Hercules (q.v.) fights on the side of the gods.

God   Fundamentally, *Consolation* seeks to define the nature of God and the operation of God in the world; called creator (q.v.), helmsman (q.v.), and Father (q.v.); Fortune (q.v.) and Providence (q.v.) are subordinate to him; equated with the Good (q.v.) and the One (q.v.); as defined by the prisoner (III.12.4–8); as defined by Philosophy (III.12.26–36); his Providence (IV.6.29–32); his eternity (V.6); his foreknowledge (V.3); controls the world (I.6.4 and 7, III.12.9–22, V.1.8) and the order of the seasons (I.m.6.16); source of all things (I.6.11) but not the source of evil (I.4.29–30, IV.1.5, IV.5.5–7); as highest good and happiness (III.10.7–17); Lord of kings (IV.m.1.20); plants Philosophy in the minds of the wise (I.4.8); people may be similar to God (I.4.39, III.10.24–25, IV.6.37); follow God (I.4.38).

the Good   A Platonic category, equivalent to God and the One; defined (III.2.2, III.2.20); equivalence of the Good and God (III.10.31, 36–43; III.12.12–22); the goal of all things (III.m.9.23, III.11.2–5, 37–41, IV.m.6.45); happiness, the goal of all people (III.2.2–12, IV.2.11–16); the source of Good (III.m.12.2).

Greek, quoted in text   Pi and theta (I.1.4), proverb (I.4.1), Euripides (III.6.1), philosophic texts (I.4.38, Pythagorean maxim; III.12.37, Parmenides; IV.6.38, Chaldean Oracles?), Homer (I.4.1, *Iliad* 1.363; I.5.4, *Iliad* 2.204; V.m.2.3, *Iliad* 3.277 = *Odyssey* 11.109, 12.323; IV.6.53, *Iliad* 12.176; II.2.13, *Iliad* 24.527–28).

Hades (the underworld)   III.m.12.26 (translating Taenarus [q.v.]).

Hades (god of the underworld)   III.m.12.40 ("the judge of the shades").

Helen   The wife of Menelaus (q.v.), the cause of the Trojan War (IV.m.7.3, the "wife abducted").

Hell   Not a Christian theological entity but an equivalent of the mythological Hades (III.m.12.46, translating Tartara [q.v.]).

helmsman   An epithet of God (I.m.5.27, 46; I.6.19, III.11.39, IV.1.3, IV.5.5, 7; IV.6.29).

Hercules   The Greek Heracles, the most popular of the characters of Classical mythology; the man who by strength and fearlessness civilizes the world, pays off the debt of his own wrongdoings, and gains a place among the gods; susceptible to spiritual allegorization in both pagan and Christian circles; and Busiris (II.6.10); labors of (IV.m.7.11–31: individual labors are listed in this glossary as well).

Hermus   A gold-bearing river in Asia Minor (the Gediz in modern Turkey), mentioned in the company of other rivers of riches (III.m.10.8).

Hesperian   Pertaining to Hesperus, the evening star; a synonym for Western (I.m.2.16, translated "Atlantic"; III.m.2.31).

Hesperides   The daughters of Night, living in the far west on the shores of Ocean, guardians of a tree with golden apples; retrieving these apples was one of the last of Hercules' labors (IV.m.7.17); returning through Africa he encountered Antaeus (q.v.).

Hesperus (= Vesper, q.v.)   The evening star (I.m.5.10, II.m.8.7); *Hesperius*, adjective, cf. Atlantic (q.v.).

Hindu Kush   The western Himalayas, viewed as the eastern boundary of the Roman Empire (II.7.8, called "Caucasus"); see also "India".

Homer   The poet of *Iliad* and *Odyssey*, with a reputation for divine wisdom that only grew in late antiquity; his writings are subject to allegorical interpretation in Neo-Platonist circles; while *Odyssey* is read as a tale of the journey of the soul, and as such has significant influence on *Consolation* (see Circe, Sirens, Polyphemus, Ulysses), it is *Iliad* that is quoted in the text (see "Greek, quoted in text"); the poet is named only at V.m.2.1; the translation has added his name where the Greek of his text is quoted.

Horace (Quintus Horatius Flaccus)   65–8 B.C.E., the foremost of the Roman lyric poets; his *Satires* are quoted from once (II.5.9); cf. Tiresias.

Hydra   The many-headed swamp snake of Lerna in the northwestern Peloponnesus, killed by Hercules as the second of his labors (IV.m.7.22); an emblem of the many-headed philosophical problem of the reconciliation of divine Providence (q.v.) and seeming evil in this world (IV.6.3).

India   The eastern limit of the known world (III.m.5.5; cf. Hindu Kush); home of tigers (IV.m.3.15) and pearls in rivers (III.m.10.9–10, the Indus) and the sea (III.m.3.3, where the Latin "Red Sea" stands for the Indian Ocean).

Iphigenia   The daughter of Agamemnon (q.v.), whom he had to sacrifice in order allow the Greek fleet to set sail for Troy; not explicitly named in the text (IV.m.7.6, "his luckless daughter").

Ithaca   Island home of Ulysses (q.v.), off the northwest shores of the Greek mainland (IV.m.3.1, translating Neritos [q.v.]; IV.m.7.8).

Ixion   Legendary king of Thessaly who attempted to rape Hera; father of the Centaurs (q.v.); tied to an endlessly revolving wheel as his punishment in the underworld (III.m.12.34–35; cf. Fortune's wheel at II.2.9).

Juvenal (Decimus Iunius Iuvenalis)   Roman satirist active in the early second century C.E.; Philosophy paraphrases a snippet of his verse from *Satire* 10.20–22 (II.5.34).

Libya   North Africa generally (II.m.2.7, translating "Phoenician"; IV.m.3.11, translating "Marmaric"; IV.m.7.25).

Love   Latin *Amor,* corresponding to the Greek *Eros;* a cosmic principle of divine harmony, the uniter of opposites (IV.m.6.16, 44, 47); such a conception of Eros may be traced back to Parmenides (q.v.); as king of heaven (II.m.8.15, 29); beyond law (III.m.12.47–48, in story of Orpheus).

Lucan (Marcus Annaeus Lucanus)   39–65 C.E., nephew of Seneca (q.v.) and author of *The Civil War,* an epic on the contest between Caesar and Pompey; called "our kinsman Lucan" by Philosophy (IV.6.33), he laments the passing of Republican freedoms and the coming of empire and tyranny.

Lucifer   Not a Christian devil but the planet Venus, when rising before dawn; the "light-bringer," in contrast to Hesperus (q.v.), which is the name for Venus as the evening star (I.m.5.12, III.m.1.9, IV.m.6.15).

Lydia   A region of western Asia Minor, west of Phrygia(q.v.), around the river Hermus (III.m.10.8, expanding on the translation of "Hermus"); the defeat of its last king, Croesus, in 550 B.C.E. by the Persians under Cyrus (II.2.11) is told by Herodotus, *Histories* 1.86 ff.

Lynceus One of the Argonauts, the pilot whose special power was his keen sight (III.8.10).

Macedonia Northern Greece, connecting the mainland to the Balkan peninsula, west of Thrace; one of its kings in the Hellenistic era was Perseus (q.v.) (II.2.12).

Marmarica Coastal area of North Africa between the Pentapolis and Egypt (IV.m.3.11, translated as "Libyan").

Menelaus Brother of Agamemnon (q.v.); the Trojan War is fought to recover his wife Helen (q.v.) (IV.m.7.3).

Mercury (the god, the Greek Hermes) Not explicitly named; as "Arcadia's wingèd god," he gives to Ulysses the magical plant *moly* that makes him invulnerable to Circe's potions and poisons (IV.m.3.17).

Mercury (the planet) Not explicitly named; as the fiery planet (IV.m.1.12), or the red planet (IV.m.6.6), its color and motion are in contrast to those of Saturn (q.v.).

Muses Nine in number, goddesses of literary inspiration in all genres, under the leadership of Phoebus (q.v.) Apollo; Philosophy functions in *Consolation* as the author's Muse; Calliope, Muse of epic poetry, is mother of Orpheus (q.v.) (III.m.12.23); known collectively in Latin as *Camenae* (I.m.1.3); Muses banished from the prisoner's cell (I.1.7); Philosophy's new Muses (I.1.11; cf. II.1.8); Plato's Muse (II.m11.15).

Nature Capitalized when an abstract principle of the created world, and not merely in reference to an individual's nature (I.m.2.23, II.5.15–16, II.6.13, III.2.20, III.m.2.1, III.3.19, III.11.20, 23).

Nemean lion The lion that terrorized the town of Nemea in the Argolid (the northwestern Peloponnese) until killed by Hercules as the first of his labors (IV.m.7.15).

Neritos A mountain on Ithaca (q.v.); in the Latin poetic tradition, a neighboring island (IV.m.3.1, translated "Ithacan").

Nero (Nero Claudius Caesar) 37–68 C.E., Roman emperor 54–68, responsible for the death of Seneca (q.v.), an influential advisor in the early years of his reign, as well as of Canius and Soranus (qq.v.); the type of tyrant (II.m.6, III.m.4) behind whom lurks the tyrant Theoderic (q.v.).

Nonius A minor magistrate and contemporary of the Roman poet Catullus (q.v.), who ridicules him as a wart sitting upon his chair of office (III.4.2; cf. Catullus 52).

North Wind Latin Boreas (I.m.3.7, I.m.5.19), Latin Aquilo (I.m.6.9, II.m.3.11).

Notus South Wind (II.m.6.12, III.m.1.7).

Ocean   Originally the river that surrounds the world, Ocean is emblematic both of violence and of regularity (IV.m.6.12, translating *Oceanus*; I.m.2.14, I.m.4.5, II.m.2.1, II.m.4.5, translating *pontus*).

One/Oneness   The source of all being, the unity (identified with God as creator) which imparts to all of creation its status of existence as particular things, and to which all things long to return; capitalization is a modern convention, and the decisions made in this translation are to an extent arbitrary (e.g., III.11.37, 39; III.12.33, IV.3.14).

Opilio   The younger brother of Cyprianus (q.v.), he regained his position in Theoderic's favor by informing against Boethius (I.4.17); son-in-law of Basilius (q.v.).

Orpheus   The legendary poet and singer of Thrace; descended, unsuccessfully, to Hades to get back his wife Eurydice (q.v.), who died on their wedding day; his story is told at III.m.12.

Papinianus (Aemilius Papinianus)   One of the most important Roman jurists, concerned with the ethical basis of law; served under the emperor Septimius Severus, late second and third second centuries; after death of Severus in 211, executed by Caracalla in 212 (III.5.10).

Parmenides   Greek philosopher of the fifth century B.C.E.; the founder of the Eleatic school, particularly concerned with the relation between language and reality; his student is Zeno (q.v.), also of the town of Elea; a verse from his epic poem is quoted in Greek at III.12.37.

Parthia   A region south of the Caspian Sea, defining the eastern boundary of the Roman Empire (II.7.8) and known for its cavalrymen who shoot arrows from their retreating horses (V.m.1.1, translating "Achaemenid").

Paulinus (Flavius Paulinus)   Consul in 498, protected by Boethius from certain of Theoderic's officials who wanted to bankrupt him (I.4.13).

Pavia (ancient Ticinum)   South of Milan, the town that was the site of Boethius' exile, though not named within the text (I.4.36, "500 miles" from Rome; alluded to at II.4.17).

Perseus (also known as Perses)   King of Macedonia 179–68 B.C.E., unsuccessfully opposed the Romans and defeated by Aemilius Paullus (q.v.) at the battle of Pydna (II.2.12).

Philosophy (character in Consolation)   The Platonic embodiment of all philosophy and the Muse of philosophers and of their writings, she displays her learning and reveals her character through the course of the dialogue. The following elements of her iconography and her nature may be mentioned: her entrance (I.1.1–11), her torn robes (I.1.3–5, I.3.7–8), her books (I.1.6, I.5.6), her Muses (I.1.11, II.1.8), her leader (I.3.13), her city/citadel (I.3.13–14, I.5.5), her martyrs (I.3.6, 9–10), recognition by prisoner (I.3.1–2), role as the prisoner's guide (I.3.4–5, I.4.32, IV.1.9, V.1.4–5), as his nurse (I.2.2–4, I.3.2,

4), as his teacher (I.4.22, I.4.38), as his doctor (I.2.1, I.4.1, I.6.1, 17), as provider of medicine (I.5.11–12, I.6.19–21, II.1.7, II.3.3–4, II.5.1, III.1.2–3, IV.6.5), her abduction by schismatic philosophers (I.3.7), charges made against her (I.4.41–42, I.5.9).

Phoebe Sister of Phoebus and identified with the moon (I.m.5.7, II.m.8.8, IV.m.5.9, IV.m.6.7).

Phoebus Seemingly a poetic synonym for the sun, Phoebus is in essence Phoebus Apollo, god of the Muses and of the light of revelation (I.m.3.9, I.m.5.9, I.m.6.2, II.m.3.2, II.m.6.9, II.m.8.5, III.m.2.31, III.m.6.3, III.m.10.18, III.m.11.8, III.12.1, IV.m.1.10, IV.m.5.16, V.m.2.2).

Phoenician Referring to the peoples of the Eastern Mediterranean, occupying the Levant in modern-day Syria and southern Lebanon; Tyre (q.v.) was a Phoenician city; colonies were sent out from Phoenicia westward from the eleventh to the eighth centuries B.C.E., including Gades in Spain and Carthage (q.v.) in Africa (II.m.2.7, translated "Libyan").

Phrygia The central and western parts of Asia Minor, containing Troy and used as a synonym for it in the Latin (IV.m.7.2).

Plato The Greek philosopher whose thought and writings, both in their original form and as reinterpreted by the Neo-Platonists, provide the central argument and design of *Consolation*; Philosophy appears at I.1.1–6 as summation of Platonic philosophy; III.m.9 is a poetic statement of key elements of *Timaeus*. Explicitly named: I.3.6, I.4.5 (*Republic*, philosopher kings), III.9.32–33 (*Timaeus*, invoking the Father), III.m.11.15 (*Meno*, *Phaedo*, doctrine of recollection), III.12.1, III.12.38 (*Timaeus*, arguments to resemble their subjects), IV.2.45 (*Gorgias*, only the wise are powerful), V.6.9–10, 14 (*Timaeus*, eternity of the world).

Polyphemus The one-eyed Cyclops of Book 9 of *Odyssey*, a terror met and overcome (at some cost) by Ulysses (IV.m.7.9).

Porch Latin *Porticus*, a translation of the Greek *Stoa*, the covered walkway in Athens from which the Stoics take their name, and used as a synonym for their philosophical school (V.m.4.1, translated as "Stoic philosophy").

Previdentia A term coined by Philosophy at V.6.17, meaning "foresight," in contrast to Providentia (Providence), claimed to mean "looking out" or "looking out ahead."

Providence Despite Philosophy's attempt to redefine the term at V.6.17, Providence is forethought, and represents the principle of divine order at work in the world, explaining the seeming power granted to unjust people in IV.6, and reconciled with human free will in V.3 ff. (I.4.43, III.m.2.3, III.11.33, IV.6.4, IV.6 passim, IV.7.4, V.1.19, V.2.11, V.3.4-8, 14–16, 26, 32; V.4.1, 14; V.6.17, 30, 37–38).

Ptolemy (Claudius Ptolemaeus) Astronomer and geographer of the second century C.E., the latest authority explicitly cited in *Consolation* (II.7.4, paraphrasing *Almagest* 2.1).

Pythagoras   The enigmatic Greek philosopher of the sixth century B.C.E. whose mathematical understanding of nature influenced Plato and Platonic thought (an aphorism is quoted in Greek at I.4.38).

Ravenna   City at the mouth of the Po River; capital of the Western Empire from 402; captured by Justinian's forces in 540, later the capital of Byzantine Italy; had administrative and judicial functions under Theoderic (I.4.17) (q.v.).

Regulus (Marcus Atilius Regulus)   Consul in 267 B.C.E., a successful general in the first Punic War, captured and defeated in 255; according to legend, he then returned to Rome to negotiate for the Carthaginians, but opposed any concessions and was tortured and executed upon his return to Carthage (II.6.11; see Horace, *Carmina* 3.5).

Saturn   The planet (IV.m.1.11, "the cold old man"; contrasted to Mercury [q.v.]).

Senate/Senators   In Boethius' conspiracy trial (I.4.20–23, 31–32, 36; III.4.15; III.m.4.5, translating "Fathers"); Senate-House (II.3.8).

Seneca (Lucius Annaeus Seneca)   ca. 4 B.C.E.–65 C.E.; Roman author, Stoic philosopher, and advisor to the young Nero, who forced him to commit suicide in 65 C.E. for alleged involvement in Piso's conspiracy against him; his Stoic tragedies are a great influence on Boethius' versecraft, both in substance and in style; named explicitly only in reference to his death (I.3.9, III.5.10–11).

Sirens   Bird-women who lure sailors to their deaths by their beautiful singing and their claims of knowledge, famously avoided by Ulysses in Book 11 of Homer's *Odyssey*; Philosophy banishes the prisoner's Muses at I.1.11, calling them Sirens.

Sirius   The Dog Star, the brightest star in Canis Major; synonymous with the hottest part of the summer, in which it rises (I.m.5.22).

Socrates   Athenian philosopher, 469–399 B.C.E.; the inspiration of Plato, his particular importance to *Consolation* is the fact of his execution on false charges and his role as one of Philosophy's martyrs (I.3.6, 9; I.4.24); *Consolation* as a prison dialogue owes much to *Phaedo*, and especially to *Crito*, set in the days in which Socrates awaits his cup of hemlock.

Soranus (Quintus Marcius Barea Soranus)   A just proconsul in Asia who thus ran afoul of Nero's anger; false allegations of anti-imperial plotting led to his forced suicide in 66 C.E. (I.3.9; cf. Tacitus, *Annals* 15.64, 16.32).

South Wind   Latin Notus (II.m.6.12, III.m.1.7), Latin Auster (I.m.7.6, II.m.3.7, II.m.4.9).

Stoics   Followers of Zeno of Citium of the late fourth century B.C.E., viewed as one of a number of Hellenistic philosophies that destroyed the integrity of Philosophy (I.3.7), or as one that adopted a materialist view of the universe (V.m.4.1); but the ethics of *Consolation* are Stoic (cf. the destructive passions of I.m.7.25–31), as is its dialogic approach to self-understanding; cf. Porch.

Stymphalian birds   Man-eating birds inhabiting northeastern Arcadia (q.v.); killed by Hercules as one of his labors (IV.m.7.16).

Sun   Father of Circe (IV.m.3.5, translating "Sol," the Greek Helios who is not the same as Phoebus).

Symmachus (Quintus Aurelius Memmius Symmachus)   A leading citizen of Rome of distinguished ancestry; adoptive father of Boethius and his father-in-law, through his daughter Rusticiana; consul in 485 and head of the Senate in 524 at the time of Boethius' downfall; also executed by Theoderic (I.4.40, II.4.5).

Taenarus   In the southern Peloponnese, the site of a cave which leads to the underworld (III.m.12.26, translated as "Hades").

Tagus   A gold-bearing river in Spain, the modern Tajo (III.m.10.7).

Tantalus   Mythical king of Sipylus in Asia Minor, famous for his wealth; father of Pelops, whom he cooked and served to the gods; punished in the underworld by the sight of food he cannot eat and water he cannot drink (III.m.12.36–37).

Tartara (= Tartarus)   The deepest region of the underworld, below Hades, reserved for legendary sinners and their punishments (III.m.12.46 and 56, translated as "Hell").

Theoderic   sometimes spelled Theodoric; Gothic king from 493–526 of an Italy essentially independent from Constantinople; creator of the Ostrogoths, in Italy from 489; unified the Gothic kingdoms in 511; an Arian Christian; his later years saw much conflict with Constantinople, which ultimately defeated his kingdom after his death; responsible for the execution of Boethius, his Master of the Offices, in ca. 524. Hatred of Theoderic is obvious in the prisoner's apology (I.4.12, 17, 32); Theoderic may be seen behind depictions of Nero (II.m.6, III.m.4, III.m5) and of tyrants generally (cf. I.m.4.11–12, II.6.8, IV.m.1.29–30, IV.m.2).

Thrace   An area of northern Greece, vaguely defined but east of Macedon; proverbial for North (I.m.3.7) and the homeland of Orpheus (III.m.12.5).

Thunderer   A synonym for Jupiter, king of the gods (IV.m.6.2).

Thule   A near-mythical land of the far north, sometimes used to refer to Scandinavia (III.m.5.7, translated "northernmost icefields").

Tigris   Along with the Euphrates to the west, one of the two rivers of Mesopotamia, and incorrectly supposed to arise from the same source (V.m.1.3).

Timaeus   Plato's account of the origin and structure of the natural world and of its creator; a crucial influence in *Consolation*, it provides the substance of III.m.9, is cited at III.9.32 (*Timaeus* 27c), and is alluded to at III.12.38 (29b), V.6.9–10 (28b ff.), and V.6.14 (37d ff.).

Tiresias   The blind seer of the mythology of the city of Thebes, appearing as a character from one of Horace's *Satires* at V.3.25.

Tityus   A son of Earth, punished in the underworld for his attempted rape of Leto by vultures who eat his liver (only one vulture at III.m.12.38–39).

Trigguilla   A Goth, palace official and agent of Theoderic; Boethius opposed some of his plans (I.4.10).

Troy   The crux of Homer's epics, the city fought for in the Trojan War appears in the Latin only beneath the much broader geographical term Phrygia (IV.m.7.2).

Tyre   The great city of southern Phoenicia, once sending Phoenician colonies to the West, becoming a Roman colony at the end of the second century C.E.; here its only importance is its manufacture of purple dye (from the myrex; cf. III.m.8.12), emblematic of the royal robes of tyrants (II.m.5.9, III.m.4.1).

Ulysses   Roman form of Odysseus, hero of the *Odyssey*, an epic of wandering and homecoming congenial to Neo-Platonic allegory; and Circe, IV.m.3 ("Ithacan captain"); and Polyphemus, IV.m.7.8–13 ("lord of Ithaca"); cf. Homer.

Ursa Major   One of a handful of stars and constellations (see also Boötes, Sirius) referred to by name (the Bear), the never-setting polar stars being emblematic of constancy (II.m.6.11, IV.m.5.1 [misnamed Arcturus], IV.m.6.8).

Vergil   Roman epic poet, 70–19 B.C.E.; unnamed in *Consolation*; *Aeneid* 12.764–65 is quoted at IV.2.28; cf. Evander.

Verona   City in northern Italy, occupied by Theoderic (q.v.) from 499 and used occasionally as a capital city (I.4.32).

Vesper   Venus as the evening star (IV.m.6.13); = Hesperus (q.v.).

Vesuvius   Volcano on the bay of Naples (I.m.4.7); cf. Aetna.

West(ern)   Translating Tyrrhenian (III.m.8.8); translating Hesperian (III.m.2.31).

West Wind   Latin Corus (properly, the violent northwest wind of winter: I.m.3.3, IV.m.5.13) and Zephyr (I.m.5.20, II.m.3.5).

Zephyr   West Wind (I.m.5.20, II.m.3.5).

Zeno   Of Elea (cf. Eleatic philosophers, I.1.10); Greek philosopher of fifth century B.C.E., student of Parmenides (q.v.) and author of the famous paradoxes; resisted torture at a tyrant's hands (variously named in antiquity: I.3.9; alluded to at II.6.8).